OUT OF THE BLUE

OUT OF THE BLUE

The Role of Luck in Air Warfare
1917–1966

Laddie Lucas

Illustrated by Michael Trim

Hutchinson
London Melbourne Sydney Auckland Johannesburg

Hutchinson & Co. (Publishers) Ltd

An imprint of Century Hutchinson Ltd

17–21 Conway Street, London W1P 6JD

Hutchinson Publishing Group (Australia) Pty Ltd
16–22 Church Street, Hawthorn, Melbourne, Victoria 3122

Hutchinson Group (NZ) Ltd
32–34 View Road, PO Box 40–086, Glenfield, Auckland 10

Hutchinson Group (SA) Pty Ltd
PO Box 337, Bergvlei 2012, South Africa

First published 1985
© P.B. (Laddie) Lucas 1985

Illustrations © Michael Trim 1985

Phototypeset in Linotron Sabon by Input Typesetting Ltd, London

Printed and bound in Great Britain by Anchor Brendon Ltd,
Tiptree, Essex

British Library Cataloguing in Publication Data
Lucas, Laddie
    Out of the blue: the role of luck in air
    warfare 1917–1966.
    1. Air warfare—History
    I. Title
    358.4′14′0904   UG625
ISBN 0 09 162410 X

Contents

Acknowledgements

I must at once acknowledge the support I have received from all those contributors, the world over, who have helped to make this collection an extensive, first-hand record of the incidence of chance and luck in the air war. A select few have reached the summit and should be mentioned ... Lord Balfour of Inchrye, successful minister in Churchill's wartime coalition, and the five defence chiefs – Marshals of the Royal Air Force Sir Dermot Boyle and Sir Michael Beetham, Generals R.F. Armstrong and R.H. Rogers of the South African Air Force, and Generale Francesco Cavalera, the Italian supremo. Their presence in this international volume adds distinction to it.

To Air Commodore Henry Probert and his staff at the Air Historical Branch (RAF) of the Ministry of Defence, in London, I offer special thanks. Their suggestions and help when this work was originally being planned were particularly valuable. The Air Commodore's own contribution on the part which chance played in the high command of World War II makes a notable addition to the historical record.

I must, at the same time, also express my indebtedness to Air Marshal Sir Edward Chilton for his narrative on the epic 'Channel dash' of the German ships, *Scharnhorst, Prinz Eugen* and *Gneisenau*, in February 1942. This minutely researched account exposes with rare authority the punctiliousness of the German high command's planning of this remarkable episode.

I do not forget the help I have been given by Group Captain Ian Madelin, British Air Attaché in Rome, in connection with Generale Francesco Cavalera's arresting story. Nor do I overlook the assistance willingly offered by Wing Commander Martin Sparkes, Air Attaché at the British Embassy in Prague, with the splendid Czechoslovak contributions.

I also have warmly to acknowledge the support which Colonel Kenneth Cordier of the United States Air Force and, until his recent retirement, the US Air Attaché in London, has provided. His important account of his aircraft's destruction by a Soviet SA–11 missile in the Vietnam War enhances the authority of the record.

Further, I am indebted to my good friend, Generalleutnant Adolf Galland, for his contribution to the Luftwaffe representation in this work, and for his advice. Likewise, I acknowledge gratefully the help which Jiro Yoshida, of the Zero Fighter Pilots' Association has provided in Tokyo, in ensuring the Japanese Air Force's presence in the collection.

The contribution of the judiciary, in which the Royal Air Force remains strongly represented, is notable. I specially wish to thank Judge Rodney Percy for having encouraged it.

Likewise, I am grateful to Helena Naylor for permission to publish two sonnets, composed by her late husband, Squadron Leader Paddy Engelbach, while he was a prisoner of war in Germany.

Finally, to Alexander Bell and his family I offer my salute for their patient assistance with foreign-language translations; and, on the same score, I am indebted to Charles Pretzlik for bringing his experience as a World War II Mosquito (night-intruder) pilot to bear in unravelling the descriptions of the German defensive system.

List of Illustrations

Luck, Fate, Chance, Destiny, Providence? They Took Their Pick

As an airman who left the ground first in 1913, I am lucky to have survived and escaped serious injury. On the few occasions when I was very near to 'buying it', fate stepped in and gave me another chance

> Kenny van der Spuy, major-general, South African Air Force,
> World War II; pilot, Royal Flying Corps, World War I

Thank you, God, for guiding 'chance' twice that morning to save my life.

> Captain Harold Balfour, pilot, Royal Flying Corps,
> World War I; Under-Secretary of State for Air, World War II

I'm not sure there is such a thing as 'chance'. . . . Almost always, what appear to be chance happenings can, on retrospective reflection, be seen to fit into the . . . plan of life . . . like pieces in a jigsaw

> The Revd Rodney Pope, flight sergeant, Air Bomber,
> Bomber Command, Royal Air Force

The Lancaster plunged earthwards . . . adding to my absolute terror until I felt that I was detached from humanity and mankind. . . . It was as if someone had whispered . . . that my wife, my mother, the great East End padré friend of my life . . . prayed for my safety every night and that my faith required me to believe that their prayers would be heard. . . . We were still bathed in the full, awesome glare of the searchlights, but now I could sit calm

> T. Bennett, squadron navigator,
> 617 Squadron, Bomber Command, Royal Air Force

Fate is a strange master, and I have always been a fatalist

> Al Deere (New Zealand), wing leader, Biggin Hill,
> Royal Air Force

The way all [my] crew were picked was a sheer gamble. I think, therefore, I was exceedingly lucky

> Johan Christie, Pathfinder, captain, Bomber Command,
> Royal Norwegian Air Force

13

'Chance', in this context, would seem to be nothing less than the benign finger of God poking into . . . human affairs and transforming them

> The Revd Canon J.B. Rutherford, flight sergeant navigator,
> Bomber Group, Royal Air Force, Southeast Asia Command

In war you have to be some sort of a fatalist, otherwise the nerves wouldn't stand it

> Jiři Maňák (Czechoslovakia), squadron commander,
> Royal Air Force

If I am not to survive . . . let me have the satisfaction of falling to the enemy's fire

> René Mouchotte, Free French squadron commander,
> Royal Air Force

As we approached Berlin . . . my 18-year-old flight engineer, Ken, spoke up. 'Should we pray, Skipper?' 'No,' I replied, 'not while we're about to kill more old men, women and children down there.' But I thought to myself, if I do survive this tour I'll try to do some type of public service — to sort of balance my personal books; good deeds versus destruction.

> H. 'Nick' Knilans, United States Army Air Force,
> bomber captain, Bomber Command

Chance, fate, karma — call it what you like, my flying career was ended and I was about to become a POW. . . . I was not intended to fly any more, nor was I intended to die

> W.R. 'Dixie' Alexander, fighter leader, Eighth and Fifteenth United States
> Army Air Forces

Any . . . [airman] . . . knows that in war it is not always the ponderables that count, but that a great deal depends on luck. After this flight [with the Messerschmitt 262, the Luftwaffe's brilliant new jet] I believed we were in luck

> Adolf Galland, Generalleutnant of the Luftwaffe's Jagdwaffe

I think that during the war we were all consciously or unconsciously aware of the part chance played in our lives. This manifested itself in some cases by a rule that one didn't change operations with someone else once the programme had been published

> George Burges, Royal Air Force's Malta all-rounder;
> Faith, Hope and Charity exponent

It was all a lottery, as we well know

> Frank Dodd, flight commander, No. 544 photo-reconnaissance
> (Mosquito) Squadron, Royal Air Force

My guardian angels — and there were certainly several of them — were standing by me. . . . I reached the safety of cloud cover. . . . For me, it was

14

a miracle that I got back to base. . . . But what had befallen the young [lone Messerschmitt] pilot who had [facetiously] been advised to 'wait for a Spitfire' [to escort him home!]? He had returned to our airfield unscathed. Beginners also had their guardian angels

Eduard Neumann, oberst, Jagdgeschwader Kommodore,
Luftwaffe

In the years that have passed . . . people have congratulated me on my *lucky escape* [picked up from a dinghy in an English Channel gale]. Call it what you like, I prefer to think that fate, and some higher destiny, decided that that day wasn't to be the end of my life

Piet Hugo (South Africa), wing leader,
Royal Air Force

Some members of a crew carried 'good luck' charms to bring them back safely. . . . I usually wore a white, roll-neck sweater for luck when operating over Germany

Aubrey Breckon, New Zealand bomber captain
and squadron commander

Chance and, perhaps, luck played a major part in aerial warfare. Every time you came under heavy fire from light, medium or heavy flak, to say nothing of angry Me 109s banging away at you, it was only by chance that you got away with it. If you survived to fly operationally for two or more years, chance was really on your side

Sir Frank Hopkins, admiral, Fleet Air Arm; squadron
commander, European, Mediterranean and Pacific theatres

Looking back on three tours of operations against the enemy – one in Europe, one in the Middle East and one in Burma, ninety operations in all – I can see how God was biding his time until I was good and ready to be called to His service!

The Rt Revd Bishop Denis Bryant (Western Australia),
bomber navigator, pilot and aircraft captain,
Royal Air Force

I stayed, suspended somewhere between life and death. I had been [so] fully consecrated to the idea of extinguishing my life that I did not know what to do with myself. Many of my friends had achieved their goal of glorious death, but I had not. They were at the gate of Yasukuni now, waiting for me so we could all enter together. But the war was over, and I had no right to enter that sacred place

Yutaka Yokota, pilot and volunteer for the Kaiten Weapon,
the human torpedo; master sergeant of the Japanese
Imperial Naval Air Forces

The miraculous escape from two SA-IIs [Soviet missiles] convinced me there was something in the grand scheme of things which I had yet to do, otherwise my story would have ended [in Vietnam] on 2 December 1966

Kenneth W. Cordier, colonel, United States Air Force;
combat leader, Vietnam;
US Air Attaché, London,
1982–84

The Air Was the Master

All aircrew who survived one or more operational flying tours in World War II have some extraordinary story of luck, fate or chance to tell, otherwise they wouldn't still be here. This was also true of World War I and, for that matter, Vietnam.

These experiences are usually known only to a few. Mostly they have never been written down, as people tend to keep these things to themselves. Forty and more years on, however, there is a recognition that unless they are recorded now, while there is still time, they will be lost forever. Passed on (if they are known) at second or third hand by later generations, they would probably never be believed, anyway.

There is another reason for making this collection. It may – just – remind our heirs and successors what their forbears endured to give them some chance of living reasonable lives. . . . And how fortunate we, in the air forces, were to have survived. It is worth pausing, now and then, to consider what might (or might not) have happened had the Allies lost the war. It bears thinking about.

WHO WANTS WAR?

This has nothing whatever to do with the adulation of war. Sometimes my generation is accused of glorifying war, of being outright warmongers, of accepting war as a means to an end, of being 'trigger-happy'. Strangely, the opposite is the fact. To live through a global war – in this context, in the air – is to learn at first hand its meaning and consequences, and thereby to be cured forever of 'wanting war'. This does not mean that, in the face of provocation, you may not at some time have to stand and fight for your own, or even someone else's, rights and freedom. Global wars are discouraged by strength and provoked by weakness. The history of this century has proved it.

To be blessed by destiny to survive a world conflict, paradoxically, begets humility. It is the antithesis of much modern preaching. Maybe we sensed this more acutely in the air forces, enemy as well as Allied, than some others did elsewhere. For us, the air was always the master of our fate. This was drilled into us from the start. Take liberties with it, push your luck with it too far, disregard its portents, put it to the touch too often, and your chances of survival were slim. The firmament would, in the end, always prevail. We were its servants. Ignore this truth, and 'the chop' was never very far away.

The purpose, therefore, of exposing these experiences and stories, told at first hand – some horrific, some humorous, some, frankly, incredible – is to put down a mark which says quite shortly: 'All this happened and we believe it should be known. How some endured their tests and challenges when they came, God, literally, alone knows. It was our destiny to survive as others were destined to fall. So, without wanting to be pompous about it, we believe we have a responsibility to say how it all struck us, and how we, in the air, saw luck at work. It's just possible there may be something to learn from it.'

FONDNESS AND AFFECTION

Aircrew, by performance, lived very close together. Personal beliefs could not be hidden for long; squadron life was an intimate existence. In most operational roles, each one was directly or indirectly dependent upon the other for survival. There was mutual trust and reliance, one upon the other. This promoted fondness, affection and respect. Friendships thus forged have endured, quite fresh, for years. These relationships after the war were even to extend to 'the other side', to the former enemy, because we each had a common master – the air – and a common interest – flying.

The bond between aircrews and groundcrews bridged the great divide between land (or ship) and air. Ground and air were both playing in the same team. They were as one, winning and losing together, with all the attendant emotions which success and failure brought.

DEPENDENT UPON DESTINY

It follows from this that individual philosophies about the likelihood of survival, and its affinity with luck and divine providence, were diverse and often vehemently held. The thinking generally rested upon four principal tenets.

First, there were those who regarded operational flying, in all its forms, as being a lottery, a game of chance. If your aircraft's letters were on a few 20–mm cannon shells that was probably 'it'. If not, so be it. You were either lucky or unlucky. The superstitious ones usually came into this category.

Then there were those who thought the whole thing depended upon destiny. Some were destined to live, some to die; all was preordained. The future was in our stars, not in ourselves. Obviously, by training and discipline you did your best, you did everything that was expected of you, but, after that, it was all in the book. The fatalists thought this way.

The third lot – and they tended to be extrovert and confident about it – believed that people made their own luck. By their performance, efficiency, ability and by *their sheer competence*, pilots, particularly, determined their fate. It was 'the more I practise, the luckier I get' syndrome of the games players. If you were on top of things, and stayed there, you were likely to survive; if you let the standards go, it was probably 'goodbye'.

Those in the fourth category were well apart from the other three. They tended to keep their thinking more to themselves. In a word or two, it was all in the hands of the Almighty. It was His purpose, His decision which determined the way things should go. Events were part of the unfolding pattern of life. There weren't such things as luck or fate or chance. It was His will which, in the end, dominated all. Play to His rules and, on the whole, you were more likely than not to be undefeated at the close.

INTOLERABLE PRESSURES

Where, then, did I stand in all this? From the beginning of my first tour of flying until the end of my third – with a couple of rests on the staff in between – I was always quite clear about the approach, otherwise I couldn't see how one would avoid being driven up the pole or, as the phrase has it, 'round the twist'. The life and the pressures would have been intolerable.

It was simply this. You did your best to prepare yourself (or your flight, squadron or wing) for an operation. Every detail had to be thought through (if there was time), and everything, as far as was possible, provided for. The discipline, the precision of the flying, the leadership – all this, where it could be influenced, had to be right; and made really tight. This was all that you were *practically* able to do as an individual or as a leader.

The rest was in God's keep. He was dealing the cards. It was no good worrying about what sort of hand you might pick up. Maybe it was His purpose that you should be 'lucky' and survive; or maybe, again, it wasn't, in which case your future would be elsewhere than on this earth. But there was nothing that you could do about it after you had first satisfied yourself that the best, all round, had been done. For me (but not, I readily accept, for others), any other thinking would have made the thing unbearable.

I could not myself see that there was a better antidote to fear, nor a more lively stimulant for courage. One needed this kind of prescription because there would always be times when you had the living daylights scared out of you and required an extra injection of willpower from somewhere to see things through. I believe this philosophy was more common than some believed.

CHANCE TO WORSHIP

In the three squadrons I commanded in wartime, I tried to see (it wasn't always operationally possible, particularly in the rough times) that, once a week, the crews had the chance of worshipping together. It was *never* a compulsory church parade; but I felt that the opportunity should be there for those who felt inclined to take it. I thought it would be appreciated, and the support *always* vindicated the belief.

For my part, there were, in retrospect, four instances, two similar and two quite different, where something or someone – luck, chance, destiny or the Deity – intervened to keep me in business when, by all normal tests, I should certainly have been seen off. It is easy now to see how the puzzle fitted together.

My over-riding good fortune was to have, early on, the benefit of exceptional mentors. There was George Clarke, the Canadian son of Desmond Clarke, the president of the Clarke Steamship Line on the St Lawrence

River. George taught me to fly in 1940 at No. 11 EFTS* at Cap de la Madeleine, near Trois Rivières, in the province of Quebec, and fastened a grip on the process which permitted no deviation at all. 'God dammit,' he would cut in. 'I have told you to climb this airplane [a Fleet Finch II] at 72 m.p.h., not 71 or 73. Now, do you hear me?' His questions were *always* rhetorical.

When I went to my first fighter squadron in 1941 – No. 66 at Perranporth in Cornwall – the CO was Athol Forbes (Air Commodore A.S. Forbes), a brilliant operator, who had commanded a flight in 303, the Polish Squadron, in the Battle of Britain with signal success. He was quickly followed by the 21-year-old 'Dizzy' Allen (Wing Commander H.R. Allen), who had also fought through, and survived, the battle. Opposites they were, but each knew the form from A to Z in the air, and could impart it. Indeed, 'Dizzy' persevered with me, just a mere wartime amateur, to an extent which my flying at the time can hardly have justified.

REDOUBTABLE CANADIAN

There followed, early in 1942, a fortnight or so in Malta flying clapped-out Hurricane IIs with the redoubtable Canadian, Stan Turner (Group Captain P.S. Turner), before the Spitfires arrived and the battle for the island had built up to its climax. Stan had survived the battles of France and Britain and the first sweeps, with the Tangmere Wing under Douglas Bader, over northern France. He took the island's flying apart, transformed it within a month, and left his mark upon it which was never, subsequently, to be erased. I was just a pupil in the class watching his mastery.

He was succeeded in 249 by the Cranwell-trained Stan Grant (Air Vice-Marshal S.B. Grant), one of the most proficient squadron commanders of World War II. I saw him at work, just as I had done with Allen in England, from the best vantage point from which to judge, that of a flight commander.

It was my luck that I fell in with these five exponents of the flying and fighting art when I was most in need of the example. I could so easily have had five ordinary counterparts to serve, in which case I would have been unlikely to have survived beyond the spring of 1942.

FRIDAY THE THIRTEENTH

Then, from among my fair share of chances, I had an escape on Friday, 13 July 1942 – the last time I flew in Malta – which could only have been fashioned by providence with an eye open for the future.

I was then commanding 249, and had just been posted back to the UK for a rest. My successor wasn't yet in place, so I took the opportunity to have one more swing round with the squadron. We had a field day with some Italian Macchi 202s, high up, ten or fifteen miles east of the island. I was just shaping up nicely for another assault when I chanced to glance in my rear mirror. Four Me 109s, in line astern, were forming up for the kill.

*Elementary Flying Training School. (Ed.)

It was always said that if you could actually recognize a 109 in the rear mirror it was too late, and here were four! The noise of cannon shells exploding all over the place sounded as if one had been hit by a bus . . . and I had deserved every one of them. After some remedial action I called up the ground station, gave a 'fix', and said I would be stepping out. The Spitfire was then beginning to burn and smoke filled the cockpit.

I pulled the toggle above my head to release the hood, and it came away in my hand. The canopy was jammed tight and nothing would move it. The situation was now interesting. For some reason unknown to me, when I had got down to 13,000 or 14,000 feet in a spiralling dive, the flames and the smoke began to subside. I had done nothing to cause it save cut all the switches.

I now reckoned I might just have enough height to squeeze a 'dead-stick' glide into Halfar, the airfield in the southeast of the island. Amid a splendid display of red Verey lights, I managed a downwind landing with wheels down, but no flaps, at precisely the moment that three Fleet Air Arm Swordfish aircraft were taking off straight towards me. Providence had turned Friday the thirteenth into my lucky day.

OUT OF BOUNDS

There was a not dissimilar experience, rather more than a year later, over the Pas de Calais in northern France. We were operating from Manston in east Kent, and had been to Lille with a couple of dozen B–26 Marauders of the United States Army Air Force. As we were coming out from the target, I was hit by a 109 in circumstances best left unsaid. Halfway across the Straits the Rolls-Royce Merlin engine in my Spitfire called it a day. The options were then obvious, and none of them was particularly agreeable. However, I still had plenty of height.

As I was hesitating (I always had a fear of baling out and finishing up in the water), I suddenly saw to the northwest, and away in the distance through the hazy sunlight, the outline of the clubhouse at Prince's, Sandwich, where I had been born in World War I. My father had been a co-founder of the club in the early years of the century, and was the principal architect of the original golf course where Gene Sarazen, the great American player, had won the Open Championship in 1932.

The clubhouse, and the open expanse of the course, attracted me like a magnet. I was overwhelmed by the feeling that this was somehow 'meant'. I seemed to hear a voice saying: 'Try for the 1st fairway and line up on your old nursery window.' But, true to all known golfing form, I missed the 1st fairway and the 2nd, the 6th, 8th and the 9th, and eventually finished up, out of bounds, in the marsh at the back of the old 9th green!

Years afterwards, my old friend, Henry Longhurst, the TV commentator and golf writer, was told the story. 'There you are,' he said, 'as in peace, so in war – inaccurate.'

BERKELEY ENCOUNTER

But of all the surprising deliverances which blessed me in those cataclysmic years, there is one which, for forty-three years, has continued to haunt the mind. It started with lunch on 4 August 1942. I was on a fortnight's leave, having recently returned from the Mediterranean. The Air Ministry had warned me that I must be ready for an interview with His Royal Highness The Duke of Kent, then a serving officer in the Royal Air Force. It was intended that, subject to his concurrence, I should be appointed His Royal Highness's personal assistant.

I had recognized instantly the honour that such an appointment, if confirmed, would imply; but I had been told that it would mean an eighteen months' tour of duty, and the last thing I wanted, at that juncture of the war, was to be away from flying for so long. Six months was the normal rest span. However, as a staunch Royalist, I knew where my duty would lie.

As I waited in London for a call, I took a girlfriend to lunch at the Buttery, in the old Berkeley Hotel on the corner of Berkeley Street and Piccadilly, a favourite haunt of my generation. By an extraordinary coincidence, Michael Strutt (Squadron Leader The Hon. Michael Strutt), one of my oldest and closest friends, was lunching with a girl at the next table. Michael was an air gunner and had just finished a tour, sitting in the back of one of Bomber Command's Wellingtons. He knew he was lucky still to be alive. Now, for a rest, he had been posted as a gunnery instructor to a station in the northwest of England, an appointment for which, temperamentally, he was totally unfitted.

I told him what the plans were for my future employment. 'My dear old boy,' he said, 'what a marvellous job! Do you know HRH? He's such a nice man. You're very lucky.' I explained my feelings.

As we talked, it quickly became plain that it was Michael, and not I, who should be offered to the Duke. He knew His Royal Highness and I didn't; it was inconceivable that the Duke would want a stranger on his staff when a friend was immediately available. There was only one snag: Michael was a flight lieutenant and it was a squadron leader's appointment.

Strutt spoke to his stepfather, Lord Rosebery, the same afternoon. Word was at once left with 10 Downing Street and the Duke of Kent's office. Within a couple of days all had been arranged. Michael, promoted soon to be a squadron leader, became His Royal Highness's PA, while I was dispatched to Stanmore in Middlesex, to serve on the staff of the Commander-in-Chief, Fighter Command, Air Marshal Sir Sholto Douglas (Marshal of the Royal Air Force Lord Douglas of Kirtleside). It was a most happy arrangement.

On 24 August I was sent up to Liverpool to give a series of talks on the Malta battle to local factory workers and to a Royal Air Force establishment. Returning to London by the early evening train the following day, I bought a copy of the *Liverpool Echo* on Lime Street Station. Turning at once to the 'fudge' (Stop Press), a journalist's habit, the stark headline, in unusually heavy type, numbed me: 'DUKE OF KENT KILLED'.

The flying boat taking the Duke to Iceland had crashed into a hillside in the north of Scotland. All save one of the occupants had been instantly killed.

Michael Strutt was among the dead.

Laddie Lucas, April 1985

The Parabola of War:
1917–1966
1917–1918

The fighting over France and Flanders in the second half of World War I established the basics of aerial warfare which were to endure for some five decades. Taken down from the shelf and dusted, the early lessons were thankfully absorbed by the Allied and Axis squadrons in the opening exchanges of World War II. The doctrines became, in their refurbished and buffed-up form, the accepted lore in the struggle for mastery of the daylight air. They registered the beginning of a parabola which was to span an astonishing half-century of development from the age of the biplane, with its open cockpits and unprotected aircrews, to the initial salvos of guided weaponry which were to become a feature of the Vietnamese and Israeli wars.

Captain Harold Balfour of the Royal Flying Corps, a spirited and twice-decorated officer in Major Sholto Douglas's* famous 43 Squadron, was frequently in combat in the formative and crucial period of World War I. He survived the holocaust to serve with special distinction as Parliamentary Under-Secretary of State at the Air Ministry for six cataclysmic years from 1938 until 1944, four of them in Winston Churchill's wartime coalition when the air war was at its peak. He was subsequently made a peer.†

The reflection which follows, written some sixty-seven years after the event, recaptures the ethos of fleeting, emotional leaves in London and those hideous, pioneering days of combat over the Western Front. It lifts the curtain on the fluctuating fortunes of war.

The Unbelted Option

The gaiety of London had never been greater. You could scarcely get a table in a restaurant. Musical and stage plays were packed out. But the audience carried in the background the thoughts of France and all that it meant, with the precious days and nights of leave dropping away so quickly. The young had to laugh and not think. It was gaiety with a background of sadness. Every night the Alhambra was packed. George Robey and

*Lord Douglas of Kirtleside.
†Lord Balfour of Inchrye.

Violet Loraine were in the 'Bing Boys'. That sad refrain Violet Loraine sang every night to encores – one, two and even three. 'If You Were the Only Girl in the World' – that tune is still nostalgic. The eyes of hundreds filled with tears. The uniformed boy with his girl beside him were both aware of a background which had no certainty of life and the probability of death in a very short time ahead. For the boy, the hazards of war, with each day of his life, could depend on his skill, bravery, competence and, above all, chances of good luck.

It was in April/May 1917 that chance was on my side, and decreed that I might live on.

43 Squadron RFC was sent to France to Trezene airfield, near Aire. Sholto Douglas was our Squadron CO. We had Sopwith two-seater biplanes. The pilot sat just behind the 110–hp Clerget rotary engine, and the gunner aft in a circular turret. Armament was one Vickers gun firing forward through the propeller, and one Lewis gun mounted on a 'scarf ring' for the gunner-observer. Our job was labelled 'offensive patrols', but as the performance of our Sopwiths was vastly inferior to the German Albatros in speed, climb and manoeuvrability, we started every fight at considerable disadvantage. Richthofen's circus, looping, rolling, spinning their gaily painted fighters, were ready waiting for us every morning. They were at a height we just could not climb to. When their formation dived on us, our Sopwiths had to be handled gingerly, for above about 160 m.p.h. the wings were liable to come off.

We had 32 aircrews, two crew to each aircraft, and in the month of 'Bloody April' our losses were 35, or rather more than 100 per cent.

On the battlefield below we watched the Canadian infantry fighting to capture Vimy Ridge, which was of great strategic importance.

The battle was on, but 43 could play no part. This was due entirely to the stupidity and obstinacy of the so-called 'experts' back at Headquarters. It is worth recording as an example how technicians, safe on the ground, were so often convinced they knew better than we who had to do the job. Our rotary Clergets used castor oil as lubricant. Without notice, Headquarters informed us 'No more castor oil'. Now we were to use a substitute pharmaceutical oil. In twenty-four hours we had seized up nearly every engine in the squadron. I, myself, had an engine seize up at 12,000 feet, but luckily over a neighbouring airfield. Mechanics from the squadron came over and fitted a new engine. By the time I landed back at Trezene, the replacement engine was almost red-hot and about to seize up. I had a third seize up a few seconds after take-off. Fortunately, I could just clear some trees bordering a wide French road which had no hedges or ditches on either side, and on which I managed to land.

Once the squadron groundcrews had our aircraft serviceable, we were all kept busy during daylight hours doing 'line patrols'. These meant flying back and forth over our section of the front line at a low height, usually 1500 feet, as protection against German fighters darting over our lines to pick off one of our army cooperation aircraft working with our gun batteries, which they were in touch with on Morse, for radio telephones had not been invented. The unpleasant hazard was a chance of being hit by either one of our own or the German shells. I remember that when a shell passed nearby one could hear its whistle, and in cases of a really near miss one could feel the air bump as it passed. My observer and I got a wonderful view of the ground battle, with the main and communicating trenches running through broken-up territory made up of water-filled shell holes, doubtless harbouring pockets of infantry, live or dead. The trench lines were so irregular and so indented that one could not tell whether a trench was ours or theirs.

Quite suddenly, I looked down to realize that the west wind had carried me over what must have been enemy territory, held against ground attack, and I was probably half a mile the German side at 1200 feet. I lost no time in turning west to regain the safety of our lines. I opened the throttle and swung the nose towards home, but my ground speed was all too slow against the wind. The Germans opened up all they had in rifle and machine-gun fire. I flew zigzag, and by luck managed to avoid being hit, except for the occasional hole appearing in one or other of my wings. I thought that in a few minutes I should reach the safety of our lines when, with a hard metallic clank, my engine packed up. One of the cylinders must have been hit. I pushed the nose down to retain flying speed, and used every bit of height left me in an attempt to reach our lines.

And here chance, that elusive thing, entered the situation. I recalled that only the night before, in the mess, we'd had a discussion – If you crash on Vimy Ridge would you or would you not keep your belt on for the inevitable crash? I had given the view that it was better to remain strapped in, and take the crash as part of the machine, rather than run the risk of being thrown forward against the butt of the Vickers gun just in front of my face and having my brains spattered over the wreckage. As I held the aircraft in a straight glide for the last hundred feet or so, it flashed through my mind that the majority were for unstrapping. I said to myself, 'Well the majority were for unstrapping so I had better go with them.' I flicked up the safety catch just before my undercart and propellor, and the front of the aircraft, hit the rim of a shell crater. We had just tipped the ridge with a few feet to spare and I had stalled the last twenty feet or so to reduce forward speed. The engine in front came back to where both my legs would have been, but I was thrown forward and shot through the centre section struts, through which I could not have crawled if I had tried to on the ground. There was chance in my remembering the discussion and chance, again, in shooting through a space through which I could not have crawled, and this without hurt or graze.

Thank you, God, for guiding chance twice that morning to save my life.*

Lord Balfour of Inchrye, 'The Balfour Papers',
Kensington, London, 1984

---

*Captain Balfour was back in combat with 43 within a few months. The squadron, re-equipped with 'lovely little Sopwith Camels' in place of the 'obsolete 1½ Strutters', achieved 13 confirmed enemies destroyed within a month for two or three casualties. 'Thus was "Bloody April" avenged for 43.' (Ed.)

Sopwith Camel crashing

British Camel in a Russian Forest

South Africa's contribution to the Allied air effort in two great wars is a glittering feature of modern military history. The deeds of the Republic's stalwarts adorn the record. Take the case of one of their intrepid Sopwith Camel pilots in the old Royal Flying Corps. His extensive and decorated Service career spanned the two global conflicts.

K.R. van der Spuy, who became a major-general in the South African Air Force, was twenty-six when, in April 1918, he was placed in charge of a newly formed Royal Air Force group whose headquarters were in the Russian village of Beresniki, 250 miles or so up the Dwina river and a Sabbath day's journey from Archangel. This group, which embraced a Slavo-British Aviation Corps unit, formed an important element of the Elope Expedition to northern Russia. The SBAC unit included men who had fled from the Imperial Russian Air Arm (and other European states) to make war against the hated Bolsheviks. General Sir Edmund Ironside was in overall command of the expedition.

Kenny van der Spuy was, for those times, already an unusually experienced pilot. He had four hazardous years' flying behind him during which he had also found time to gain an A1 certificate on one of the Royal Flying Corps' Instructors' Courses.

'Had I not gone through that course,' he has written, 'I would probably never have survived the crash which I shall now describe. There, one learned to execute what could almost be described in those days as the 'impossible'.

Despite his ninety-three years, the General still retains an acute recollection of his unnerving experience sixty-six years ago.

I was on an inspection visit to the front, and due to fly my Sopwith Camel back to Archangel the following day, when Dame Fortune stepped in.

The Dwina Headquarters had for some time been concerned about the location of an enemy battery which was harassing our lines on the Vaga river section, but until then they had not succeeded in locating it. Unhappily for me, on the afternoon before, a Bolo* who had deserted had disclosed the required information. After interrogating him and after consulting General Finlayson, the commander on that front, I decided to lead a formation to bomb and machine-gun the battery position. . . . It would provide the SBAC lads with an opportunity of getting their own back on the Bolsheviks.

As my Sopwith Camel was undergoing repairs at the time and would not be ready, I asked Kozakov, a well-known former colonel in the Imperial Russian Air Force, if he would lend me his Camel, which he willingly did. This provided a cue for chance to slip onto the stage and do her dirty work, for, as I was taxiing out for take-off, a SBAC ack-emma† stopped me by holding up his arm. He shouted out something which I couldn't hear, unscrewed a panel, did something to the engine's insides, refastened the panel and then waved me on. It was only later that I realized he had probably loosened some electrical leads which would cease to function after I had flown some distance. The next step in the game of chance was that, when I reached our rendezvous, there was no sign of the other members of the formation. . . . I was alone . . . however, I decided to push on hoping that we would meet later. . . . I reached the location we were looking for . . . came in low and dropped my bombs on what I believed to be the battery area. I circled, did some machine-gunning – more or less for fun and to scare the Bolo – and then made a beeline for home, climbing to about four thousand feet.

Just when I thought I was home and dry my engine cut out completely. . . . This registered the fact that the mechanic, just before take-off, had probably done some dirty work. . . .

I was now in a really tight spot, with only the Vaga river and enemy ground on the left, and vast forests stretching for hundreds of miles on my right. I could not go for the river area because the current was flowing strongly carrying huge ice chunks with it, and along its banks were a few small holdings and an enemy waiting to receive me with pitchforks and long rifles.

I had no alternative but to head towards the forest – not a pleasant prospect as I did not relish landing in the only very small clearing I had spotted. I would be lucky to get out of the situation alive. I had seen some of these small clearings before and had, in fact, once found and carried a dead airman out of one, after hacking his frozen body out of the crashed machine. . . .

It was now that my guardian angel cocked a snook at chance, so saving my life. Coming in as low as I could over the trees, with a dead engine, I called into play every trick I had learned at Gosport – side-slipping, tail-wagging, wind-breaking and the rest. I only just avoided crashing into the trees at the far end of the clearing as the Camel dropped in a flat pancake.

*Red soldier.
†Ack-emma, air mechanic.

The undercarriage hit the snow with a crunch, the nose followed, and the aircraft whipped over onto its top plane in a perfect half loop – just as I had hoped it might – so that I could then loosen my safety belt, drop out and, hopefully, get away into the forest.

Unfortunately something then happened which I had not anticipated. The impact was so severe that the bolts had sheared. The top plane collapsed and, instead of hanging about five feet above ground, I found myself flat on my back in the snow, with only the small curve of the pilot's cockpit around me. To make matters worse, the petrol tank had burst and its contents was pouring over me. If ever I prayed, it was then! Fire is an airman's greatest fear and I was terrified that the fumes would reach the hot engine. I heard myself shouting for help. . . . I made every effort to get out of the wreck and be on the move before the enemy turned their machine guns onto it. I managed to get my forearm out of the cockpit and, digging furiously in the hard snow and ice, I succeeded in getting my head and shoulders through, forced my body out, and was away as fast as my cumbersome flying coat and boots would allow, towards the cover of the trees. . . .

Hope is a wonderful friend in such circumstances. It provides added energy, wards off exhaustion and gives speed to one's feet. . . . But having cleared my pockets of rations of chocolate and biscuits a day or two before, I had not had a morsel to eat; I had hurt my leg when swimming a deep stream, and it had become bitterly cold. And then my guardian angel, who had stood so staunchly beside me, decided to desert me – or destiny took a hand. (And we have to agree that destiny's will is finite!)

I became very fatigued, and during the third night after my crash I was captured by the Reds. They marched me back through the forest for many miles to the Red Army HQ at Vologda, where I was grilled for three days and then taken to Moscow. There, I languished in a Russian criminal jail for two years. This sounds grim – and it was! During this weary period, the record I had planned to establish for the first flight from London to Cape Town – with £10,000 and a knighthood awaiting the successful pilot – was achieved by two fellow South Africans a week before my release. Destiny hatches its plans craftily, and smiles at the results, be they good or bad.

On the other hand, it was only by chance that I was not executed by my captors, since the rules of war did not apply in my case. In the formal language of diplomacy, Russia was in the hands of a Revolutionary government and the White Russians, whom we were aiding, were dissidents and not a recognized enemy. I was not, therefore, regarded as a combatant but as a criminal making unauthorized war!

I had plenty of time in those two years to ponder the imponderables of chance, fate, destiny, good angels – or any other such outside influences.

Major-General K.R. van der Spuy, 'The van der Spuy Papers', Stellenbosch, Cape Province, Republic of South Africa, 1984

The Luck of the Irish?

Major James Byford McCudden, VC, son of an Irishman from County Carlow, but of Northern Irish descent, was one of the 'immortals' of the Royal Flying Corps and World War I. What he accomplished in five extraordinary years' service, first, as an engine fitter and, later, as a pilot, with 57 confirmed victories, is secured by the record. But his luck and, indeed, that of his family, which had been an ally through months and years of rugged fighting, ran out in the end. He was killed, only weeks before the Armistice, in an accident from which seven times out of ten he might have expected to escape.

Was it destiny, fate or just plain ill luck? Or was it, again, uncharacteristically bad judgement, born of overconfidence – it had happened before and would happen so many times again?

What is here of interest is that Jimmy McCudden kept a daily note of his wartime service. The final passages, written only shortly before the chopper fell – and only a few weeks after his own brother had been shot down and killed, with 11 German aircraft to his name – offer a valuable insight into the magnanimity of the air and into fortune's strange and unyielding ways.*

I think it is my duty . . . to give . . . my views on the German aviators who have been my enemies since 4 August 1914.

The German aviator is disciplined, resolute and brave, and is a foeman worthy of our best. I have had many opportunities of studying his psychology since the war commenced, and although I have seen some cases where [he] has on occasion been a coward, yet I have, on the other hand, seen many incidents which have given me food for thought and have caused me to respect [him]. The more I fight [him] the more I respect [him] for [his] fighting qualities. I have on many occasions had German machines at my mercy over our lines, and [the pilots] have had the choice of landing and being taken prisoner or being shot down. With one exception they chose the latter path. . . .

. . . It is foolish to disparage the powers of the German aviator, for doing so must necessarily belittle the efforts of our own brave boys, whose duty it is to fight them. The marvellous fight which Voss put up against my formation will ever leave in my mind a most profound admiration for him, and the other instances which I have witnessed of the skill and bravery of German pilots give me cause to acknowledge that the German aviators, as a whole, are worthy of the very best which the Allies can find to combat them. . . .

I will carry my readers as far as the month of April 1918, so as to complete my five years with the Royal Flying Corps. In March I had leave, and at the end of March my brother was reported missing. Now he is buried near Le Câteau, where he was killed over thirty miles behind the enemy's lines, while engaged in escorting a bombing formation on his SE5.

No more words are needed in praise of one of the bravest and most

---

*James Byford McCudden, *Flying Fury* (John Hamilton, 1930), originally published as *Five Years In the Royal Flying Corps*, 1918.

gallant boys who ever died for his country than to refer to the spot where he fell, nobly carrying on that offensive spirit which has ever been the most splendid feature of the Royal Flying Corps.

On 2 April I was gazetted with the Victoria Cross, and there was not a prouder man living when, on 6 April, I went to Buckingham Palace and received, at the hands of the King, a bar to my MC, the DSO and bar, and the Victoria Cross. I will ever remember how the King thanked me for what I had done.

I am now in England training the young idea, but my heart is in France amongst the gallant boys who are daily dying, and those who are dead, having given themselves to that most wonderful cause.

McCudden's editor, C.G. Grey, former editor of the Aeroplane, *and once the doyen of all the air correspondents and commentators, then added this poignant postscript:*

Three days after James McCudden had written these words he was appointed to command one of the most famous wartime fighter squadrons – No. 60 – the greatest honour which he could have asked. He left England full of joy at returning to the work he loved. He flew across the Channel in a machine which he had specially chosen for his own particular style of fighting, and landed safely in France. On starting again on the last stage of his journey he was killed in a trivial accident of the kind which had cost us so many of our best pilots. On leaving the aerodrome his engine stopped, and in trying to turn to get back into the airfield* he side-slipped into the ground. He lies where his heart was always, amongst those who died in the King's Service.

This ill-fated ending was to find countless similar echoes two decades later in the next great war that followed.

---

*Trying to turn back for the airfield, if the engine(s) cut on take-off, was the one manoeuvre which World War II pilots, from the very beginning of the elementary flying stage, were instructed never, never to attempt. (Ed.)

Chucked in at the Deep End
1939–1940

The air war of 1939–45 was a period of progressive change. One phase of it ran on into another as the seasons blend into a year. The divisions between the various stages did not appear, at the time, to be clear cut. Only the theatres stood out in distinct relief.

Air battles and campaigns were fought out and disposed of, and yet we did not see them with a definitive beginning and end. They were not ticked off like items on a shopping list. Rather did we regard them as periods of intense activity sandwiched in between spells of relative quiet.

Things are seen quite differently in retrospect. We look back after nearly half a century and view the battles, the phases and the campaigns separately. They take on the panorama of a stage play with its acts and scenes. The story is there in its unfolding sequence, but the chapters are readily discernible.

The opening act of 1939–40 was as different in character from the closing operations of 1944–45 as the theatres in which the dramas were played out. The actors who moved across the stage in the first sixteen months of war were learning their parts as they went along. They had no prompters in the wings. They were in front of the footlights and expected to say their lines. In terms of operational experience, it was one of the roughest periods of the war. The hazards were very great because the odds were so poor and because of the pioneering nature of the work. The aircrews and, with them, the groundcrews were chucked in at the deep end. They had to swim for it – or sink.

It follows that the element of luck was much in evidence at this time. Because the stakes were so high, the chances matched them. Fortune smiled and frowned.

Squadron Leader Raymond Chance, now a Recorder of the Crown Court, but then the pilot of a Whitley bomber of 77 Squadron, based at Driffield in Yorkshire, and temporarily deployed at Kinloss on the shores of the Moray Firth in Scotland, was one of the early ones to roll the dice.

'The Trumpets Had Sounded . . .'

It was the night of 18/19 April 1940, and the Norwegian campaign was following its predictable course. An attack had been ordered on the enemy-

31

held airfield at Trondheim, the port which lies just to the south of the Arctic Circle.

Disaster struck thirty miles short of the target while the aircraft was flying at 10,000 feet. The port engine spluttered and stopped; a flame started flickering from it. The Whitley quickly lost height. At 23.40 it hit the turbulent Arctic waters. ('To the best of my knowledge no one had ever survived, up till then, from a Whitley that had crashed in the sea.')

Chance's formal report, written a few weeks after this dreadful incident, picks up the narrative.

. . . Events seem to have belonged to another world. I remember a noise like a thousand panes of glass being shattered, and that a steam roller had landed on my feet and, working up, was crushing my head. I must have gone unconscious. I was aware, later, that I was in heaven. A long dim corridor stretched before me and at the end, on the right, was a large double door which led to a ballroom, the dazzling lights of which shone into the corridor. No one was about so I decided to make my way towards it.

This experience then faded, and later I thought, without any qualms, that I was in the aircraft on the bed of the ocean, and if I could get to the back door I would hold my nose and try to reach the surface. I would then search for the others. I started to crawl along the fuselage. This experience then faded and I was back in the corridor in heaven. I was nearer the ballroom now. I reached the door. With sudden fierceness the reality of the situation hit me. I was in an aeroplane on fire.

I was stung into action. The engine and wing were on fire, and the water seemed on fire from fuel spreading. I could see no one in the aircraft and was about to jump into the sea, when I saw the dinghy still folded lying down towards the tail inside the fuselage. My reactions were instantaneous. I knew the men were outside somewhere but hadn't got the dinghy. I dived for it like a rugger tackle, dragged it to the door and – with one idea uppermost, that fire would destroy the rubber and no one would then get away – flung it with all my strength into the dark towards the tail, and immediately plunged in after it.

My mae west shot me to the surface; I found the dinghy, pulled the cord, and it started to inflate. As it did so the two whom I understood couldn't swim* started to climb in (I think they had been hanging on the tail) . . . I did not know then that I had smashed my right foot. . . . We were joined by Sergeant Tindall, the bomb-aimer, who, I was told, was now hanging on the other side of the dinghy. . . .

There then followed tense, desperate moments of superhuman effort to gain release from the cords under the dinghy, push it away from the flames of the sinking aircraft and give succour to the struggling navigator, Pilot Officer Hall, who was some fifty yards away in the darkness, crying for help.

I told the survivors I would have to wait outside [the dinghy] to get my

*Aircraftman O'Brien, the wireless operator, and Aircraftman Douglas, the tail gunner.

breath back. It may have been fifteen minutes before I could try again to clamber in. . . .

Eventually I was hauled in and collapsed inside the rim of the dinghy. I hadn't the strength to lift my head out of the water in the bottom, and was saved from drowning no doubt by one of the survivors putting his boot under my chin. I heard P/O Hall shouting, but more faintly, and conceived the idea of going over the side and trying to drag the dinghy towards him. I got up on one elbow but fell back exhausted. I had the agony of listening to him drown. . . .

In the small hours, A/C O'Brien and A/C Douglas appeared to be on the verge of passing out so, sitting on the rim, I supported both with an arm around each neck. I thought they would fall backwards into the sea which was getting choppier now. . . .

It was unbelievably cold. Teeth and knees were chattering and knocking. . . . I saw one of the two I was supporting was going to be sick. . . . As he was being sick I put my hands in front of his mouth and found that it warmed them. . . . About half an hour later I noticed the other was also about to be sick. This time I pushed my face in front of his mouth. . . .*

Song has always been a stimulant and reviver in the face of mortal danger. This was no exception.

To try to keep up our spirits – and our warmth – I led the crew in singing 'Roll Out the Barrel'. It must have sounded strange in the dark in the choppy North Atlantic. . . .

In the hour before dawn I heard a noise which I thought was an aircraft. Suddenly Sergeant Tindall pointed to a dark shape in the water. . . . A searchlight came on and started picking its way over the water and finally settled on us. . . . It was a British destroyer, HMS Basilisk.†

A whaler was lowered and started to row towards us. . . . On reaching the destroyer a rope ladder was lowered. My crew scrambled up, but on putting my foot on it I promptly fell back into the whaler. . . . [In the intense cold] I had become unaware of my broken ankle and crushed foot. . . . I was carried to the wardroom where I found the rest of the crew on mattresses. There being no doctor, my foot was put in a box of cotton wool. . . . It was jet black and barely recognizable. . . . A bottle of whisky and two hundred cigarettes were put at my elbow. . . .

The First Officer told me they were in action against a submarine and were some 100 miles off course chasing it. He added that, with a break in the cloud, a moonbeam had shone on the water and an AB had shouted to the bridge on seeing us, thinking that we were a floating mine. . . . That's when they put the searchlight on the water. . . . It was thought there wasn't another British ship within 400 square miles of us. . . .

It was on the second day that we reached Scapa Flow. . . . I was in hospital for a long time.

---

*Forty-four years on, Squadron Leader Chance offers a reflection on that awful moment. 'Looking back over my life, that, I think, was when I had reached rock bottom. I believe it is called survival.' (Ed.)

†Later sunk off Dunkirk.

Ray Chance eventually returned to operations – on Blenheims with 21 Squadron in 2 Group during its most lethal period. A spell on the staff at the Air Ministry was followed by a posting to Bengal and Burma. He was called to the Bar in 1958. He has now written this moving postscript to his crew's extraordinary escape forty-four years ago.

One may ask how it is possible to survive for so long in the water in those latitudes with severe head injuries, a crushed foot and a broken ankle. The answer is really quite simple. You decide quite calmly whether 'to go now', in which case that's it. Or you look at the vast black ocean and say to yourself 'You'll get me sometime, but I'll give you a run for it. You will have to get me. I will never surrender.'

There is also a spiritual quality in it. You know there can really be only one answer – death. You are looking straight into eternity. You are quite peaceful. You are not brave or courageous because there is no fear. That is over. You look into eternity and just wait. You feel a growing closeness to the forms of the universe. . . .

In this experience, suddenly there was the blinding flash of the searchlight from nowhere. . . . The trumpets had sounded on the other side. But it was not to be. If it be the hand of God, I know not – but I like to think, and believe, it was. . . .

Squadron Leader Raymond Chance, 'The Chance Papers',
Norwich, Norfolk, 1984

'Sonnet'*

I have been near that state which men call death,
And given up my life ere now as lost.
In fact I have, with truth, been known to boast
That once I thought I'd breathed my final breath.
Yet cabin-trapped, or hanging underneath
A silken billow above a hostile coast,
I cannot say what thoughts were uppermost
In my mind. I did not feel my teeth
Begin to chatter, or the tight'ning cord
Of panic bind my brain, and seemed to miss
The awful stab of late contrition's sword.
The next time may be different, but this
I know, that as you go to meet your Lord
A strange, warm comfort calms you with its kiss.

P.S. Engelbach

Flight Lieutenant Paddy Engelbach, ex–141 Squadron and an exceptional linguist from his Oxford days, wrote this sonnet, and other poetry, in prison camp; he was then twenty-two. He returned to flying after his release, eventually becoming the commanding officer of No. 23 Squadron. He was killed on 15 February 1955, while flying a Venom at night.

*See 'Sonnet', page 278. (Ed.)

Arctic Kiwis

There was always a daunting severity about those early operations from northern Scotland across 1000 miles of turbulent sea to Norway and the Arctic. Such was the extremity of the range, and the variety of hostile circumstances, that each mission was a hazardous challenge.

Aubrey Breckon, one of New Zealand's exceptional and longest-serving captains and squadron commanders (he was still 'in play' five years later in the closing stages of the Pacific war), knew their character all too well. A stalwart of Bomber Command's No. 75 (New Zealand) Squadron, based then at Feltwell, on the borders of Norfolk and Suffolk, he was ordered by his commanding officer, Wing Commander M. Buckley, to collect, on 10 April 1940, a specially prepared, long-range Mk I Wellington, No. 4387, from Bassingbourne in Cambridgeshire, and fly it up to Wick, on the northeastern tip of Scotland.

[The Royal Navy wanted] an important and highly secret reconnaissance flown to the Lofoten Islands, then to Vest Fjord, by Narvik, and along a coastal strip of northern Norway. No member of my crew – Pilot Officer Harkness, co-pilot, Sergeant Hughes, navigator, Leading Aircraftman Williams, wireless operator, and Aircraftman Munby, air gunner – was to be made aware of the intended mission before reaching Wick. The Germans had just attacked Norway and, in a daring stroke, had entered Narvik, the vital iron ore port, some 200 kilometres north of the Arctic Circle. An urgent report was now needed on enemy naval and shipping strength in the area. A Royal Navy specialist observer, Lieut-Commander F.O. Howie, was to accompany us. . . .

Breckon's deadpan and deliberately underplayed account of this operation cloaks its tense nature and the prolonged strain it had upon the crew. None had ever before had to face a mission of such duration – or one which depended so acutely upon professional competence, flavoured with liberal dashes of luck.

Take-off was scheduled for 08.00 hours on 12 April with an estimated flight time of 14½ hours for the trip of 2000 miles. To lighten the aircraft and maximize its range, no bombs were carried, only a generous supply of ammunition. We knew we should be stretching things and that, on return to Wick, the fuel position would be critical. . . .

Weather conditions were of the worst – snowstorms, rain, ice, spasmodically low visibility, varying winds, and, always down below, there was the grey, treacherous and foam-flecked sea. . . .

Breckon doesn't say it, but it was, in a phrase, one hell of an operation to have to undertake on a couple of engines, and without any of those comforting navigational aids on which we were so content to rely in the later stages of the war.

Five-hundred miles out to sea on the outward leg we sighted a large naval task force. At first blush, Lieut-Commander Howie thought they were ships of the German navy. Closer inspection, however, confirmed that they were ours. His face (no doubt like mine) turned from a scared shade of white into a relaxed and rosy smile.

'Why don't we fly a bit closer to them,' I said, 'it would be good for morale?'

'Not on your life,' he retorted, 'they might shoot!'

I settled for waggling my wings in salute. . . .

As we approached the Norwegian coast we sighted a German Ju 52 transport aircraft. We thought of attacking, but then remembered the need to conserve fuel. Anyway, we didn't want them to alert their fighters; we were pretty sure they hadn't seen us. . . .

In cold, squally, typically Arctic weather, we completed our mission successfully. Relieved, we set course for home. It was when we neared the coast of Scotland that our troubles began. It was by now pitch dark. The weather, which had been getting progressively worse, was closing in with rain squalls and clouds lowering to near the deck. We were critically short of fuel, and the whole crew was utterly exhausted after the strain of the long flight. We had real difficulty in locating Wick. . . .

We had no margin left. Our Royal Navy companion suggested it might be better to ditch in the sea near the coast. I felt that would be too hazardous an option in the dark. Better, I said, to parachute, even low down, over the land. Fancy coming to this, I thought, after more than fourteen testing hours and a successful mission. . . .

I set course from the sea, inland, for what the navigator and I thought would be the position of the airfield. I warned the crew to be ready to jump if the motor cut for lack of fuel. Flashing our navigation and landing lights on and off in case a fighter might have been sent off to search for us and lead us into base, I made a final, committed run for our destination. There was no panic – first-class, well-trained and disciplined crews don't panic in a crisis; they hold steady.

Just then, remarkably, a fighter – a single-engined Hurricane it turned out to be – spotted our flashing lights in the murky darkness. With his own navigation lights on, and profiting from local knowledge, he led us straight into our landing path. It was a notable piece of airmanship for which, afterwards, we offered the pilot suitable thanks. . . .

But the hazards – and the tensions – had been well worthwhile.

The sortie had been the longest undertaken by a Wellington. The Royal Navy were satisfied, and our findings had an important bearing upon the seaborne operations that followed. We had had our share of luck. . . .

Group Captain A.A.N. Breckon, Glendowie,
Auckland, New Zealand, 1984

Does Fortune Run in Families?

Was Aubrey Breckon really luckier than most? Indeed, was his family destined to be specially favoured? Ivan, the younger brother, who died in 1981, survived his full share of Bomber Command's offensive with a tour with 75 Squadron and a spell with the Pathfinder Force.

'We must *have been lucky*,' says Aubrey, 'to have got away with that lot.'

And what does this specialist in good fortune rate as his 'luckiest' trip?

Like many others, I experienced plenty of dicey flights. But if I was to pick out one it might be the night my crew fell asleep over Germany. We had been on a deep penetration raid. All of us were exhausted from a run of operations. We were returning at altitude in thick cloud and not thinking much about fighters. . . .

We must have dozed off pretty well together. Suddenly, I came to and found that we were losing height rapidly, diving earthwards. Searchlights under the clouds were groping about for us, with the ack-ack gunners very active. . . .

Later, we found ourselves in bad weather over London being fired on. We had given the correct identification procedure, but to no avail. . . . We switched off our navigation lights and took positive evasive action. . . .

We were lucky not to be shot down over Germany – or England – that night. . . .

Group Captain A.A.N. Breckon, Glendowie,
Auckland, New Zealand, 1984

Times go by turns, and chances change by course
From foul to fair, from better hap to worse

Robert Southwell (1561–95)

Chancing Their Arm

No group of aviators 'put it to the touch' more often – or with greater nerve – in World War II than the crews of the Fleet Air Arm. They were an admirably aggressive lot. None outside their Service envied them their tasks; rather was it a case of thanking the Almighty that it was 'them and not us'.

Major R.T. Partridge, Royal Marines, was one of a select group of some forty Marines who, both land-based and seaborne, chanced their arm in the air. CO of 800 Squadron, he was shot down on 13 June 1940, near Trondheim, and thereafter spent the next five years at Hitler's pleasure. Before that, he had the signal honour of being awarded the first Distinguished Service Order of the war, and with good reason. He has told his story in Operation Skua (FAA Museum and Picton Publishing (Chippenham) Ltd), but here, in a specially written narrative, he describes three incidents which leave one wondering what supernatural power it was that allowed him to survive.

Dick Partridge opens with the stunningly successful, dive-bombing attack by Skuas of 800 and 803 Squadrons*, based at Hatston in the Orkneys, on the German cruiser Königsberg, lying alongside in Bergen harbour.

At 05.00 hours on 10 April 1940, sixteen aircraft from the two squadrons

*Lieutenant 'Bill' Lucy, RN, was the CO of 803. (Ed.)

37

were airborne for a round-trip that was going to last 4½ hours, *about ten minutes over our official endurance* (editor's italics). Arriving at Bergen at dawn, we attacked the *Königsberg* out of the rising sun, scoring three direct hits and several near misses. Later reconnaissance showed that the ship had broken in two and sunk.

For the loss of one of our aircraft it had been demonstrated that major warships were readily vulnerable to attack from the air. . . .

. . . A little later in the Norwegian campaign I was patrolling with a sub-section of three Skuas from *Ark Royal* over the coast near Aandalsnes. We spotted a Heinkel 111 bombing HMS *Flamingo*. After some twenty minutes we were able to attack and the Heinkel was seen going down with its port engine on fire. . . .

Suddenly, my engine cut and I was confronted with a forced landing up in the snow-covered mountains. . . . Fortunately, we made a successful wheels-up landing on a frozen lake alongside a mountain, set fire to our Skua, and struggled through the deep snow to a hut we had seen from the air.

Unknown to us, the Heinkel had crash-landed on the other side of the mountain. As we were settling down in 'our hut' for the night, we heard a whistle blowing. To our consternation we saw three German aircrew advancing towards us. They were quite friendly and claimed to have been shot down by three Spitfires. As Skuas were the only single-engined mono-planes in the area, it dawned on me this was the surviving crew of the Heinkel I had shot down.

My observer and I moved on to another hut for the night, but, next morning, as the Germans rejoined us, we were surrounded by a Norwegian ski patrol. One of the Germans was shot as he tried to draw his pistol, the other two were taken prisoner.

That night we walked twenty-one miles over the mountains, and after a further three days of remarkably adventurous travel, we managed to join up with British troops being evacuated by sea from Aandalsnes. . . .

I was soon back flying again from *Ark Royal*, this time right up north at Narvik. . . . With the sinking of HMS *Glorious*, and, presumably, with the successful attack on *Königsberg* in mind, it was decided at high level to send in 800 and 803 to revenge-bomb the German fleet in Trondheim.

This time, with twenty-four hours' daylight in these northern latitudes, there could be no surprise that it turned out to be a 'suicide' run. Me 109s and 110s were waiting for us, no hits were scored, and only four Skuas got back to *Ark Royal*.

I was shot down in flames by two 109s and taken prisoner. My observer was killed. . . .

The story, however, didn't end there. In 1984 the remains of Dick Partridge's second crashed aircraft were located a few hundred miles off Bessholmen, Stjorhfjorden. . . . A wheel, tyre, oleo leg, radio and bits of wing and fuselage were found. The engine was discovered nose down in the mud. Nearly ten years earlier – thirty-five years after the event – the first Skua, which had sunk to the bottom of the lake near Aandalsnes when the snow and the ice melted, was found in good condition by a Norwegian sub-aqua club. It was raised successfully and now, as the only remaining aircraft of this type in the world, rests in the Fleet Air Arm museum at Yeovilton. The publicity which this recovery aroused in Europe had a happy by-product.

It resulted in my receiving a letter from Neukirchstockach, Brunnthal, in Germany, from the pilot of the Heinkel, Oberstleutnant Horst Schopis. . . . Now we often meet and have become the best of friends. My wife proposed a toast at our first meeting: 'Thank God you didn't kill each other!'

Major R.T. Partridge (Royal Marines), (Retd), Piltdown,
East Sussex, 1984

Rallying to the Colours

Each man the architect of his own fate
Appius Caecus (fourth century BC)

With the advent of war, volunteers* from all over the world, from Europe and the Commonwealth, and from South Africa and the United States, were clamouring for the opportunity to make the air their battleground. They did not always succeed. Sometimes it needed a touch of luck, a brush of chance, a smile from providence (and even, now and then, a splash or two of subterfuge), to make it. Some held that destiny had much to do with it.

A pair of spirited Australians, Clive Caldwell, from Sydney, and David Shannon, from Adelaide, between them Desert fighter and Dambuster extraordinary, made unpredictable starts which certainly gave no clue to what was later to follow. Take Caldwell first.

I was accepted by the Royal Australian Air Force, early in March 1940, as a cadet officer for pilot training. Ten days later I was introduced to the Minister for Air, in real life a grazier from Victoria, who was soon to be killed in an air accident. He was visiting my club in Sydney. From him I heard the alarming news that those concerned with the expansion of the RAAF were to become flying instructors in the Empire Air Training Scheme which was soon to start. . . . I was determined never to do that. . . .

I immediately sought my release from the Service. This was achieved not without difficulty – and to the accompaniment of some very uncomplimentary remarks.

In May 1940 I was included in No. 1 Course of the Empire Air Training Scheme (EATS) as an aircraftman second class for pilot training. I was commissioned a pilot officer on completion, and in late January 1941 we took the ship for Egypt.

That purely chance meeting with Mr Fairburn after dinner in the Australian Club in Sydney was to change radically the whole course of my 'hostilities only' war service.

---

*Every member of aircrew of every Allied air force was a volunteer. None was conscripted or drafted into the job. It gave the air its enduring strength. (Ed.)

It is worth noting here, as a postscript to his bizarre entry into the Service, that Clive Caldwell, who was to finish 'his' war in the Pacific as a much-decorated group captain, consulted a clairvoyant on arrival in Egypt. He was then on the threshold of a brilliant operational run.

Four of us who were friends from No. I (EATS) Course in Australia were on a short leave, staying at Shepherds Hotel in Cairo. . . . We decided that we should consult a Hindu palm reader who was in the hotel about our future glittering careers as fighter pilots in what has been called 'the greatest game of all'. Maybe we had had a bit too much grog as none of us believed such nonsense anyhow.

I was the last of the four to go in. The other three had all been told in effect 'you will soon see much action'. I expected the same story, and said so. . . . Far from it; I was told 'each of your friends will be killed while flying with you – and very soon. You will have harsh experiences and will suffer wounds. But you will survive this war and live beyond seventy years.'

Each of the other three was soon to be killed flying with me in the Western Desert in June and July 1941 – Dave Gale, while attacking Gazala airfield, Don Munro, while strafing the Bardia-Tobruk road, and Jim Kent, while he was covering a Tobruk convoy off the Gulf of Sollum. For them, the great game was soon over. . . .

I was to live on, passing the seventy mark some years ago. . . . A prophecy fulfilled – or just odd coincidence?

Group Captain C.R. Caldwell, 'The Caldwell Papers',
Sydney, New South Wales, Australia, 1984

One of the Vertebrae

The backbone of the squadron were Martin, Munro, McCarthy and Shannon . . .

Leonard Cheshire, VC, Officer Commanding,
No. 617 Squadron, Bomber Command, Royal Air Force

David Shannon wouldn't have been among that 'impregnable quadrilateral' but for one of those curious chances which were so often to mark the early careers of the great operational leaders.

I suppose it was a quirk of fate that I joined the Royal Australian Air Force in the first place. . . .

Some short while after my eighteenth birthday in 1940, I, together with a great chum of mine, Batty Marks, presented ourselves at the Royal Australian Navy's recruitment office for volunteers in Adelaide. When we were told that we could expect a long wait before being called up for training, I walked round the corner and signed on with the RAAF to train as aircrew.

Batty awaited his call from the navy. He was to spend a great deal of his war service in Arctic waters protecting the Russian convoys. I graduated as a pilot on single– and twin-engined aircraft and was shipped off to England. . . .

It was my destiny to be seconded to Bomber Command of the Royal Air Force. . . .

Squadron Leader David J. Shannon, Dulwich, London, 1984

Presumption Paid

Nowhere was there a stronger desire to volunteer for service in the air — and be prepared to hazard a few chances to get there — than in South Africa. The intensity of this support shone through in the telling and magnificently resilient activities of the South African Air Force in the Western Desert, the Mediterranean and Italy.

Charles Barry, for years after the war a familiar figure with the Republic's Argus Press, flew two tours of operations with 60 (PR)* Squadron and its Mosquitoes, becoming the unit's senior flight commander towards the end. If he hadn't been prepared to chance his youthful luck at the outset — and go to unorthodox lengths to do so — he might never have put a foot on the stairway to the stars.

The first chance I took at becoming a pilot was nearly my last. It was in the early days before the Empire Air Training Scheme got underway in South Africa. All pilots' courses were full, so it was no use trying to join up as a pupil; you would wait months to be accepted. But there was a reputed short cut: join the SAAF in another category and immediately put in for a transfer.

I joined as an air-mechanic photographer and waited gloomily for my transfer to come through. Finally, sick of square-bashing and terrified I would be posted elsewhere on photographic duties, I decided to try my own hand at solving the problem. I wangled a morning off to attend to 'an urgent family matter', and hitch-hiked the five miles to SAAF HQ, Pretoria, dressed in blazer and flannels.

I got through the guard and reported to the office of Colonel Rod Douglas, the huge, genial but formidable head of personnel.

'I have come to see the Colonel on a personal matter,' I told the surprised clerk, trying to look a bit older than my eighteen years. He disappeared, and a moment later beckoned me to an office.

'Who are you?' asked Colonel Douglas.

'Air Mechanic Barry, sir. I have come to inquire about my application for transfer to pupil pilot.'

He stared in amazement.

'You can't just come barging into my office like this,' he thundered. 'Why aren't you in uniform?'

'I haven't had a full kit issue, Sir,' I said, beginning to feel naked.

He glared. 'Just like my son. No discipline and always has an excuse.'

'Yes, sir.'

'What's this "Yes, sir?" Do you know him?'

'Yes, sir. I was at school with him. Lots of spirit.'

'What do you mean?'

'I mean I think he would have done what I have just done, sir.'

A long glare, then a not unkindly nod.

'Take your spirit back to camp, and don't try this again or I'll have you on the mat for insubordination.'

---

*Photographic-reconnaissance squadron.

41

'Yes, sir.' I almost saluted with relief, but then remembered how I was dressed.

A couple of days later I was summoned before a selection board and remustered as a pupil pilot.

Charles Barry, Johannesburg, Republic
of South Africa, 1984

Making Hay . . .

Wherein lay the stimulus to fly, to be part of a crew, to be alone in an aircraft in the limitless sky? Often, in youth, there was some touchpoint, a totally unpremeditated event, maybe, which set it all going.

John Moutray (Flight Lieutenant John Moutray), the Canadian wireless operator, won glory and recognition in sixty-five operations with Bomber Command. His artistic talents have been made manifest in peace in his lovely aircraft paintings and, before retirement, in his record as art director of Canada's Evergreen Press. For him, the light shone early.

I was raised on a small cattle ranch at 4100 feet in the interior of British Columbia. . . . One summer, while making hay, a small biplane flew over at a great height, and from then on that was all I could think about. On a visit to town* (a day's drive over the mountains), I sat on my father's lap in the front cockpit of a barnstorming visitor giving rides at five dollars for fifteen minutes. . . .

I arrived in Northern Ireland in the late summer of 1938, as did many others at this time, and eventually joined the Royal Air Force in the Belfast recruiting depot. Later, it was on to Uxbridge and Cardington for the usual ten-week square-bashing, then to Yatesbury and the wireless school. I did not have the education for pilot training. . . .

On to Cranwell where I had my first and one of my most interesting rides in a Royal Air Force aircraft, a Vickers Valencia troop carrier, used in the Middle East. We were all given helmets and sat along the sides of the fuselage like paratroopers trying to look interested. The engine noise was marvellous, as was the bumpy ride over to the far side of the grass airfield where we turned into wind. More loud engine noise while everything, wings, wires, struts and us, all shook like hell. Then the sudden thrill of being airborne. . . .

This ride was supposed to tell the RAF who wanted to fly and who didn't. There is no doubt in my mind what I wanted to do; at least I would be aircrew. . . .

John H. Moutray, Richmond, British Columbia, 1984

Guarding the Home?

Some keen fellows, trying to antedate the magical eighteenth birthday and thereby accelerate their entry into the service, resorted to all sorts of

---

*Kamloops – a Red Indian name for the town, meaning a meeting of the waters. (Ed.)

ingenious ruses to hoodwink the recruiting sergeants and disguise their true age.

Others, in the rush to 'get into it' before they were eligible, found temporary salvation in Britain's Home Guard. The transparent and effervescent enthusiasm of the teenagers made an interesting mix with their older, staid and well-tried colleagues. If they were particularly keen – and lucky – the likely lads got into the business of air warfare early on in one of the Home Guard's newly operational 'Z' rocket batteries. Here, the endless evening training sessions in the local drill hall seemed to pay off as they went patriotically to work with the recently acquired, rocket-propelled, anti-aircraft shells against the enemy's high-flying bombers.

A good example of it was on Tyneside, a customary target for German attack. Judge Rodney Percy, then awaiting his youthful chance of serving king and country, recalls an untypical incident which, if the fates had decreed otherwise, could have ended in utter disaster.

It happened early in the war when the Home Guard's 'Z' batteries at North and South Shields, on either side of the River Tyne, went smartly into action in support of the 'professional gunners of the Royal Artillery, firing their predictor-controlled, anti-aircraft guns'.

But there was a lot of difference between the quiet of the drill hall and the rough reality of the launching site on a cold, pre-dawn morning with the sirens heralding the approach of the enemy.

About a hundred sleepy, confused and incompletely and improperly dressed, part-time soldiers ran out to the rocket site in the park of Westoe. . . . Soon we could hear the distant drone of aircraft. The excitement increased. . . . This was 'it'.

With headphones on beneath my steel helmet, I bawled out to my No. 2 man the dictated fuse setting. With . . . icy fingertips and trembling hands, I fiddled about with the circular key and supplied it to the stubborn, grease-congealed fuse ring on the nose of the shell. . . .

Confidently, I expected my No. 2 to complete the fuse-setting on the shell, slung on his side of the frame, and follow the precise procedure of grabbing the 5-foot-long rockets, cradling them in both arms and thrusting each in turn securely onto the launching rails. These were set in their horizontal loading position.

Then, crisis! Nothing happened! He never appeared, as he should have done, round my side. I peered around the frame, fully expecting the anticipated order to fire to be given within the next thirty seconds. . . .

My heart missed a beat. There was my No. 2 man, on his hands and knees in the mud, groping about in the darkness, hunting for his spectacles. He was an elderly man, by occupation a shipyard worker. While making his fruitless search, he was complaining volubly in colourful language. . . . He couldn't 'see the 'effing fuse ring without, first, finding his 'effing glasses and wearing the bloody things. . . '.

Expediency determined that I should help him. Urgently, I dashed forward, nearly strangling myself in the process. I had forgotten to detach the cable linking my headphones to the framework. It pulled taut, knocked my helmet askew, and swiped my own spectacles from my face; they, too, plopped into the mud. . . .

It didn't matter; my near-sight was excellent. Successfully, I set the fuse for my No. 2 and then dashed back to my own position. . . . Relieved, I saw him loading up our rockets as cones of light from the searchlights were probing the darkness to illuminate one or more of the oncoming aircraft. . . .

Suddenly, the order to fire was received. I slammed down the plunger hoping that our two rockets would join with the others in a massed and dramatic ascent into the night sky. But no! What horror! Instead of soaring upwards, our pair of rockets hurtled diagonally across the site, cutting a fiery passage through the air, just above head height, to disappear ignominiously into the North Sea!

My No. 2 man had *forgotten* to set the elevation from the launching platform's horizontal loading position. . . .

With far too many of my erstwhile 'rocketeers' lying prostrate in front of their platforms, I never did bother to search for my own glasses. . . . Maybe they are still buried beneath the surface of Westoe's public park as a wartime souvenir?

His Honour Judge R.A. Percy, Alnmouth, Northumberland, 1984

Editor's note: *Undeterred, Rodney Percy was called up at eighteen and commissioned in the Royal Corps of Signals, later to command No. 242 Medium Wireless Section, XIV Indian Army, Burma.*

You've got to be young to be lucky.

H.R. 'Dizzy' Allen, Officer Commanding, No. 66 Squadron,
Royal Air Force

There, but for the Grace of God . . .

There was often a sizable helping of luck (pro and con) in a posting, just as there was in a man's decision to volunteer. 'Never volunteer' was the old hands' cry; but it never stopped the keen ones from placing their future on the altar of chance. Then, one thing seemed to lead to another . . . and another . . . without control over their outcome.

Group Captain Kenneth McDonald, who flew a tour on Halifaxes as a flight commander of 78 Squadron in 4 Group of Bomber Command, and in the peace that followed became a sales director of Canadair, makes an interesting example. His 'chances' formed a chain of coincidence.

The first squadron I was posted to in May 1937 was 105, based, then, at Harwell. Geoffrey Tuttle (Air Marshal Sir Geoffrey Tuttle) was the CO. . . . One of our number returned to the squadron after doing a navigation course at Hamble. My mother, recently widowed, was living in Southampton, so the idea of spending two months near her appealed. I, therefore, put in for the course. . . .

I wasn't sent to Hamble, but to Manston [in east Kent], and instead of returning to the squadron I was posted as an instructor, first to No. 2 Flying Training School, then to No. 7 and, later, in 1938, to No. 11. At

No. 11 FTS a notice appeared in daily routine orders about instructing in South Africa, Rhodesia and Canada. . . . Desmond McGlinn and I put our names in – and then forgot all about it. But, in July 1939, two months before the outbreak of war, we were both posted to Canada. . . .

Meanwhile, 105 was re-equipped with Fairey Battles and became part of the Advanced Air Striking Force in France. . . . Very few of the chaps survived the 1940 battle.* That was lucky chance number one.

In June 1942 John Archer and I were waiting at Dorval [Montreal], to fly a Ventura across the Atlantic. We were both qualified navigators as well as pilots. While I was fogbound at Pennfield Ridge, on a cross-country flight, word came through for a pilot/qualified navigator to take a Liberator (B–24) to the Middle East. John got that job, and the aircraft was lost. That was lucky chance number two.

In April 1943 at the end of my tour on Halifaxes with 78 Squadron at Linton-on-Ouse, we applied, as a crew, to do another fifteen trips with the Pathfinder Force. We thought we were pretty good, and this was a recognized option. . . . Nothing came of it. Instead, I was promoted to command No. 1652 Heavy Conversion Unit, also in 4 Group, Bomber Command. . . . When I look now at the casualties of the Pathfinder Force at that time, I incline to think that was lucky chance number three.

Group Captain Kenneth McDonald, Willowdale,
Ontario, Canada, 1984

> Yet they, believe me, who await
> No gifts from Chance, have conquered Fate
> Matthew Arnold (1822–88)

Return to Go

The well-trained peacetime professionals, who turned their hand to war, initially made the air forces' wartime intake of aircrew look, just what it was, an enthusiastic bunch of amateurs. But the comparison didn't last long. The amateur airmen, who were 'in for the duration', had to learn fast if they were to endure. If they hadn't 'signed professional forms' by the time they were halfway through their first operational flying tour, the chances of ultimate survival were slim. On the other hand, the longer they stayed out of trouble, and the wider their accumulated experience, the greater was their expectation of life.

There was something admirable about the select band of pre-war professionals who were 'at it' in 1939, and whose resilience, keenness and tenacity – and luck – sustained their operational effort right up to the final

---

*The carnage in the Battle (light-bomber) squadrons was appalling – possibly the worst of the war. 'Shocking casualties, sometimes reaching 100 per cent . . . against a particular target . . .' is how Air Chief Marshal Sir Christopher Foxley-Norris, a Lysander pilot in France in 1940, has described it. (Ed.)

curtain in 1945. Six years was a long haul; few carried their bat right through the innings.

One who covered the divide was Squadron Leader W.C. Duncan, a decorated officer, with a peacetime short-service commission granted in 1937. His operational span began, tenuously, in 1938/39 with 28 Squadron and its Hawker Audax aircraft at Kohat, up on the North-West Frontier of India. It stretched, with one disagreeable interruption due to wounds, right on into the closing stages of the war in Europe. There, as a flight commander of No. 613 (City of Manchester) Squadron, flying low-level day- and night-intruder missions with 2 Group's Mosquitoes, he remained undefeated at the close.

Then, to the astonishment of his colleagues, Bill Duncan resigned his commission and became, at the age of twenty-eight, a medical student. He qualified (extensively) in 1951, emigrated with his wife, Alison, to New Zealand, and made a new and successful career in practice in Palmerston North. ('I had started to think about medicine during the war.')

Chance was mixed liberally with courage, but his operational start with the Royal Air Force was hardly propitious.

The squadron had moved from Kohat to Miranshah, a fortified outpost in Waziristan. On 9 July 1939 I was flying K 5566 with my Canadian air gunner, Aircraftman Baxter, on an operation. During the flight, Baxter had a stoppage in his Lewis gun. Instead of placing the gun in the safety position, pointing away from the aircraft, he brought it into the cockpit. It was difficult to work on it with the slipstream blowing around him.

Unfortunately, as he was working on the gun, the blocked round was fired. The bullet shot through the side of the fuselage. By a most unusual chance, it hit the wire cable controlling the rudder on the port side of the aircraft, severed it and left no way of turning to the left.

It was possible to fly the aircraft back to Miranshah, thirty miles away, despite having no rudder control. But then, as we reduced height and began a gliding approach, the aeroplane went into a flat spin. The offset fin which, in an Audax, was designed to counteract the engine torque,* had come into play. We were too low to recover and the aircraft crashed into the boulder-strewn terrain, killing my air gunner and knocking me unconscious.

I was told later that an old Waziri woman, who was grazing her cattle nearby, saw the crash and ran to give help. Apparently, she dragged me out of the wreckage after seeing that the air gunner had been killed. She then made off to a nearby hill, waved her skirt, and succeeded in attracting the attention of the Tochi Scouts, the local militia, who came to the rescue. The tribeswoman was later rewarded in a suitable ceremony by the governor of the North-West Frontier Province.

I suffered multiple injuries, including a fractured right elbow. However, I returned to flying in May 1941, and was then posted back to the United Kingdom, where I was sent to a Heavy Conversion Unit equipped with Wellington aircraft.

One day, doing a practice overshoot† with an instructor, I found I was

---

*Tendency of the aircraft to pull to one side.
†Overshooting a landing and taking remedial action.

unable to hold the aeroplane, with landing flaps down, owing to my weak right arm. I was taken off heavy bombers, but, later, was allowed to convert onto Mosquitoes. I completed my tour, flying from bases in the UK and France. . . .

Five years or so after the war's end, and some twelve years after his pulverizing experience on India's North-West Frontier, Dr Duncan, by an extraordinary chance encounter, was reunited with one of his former rescuers.

Soon after we had reached New Zealand, I was walking down the stairs in the Palmerston North squash club. Coming up was someone whose figure seemed to be familiar. It was Flight Sergeant Murray, then stationed at a local Royal New Zealand Air Force base. As Leading Aircraftman Murray in 1939, he had been put in charge of a party at Miranshah ordered to pick up the wounded survivor from a crashed aircraft – name of Pilot Officer W.C. Duncan.

Dr W.C. Duncan, Palmerston North, New Zealand, 1984

The Cult of the Reciprocal* 1†

Very early in the war, a bomber crew‡ flew a reciprocal course in error and bombed a West Country seaport in mistake for Germany.

The authorities, while of course regretting the error, felt that here was a chance to examine at first hand the reliability of our bombers and their effectiveness.

An unfortunate air-force armament officer was dispatched to the scene. Knowing that he was likely to be unpopular in the area, he travelled in mufti and as inconspicuously as possible.

During his investigations his identity was discovered, and he was immediately beset by a crowd of hostile locals. They were angry not because the Royal Air Force had bombed their city, but because the bombing was so ineffective!

Marshal of the Royal Air Force Sir Dermot Boyle,
Sway, Hampshire, 1984

Spanner for the Job

The engineer officers who sustained the squadrons and wings of the Royal Air Force needed a nice mix of attributes, and a dash or two of luck. Those who had started as apprentices in the 1920s and 1930s, and had then travelled the long road through the ranks, could claim to be the best-trained aircraft engineers in the world. Their wartime performance, at home and overseas, justified the contention.

*Flying, mistakenly, in the opposite direction to that intended. It was a pilot's ultimate bloomer; the 'black' to end all 'blacks'. (Ed.)
†See pages 97, 99, 160, 218 and 278.
‡Based in East Anglia. (Ed.)

Their lot was to keep the aircraft flying irrespective of the difficulties, to keep the serviceability state above the top line – no matter what the excuses. They took the kicks (plenty of them) with an outward equanimity which made one wonder what must be going on inside. Humour, patience, first-class mechanical skills, and a modicum of ribaldry, were their stock-in-trade.

'Spanner' Hendley (Wing Commander W.J. Hendley) possessed these characteristics to a point. He rose, on merit, from Boy W.J. Hendley of the Boys' Wing, No. 2 School of Technical Training* at the Royal Air Force College at Cranwell from 1920–23, to be one of Fighter Command's most able wartime engineers. It was as the station engineer officer at Coltishall, 12 Group's base near Norwich, that he made his mark. To the squadrons and wings which were deployed there, and to the shot-up victims of the enemy, both American and British, who seized on this as the first haven from the storm, he became a rather special Spanner.

Hendley had been right through the mill. He knew the tricks because, as the old senior NCOs would tell you, he hadn't been averse to using a few himself. He also knew how fortune and misfortune could blend.

I could claim the early intervention of Lady Luck when a posting to the aircraft carrier, HMS *Glorious*, was cancelled by my squadron commander at the beginning of September 1939. *Glorious* was sunk off Norway less than a year later with the loss of 1474 officers and men of the Royal Navy and 41 of the Royal Air Force. Only thirty-nine of her complement were rescued. Instead, I went to France with the two Hurricane squadrons from Debden in Essex, Nos 85 and 87. We formed part of the Air Component. I was WO Eng.† for 87 and my old pal, Dan Newton, held a similar spot in 85.

We arrived at Boos, a small French airfield, four or five miles from Rouen, on 3 September. Within three weeks orders were issued to move to Merville, but, before moving, the two squadron commanders, Squadron Leaders David Atcherley (Air Vice-Marshal David F. Atcherley)‡ of 85 and W. Coope of 87, flew Dan and me over there to 'case the joint'. We were wined and dined sumptuously at a hotel named the Seraphim. This was renamed the Paraffin when the squadrons arrived.

After farewell salutes and handshakes, we left in our two Magisters§ for the run back to Boos, travelling at nought feet and scaring chicken, cattle and peasants as we went.

Approaching Rouen, David Atcherley pointed to the transporter bridge over the river, obviously intending that we should fly under it. The transporter looked like a large-scale pan, suspended from a beam perched on the top of two towers, one on each riverbank.

When we got to within 300 or 400 yards of the bridge, I noticed the

---

*The Boys' Wing at Cranwell was later transferred to RAF Station, Halton, where the designation of aircraft apprentice was then established. (Ed.)
†Warrant Officer, Engineer.
‡One of the illustrious – and quite eccentric – Royal Air Force twins; Dick 'Batchy' Atcherley (Air Marshal Sir Richard Atcherley) was the other. Both thoroughly accomplished officers, the stories about them – apocryphal and otherwise – are legion. (Ed.)
§Light training and communications aircraft.

transporter was moving slowly, but inexorably, from left to right. My pilot had spotted this too and yanked viciously back on the stick, clearing the right-hand tower by only a few feet. 85 Squadron got through with little to spare.

We landed together, and as I stepped out of the Maggie Dan yelled across: 'So 87 Squadron chickened out!'

I thought that 87 had been particularly lucky.

But much later, back in England, Hendley's luck turned – or rather, he saw at first hand how negligence could mix with fate to kill.

Aeroplanes could be unforgiving devices, and many cases could be quoted. One happened at Coltishall. The pilot of a Merlin-engined Beaufighter,* on a routine flight, radioed that an engine had failed and he was returning to base. A few minutes later, the aircraft crashed when within sight of the airfield, killing pilot and radio/navigator and a met. officer, who was also on board.

We soon established which engine had failed first from the position of the bias tab on the rudder.† The other engine hadn't survived the thrashing the pilot had had to give it to reach base on one motor.

We could find nothing at the scene of the crash to tell us why the first engine had failed, so we took it back to the station workshop to give it a complete strip examination.

We soon found the answer when the front casing of the engine was removed. . . . A tab on the locking washer for the wheel that operated the cam drives had not been turned up. The rotation of the wheel had allowed its retaining nut to unscrew, and disengage the cam drives. . . .

It was a cruel piece of luck for the crew to have picked this aircraft. The loss of three good airmen was a terrible price to pay for the negligence of some assembly worker failing to turn up the tab of a locking washer. . . . I was to learn later that this wasn't the first case. . . .

Wing Commander W.J. Hendley, March, Cambridgeshire, 1984

The Light to Lighten the Darkness . . .

Group Captain Patrick Foss was another of the Royal Air Force's peacetime professionals who, having entered the Service with a short-service commission, made his mark in the opening stages of the offensive against Germany. His progress from such a base was predictable and adventurous. . . . Bomber Command in the hideous times of 1940. . . . Bombers, again, in Malta and the Mediterranean in the equally hazardous days and nights of 1940/41. . . . Thence to the ferrying and air transport staff at the Air Ministry until 1943. . . . Thereafter to Transport Command HQ as group captain, operations, followed by a spell at the School of Air Transport.

Against such a background, Pat Foss's account‡ of his crew's second

---

*Versatile twin-engined aircraft used for night fighting, shipping strikes, long-range fighter escorts etc.

†Pilot would have trimmed the tab to balance the loss of engine on one side or the other.

‡Taken from his manuscript 'Climbing Turns'.

Wellington Bomber under attack

operation in July 1940 – against a petrol plant at Wesseling, near Cologne
– deserves a place in the record.

They were in a well-loaded Wellington 1c, based at Marham in Norfolk.
It was 'a murky night with a layer of cloud at 12,000 feet', their operational
height. As they approached the target, Foss saw a Whitley bomber ahead
and just below, coned in the searchlights. 'They lit the aircraft up like
daylight' to the accompaniment of a heavy bombardment.

I decided to glide in low just beneath him in the hope that the defence
would not pick me up while they concentrated upon him. . . . In no time
after our flash bomb [for the photograph of the target area] had exploded
very low, four or five searchlights bracketed us at about 8000 feet. . . .
Shells began bursting all around us. . . . I twisted and turned to shake off
the lights. . . . At that moment our rear gunner shouted that he could see
a light which he took to be a fighter approaching. . . . Any second now
could be our last. . . .

As I sweated at the controls, I offered up a prayer that I might be shown
what to do to take us out of danger. . . .

An extraordinary impression came over me. I found myself outside the
Wellington and away in the sky, from where I could see the aircraft lit up
and surrounded by shell bursts, just as if I was a spectator. . . . I saw then
how I might throw off the defences if I did a highly dangerous
manoeuvre. . . . I had the feeling of confidence to execute it. . . .

Then I was back in the cockpit and at the controls again, bathed in cold
sweat. I pulled the Wellington up into a vertical stall turn, fell out of it

and into a spiral towards the earth. Almost at once the lights left me and we were falling in the darkness. I eased out of the spiral and levelled off as best I could with an invisible earth. . . .

A single searchlight now came on and was laid along the ground, lighting up our track and illuminating the hills immediately in front of us. . . . We were only a few hundred feet up. . . .

We climbed over the hills and, as the light went out, we made our way back to Marham. . . .

Group Captain P.S. Foss, Beaconsfield, Buckinghamshire, 1984

'Dusk Take-Off, 1940'

At the end of the runway
The WAAF corporal lingers,
Nervously threading
A scarf through her fingers

Husband? Or lover?
Or friend for a night?
Her face doesn't tell
In the dim evening light.

The Squadron is airborne,
But still the WAAF lingers,
Nervously threading
A scarf through her fingers.

Ronald A.M. Ransom,
Cheltenham, Gloucestershire

Blood Orange and the Radar 'Miracle'

The part played by radar and ground control in the great defensive air battles of World War II – the battles for Britain and Malta and, in the last couple of years, for Germany – has been consistently understated. It has been overshadowed by the more glamorous activities of the airmen whose endeavours it was designed to assist. Yet the day– and night-fighters on both sides would have been largely ineffective without it. A first-class reporting and control system was an essential prerequisite for the successful operation of fighter defence – and offence. The Germans knew this as well as the British. The Women's Auxiliary Air Force's contribution to its organization was one of its glittering features.

The accomplished sector or group controller, conducting operations from the ground, was as important to aerial defence as the able squadron or flight commander deftly manoeuvring his formation in the air. The ground and the air were complementary to one another. The relationship between senior controller and formation leader was intimate and founded upon confidence, trust and respect. It blossomed with success, and success in the miraculous sphere of fighter direction and control depended, in the controller, upon an amalgam of skill and knowledge, intuition and luck.

The exceptional senior controllers, both at sector stations and at group headquarters, were few in number, and they left their indelible mark. Wing Commander W.R. Farnes was such a one – as those who worked with him during his periods with No. 11 Group of Fighter Command, including the Battle of Britain, and in the battle for Malta in 1942, will testify.

Bill Farnes was a Royal Air Force pilot with a short-service commission. His entry into the rarefied field of radar* at the start of the war was unanticipated and unorthodox. When he eventually left it in the Far East, with the defeat of the Japanese, and with his achievements thick upon him, his subsequent progress to the top echelon of the Bristol Aeroplane Company was predictable. Some might claim that he was destined to succeed.

It was chance that led me into becoming a controller in the fighter-defence system. I was off flying duties in the summer of 1939 and serving as the adjutant of No. 1 Recruit Training Wing at Uxbridge. A few days after war was declared on 3 September, I received, 'out of the blue', a signal posting me to the Royal Air Force station at North Weald in Essex, for 'fighter-defence duties'.

RAF, North Weald, and RAF, Debden, composed the northerly sector headquarters in the No. 11 (Fighter) Group area, the others being at Hornchurch, Biggin Hill, Kenley and Tangmere. . . . I was given the task of learning all I could about the radar defence reporting organization during two detachments from North Weald, the first during the winter of 1939/40 and the second in the spring of 1940 before the Battle of Britain.

On each occasion I was sent to Bawdsey Manor, a property on the Suffolk coast near Felixstowe, which had been taken over by the Royal Air Force before the war. It was here that the original RDF station had been built under the supervision of Sir Robert Watson Watt, who had pioneered the invention.

Radio Direction Finding (RDF), as it was known in those days, had been developed as two systems – 'Chain Home' (CH) and 'Chain Home Low' (CHL). Both were designed essentially to report the movement of aircraft over the sea, and to give early warning of the approach of potential enemy aircraft to the shores of the United Kingdom.

In addition to the CH station at Bawdsey, and others that had been installed at strategic points to guard the approaches from Europe, there were also the CHL stations. These provided protection by detecting low-flying aircraft, and had been specially developed for this purpose.

Let me explain, simply, the difference between these two systems. The CH coverage emitted and received transmissions from fixed high towers and 'carpeted' an area of several hundred square miles to seaward. It is probably best visualized as a wedge cut from a whole Cheddar cheese.

The CHL system, on the other hand, transmitted and received responses from equipment which could be rotated – rather like a searchlight beam sweeping an area to detect the presence of low-flying aircraft.

The Bawdsey CH station, and other similar installations, had their limitations. While the detection of *range* of an aircraft from the station was

*Originally called RDF (Radio Direction Finding).

52

very reliable, there were often difficulties in determining its *bearing* from the station and in obtaining an accurate assessment of its altitude. In the circumstances, it was necessary to fly, periodically, what were called 'calibration flights' offshore to test bearings and altitudes.

CHL systems, however, were far more accurate because they could detect more precisely *bearing* as well as *range*. This type of station had the added advantage of being transportable, and CHLs were later to provide the basis of the development of Ground Control units (GCIs) which, together with CHL mobile systems, began to achieve some success against German bombers during the night blitzes of British cities in 1940/41. Similar effects were felt by mine-laying aircraft operating in the Thames estuary. . . . These stations were later used successfully in the invasion of Europe and elsewhere overseas.

Two serving officers, Squadron Leaders John Tester and Walter Pretty (Air Marshal Sir Walter Pretty) were in charge of the CH station at Bawdsey and the CHL station at Clacton, in Essex, respectively. Both were regular general duties officers who had specialized in Signals and RDF. They were assisted by a civilian technical officer, Mr Cole.

When both types of RDF stations were supplying details about aircraft movements over the sea to the filter room for the information of the C-in-C, Fighter Command, and his group commanders, all three of these brilliant and energetic individuals had become convinced that it must be possible to effect interceptions many miles out to sea by direct control from what was called 'the trace' – the information shown on the cathode-ray tube.

The benefits of this would be immense. Not only would it save vital time in warning and marshalling the defences, it would also bring great tactical and psychological advantages over the enemy. . . .

Bawdsey's calibration aircraft was a Bristol Blenheim, based at Martlesham Heath, the historic home of the Royal Air Force's development flying. Its pilot was Flight Lieutenant Smith – 'Blood Orange' Smith they called him, after his personal call sign.

John Tester and Walter Pretty were often busy on other duties at this time, and although Mr Cole was always present, he was not allowed, being a civilian, to give directions to RAF aircraft. . . . I was grateful that all three spent so much time instilling in me their knowledge of the RDF system, its capabilities and limitations, and their hopes for the future use of direct control from the set itself. . . .

That was the background to this almost incredible new development as Bill Farnes, in his fortunately privileged position, was able to see it. Luck, fate, destiny, chance, or the tide which runs in the affairs of men, had allowed him to be in at the start of an operation which, with its subsequent developments, and over the next five years, was to transform the use and control of air power.

There followed, on 5 February 1940, the opportunity which, even in his moments of extreme fantasy, Farnes could hardly have foreseen. He recalls the incident which was to make history. The thrill, responsibility and poignancy of it must have been hardly bearable. Tester and Pretty were away from the station and unavailable. Farnes was thus on his own, calling the shots.

I was in our hut at Bawdsey. This was a completely blacked-out building which housed the CH equipment and the cathode-ray tube. The four airmen technicians were on duty on the morning shift. Suddenly the airman scanning the tube reported an aeroplane at fifty to sixty miles' range. The best bearing we could get was south-southeast. . . .

I suspected the aircraft was German, looking for targets in the shipping lanes off the East coast. . . .

Blood Orange Smith was always at readiness, armed up, refuelled and ready to scramble. I alerted him at once, and within five minutes he was airborne and setting course. . . . I knew that if there was a lot of chatter on the VHF,* the Germans' control station in France would pick it up and he would be recalled. But I needed to get Blood Orange beyond the 'ground effect' and interference of Bawdsey, and far enough seawards both to identify him and work out the track of the enemy aircraft. . . .

After we had picked up our fighter on the Trace, I gave Blood Orange the briefest of directions and course to steer to ensure that I put him south and up-sun of the target, and well above it. . . . We had tracked our adversary to a point forty miles or so east of Aldeburgh, off the Suffolk coast, when Smith transmitted his excited 'Tally Ho!' over the R/T.† He had sighted a Heinkel 111 below and was going in to the attack.

Two or three minutes later (it seemed an age) Blood Orange called again. He was clearly distressed. He urgently requested an emergency course to steer for base. I gave him the answer: 'Steer Two Five Zero [250 degrees] for base.'

Luck had taken a hand again, this time badly for Smith. He had followed the enemy down to confirm his kill, and the rear gunner of the Heinkel, courageously, had opened fire hitting Blood Orange in the chest and upper arm. . . . He just made Martlesham where, after crash-landing the Blenheim, the emergency crews were ready to remove him from the aircraft and transfer him to the waiting ambulance. He recovered in hospital.

Blood Orange had made history. He was the first man to destroy an enemy aircraft, many miles from land, as a result of a controlled interception. . . . I had the good fortune to be the chap who helped him do it – and to prove that the theories of Tester, Pretty and Cole could be turned to practical advantage in the future development of direct radar control. . . .'

Wing Commander W.R. Farnes, Marshfield, Chippenham,
Wiltshire, 1984

Own Goal!

What odds would you lay against the crew of a Whitley of Bomber Command of the Royal Air Force, briefed to bomb targets in Germany in 1940, getting utterly lost, crossing and recrossing the English Channel into enemy territory, and finishing up, some hours later, bombing an airfield in Cambridgeshire, England?

*Very high-frequency radio telephone.
†Radio telephone.

Ten million to one? Even money? Take care, strange things – very strange things – happened (on both sides) in war before the days of worthwhile navigational aids.

Jack Dixon, the contributor of the following dialogue, is well qualified to write it. He is the distinguished Professor of French Literature at the University of Winnipeg, holder of an Oxford degree and a PhD at Stanford. He writes on literature, education, rights and freedoms, politics and principles, and on philosophy.

There is more that should be known. In 1940 Jack joined the Royal Air Force as an aircraft apprentice at Halton. He was then sixteen and in time became a fitter armourer. In 1943 he remustered as aircrew, and did his pilot training in South Africa. He was commissioned, first, in the Royal Air Force, and then in the Royal Canadian Air Force. He has had quite a life.

The story which the Professor now recounts is true. It has, moreover, been seen and confirmed by the member of the Whitley crew engaged on that fateful 'operation' who now appears in the cast. It has also been read and checked by another member of the cast, a fellow citizen of Winnipeg who, by chance, was on the ground staff of the Cambridgeshire base the night it was bombed by 'one of ours'.

NO.10 SQUADRON, BOMBER COMMAND, ROYAL AIR FORCE, DISHFORTH, YORKSHIRE, ENGLAND   17 May, 1940

21.00 hours. Take-off of Whitley V for targets in the Ruhr.

Pilot to crew: 'There's the green light. Hold tight for take-off. Here we go! And look out, Jerries!'

22.20 hours.

Pilot to crew: 'I don't like this weather. That was some thunderstorm we tried to break through off Flamborough Head. We must have tried to get round it four or five ways.'

Navigator to pilot: 'Five times, at least. The weather's crazy. My new course to the Dutch coast is 140 degrees. ETA target 22.30 hours.'

'In this weather [said the second pilot] we might not see it . . .'

' . . . and if we see it [added the rear gunner] we won't recognize it!'

Pilot to crew: 'The weather is thick as Dishforth tea! Last night the op was cancelled and the weather cleared; tonight it's on and this kite has to swim through it. Keep your eyes peeled.'

22.22 hours.

Second pilot to pilot: 'Coming up to coast now.'

22.25 hours.

Pilot to navigator: 'That doesn't look like Amsterdam to me. More like Rotterdam.'

22.30 hours.

Navigator to pilot: 'Course to first target is 138 degrees.'

00.20 hours.

Pilot to crew: 'Well, that's it! We haven't found any of our targets. Navigator, give me a course for the coast and we'll look for a target of opportunity.'

Navigator to pilot: 'Put her in a 360–degree turn to port and I'll have

a good "butcher's". . . . Turn now to starboard, 360 degrees. . . . I'll get another view. . . . No, not a damned thing! Right, steer 275 degrees. When we hit the coast follow it west. We might find a target there.'
01.00 hours.
Second pilot to pilot: 'That looks like an airfield coming up now. Over to starboard. Hell, they just turned the lights off!'
01.40 hours.
Pilot to crew: 'Lots of searchlights around. Keep your eyes open. I'm going to take evasive action.'
01.42 hours.
Rear gunner to pilot: 'I can see fighters about, but there's no ack-ack.'
01.50 hours.
Pilot to crew: 'That was pretty hot back there! Wonder what target it was.'
01.55 hours.
Navigator to pilot: 'Airfield coming up ahead. Do a dummy run over it.'
01.57 hours.
Wireless operator to pilot: 'That doesn't look like a Jerry airfield to me.'
Pilot to wireless operator: 'One flarepath is much like another.'
02.02 hours.
Navigator to pilot: 'Steady, steady. . . . Left a bit. . . . Steady. . . . Hold it. . . . Bombs away!'
02.05 hours.
Pilot to wireless operator: 'Get me a fix.'
02.07 hours.
Wireless operator to pilot: 'First-class fix forty miles north of London.'
Navigator to crew: 'Longitude is right but latitude is all wrong.'

RAF, BASSINGBOURN, CAMBRIDGESHIRE,
ENGLAND   17–18 May, 1940

02.00 hours.
'Christ, take cover! Another bloody Jerry!'
'No, it's not, it's one of ours. Nothing to get your knickers in a twist over. It's just a goddam Whitley. Probably lost!'
'You're bloody cocksure, Greenburgh! We've been bombed twice already, and even your mate was killed in his bed next to you. That's another Ju 88! I'm not taking any chances!'
It was a dark night. A few airmen were posted here and there on guard duty at the Wellington Conversion Unit when they heard the drone of an aircraft approaching. There had been heavy cloud and rain, but now it had cleared a bit.
The second speaker was Aircraftman Lou Greenburgh, a Canadian, who had joined the Royal Air Force in 1937, partly to escape the depression in Canada, and was now an airframe mechanic.
'I know the sound of a Whitley, goddammit! It has two Merlin engines and a coffin-like fuselage, and nothing makes a noise like a Whitley!'
He was about to boast that he had a 100 per cent record of aircraft recognition, by sight *and* by sound, but realized it wouldn't go down well.
Thirty seconds later there was a tremendous explosion close to them: a

250–lb HE bomb. It landed a few yards from the bomb dump! Then another bomb. And more! The aircraft may have been lost, but it was a Jerry and it was dropping bombs.

'You and your "goddam" Whitley!' The sarcastic mimicry hurt.

Lou Greenburgh, who was to remuster to aircrew and have a distinguished career as a Bomber Command pilot,* did not live it down. Not at Bassingbourn, at least. His a/c recognition record lay in ruins among the rubble.

CANADIAN AIR FORCE BASE, PORTAGE LA PRAIRIE,
MANITOBA, CANADA   15 September 1984

Two friends were chatting, quaffing ale, and watching the air show, by courtesy of Air Command, Canadian Armed Forces, on the occasion of the Fourth Commonwealth Wartime Aircrew Reunion. One of them, a Winnipegger, saw a friend, also of Winnipeg, approaching and hailed him:

'Lou, meet my friend from Pennsylvania. Alex Miller – Lou Greenburgh.' Turning to Alex: 'Lou had an extraordinary career in the RAF – Bomber Command. After the war, too, on the Berlin airlift. Shot down, ditched, rescued; shot down, evaded, got back.' Turning to Lou: 'Alex was shot down before the Battle of Britain and spent four years and ten months in the bag. Escaped twice, caught twice.'

Lou: 'I was groundcrew then, in England. That was before I remustered, in a fit of insanity! What squadron were you on?'

Alex: '10 Squadron. Whitleys.'

Lou: 'Whitleys? I was bombed once by a Whitley.' (Lou had never abandoned his conviction.)

Alex: 'When was that?'

Lou: 'I'll never forget it. It was on 17 May, 1940. I was on guard duty and my mate had been killed the night before.'

Alex: 'Where did that happen?'

Lou: 'At Bassingbourn.'

Alex: 'Meet one of the crew who bombed you!'

Lou went into paroxysms of thigh-slapping mirth, disbelief, hilarity, vindication and joy. They told their stories.

Lou's aircraft recognition was restored to its perfect 100 per cent.

                                        Jack E.G. Dixon, Winnipeg, Manitoba, Canada, 1984

The Fortunes of a Quartet

The spring, summer and autumn of 1940 produced a rising crescendo of aerial activity. The battles over France, Dunkirk and Britain brought diverse individual experiences for the Allies. It was a time when names were being made – and when the fates were dealing a strange variety of cards.

In the class of 1940 there were some remarkable stories to tell. Four of the classmates – Jean Accart (Général J.M.J. Accart) of France, Colin Gray

*Twice decorated by HM the King at Buckingham Palace. Ditched in the North Sea on 31 December 1942 in a Lancaster II and survived with all his crew. Shot down over Occupied Europe in 1943 and 'walked' back to England. (JEGD.)

57

(Group Captain C.F. Gray) and Alan Deere (Air Commodore A.C. Deere) of New Zealand and Robert Stanford-Tuck (Wing Commander R.R. Stanford-Tuck) of England, had already begun to make their respective marks.

JEAN ACCART

Jean Accart, who was later to take his place in 345 Squadron, the Free French unit in Fighter Command, fought with distinction through much of the Battle of France. He is as good an example as any of the way some were to survive apparently fatal wounds. It was on 1 June 1940, within three weeks of the final collapse, that he was on the receiving end of a bullet which, in 999 cases out of 1000 would have killed instantly.

The shell struck him between the eyes and became embedded in his skull to a depth of five centimetres. It missed his brain by a whisker. Sixty other fragments were pitted in his face. The circumstances suggest that fate was keeping an eye on him that day.

Accart, flying a Curtis P–36 fighter, had attacked a Heinkel 111 in a formation of forty German bombers which were heading up the Rhone Valley, south of Lyons, at around 15,000 feet. After registering strikes on the aircraft, he saw the enemy begin to smoke and lose height rapidly – then a bullet hit him. He lost consciousness.

. . . I recovered momentarily, and passed my hand across my face. It was covered with blood. . . . My movements were slow and took an immense effort. . . . I gazed at the dashboard and, through a pink haze, saw vaguely that the airspeed indicator needle was going 'off the clock' . . . I was diving vertically. . . .

I had but one thought now – get out and jump. With a supreme effort I wrenched myself clear of the cockpit. . . . My body hit the tail plane. . . . I had enough sense still in me not to pull the rip-cord too soon to risk the parachute opening and tearing in the violent slipstream. Then I passed out completely. . . .

I came to in an ambulance which, seemingly, had no springs. I had to tell the driver to slow down to reduce the bumps and the jolts. . . .

At Pontarlier hospital, the doctors told me that my face was pock-marked with shell splinters and that a bullet had gouged a hole between my eyes the size of a 10–sou coin, and was lodged there. . . . My teeth were broken and my jaw ached; my left arm was almost completely paralysed; there was an open fracture of my left leg, and the whole of my body was lacerated and bruised. . . .

My leg was operated on immediately. . . . The next day I was evacuated to Lyons for the head operation. But my excitements had not ended.

We set off in a small hospital aircraft. Its slow speed and painful vibration made the journey seem interminable. . . . I heard the pilot remark that there would be fog round the airfield when we arrived at dusk. . . . I was now entirely blind, but I mentioned to Lieut Dr Brochard, who was accompanying me, that I knew the district well and Ambérieu was often open when the field at Bron was closed. . . .

Then, just as we were approaching Lyons, I heard the pilot saying that he was exhausted, that visibility was closing in and that he had never flown at night! His admission greatly annoyed me, for weak and tired though I was, I felt I could not endure another accident. I tried to visualize the position, and then I told the pilot (he was a reservist who had only flown for fun) that he should let down with a little throttle and at minimum speed. . . .

Suddenly, contrary to my advice, he cut the throttle completely. . . . The aircraft hit the ground hard, shaking me horribly; it bounced so high that the pilot had to open up and go round for another circuit in the darkness. . . . He got down on the second attempt with some bumps and bounces; but nothing was broken.

Half an hour later, I was in the operating theatre of Grange-Blanche hospital in the hands of two fine surgeons and in the care of the devoted sisters. . . . From my bed I heard, daily, the saddening news of the fighting. I soon gave up hope of ever getting back in time to lead my squadron again. . . .

The war was over for my trusted Curtis, too. It had hit the ground at terrific speed and shattered into a mass of pieces. . . . At least, I thought, the Germans wouldn't get it.

Editor's note: *In 1943, three years after this shattering experience, Jean Accart, risking much, escaped to England via the Pyrenees, Spain and North Africa, leaving his wife and five children in Savoy in Occupied France. To obscure his identity from the Germans and safeguard his family, he adopted the pseudonym, Francis Bernard; Commandant Francis Bernard was the name by which the Royal Air Force came to know him.*

Forty-five 'borrowed' years on, the bullet is still lodged in Accart's skull. The surgeons concluded that it was impossible to remove it without taking unacceptable risks.

Général Accart offered the foregoing, specially condensed version of the story which appeared in his book Chasseurs du Ciel *(Arthaud, Paris, 1946).*

COLIN FALKLAND GRAY

Colin Gray was now on the threshold of a run of uninterrupted success which, in the next five years, would take him to a place among the elite of World War II's fighter pilots. But, like the rest of them, he had to face the swings of the pendulum. Towards the end of April he was taking a short leave from his squadron (No. 54) based, then, at Hornchurch in Essex.

I was in Edinburgh and rang my twin brother, Ken, who, at that time, was flying Whitleys from Kinloss in Morayshire, on operations over Norway. Apparently he had been having a rather taxing time. He told me he was going on leave the next day, 1 May 1940, and was taking a Whitley down to his home base at Driffield in Yorkshire. He offered to pick me up from Leuchars, near St Andrews in Fifeshire, and we arranged to go on leave together.

I arrived at Leuchars the following morning, and some time later was told that a Whitley had crashed into a hill northwest of Dyce (near Aberdeen) in bad weather, and that the officer flying the aircraft had been killed. If we had not made this arrangement to meet at Leuchars, Ken's route to Driffield would have been nowhere near this area. He had already been awarded the DFC and a Czech War Cross at the time of his death. . . .

It used to be said in those days that nothing endured for long, neither the good nor the bad. The family had now suffered a hard loss, but two of Colin's subsequent experiences that summer suggested, in the fatalistic idiom of the times, that he was being 'kept for something'.

Consider Dunkirk towards the end of May.

The squadron was patrolling in the Gravelines area when we came across a couple of dozen Me 110s escorted by a dozen or so Me 109s.

During the ensuing melee I had a good squirt at a 109, and was wondering what to do next when I heard a tremendous clattering interspersed with a couple of lusty crumps. It took a moment or two to realize that the noise was caused by bullets striking the aircraft all along the fuselage and that the crumps were obviously cannon shells. The first of these exploded at the rear of my Spitfire, severing the elevator and the rudder trimmer wires, knocking out the hydraulic system and, as I discovered later, the air bottle. The second cannon shell missed my head by a cat's whisker, exploded in the port aileron neatly removing the pitot head and, with it, my airspeed indication, and throwing the aircraft into a spiral dive.

This was a most fortunate chance as it was probably better and quicker than any escape manoeuvre I could have devised. Indeed, I saw no more of my attacker – not that I had seen him in the first place!

My second piece of luck was that neither the cannon shells nor the fifty or so bullets which we subsequently counted, seemed to have done any vital damage, to the coolant system for example, or to me for that matter; and everything held together for the thirty-minute flight back across the Channel to base at Hornchurch.

The loss of air pressure meant that I could not fire my guns, which were air-operated in the Spitfire, but, frankly, I was not very interested in hanging around to try them out anyway. It also meant that I had no flaps or brakes, which made landing tricky especially as I had no airspeed indicator. The loss of hydraulic fluid meant the undercarriage would not come down in the normal way. However, the emergency CO_2 bottle worked like a charm.

Subsequent investigation showed that the main elevator controls were almost severed and were only hanging on by a few strands. . . .

Having walked away from that, Colin Gray now had, on 31 August, what he calls 'perhaps my most fortunate experience'. The battle for the control of British skies was moving on fast to its climax. The Luftwaffe were still concentrating their attacks on the fighter airfields in 11 Group and on the radar installations. Now it was once again the turn of Hornchurch and 54 Squadron to catch it.

The airfield was bombed just as we were taking off. Twice the squadron was ordered to scramble, and each time the order was cancelled after we had started our motors. We had stopped them for the second time when we were again ordered off. By this time the engines were getting really hot and were difficult to start. I was leading a subsection of three aircraft. We managed to get going and taxied into position on the airfield where, according to flying discipline, I was supposed to wait for my flight commander, Georgie Gribble, to lead the way.

However, by this time my R/T had warmed up, and I heard the controller panicking: '54 Squadron take off, take off, for f—'s sake take off.' So for f—'s sake I took off, hotly pursued by George and his section who had not heard the message but figured there must be something very wrong for me to act like that. As I reached the far boundary I looked back and saw the whole airfield covered in the smoke and dust of exploding bombs. . . . Three of our aircraft didn't make it. . . .

Group Captain C.F. Gray, Waikanae, New Zealand, 1984

ALAN CHRISTOPHER DEERE

Some fighter pilots always seemed to be in the thick of it. One of them was Al Deere, another rugged and popular New Zealander, who, after an eventful Battle of Britain, was to lead, first, No. 54 Squadron from Hornchurch and then the famous Biggin Hill Wing in Kent.

Al made lucky escapes his business. He wrote a book after the war and called it Nine Lives *(Hodder & Stoughton, London, 1959). It was well named. There wasn't a leader in the Royal Air Force who survived more potentially lethal situations.*

One of his closest calls came in September 1940, at Catterick in Yorkshire. After weeks of pounding in the Battle of Britain, his squadron had been sent north to rest, regroup and train new recruits. The battle casualties had to be replaced. One of the most promising newcomers was a sergeant pilot named Squires. Deere took him up for his final squadron test – thirty minutes' combat with one of the exceptional exponents of the fighting art.

The job of putting Sergeant Squires through his paces had, in fact, been allotted to my deputy in the morning's training programme, but when he woke up with 'flu I stood in and took Squires up instead. I might have known what such a change of plan could mean!

After the first encounter, which began at 10,000 feet, we found ourselves down to 3000 feet. 'OK, Red 2,' I said, 'I'll climb up to 10,000 feet again and we'll have another go.'

After a series of hectic manoeuvres, I saw the nose of Squires' aircraft right on top of me. The next second he had flown into me and chewed clean through my tail. The Spitfire whipped into a vicious spin, completely out of control. The centrifugal force kept me anchored to my seat. I was stuck fast.

At some point the force must have lessened. After twisting and turning, kicking and fighting, I was released for a couple of seconds from the cockpit, only to be blown onto the remnants of my tail plane where, again, I stuck fast.

I reached for my rip-cord handle, only to realize that my parachute had been partly ripped from my back, and the handle was out of my reach.

'Fancy,' I remember saying out loud, 'after all that fighting, being killed this way.'

Then, suddenly, and miraculously, with the ground now uncomfortably close, my parachute opened, only partially, but just enough and just in time. Almost at the same moment came the impact. I was submerged horizontally in a thick, foul, stinking farmyard cesspool. I nearly drowned in the muck, as my back was agony and I could barely move.

A passing motorist and his wife came running to my aid. Despite the stench and filth, they put me on the back seat of their car and drove me seven miles back to Catterick from where I was rushed to hospital.

The 'soft' landing in the farmer's cesspool – a million to one shot – had undoubtedly saved my life.

Air Commodore A.C. Deere, 'The Deere Papers',
Wendover, Bucks, 1984

ROBERT ROLAND STANFORD-TUCK

Ask the fifth form at St Dominic's (the sixth might be otherwise occupied) to name a well-known fighter pilot of World War II and as likely as not they would plump for Robert Stanford-Tuck. The name has rolled round the globe for forty years and more. Talk to him now on the telephone and he will just have returned from Sydney, or be taking off in a couple of hours for Salt Lake City, Utah, Johannesburg, Winnipeg or Auckland. His lectures and his record create the demand.

Squadron commander and wing leader, Bob Stanford-Tuck's war was stopped uncomfortably short by a burst of flak at low level over France in January 1942. At that point he had 27 victories to his credit with 8 more probably destroyed. He was on his way to the treble chance. He had also baled out four times. For Bob Tuck, life has never been dull.

There was, however, one experience which, coming as it did right at the end of the Battle of Britain, was a cruel and personally deranging misfortune.

In late September 1940 92 Squadron was stationed at Pembrey, and our time was mostly spent chasing reconnaissance aircraft, hit-and-run raiders on the docks, and various other targets.

At 22.00 one dark and drizzly evening, I was being plotted onto a Ju 88, which I had been stalking around Wales, mainly in the Porthcawl area of Glamorganshire, when I suddenly sighted it flying from one large cumulus to another. Above the clouds the moon was so bright it seemed like daylight. The Junkers was at 500 yards' range passing directly in front of me, which is a very difficult shot. However, I was able to get in a 3–second burst as he dived fast for cover. I don't think I hit him, but before he went into cloud, I distinctly saw a cluster of black dots – his bombs – fall from the belly of the aircraft. I called up the controller at Pembrey informing him briefly of this action, and further told him that I was getting dangerously low on fuel, and would he give me a bearing for base immediately. This he did, and a few minutes later I was letting down through cloud, which was 10/10ths. I landed safely at Pembrey, having been airborne two hours exactly.

Early next morning I received a telephone call from my father, who had sad news to report. My brother-in-law, John, had been killed the previous night. John, twenty-three, was a Territorial, called up at the very start of the war and posted to the Queens Westminsters. I told my father that in these circumstances I would have no difficulty in getting three days' leave and would fly down to be with the family.

Later on in the morning while patrolling over the Bristol Channel, I suddenly had a dreadful fear that I might be connected with my brother-in-law's death. Immediately after landing at Pembrey, I grabbed a telephone, got through to my ops room and spoke to the officer who had been controlling my flight the previous night. I told him that I wished to know immediately what other actions had taken place, as I had suddenly realized that John had been stationed under canvas not far from St Donat's Castle. The controller told me that a stick of bombs had landed in this area, and it was the only action in Wales that night, as the weather had been appalling. I then asked if there had been any casualties from the jettisoned stick of bombs, and after an appreciable pause – I could hear a lot of paper rustling – he told me that one soldier had been killed in the camp outside St Donat's Castle.

As I considered this news, I was stunned by the terrible chance that this one stick of bombs had killed my own brother-in-law.

The odds against this were millions to one. If that Ju 88 had taken off from its French base just two seconds earlier, or two seconds later. . . . If the wind had been a shade stronger or lighter. . . . If the German pilot had flown 100 feet higher or lower. . . . If that break in the cloud had been smaller or larger. . . . If I had held my fire for one more second, or opened up a moment sooner. . . . But the astounding fact had to be faced, had to be lived with: out of all the millions of people in Britain, those jettisoned bombs had wiped out John's young life. . . . I could not avoid the awful truth that, quite innocently, I had caused his death.

Wing Commander R.R. Stanford-Tuck, Sandwich Bay,
Kent, 1984

Dyeing to Live

'The more I practise, the luckier I get . . .'

Gary Player, the South African golfer, may not have been the first to say it, but he was certainly the one who made the old saw stick. The principle had its adherents in wartime. . . . Plan the detail meticulously. . . . Work at it. . . . Think the eventualities through. . . . Heed the briefing. . . . Follow the rules. . . . Check the equipment. And the luck will take care of itself. So the teaching used to go.

Wing Commander Jack Rose, who kept going longer, operationally, than most, was the archetypal protagonist of the cult; and with reason. France and the Battle of Britain in 1940; Spitfires with the Poles in 1941 and 1942; command of 184 Squadron in 1943 with its rocket-firing Hurricanes and Typhoons; then, finally, from 1944 onwards, Hurricanes again, this time with 221 Group in Burma in support of General Slim's XIVth Army. . . . It was a war, seemingly, of almost perpetual motion which spilled over into the peace with an active and distinguished career in the Colonial Service – Rhodesia, British Guiana, the Cayman Islands and the rest. . . .

There was one incident with 32 Squadron at the end of August 1940, which, if it didn't say it all, at least threw down a challenge to luck. Based with its Hurricanes at Biggin, 32 was commuting daily to Hawkinge, the forward airfield on the Kentish coast, just behind the Folkestone cliffs.

On the morning of 25 August, each pilot was issued with a square, cloth-covered pack of fluorescein, a greenish-yellow dye in powdered form. These packs were to be sewn to the pilots' mae wests, and thereafter anyone who was shot down and left floating in the sea could hope that the rescue services would be attracted by the telltale stain from the fluorescein in the water. . . .

While we were waiting at our dispersal for the next scramble, I decided to pass the time sewing on my newly issued fluorescein pack to my mae west. A friendly parachute packer lent me an outsize needle and thread, and the job was soon done. So far as I remember, all my companions delegated the sewing operation later on to the parachute section or their wives or girlfriends.

Soon after I had finished my sewing, 'A' flight was scrambled, and within minutes our six Hurricanes, led by Flight Lieutenant Michael Crossley, were airborne. After climbing through thin cloud at 6–7000 feet, we were given several changes of course by the Biggin Hill controller.

At 12,000 feet we sighted a formation of some twelve Dornier 215s heading for France. High above and behind them were a number of escorting Me 109s dancing in the sun like a swarm of gnats on a summer evening.

. . . We quickly closed with the bombers, hoping to be in and out before the 109s could reach us. Mike Crossley, on the extreme left, attacked his target which soon poured smoke and began to lose height. . . . I closed with the Dornier next on the right and fired a 4– or 5–second burst. . . .

The engagement then followed a customary pattern – counter-attacks by the 109s; strikes on the tail unit and fuselage of Rose's aircraft which then became uncontrollable; then the bale out into the Channel and a couple of hours in the water before being spotted, fortuitously, by another Hurricane of 32 Squadron engaged, not on a rescue flight, but on a quite different operational mission. The fluorescein had served its purpose. . . .

Without the pack that I had sewn to my mae west earlier that day my chance of rescue would have been slim. Almost certainly I would have drifted down the Channel, out of sight of land . . . and joined the lengthening list of pilots 'missing believed killed'.

There was pathos in the ending.

Although the outcome was fortunate for me, on the same operation Pilot Officer Keith Gillman was shot down and reported 'missing believed killed'.

His body was never recovered. . . . A week later his portrait was displayed throughout the country on a Royal Air Force recruiting poster. . . .

I have often since wondered whether Keith, too, might have been rescued if his fluorescein pack had been sewn to his mae west before he took off on his last flight that August afternoon. . . .

Wing Commander Jack Rose, Broadway, Woodbury,
Devonshire, 1984

'Dizzy' Allen's Secrets*

. . . I baled out once when a half-witted sergeant pilot collided with my Spitfire and I landed up an oak tree near East Grinstead†. . . . As it was a Sunday and the pubs were not yet open, the whole of East Grinstead looked at this apparition drifting down from heaven, and the Home Guard thought that as I was so obviously a bloody German, they would take potshots at me as I tried to avoid some very high-power electric cables. Their blunderbusses, needless to say, got nowhere near me; their hands were shaking so hard, possibly from senility, or DTs, or fright, or excitement – I don't know what – but they missed me by a mile. . . .

Bodie was our local ace, and a true one at that. He didn't claim anything he didn't see explode in front of his very eyes. He was, was 'Bogle', a bloody good hombre. He should never have been promoted out of 66 Squadron. . . .

. . . Bodie recounted his experiences of one of his last days with 66. . . . These are his own words, take a lot of trouble reading them:

The second [enemy aircraft] was spinning. There was a piece off one wing. He spiralled crazily down into the water. It reminded me of chestnut leaves in the autumn, fluttering down onto the school playing fields. He hit, exploded, and petrol and oil burned fiercely on the surface of the sea. The flames died away; only a few bits of wreckage remained floating.

I then remembered having seen another Dornier explode and burn – let me think, when was it? Why, only that very morning! It was still Sunday, 15 September. The day had been a year.

I flew to the coast and set course for home. Passing low over fields and villages, rivers and towns, I looked down on labourers working, children at play beside a big red-brick schoolhouse, a bomb crater two streets away; little black heads turning to white blobs as they heard my engine and looked up. I thought of workers in shops and factories, of stretcher-parties and ARP‡ wardens. I hoped the All Clear had gone. I was tired. I'd done my best for them. . . .

Cor, stone the crows! Could John Milton have written better prose than that? ' . . . Thrones, Dominations, Princedoms, Virtues, Powers. . . . No fear lest dinner cool. . . . All night the dreadless angel unpursu'd. . . . Arms on armour clashing bray'd horrible discord, and the maddening wheels of brazen chariots rag'd; dire was the noise of conflict. . . .'

*See page 20.
†In Sussex. (Ed.)
‡Air-raid protection.

Don't ask me whether Bodie did any better than Milton. That is my secret. . . .

Wing Commander H.R. 'Dizzy' Allen, Adderbury, Oxfordshire, 1984

A Question of Identification

Security in the Home Counties of England during the Battle of Britain was super-tight. The public supported the official line with its own brand of enthusiastic, free enterprise surveillance. Group Captain Lord George Douglas-Hamilton (The Earl of Selkirk), one of the four Douglas-Hamilton brothers all of whom were, at one time, squadron commanders in the Service, had his own taste of it. He was then the Chief Intelligence Officer at the Headquarters of Fighter Command, and the C-in-C's (Air Chief Marshal Sir Hugh Dowding) close confidant. As such, he was required to pay frequent visits to the battle stations.

I was returning from Hornchurch to Hendon and had been delayed by an air raid. By that time the evening was turning to nightfall and the visibility murky, so without night-flying equipment I decided that land was on the whole a more satisfactory location. I settled on a playing field in Cricklewood,* in spite of goal posts and other obstructions which were obligatory at that time.

Rather satisfied with myself, I was surprised to see a sturdy young man advancing menacingly towards me waving a cricket stump. He was quickly followed by an officer of the police who politely but firmly required my presence at the police station. He was not impressed by my uniform nor by the papers which I carried, so I rang my office at Fighter Command where my voice was recognized. This made no impression on the officer so strict were the instructions issued to the police.

He then asked did I know anyone at Hendon, to which I could only say that I had no reason to believe that I did. However we proceeded to Hendon and there my luck changed; by pure chance I met Squadron Leader Urie whom I had known in Glasgow with 602 Squadron, formerly commanded by my brother, Douglo.† At last the diligent police officer was content.

If anyone doubts the value of such strict policies, their views would I believe change following even a cursory glance at the book *Double Cross*, by the late Sir John Masterman. Therein is very convincing evidence how valuable these policies were.

The Earl of Selkirk, Wimborne, Dorset, 1984

Anglo-German Triumvirate

It is usually worth looking back and seeing how the successful and highly publicized wartime figures – Allied and German – began their climb to the

---

*In northwest London.
†Group Captain The Duke of Hamilton, 14th Duke and eldest of the four brothers.

summit. The start, quite often, was inauspicious. The three characters who follow, Johnnie Johnson (Air Vice-Marshal J.E. Johnson) of the Allies, and Werner Schröer (Oberstleutnant Werner Schröer) and Edu Neumann (Oberst Eduard Neumann) of the Luftwaffe, gave no hint by their initial experiences of the accomplishments that were to accrue.

Johnson became, in the second half of the European war, the highest-scoring Allied fighter pilot, with 38 confirmed kills falling to his guns. He led the Kenley and 122 Canadian wings with an aggressive verve which made him a legend in his time. He was never shot down; indeed, it is said that only once in all his combat experience did the enemy register so much as a single strike upon his aircraft. When asked once how he managed to preserve such a record, Johnnie had ready a typically quick and unabashed reply. 'I was too f— smart,' he said. And it was probably true.

Here he tells in his own direct words how fortunate he was ever to get the chance to achieve lasting greatness.

SOME LACK! SOME MORAL! SOME FIBRE!

In his excellent autobiography that superb test pilot, Jeffrey Quill, relates how, during the Battle of Britain, the Spitfire's ailerons were much too heavy at speed and writes 'of struggling with both hands on the stick at well over 400 miles per hour and swearing and sweating profusely . . .'.*

In 1938, whilst playing rugby, I was brought down heavily and broke my right collarbone. Although I did not know it at the time the break was improperly set, and the nerves to the forearm were imprisoned below the bone. A Spitfire crash at Sealand in the summer of 1940 had given it a nasty wrench, and the old break was tender and sore. I had to be very careful when I swung the parachute straps over my shoulder, and when I tightened the harness straps in the cockpit.

I began to pack the shoulder with wads of cotton wool, which I wore next to the skin held in place by strips of adhesive tape. But the trouble did not finish with the shoulder, for sometimes the fingers of the right hand seemed cold and lifeless and had little feeling in them.

I could fly the Spitfire with one hand, but dogfighting with those heavy ailerons was very much a two-handed affair, and as that fateful September wore on the pain increased. I approached a young reserve doctor in the mess, unofficially, on what I hoped would be on the 'old-boy' basis. Could he give me some heat treatment and massage without the usual form-filling?

On the following morning my Commanding Officer, Billy Burton (Squadron Leader H.F. Burton) said that the station commander, Stephen Hardy (Group Captain S. Hardy), wanted to see me, but he would not tell me what it was about.

We were shown into the station commander's room. Hardy shifted his 6½-foot frame in his chair and acknowledged my salute with a nod, did not invite me to stand at ease, and even Burton stood rigidly at attention a pace behind. It was a formal interview and the atmosphere was cold. Hardy came straight to the point.

'The docs tell me that you are suffering from some sort of affliction to

*Spitfire: A Test Pilot's Story, page 175 (John Murray, 1983).

your right shoulder so I am grounding you, and as I see it there are two alternatives open to you. Apparently your shoulder did not trouble you during your training when you flew light aeroplanes, so I could have you transferred to Training Command where you could be an instructor.'

Hardy paused and looked out of the window. He eased the neckband of his shirt with some irritation, and I suddenly knew why the incident was so distasteful to him. During my training days, several of my colleagues had opted for instructor-duties rather than operational flying, and it was not unknown for operational pilots to request postings to less hazardous tasks. This was known as 'lack of moral fibre', and Hardy was about to slot me into this category.

'Or,' Hardy continued, 'you can take the chance on the operating table. The docs think that if your shoulder was opened up and reset there would be a good chance of getting it right once and for all. The choice is yours.'

I did not hesitate, and elected to go to hospital where my shoulder was fixed up by a brilliant young surgeon. At the end of 1940 I was fit for full flying duties and rejoined my squadron, grateful to the Service and the understanding officers in it. They had offered me a second chance, and the opportunity to live and fight with men who knew how to conduct themselves in war.

Air Vice-Marshal J.E. Johnson, Hargate, near Buxton,
Derbyshire, 1984

DESTINED TO SURVIVE?

Werner Schröer was a 22-year-old Luftwaffe leutnant when, in August 1940, he joined his squadron in the Pas de Calais. The attacks across the Straits to targets in the southeast of England were warming to their climax. The Messerschmitt squadron to which he had been posted was, daily, in the forefront of the fighting. It had had many successes, but so, too, it had had its losses. Schröer and his two companions, freshly trained and totally inexperienced operationally, had been sent to fill the gaps.

The mischances which Schröer now modestly recounts should be seen against a later, and unusually successful, Service career. After an unlikely start on the Western Front, he moved, in the next five, relentless years, to North Africa, and the Western Desert, back across the Mediterranean to Sicily and thence to Germany, finally ending up on the Eastern Front. By the end of the war, this proved leader had amassed a total of 114 enemy aircraft destroyed, 102 of them in North Africa and the Mediterranean theatre. He had survived being shot down three times.

Subsequently it was an acute intellect and judgement, and a flair for languages, that enabled Werner Schröer to rise, in three decades of peace, to a senior executive appointment with the Messerschmitt-Bolkow-Blohm company in Germany. Here, indeed, was a lifetime of endeavour.

The very first operation which Werner flew with his squadron, on 28 August 1940, could well, but for an act or two of fate, also have been his last. He wrote this personal account of it only a few months before his untimely death on 10 February 1985.

We were living at the time in a picturesque old castle near Calais which the squadron had aptly named 'Château Schloss'. But, as newcomers, we could only listen in the evenings to the battle-tried pilots' stirring tales of the day's operations. Players and Woodbines, abandoned by British troops as they evacuated Dunkirk, did not come our way. The cigarettes were jealously guarded by the CO who distributed them personally to the squadron. Having not flown a single sortie, we did not qualify for such largesse.

However, as the ranks continued to thin, our chance eventually came. It wasn't a happy start. Flying with my leader, I was hit at about 30,000 feet over London either by a Spitfire or a Hurricane; I don't know which. I never saw it!

It was a miracle that I got back to base with my No. 1 shepherding me. Having been hit in the radiator, and with the resultant loss of coolant, my engine seized and I had to glide the last five minutes with a feathered propellor.

That was chance number one. Number two followed quickly afterwards.

As a punishment for my somewhat inferior flying ability, I was 'privileged' to fly the second-in-command's aircraft back to the maintenance depot at Krefeld; it couldn't be repaired by the squadron.

After I took off I found to my surprise that the undercarriage wouldn't retract. Other pilots will understand how one feels flying over land with a lowered undercarriage. It was a painful process for me – particularly when I had to land at Major Wilhelm Balthasar's JG 3 airfield. It was just my luck that the Major should be there to see me arrive. Experienced in the Spanish Civil War, he was now one of our exceptional pilots and leaders.

'Why are you flying about with your undercarriage permanently lowered?' he asked.

'Because, sir, it cannot be raised,' I replied.

'How many operational sorties have you flown?' he then enquired.

'One, sir,' I answered.

'I see,' he said. 'Well, next time just try pressing the undercarriage retraction button after take-off.'

I refuelled and departed feeling hurt, humiliated and dejected.

Somehow this unfair reproach had been very unsettling. I had just passed south of Brussels when the radiator temperature 'went off the clock'. It was the last straw! Memories of the strikes in my radiator at 30,000 feet over London were fresh in my mind. I decided I must find an airfield . . . fast!

Between anxious glances at the 'rad' temperature, I spotted a landing strip, apparently with parked aircraft beside it. As I made my approach someone fired a red Verey light. Whatever's up? I thought. Can't they see I want to land urgently? I tried again . . . only to receive another red flare.

I made a third attempt. This time I could see the 'marksman' as he fired yet another 'red'. I was at 500 feet. I don't care, I concluded, I'm going in to land . . . What the hell!

Suddenly, I realized my mistake. This was a dummy airfield with mounds and dips and obstructions. There wasn't a runway there at all. I touched down and bounced and bounced again. The 109 swung from left to right, touching a mound with the wing tip. With the throttle closed and the control column pulled right back into my stomach, the aircraft rolled to a standstill. I got out and walked round it. Apparently it was undamaged.

The flabbergasted soldier came running up with his rifle. 'Whatever were you doing?' he asked. 'This is a dummy airfield!'

I explained my predicament. 'Here,' he said, seeing my anxiety and pulling a bottle of French cognac from his pocket, 'take a swig of this.' He gave me a cigarette.

I was overcome with worry. Would they now have to come and dismantle the aircraft and then cart it away? It would be the end of my flying career. I'd be banished to the infantry or, at best, the paratroopers. That would be my fate. I had already had a bad experience during my training, landing prematurely on a cross-country flight. I had lost the way with other pupils. Another black mark would probably mean the end.

The poor soldier gave me a spade, and for the next few hours I toiled away trying to level off the worst of the bumps. 'I must aim to use the same path for take-off,' I said.

Swinging the propeller to try to start the engine was as much of a trial for me as it was for the soldier, but, between us, we succeeded. I taxied back to the start of the strip taking extra care to watch out for obstacles and noting special features for the take-off.

. . . A hand wave, and I steadily opened the throttle against the brakes until they wouldn't hold it any longer, and away I went. . . .

After a hazardous run, full of bounces and death-defying balancing acts, I was airborne – soaked in perspiration. I might even have forgotten to raise the undercarriage, but that was no longer, it seemed, important. . . . I was off the ground.

I circled the strip, waggled my wings at the worthy soldier, and headed east for Krefeld. Once there, I did not dare to travel even the forty kilometres to my home; I was too scared lest, in a moment of weakness, I might reveal my true story. And when, eventually, I got back to the squadron I still didn't tell anyone of my experience. . . .

It wasn't until after the war that I actually divulged my secret to my former squadron commander. . . . By then, he had a lower rank than I. . . .

Such were the chances of war.

Oberstleutnant Werner Schröer, Ottobrun, Germany, 1984

Postscript: Almost an Unfair Cop

Werner Schröer mentions his embarrassing brush with one of the Luftwaffe's elite, Major Balthasar. Wilhelm Balthasar had been blooded in the Spanish Civil War and was now an acknowledged star. 'Efficient and reckless' was the epithet the dark, suave and strikingly good-looking Adolf Galland once applied to his comrade. Mölders, Galland, Wieck and Balthasar were the German stand-outs at the time. . . .

There had previously been an explosive and potentially lethal exchange between Galland and Balthasar during the last days of the Battle of France. Those who interrogated Galland immediately after the war have recorded a note of the incident. It shows how lucky he was to be alive to recount the tale.

. . . Galland [was flying] an olive-green Me 109E . . . [He was] experimenting to see whether it was less visible than the usual blue model. One day, when flying alone, he heard Hauptmann Balthasar, a young gruppenkommandeur of JG 3, talking over his R/T to the gruppe, showing them how to attack an enemy aircraft.

Balthasar said: 'Below is a Hurricane on its own.* I will shoot it down. Watch closely. I dive and approach fast from the rear and slightly underneath. . . . The range is 600 metres – 500 metres – 400 – 300 – 200. . . . The fool's asleep. I will close to 50 metres.'

Galland listened admiringly to the thorough teaching technique of Balthasar. Suddenly, he saw specks of light flying past him. . . . He dived away, cursing and roaring with anger. Balthasar was taken aback to hear an unmistakable and very familiar voice saying over the R/T: 'That's enough of this bloody nonsense!'†

ON A WING AND A PRAYER

There were, broadly, two types of wing and gruppe leaders in the Allied air forces and the Luftwaffe, and each attracted adherents and success. On the one hand, there were those who reckoned that the primary task was to seek out and destroy the enemy without being too much concerned about the cost. On the other, there were the counterparts who led less dramatically from the front and whose prime aim was to seize whatever opportunities were going – but not at the expense of undue losses. Their anxiety was to create the openings that others might score the points.

It was largely a matter of preference and style, and it usually boiled down to a leader's temperament, and the equipment he had to work with.

Edu Neumann, at one time the Kommandeur of 1 Gruppe of Jagdgeschwader 27 and, later, the highly regarded Kommodore of JG 27 in North Africa, fell readily into the second category. He became one of the Luftwaffe's ablest and most effective fighter leaders. For him, with his selfless approach, the team was the thing with as many members of it being given the chance to kill. It was the gruppe's total that mattered, not his own.‡

On the strength of his leadership in the Western Desert, Neumann was appointed, early in 1943, to Adolf Galland's staff in Berlin after Galland had become the head of the Fighter Arm of the Luftwaffe (General der Jagdflieger). As such, he was effectively the General's right-hand man. They have remained close friends ever since.

At the beginning of 1944, Edu was transferred to Rumania to head up the day- and night-fighter presence in that theatre. His tactical ability in this role was confirmed by a successful defence of the Ploesti oilfields. Subsequently, from the autumn of 1944, he performed the same service in

*Balthasar had mistaken the newly camouflaged 109E for a Hurricane; understandable in the circumstances. (Ed.)

†Forty-four years on, 'Dolfo' Galland (the nickname is what his Royal Air Force friends call him; Douglas Bader started it) made this comment: 'Wilhelm Balthasar, who was one of our best fighter pilots, had been a friend since we served together in Spain. I was lucky that day because I was on the same radio frequency. I realized only just in time that I was Wilhelm's target. My new camouflage had "foxed" him.' (Ed.)

‡This is born out by his own record of 17 Allied aircraft destroyed. (Ed.)

northern Italy; this embraced the reorganization of the Regia Aeronautica whose remnants were then equipped with German aircraft.

Neumann, who was to bring to his post-war business interests both in the distribution of manufactured products, and in the automatic lift (elevator) field,* many of the qualities he dispensed to the Luftwaffe, might never have had the chance to shine. Had his guardian angel not lent him a hand at the height of the Battle of Britain, he could well have spent the next five years as a prisoner of the Allies, thus denying his Service the use of his special talents.

The traumatic experience he now describes shows the part that luck played in the fighting. It also reveals how differently from the Royal Air Force the Luftwaffe saw the battle tactics.

September 1940 . . . an autumn day when our fighters were to escort the bombers on their way to the London area. The attacking formations were well positioned and on time for the rendezvous. This was vital for us. With such a short endurance, the single-engined fighters had only a small safety margin to play with. We could stay airborne for around 1 hour and 30 minutes. If we were engaged in combat this came down quickly to about 1 hour 15. . . .

There were, for us, two types of bomber escort. There was the close escort when we stayed near the formations throughout a mission; and then there was the looser, wider-ranging cover when we remained above and in visual contact with the bombers. This gave rather more freedom of action.

We always wanted to do our best to support the bomber crews, but we were placed in an almost impossible position. If we stayed with the formations and remained close to them all along the route, we had to cut back our speed. This gave little scope for manoeuvre. It also made us more vulnerable to attack from behind.

Normally, the defending RAF fighters attacked at speed from a considerable height,† cutting straight through the mixed formations and firing at anything in their sights, before diving away fast towards the ground. By the time we had recovered, the enemy was nowhere to be seen. After this nightmare was over, and we had regrouped, it was soon clear that both bombers and fighters had suffered losses. Our crews, if they were lucky, would become prisoners of war.

The RAF, on the other hand, were fighting over their own territory. If their pilots baled out or force-landed unhurt, they could quickly return to their bases and find other aircraft to fly. It was only a matter of time before this kind of unequal attrition had to cease. . . .

We often flew into the London air space with the bombers which would drop their loads on targets along the Thames. Then they would turn away south at around 14,000 feet. Sometimes they would hold this southerly heading for too long, forgetting how critical was our time factor and how short we were of fuel. . . .

*There was a short spell after the surrender when Edu Neumann became a truck driver for the US forces! (Ed.)

†The Luftwaffe's impression – and a most interesting comment. Paradoxically, the RAF's concern was that so often the squadrons were underneath the incoming raids and, therefore, liable to be 'bounced' from above.

On this September day, then, I was stationed, as the gruppenkommandeur, immediately behind the bombers, with my wingman, a young Bavarian NCO, flying beside me. He had been allotted to fly with me by 1 Staffel.*

As we headed towards the target area I spotted enemy fighters climbing up towards us from below, while another squadron was starting to dive down on us from seven o'clock above. My instinct told me to turn into the aircraft which were attacking from above, and meet them head on. . . .

I fired a short salvo of 2–cm cannon and all at once my Me 109 shook and then veered sharply off to the right. A large, gaping hole, big enough for a man to put his arms round, had appeared in the starboard wing just above the ammunition magazine. There had been an explosion, but I never discovered whether I had been hit by a fighter or if it was the result of a spontaneous ignition when I fired my guns. Whatever it was, the damage compelled me to reduce speed and height. . . .

Above the southern English countryside there was a solid layer of cloud, the top of which was some 3000 feet. This acted as a backcloth against which one's aircraft was silhouetted from above. The closer one got to it the more clearly one could be seen.

With my reduced speed I now sought the cover afforded by the layer of cloud which was some 1000 feet thick. However, with the large hole in the wing, the aircraft was pulling so hard to starboard that I came out of the cloud heading west instead of east.

I was now roughly over Eastbourne, but the Channel was too wide here to attempt a crossing. I, therefore, decided to try to work my way along the coast. I could see the outline of the headland at Dungeness, known to our pilots as the 'thin shit', a vulgar expression relating to diarrhoea! I felt, however, I could still find protection in the layer of low cloud which stretched along the coast so it seemed to be safe to stay over the land.

My wingman, who had put up a fine performance in staying with me after momentarily getting separated in the combat, was now critically short of fuel. I thus gave him a direct order to return to base. If he was going to stand any chance of getting back, he would have to break off at once.

Reluctantly, he acknowledged the instruction. 'Message understood,' he replied.

Now I was alone. Ironically, over the R/T, I heard one of the young pilots calling out plaintively that he was on his own and wanted to know what to do.

'Fly east,' I said, slowly and with emphasis. 'Fly hard east.'

The next moment I recognized the voice of my friend, Hauptman Adolf, adding his comment. 'Just wait, laddie, a Spitfire will be along in a minute and then you will no longer be alone.'

Then there was silence. This little exchange, and the protection which the cloud layer offered, made me forget the fear which had haunted me since the explosion in the wing. After an eternity of threading my way along the coast, I pinpointed myself just south of Dover. At last, I thought, the shortest stretch of water across to France lay ahead of me.

But it wasn't my day. Luck wasn't with me. To my horror I now saw

*No. 1 Squadron. (Ed.)

that the cloud layer which had befriended me along the coast had broken up over the water; out to sea there was clear, bright sunshine. Only one white cloud was visible in the distance. Lord! I thought, if only I could reach it!

Now my guardian angels (and there certainly seemed to be several of them) stood by me. I reached the protecting cloud, but no sooner had I come out the other side than another shock awaited me. Down below, I saw a number of single-engined fighters circling just above the water. What a life! But in a moment, and thankfully, I identified them as friendly. They were covering an air/sea rescue pick-up. . . .

I felt there wasn't anything else that *could* happen now. I crossed the coast south of Calais and prepared to land at the airfield at Guines.

The 109 was extremely difficult to control laterally and directionally. As I touched down it began to swing violently. The starboard wing had dropped and hit the ground. . . . And yet it didn't seem to matter. . . . At last I was down safely *on land!*

When I got out of the aircraft I saw the actual size of the hole in the wing. It would have taken two men to have got their arms round it, not one. Had I known the extent of the damage I might well have baled out. . . . Sometimes it was better not to know one's danger!

What of my brave wingman? He had landed safely just before me. I walked over and commended him warmly for his devotion to duty. When one thinks that he was new to this kind of warfare, and had never flown with me before, it was a miracle that he had been able to stay with me throughout that horrific return flight.

But the greatest miracle – for me – was my safe return. I could hardly believe my luck that an aircraft so badly damaged was capable of remaining even remotely airworthy. . . .

And what of the young 109 pilot who was advised to await the arrival of the Spitfire? He had returned to our airfield unscathed. . . . Beginners also had their guardian angels!

Oberst Eduard Neumann, Munich, Germany, 1984

Good luck reaches farther than long arms
Proverb

Destined to Rise?

By the end of the Battle of Britain, Adolf Galland was on course for the upper reaches of the Luftwaffe. Few doubted that, with his background and training, with the experience he had amassed in the Spanish war, in Poland, France and now in the daylight air over Britain, and with his ability as a pilot and leader, he would rise fast. A winning, but tough, character would serve him in the in-fighting which infests every service. When Göring, with whom he was later to fall out, appointed Galland General of the Fighter Arm of the Luftwaffe no one was particularly surprised. It was a natural.

Apart from his passing brush with Wilhelm Balthasar, 'Dolfo' Galland had had other near misses from which Providence had alone appeared to shield him. It was as far back as October 1935, when he was practising aerobatics for flying displays in Germany, that he first escaped with his life.

I hit the ground at an angle of about 45 degrees after recovering too late from a spin. I was then a young leutnant in the Richthofen fighter gruppe. I survived, first, because my seat broke clear of the fuselage, thus softening the impact and, second, because a famous surgeon, Professor Dr Walter Sauerbruch, was, by chance, doing his temporary national service at the hospital to which I was rushed after the crash. . . .

Almost five years later, 'Dolfo' was mixing it again with death when, on 3 June 1940, he took part in the big attack that the Luftwaffe mounted against airfields and air installations around Paris. The operation bore the code name 'Paula'.

During an intense and vigorous combat with French Morane 406 fighters, I collided with an already damaged aircraft, losing my antenna mast* and twisting my vertical stabilizer.† I was lucky to be able to land OK at my airfield. . . .

Then there were the ups and downs of the Battle of Britain itself. Fortune favoured him in one bizarre happening.

Quite early in the battle, I was leading my staffel when we got involved in some violent dogfights with the Royal Air Force. I had expended a lot of ammunition for little apparent result when all my guns jammed. As so often happens in such engagements, I had got separated both from my No. 2 and from the rest of my staffel. I therefore took the first opportunity to clear off back to base.

With my nose down, and at full throttle, I was in a shallow dive going home fast, when suddenly I was conscious of a shadow coming up on my right. It was a Spitfire going even faster. When it was no more than thirty feet or so away from me, the pilot waved his hand before breaking sharply to starboard and disappearing altogether.

Years later, by an extraordinary coincidence, I encountered the pilot again. He was an Australian. He told me he had intended to shoot me down when, to his disgust, he found that he had already used up all his ammunition. . . .

It reminded me of an old German proverb: 'If you aren't lucky, you'll die.'

Generalleutnant Adolf Galland, Bonn, Germany, 1984

*Aerial.
†Fore and aft trimming (balancing) device.

St Paul's Flight

And now abideth faith, hope, charity, these three . . .

Corinthians 1, chapter xiii, verse 13

While the eyes of the world were fastened upon the fighting over southern and southeast England, things in the Mediterranean and the Middle East were now hotting up. Italy's entry into the war on 10 June 1940 had transformed the theatre. And nowhere did this event strike harder or with greater reality than in the fortress island of Malta, where a handful of Gladiator pilots were to win international acclaim.

Faith, Hope and Charity were the names given to three of this flight of stumpy biplanes. The heroics of the men who flew them are now a part of the island story. Yet it was a combination of chance and coincidence which provided the Royal Air Force with these aeroplanes in the first place and allowed a scratch team of gallant enthusiasts to fly them. George Burges (Group Captain George Burges), then personal assistant to the Air Officer Commanding, and later to become, with 'Titch' Whiteley (Group Captain E.A. Whiteley), the Australian, Adrian Warburton (Wing Commander Adrian Warburton), of Britain, and Harry Coldbeck (Squadron Leader H.G. Coldbeck), the New Zealander, one of the best known of the island's reconnaissance pilots, has recorded a note on the formation of this historic force. He was a founder member and prime instigator of it.

Our illegitimate birth took place in April/May 1940. Someone had discovered, at Kalafrana, some Gladiators in crates left behind by HMS *Glorious*. Why they were not taken on board was a mystery. Perhaps the ship had to leave in too much of a hurry. Possibly they were overlooked, or maybe, again, there just wasn't room for them. All we know is that somebody found them. The C-in-C Mediterranean Fleet, Admiral Sir Andrew Cunningham, gave Air Vice-Marshal F.H.M. Maynard, Air Officer Commanding, Malta, permission to use them. I feel this owed much to the friendship between the two; they worked so well together. So the flight was formed at Halfar, close to Kalafrana. It had no birth certificate and was popularly known as the 'Fighter Flight'.

We operated from Halfar for about two months, then one or two Hurricanes, on their way to Egypt, were 'hijacked' and we moved to Luqa and later to Takali. By the beginning of 1941 we started to get some *real* fighter pilots and a *real* fighter squadron was formed.

At this time I went back to the job for which I had been trained – general and photographic reconnaissance – and joined the 'Maryland' Flight which became No. 69 Squadron. I finally left Malta in the middle of 1941, after about 4½ years on the island. . . .

Group Captain George Burges, North Stoke, Oxfordshire, 1984

Another stalwart member of this curiously motley flight was Peter Hartley (Wing Commander P.W. Hartley). Whether it was his good luck or misfortune to find himself, through an unforeseeable set of circumstances, in a position to make a distinctive mark upon it is for the reader to judge.

Gladiator being attacked by Italian fighters

Here, to complement Burges's reflection, is Hartley's recollection of his experience.

Frank Harrison and I had fallen out with our CO in 21 Squadron following a nocturnal binge when the unit was blown out of Abbotsinch, in Scotland, by a gale in 1938, and then moved down to Lympne in Kent. As a punishment we were posted to a target-towing flight in Lincolnshire. Had this not happened I wouldn't then have been available for posting as adjutant to Halfar in Malta.

Between 1938 and Italy's entry into the war I was doing adjutant's duties at Halfar, interspersed with occasional practice flights for the local searchlight batteries and the Royal Navy.

I remember we regarded Italy's intervention that summer as a confounded nuisance, for we all knew that it would interfere with the pleasant lotus life we had been leading with its swimming and golf and the social visits to Valletta.

Our fiery CO, Group Captain 'Ginger' O'Sullivan, had his own ideas about how to prepare the defence against Italian bombs. He set us to work dispersing the aircraft around the airfield perimeter amid the prickly pears which were the local, staple crop. Daily our legs and arms were spiked as, in the heat, we were all in summer rig.

It was thus a relief, and a surprise, to get the chance one day to join the Fighter Flight of five Gladiators. It was an exciting, but not a difficult, change after the Swordfish we had been flying.

Day after day we went up in these wonderful machines; but it was always too late to catch the enemy's Savoia Marchetti 79s. Then, on 31 July, I was leading a flight with Eric Taylor and Timber Woods and we were jumped by Italian fighters.

Suddenly, the great radial engine in front of me erupted in flames as the forward fuel tank was hit. Fire soon enveloped the cockpit, and as I was wearing only shorts and shirt I was quickly in such agony that I would have jumped even without a parachute.

However, after baling out, I landed in the sea and was picked up by Pilot Officer Jordan in our own RAF Air/Sea Rescue launch, and taken to hospital at Imtarfa.

It is interesting now to reflect that, had Frank Harrison and I not gone out on a binge that night and upset the CO of 21, I would not have been posted to Malta and so had the chance to become an original member of the 'Faith, Hope and Charity' Fighter Flight.

Wing Commander P.W. Hartley, Exeter, Devon, 1984

Splintered Survival

Nine hundred miles away in Egypt, the cry from the squadrons was the same as the plea from Malta. Send us more and better equipment. With the units' workload now stepped up to the maximum, the need was urgent.

The Gladiator biplanes, no matter how well flown, could not match the speed of the Italian Savoia Marchetti 79 bombers. Only a handful of freshly supplied Hurricanes had the advantage of the new constant-speed airscrews, armour-plating behind the cockpit and bullet-proof centre panels in the windscreens.

For John Lapsley (Air Marshal Sir John Lapsley), who was fast becoming one of the Royal Air Force's 'names' in the theatre, the advent of the bullet-proof windscreen had a most fortunate meaning. It spelt survival.

On 10 September 1940 Lapsley was ordered, with his No. 2, Sergeant Pilot Clarke, to move with their 274 Squadron Hurricanes from Amiriya up to Maaten Bagush and then to patrol Mersa Matruh, an important forward base for the land forces.

On patrol at 14.00 hours, the pair soon spotted (there was no effective ground control and reporting system) a formation of five SM 79 bombers. On the first attack, Clarke's luck – and his guns – jammed. It was then up to Lapsley. After neatly picking off the first two bombers (he destroyed 11 aircraft in the Desert) and forcing the attackers to jettison their bomb load, he concentrated on the right-hand 79 which had now turned to starboard and was going 'full bore' out to sea.

I took careful aim through my reflector sight, and just as I opened fire there was an enormous bang right in front of my nose as my bullet-proof windscreen took a direct hit and shattered.

I could no longer see through the gunsight, so I broke away to one side keeping up with the fleeing enemy. Having checked that all seemed well with my Hurricane, except for the windscreen, I decided to come in again from above and astern. I hoped to be able to line the bomber up sufficiently through the windscreen side panel to aim the rest of my ammunition as

78

accurately as was now possible. However, my long, final burst appeared to have no effect, and as I broke from close in the gunner put another burst of return fire, dead centre, through the roundel of my starboard wing – probably holding two fingers up!

As I flew back to base, looking at my shattered windscreen with its inside surface still intact, it sank into me what a lucky chance it was that I had been in one of our newer aircraft equipped with this windscreen. Without it, I must surely have been without my head! Thank you Mr Pilkington/Triplex or whoever!

I hope the Italian gunner survived the war, for without that chance shell into my windscreen I might well have spoiled his day!

Air Marshal Sir John Lapsley, Benhall, Saxmundham,
Suffolk, 1984

Widening the Odds
1941–1942

As the air war broadened to cover new areas of the globe, so the fortunes – and misfortunes – of the aircrews gained in variety. It wasn't only the operational commands which attracted the fates. The flying schools and other training units came increasingly within their purview. A rising number of pupils, flowing into the teaching establishments, were now accepting, often naively, what destiny and wartime flying might hold. All were volunteers and, generally, they thought little of the future. They lived for the moment, and it was the gaining of their 'wing' or 'wings' which, at this early stage, was the thing. All else was subjugated to this end. Failure hit very hard. Success brought innocent elation.

The ability of the Allies to ensure the flow of their aircrew resources from the great Commonwealth Air Training Plan and from the United States, was a match-winning card to hold. For trainees in the initial stages to be able to get on with the job, largely untrammelled by war, and in climates and conditions which promoted, rather than impeded, advance, was a massive bonus. Navigational problems in the operational theatres came later.

All this effort and output, whether from the United Kingdom or abroad, brought in its train arresting tales of luck and chance, tinged, here and there, with humour. Even those who were later to achieve high operational distinction were not immune in the initial stages of the climb.

Avro Piggyback

There came from No. 2 SFTS* at Forrest Hill, Australia, and then from No. 7 SFTS in Alberta, Canada, successive incidents which had no parallel in the early Commonwealth flying training programmes.

The Australian experience, which involved two twin-engined Avro Ansons landing in daylight one on top of the other five miles southwest of Brocklesby, near Albury, was, at the time, unique. The brief account which follows is reproduced by kind permission of Group Captain N.A. Smith, President of the Mess Committee, RAAF Support Unit, Melbourne, Victoria.

*Service Flying Training School.

80

The two aircraft collided in perfectly clear weather at 2400 feet. . . . N 4876 [piloted by LAC Fuller with LAC Sinclair as second pilot] became firmly embedded on top of L 9162 [piloted by LAC Hewson with LAC Fraser in the second pilot's seat]. . . . Its portside propellor carved into the fuselage of the bottom aircraft, cutting away the seat from behind LAC Hewson, slightly injuring his back. Both engines of the upper aircraft stopped, but those in L 9162 kept operating normally.

The situation was decidedly unpleasant, and the two airmen in the lower Anson baled out. LAC Sinclair also parachuted to safety, but LAC Fuller stayed in the top aircraft and tested his controls with the idea of landing the two aircraft. He became convinced that, by using his own controls and the thrust of the lower engines, he could . . . control his unwieldy flying combination. . . . After a number of descending turns, he made a perfect forced landing in a paddock, the bottom aircraft receiving only superficial further damage.

. . . LAC Fuller received high commendation. . . . Ironically, he received fatal injuries later in the war when his bicycle . . . collided with a bus in Sale, Victoria.

In the Canadian version two Ansons were again involved, and they also were landed by the pilot in the upper aircraft. There was, however, one major difference: The incident took place at night.

That Made the Two of Them

Tony Holland (Flight Lieutenant A.C.W. Holland) is a good example of a successful wartime officer who, selected originally for a flying instructor's course at the esteemed Central Flying School, Upavon, was eventually able to break free from his Training Command bonds and apply himself to a rigorous operational role. He became one of the very few members of Lord David Douglas-Hamilton's 603 (City of Edinburgh) Squadron to survive the fluctuating fortunes of the Malta battle. But nothing in the prelude to squadron service gave a clue to the decorated future which lay ahead.

After completing the course at Upavon, I turned a blind eye to the sage comments of Wing Commander 'Speedy' Holmes on the 'average' assessment I had been given. 'This officer must pay more attention to his airmanship. He must not hurry his demonstrations or explanations.'

A month later, my log book bore a red endorsement. 'This pilot has been involved in an accident due to faulty cockpit drill and to gross carelessness.' It was signed by Group Captain W.B. Farrington, officer commanding No. 1 SFTS.

My crime? My pupil was making such a perfect precautionary landing approach to our satellite airfield at Shrewton that it seemed right to let him finish it off and put the Fairey Battle down. . . . The pity was that both of us forgot the undercart!

A month later, another – and more penetrating – experience made its mark which I have kept strictly to myself until now. Like other service flying training aircraft in those days, the converted Fairey Battles were not equipped with radio, just a Gosport tube through which to punish the ears of some unfortunate pupil in the front cockpit.

Exercise 19 in the flying sequence was instrument flying.* We stooged around with the pupil flying various courses above loose cloud. From where I had last taken a visual fix we were just south of Netheravon; but then the weather closed in with 10/10ths cloud while I basked in the clear blue sunshine above, and the pupil sweated it out under the hood.

'OK,' I said, 'time to go back now, let down at five-hundred feet a minute.'

Into the grey, swirling opaque we flew. Below 1000 feet I began to feel a twinge of anxiety. I forget now how low we were when the aircraft broke clear, but very solid slopes of hard ground on either side of us disappeared into the cloud above. . . . Amazingly, we were flying down a valley west of Salisbury!

'I've got her,' I said, summoning as much vocal nonchalance as I could, and we groped our way back to Netheravon, feeling very humiliated, but grateful for whatever chance had positioned us during our descent.

A.C.W. Holland, Heads Nook, Carlisle, Cumbria, 1984

Red-faced Academic

Robert Harriss was a wartime flying instructor. This, and his subsequent years spent in close proximity to the Law, have instilled in him the merits of caution. So here, in a reflection upon his training days, he recalls the embarrassment of the luckless senior flying instructor whom he prefers, out of compassion, not to name!

The airfields at RAF Cranwell and RAF Wellingore [in Lincolnshire], were very close to each other. Wellingore, long since reclaimed by the plough, was the relief landing ground for Cranwell.

Night-flying training was in progress. It was wartime, the countryside was blacked out and the airfield lighting consisted of a few paraffin flares.

Cranwell's Chief Flying Instructor was testing a pupil before sending him on his first night-flight solo, if found suitable. The Tiger Moth took off from Cranwell, turned to port to join the circuit for landing. However, probably due to the wind, the pupil (unnoticed by the CFI) lined up with the Wellingore runway, indistinguishable from that at Cranwell, and made a safe landing.

Well-satisfied with the pupil's performance, the CFI had no hesitation in leaving the aircraft and sending the pilot off solo.

The *ab initio* pilot took off. He unwittingly rectified his previous error – and landed back at Cranwell.

When, at length, the pupil did not return, a very embarrassed Wing Commander, CFI, wandered across to the duty pilot sitting at the end of the flare path. 'Where in Heaven's name am I?' he enquired.

H. Robert Harriss, Eaglescliffe, Stockton, Cleveland, 1984

---

*The pupil was put under a hood so that he couldn't see out. He then had to rely on the dashboard instruments to fly the aeroplane while the instructor watched from the back. (Ed.)

Conscientious Luck

The good instructors blended a firm discipline in the air with compassion and understanding. The poor ones should never have been made flying instructors, anyway. The borderline pupil of a doubtful mentor could, however, usually rely on a check by a senior instructor before he was finally turned down. The slower but conscientious trainee was normally given the benefit of a split-line decision.

Derek Waterman, who flew Halifaxes with 158 Squadron at Lissett in Yorkshire, knows that without a fair helping of luck (and resolve) at the elementary stage he would not now be able to look back upon an operational tour of merit with 4 Group of Bomber Command.

His start was chequered. 'I found with utter dismay that I was slightly colour blind, but I managed to scrape through in a "lantern test" and my records were marked "safe lantern"!'

A bad instructor plus a doubtful intermediate check at grading school which suggested that he needed 'a few more circuits and bumps' left him convinced that, in the face of all the competition, this was 'the end of the road for me as a pilot'. Derek hasn't forgotten the feeling.

Only those who experienced the anguish and worries of pilot training would know just how depressed I was. The probability of being switched to another aircrew category was unthinkable, as all my close friends, older than myself, had either gained their wings or were well on the road to doing so.

(Six of us, school chums, actually all became pilots and we all survived the war.)

Sitting in the Flight Office, shortly after the wretched solo check, the flight commander approached me and said if I had nothing else to do, would I update his log book from the Authorization Book* as it was some six months behind! This I did, and on handing the log book to him he asked whether I had flown solo. I told my sad story. He promised me another check and an extra thirty minutes' solo!

Somehow I managed to convince the check instructor that I could be trusted to bring the aeroplane back on my own in one piece, and I managed a circuit and landing without too much difficulty; and then came a bonus – the promise of three more circuits and bumps!

That placed me ahead of my course mates, changed the course of my RAF career and convinced me that luck plays a large part in our lives.

Those superstitious people who avoid having anything to do with the numeral 13 will not find comfort in Derek Waterman's subsequent story. It was after surviving Course No. 13 *at No. 4 Bomber Flying Training School at Mesa, Arizona, that he was eventually posted to 158 Squadron in Yorkshire. After completing some eight operations on 'assorted Halifax III aircraft', Waterman and his crew were allotted an aeroplane which*

---

*Book in which all flights had to be authorized either by a flight commander or his deputy. Pilots were required to enter their flights in their own log books. (Ed.)

carried the defiant name, 'Friday 13th'. They flew a further twenty-six (13 x 2) missions in it, and so finished their tour.

This aircraft had completed 128 operations by the end of the war. The panels showing name and bombing tally, are now displayed in the RAF Museum at Hendon, with our crew photograph. So, I am never too concerned about the number 13. In fact, it brought us exceptional luck because we completed our tour of operations without any injuries. . . .

D.A. Waterman, Barfield End Green, Thaxted, Essex, 1984

Recalled from Calamity

A morning in 1941. . . . The crewroom of a Coastal Command Operational Training Unit at Silloth on the Solway Firth. . . . Pilots are sitting about in armchairs waiting for their detail. One of their number is Derek Bielby who is soon to join a squadron. A gramophone is playing a current hit. . . . Wellington aircraft are parked on the tarmac beside the hanger. . . . Flying Officer 'Taffy' Evans, an ex-Halton apprentice and now a technical officer on the station staff, is about to accompany the crew of a Wellington on an air test following a major inspection. . . .

Nearly forty-five years on, Bielby here describes the circumstances of Evans's 'incredible escape' that day.

Flying Officer Evans was a very popular officer with the aircrews who formed the instructional staff of the OTU. His sparkling eyes and chubby, faintly roseate face perfectly complemented an enthusiastic, buoyant personality. . . .

There seemed nothing unusual in the sight of a black Wellington, in which Taffy Evans was by now a passenger, taxiing along the perimeter track on its way to take off. . . . What did attract our attention was an airman, running across the wide grass verge separating the perimeter track from the hangar, and making for the oncoming aircraft.

The airman was vigorously waving his arms, signalling the trundling Wellington to stop. . . . As it came to a standstill, the nose was opened and the wooden aircraft ladder was lowered. The airman quickly mounted it until only his legs were visible.

Presently, he reappeared, closely followed by Flying Officer Evans who was wearing his parachute harness and carrying the pack. Both men made hurriedly for the hangar and disappeared. Meanwhile, the aircraft's ladder was withdrawn, the hatch closed and the Wellington proceeded to the runway for take-off.

A few moments later, with the tail in the air, it was gathering pace, with its wheels still in contact with the runway. Just as it was becoming airborne, but before it had gained sufficient flying speed to give single-engine control, there was a sudden engine failure causing the aircraft to cartwheel into the ground. . . . All on board were killed.

At the last moment, the unit's chief technical officer had sent an urgent message for Taffy Evans summoning him immediately to his office. . . .

Was it chance, fate or divine intervention that allowed the summons to reach Taffy before calamity struck?

Derek Bielby, Stokesley, North Yorkshire, 1984

St Cyrus 1 Scottish Haar 0

I never pass along the coast road from Dundee to Aberdeen, but I look at the slim steeple of the Church of St Cyrus, north of Montrose, and say a little prayer of thankfulness.

Pupil pilots who did their flying training in the United Kingdom, particularly up on the northeast coast of Scotland, were presented with a dual challenge – to master the aeroplane, and at the same time match the worst that the weather, and the enemy's sneak raiders, might do.

Winter winds, rain, snow and ice, and that local hazard which the Scots, in their wisdom, call a haar (others deem it a thick sea mist), all combined to test to the limit the hesitant learner.

It was the haar that could be the devil as McInnes Wilson (Warrant Officer R. McInnes Wilson), known to the air force as 'RM', found to his cost in February 1941. He was doing his service flying at the time, stationed at No. 8 SFTS at Montrose. The happy days with docile Tiger Moths were behind; now it was the somewhat temperamental Miles Master that the trainee was confronted with. He had been detailed by his instructor 'to fly up to Aberdeen, carry out a navigational exercise over the Keith area and then return to base'.

All went well up to Aberdeen, but then the damnable haar started rolling in fast, blotting out the friendly coastline and much else besides. The pupil was now 'on his own', without radio or other navigational aids of any kind. It was the classic challenge. How to find the way back to base and, once there, to get the aircraft down in one piece. This was the single, exclusive aim which riveted Wilson's mind. With little more than 50 hours' flying in his log book, and an aeroplane which he regarded with some apprehension, it offered an unenviable prospect.

I was beginning to feel that the whole episode was going to finish with an entry in the 'Killed on Active Service' columns in the newspapers, as I turned north again into the deepening gloom. . . . I stooged on full of foreboding and then, suddenly, sticking up out of the haar, I saw the distinctive steeple of St Cyrus kirk. The village of St Cyrus was located on a high cliff, three miles to the north of Montrose airfield, and we all knew it well. . . .

I did not hesitate. I did a steep circuit round the steeple, and then plunged straight down in the direction where I guessed the airfield to be, lowering my flaps and my undercarriage as I went. I had an anxious moment or two when I could see nothing . . . then parked aircraft showed up suddenly below, a good deal closer than comfortable. But my luck held, and I landed all in one piece.

I have no idea who St Cyrus was nor what was his particular line of goodness, but I certainly feel his canonization was well deserved.

R. McInnes Wilson, Newton Stewart, Wigtownshire,
Scotland, 1984

Editor's note: *With that experience behind him, Wilson joined 260 Squadron and its Hurricanes, flew off an aircraft carrier en route for Malta and the Middle East, and after an extensive run of operations was eventually shot down in a transport aircraft in the Western Desert, nearly landing on top of Rommel ('one of the few "top brass" I ever saw') in the process. He was taken prisoner, but was repatriated because of his injuries and later returned to his solicitor's practice in Scotland.*

Deliverance in the Sun

By contrast with Montrose, there was much to be said for the sunshine and quiet of Kenya as a training ground. David Bennett (Wing Commander D.E. Bennett) was posted there to instruct at No. 70 Operational Training Unit at Nakuru, immediately after surviving a tortuous tour with Bomber Command's 2 Group Blenheims, based in East Anglia. With 600 hours on these Bristol aircraft, he was then highly experienced – and lucky. And it was Blenheim crews that he had been sent to Africa to prepare for operations.

The prospect of a rest in such an environment, after the traumas and hideous casualties of 2 Group's low-level operations, must have possessed an appeal. However, a simulated operation flown on 7 September 1941 from Nakuru, in the Rift Valley, to a target near Malindi, now an agreeable tourist resort on the Indian Ocean, provided an unpleasant reminder of perils just past. It was to be, as the terrain allowed, a round trip of some 900 miles at low level.

With the bombing and air-firing completed, Bennett and his crew of trainees, Gordon Keys, the navigator, and Jock Ramsey, the gunner, with John Barry, a passenger, set course for home.

[The country over which we passed] varied from the blue of the ocean and Malindi's inviting white sands with the lush, tropical green of the coastal region, to scrub and plains and veldt, full of game, and then the mountains. We photographed a huge herd of elephant in the Tsavo area, pink in colour from the red dust, a sight never to be forgotten. . . .

Then, approaching the Makindu area, fuel tanks were changed for our last 180 miles or so to base. . . . Almost at once, and with no warning, the starboard engine faded out followed by the port motor. Remedial action brought no success, and we were instantly confronted with a forced landing in an area of baobab and fever trees, huge anthills and tussock grass. . . .

Pulling up to 500 to 600 feet above ground with the surplus speed and putting down 20 degrees of flap . . . I decided to try and flop in between trees, but at the last moment I saw a dirt road running through the trees. . . . Banking to starboard, I elected to try this as a landing spot. . . . The approach was looking good when there was an almighty bang – and that was the last I recall until finding myself in a Nairobi hospital.

I learned afterwards that we had, indeed, made the road, but, hitting some trees at around 80 m.p.h., the Blenheim had somersaulted, broken its back, shed both engines and lay inverted in the road. Jock Ramsey had been able to struggle out of his turret to find an utter shambles that had once been the cockpit. . . . He pulled Gordon, Barry and myself from the wreckage. . . .

Miraculously, there was no fire, and help was not long in arriving. A few miles down the road by an extraordinary chance, was an Italian prisoner-of-war camp, populated mainly by members of the Regia Aeronautica who had been captured in the Ethiopian and Eritrean campaigns, to the north of Kenya. It was commanded by Lieut-Colonel Denis Wheatley of the Nigerian Regiment. He had seen the Blenheim go down in the bush country and, guided by the great column of dust as it crashed, he organized a truck, stretchers and medical aid provided by one of the Italian doctors and his orderlies.

The crew were taken back to the CO's bungalow. . . . Later that night, John Barry and Jock Ramsey, fortunately not seriously injured, were put on the Mombasa-Nairobi train at Makindu. . . .

In the subsequent court of enquiry, it was concluded that the principal cause of the crash was water in the fuel system causing double engine failure. . . . But it was almost a miracle that none of the crew was killed. The split-second chance to try a landing on the road, and the fortuitous proximity of the Italian POW camp, probably saved us all. . . . Sadly, Gordon Keys had to have his right leg amputated, and we were each in hospital for two months. . . . Later I was able to return to flying.

After 4000 hours as a pilot, I count myself lucky to be alive at all. Chance is, indeed, a fine thing.

Wing Commander D.E. Bennett, Shirley, Southampton,
Hampshire, 1984

Air Gunner's Allergy

The presence of a steady, competent, well-ordered mind in the pilot's seat was of signal importance to a good bomber crew. It made for cohesion and confidence; and confidence could be transmitted individually and collectively. Conversely, an imprecise and indeterminate disposition could breed doubt, even apprehension.

A trainee pilot was lucky if he had as his first instructor a man who was firm and demanded accuracy. Punctiliousness and precision in the air, once learnt, always stuck. This was the way that able, dependable, disciplined minds were trained. Even so, there were inevitably the exceptions which penetrated the system.

Mike Henry (Flight Lieutenant F.M. Henry), one of the best air gunners in the wartime business, was allergic to incompetence in a pilot. He had developed a nose for it. He had seen enough from his own experience, and, but for a smile or two from fate, it could have spelt disaster.

Henry passed so well out of his gunner's course that he was grabbed at once as an instructor. It was the last appointment he wanted. 'I flew with staff pilots. It was a form of torture, leading a vic [formation] of three Blenheims, with a student pilot on either side, each trying to maintain formation by tapping his wing tip on my turret. . . .'

Having talked his way out of instructing, he was sent to 110 Squadron (Blenheims) at Wattisham in Suffolk. In no time, his pilot was himself posted to the aircraft testing establishment at Boscombe Down for test pilot's duties. Henry thus became 'spare'. The accounts of his subsequent experiences with other pilots capture vividly his misgivings. Written in the style that made his Air Gunner *(G.T. Foulis, London, 1964) and his work for Shell's* Aviation News *so readable, he leaves the student in no doubt of his emotions.*

' . . . I was crewed with Flight Lieutenant Lyon, pre-war Cranwelltrained, who had yet to be "blooded". He was soon to be covered with the stuff at the end of his first, and only, sortie. . . .' It also left Henry in station sick quarters.

Then, in the middle of 1941, with 2 Group's cataclysmic losses at their peak, he moved to 107 Squadron, with their Blenheims, at Massingham, in Norfolk.

. . . .My new pilot's flying left a lot to be desired. I will, therefore, refrain from mentioning his name. . . . Our first sortie nearly ended in catastrophe at take-off. RAF, Massingham, was a grass field of limited run. We were bouncing across the turf when the engines became ominously quiet. God forbid, I queried, are they cutting (dreaded by all Blenheim crews)? . . .

He managed to stop before hitting the boundary hedge. I asked him what had happened as he was taxiing back for take-off. 'I forgot to close the gills and to lower the flaps,' he answered on the intercom.

. . . Mac, the navigator, and I spent many unpleasant, 'twitching' moments in the air. However, we were now on our way to Malta. From Cornwall, our trip to Gibraltar was marred by spluttering engines. The driver was getting rather worried and threatened to land on a beach in Portugal. We talked him out of that. . . . It was miraculous how we 'threepointed' with a few inches to spare on the short runway at Gib. The stern frame of the Blenheim must have got the shock of its life. . . . The groundcrew told us later that the engine trouble had been caused by flying on too weak a mixture.

The next leg wasn't much happier for Mac and me. . . . An error took us (we were flying right down on the deck* to avoid a fighter screen between Pantelleria and Tunis) to starboard of Porto Farina instead of Cap Bon. This mistake almost cost us the price of a dinghy ride short of Malta. . . .

Operating from Luqa, we completed four daylight low-level sorties against shipping, and one reconnaissance which, again, nearly ended in tragedy. On our return, from a protracted flight, with fuel tanks registering empty, the pilot landed across the runway in use, ignoring a red Verey light. . . . Wellingtons of 38 Squadron were taking off on their milk run to Tripoli. . . .

*Down on the water. (Ed.)

Approaching a dispersed Wimpy on the ground, he opened the port throttle to avoid hitting it; our wing went neatly under the Wimpy's. Throttling back, a shower of sparks from the port engine's exhausts must have given the pilot the impression that it was on fire . . . I was looking out of my hatch ready to leave. . . . To my amazement, the pilot came sliding down the port wing and Mac was doing his equal best on the starboard wing. I didn't hesitate to follow them, nearly getting my head knocked off by the tail-plane as *the aircraft was still travelling along the rocky surface*. [Editor's italics.]

The pilot was put under close arrest. . . . The fuel tanks were tested and found to contain enough fuel for only two or three more minutes' flying. . . .

I flew my next two sorties with another pilot. . . . I felt ten years younger. . . . Then, to my horror, my former pilot was released to fly again (a shortage of crews in Malta was responsible for many a wrong decision). I did three more sorties with him, one of which was terrifying, and I decided to ask the CO for a transfer to another crew.

'I'm willing sir, to continue with another crew,' I said, 'but I cannot stomach much more of X. . . .' He was sympathetic, and asked how many ops I'd done. 'Thirty-nine, sir,' I replied. 'I'll see what I can do,' he retorted. 'You have more than completed your tour, anyway.'

Shortly afterwards, my posting back to the UK came through. . . . Later, I heard that Mac and Chuck Widdon, the air gunner who had taken my place, had both perished with my former pilot. . . . Apparently they flew into the side of a ship they were attacking. . . . It would have been my fortieth, and last, sortie. . . . Thank God for odd numbers. . . .

F.M. Henry, Putney, London, 1984

'If I Must Be a Gunner'

If I must be a gunner,
  Then please, Lord, grant me grace,
That I may leave this station
  With a smile upon my face.

I wished to be a pilot,
  And you along with me,
But if we all were pilots
  Where would the Air Force be?

It takes guts to be a gunner,
  To sit out in the tail,
When the Messerschmitts are coming
  And the slugs begin to wail.

The pilot's just a chauffeur,
  It's his job to fly the plane;
But it's we who do the fighting
  Though we may not get the fame.

If we must all be gunners,
    Then let us make this bet;
We'll be the best damn gunners
    That left this station yet.

George Harding,
Royal Canadian Air Force

Corporal George Harding volunteered to be a pilot in the Royal Canadian Air Force. He could not complete his course because of air sickness. Mortified by his misfortune, but still buoyant, he then offered, with commendable spirit, to remuster as an air gunner, and was accepted.

Berlin by Moonlight

For while the tired waves vainly breaking
Seem here no painful inch to gain

Arthur Hugh Clough

The years 1940 and 1941 were rough times for Bomber Command in Europe. Harris's great bombing stretch from 1942 to 1945, with its mounting crescendo of night attacks, its gathering force of four-engined aircraft and the progressive improvement in radar and navigational techniques, still lay ahead. And the searing impact of the 8th United States' Army Air Force's complementary daylight campaign, initially under Eaker and later under Doolittle, still lay well in the future.

For the bombers of all types, this, then, was a period when the investment of prodigious resources of courage and sacrifice brought, if truth be told, relatively small return. Suffice, however, to say that the Royal Air Force's resolution and enterprise were keeping the enemy defences on the alert for much of twenty-four hours in every day.

Berlin – the Big City – was always the prestige target. Ken Batchelor (Group Captain K.S. Batchelor), a Bomber Command stalwart, recaptures the sense of chance which enveloped any bomber crew on a mission against the Third Reich's capital in those pristine days.

... 9 April 1941. ... No. 9 Squadron, based at Honington in Suffolk. ... Aircraft: Wellington 1c T2973 WS-S. ... Take-off: 20.25 hours. ... Estimated time airborne: 8 hours. ... Weather: mist clearing to perfect visibility. ... Nearly a full moon. ...

The sequence was, at this stage, familiar – for those lucky enough to survive.

Just after crossing the Dutch frontier we could see the searchlight barrier, running right down from Emden. ... As we got closer we could see also that they were coning one or two of our chaps with about thirty searchlights. ... We had seen five aircraft downed in about ten minutes. ... Later, another crew reported having seen six parachutes from one. ...

On and on we went on track ... over the huge lakes and on to the north of Hanover which was very busy pasting someone. ... Came in south and saw plenty of activity over Brandenburg. . . . We stooged on, fairly unmolested, picking up a railway to 'Bradshaw'* in. . . . Over the centre of Berlin, with the Wilhelmstrasse plainly visible, when suddenly – ching! A wandering master searchlight found us and immediately thirty more coned and caught us perfectly. . . . It was as bright as daylight in the cockpit, and we were completely blinded. . . .

We bombed and then began weaving round and round and up and down to lose them . . . but still they stuck fast and then the apex, with us in it, was filled with all the heavy flak they could put up. We could see the yellow bursts everywhere with red-hot shrapnel, the puffs lit up by searchlights, and the concussions bumping us all around as the close ones crumped and cracked in our ears, above the roar of the engines. . . . We could not get out. . . .

After what seemed like hours we cleared . . . and got out south. We had been thoroughly pasted and it scared all of us more than any of us had been scared before!

The squadron lost one aircraft on this raid. . . . Three months later, on 9 July 1941 our WS-S, T2973 failed to return from a raid. . . . The aircraft had completed thirty-five operations. . . .

Group Captain K.S. Batchelor, Gerrards Cross,
Buckinghamshire, 1984

Navigating for Survival

75 Squadron, the New Zealand unit in Bomber Command, contained some exceptional aviators, and some specially 'hard nuts'. They were a finely resolute and persistent lot. Many of them were in at the start of things in Europe and, five years later, were still slogging it out with a different foe in the Pacific.

'Joe' Lawton (Squadron Leader L.A. Lawton), the observer, was one of this rare bunch. It would be difficult to accept that he had a counterpart in the British and Commonwealth air forces who surpassed his record or who 'walked away' from more potential calamities. Destiny had him marked. Rather unusually, he had a spell with 38 Squadron (Wellington 1as) at Marham in Norfolk, before joining 75. It was an eventful time. Dunkirk was past, the Battle of Britain was at its height and the Germans were massing barges in the Channel ports. Operation Sea Lion† looked a possibility.

'I was in one of the crews which had been trained in the use of mustard gas in the event of an invasion. . . .'

Lawton's aircraft was hit by a Ju 88 over Boulogne in September 1940, and he himself was badly wounded by a 20-mm cannon shell. 'I was totally incapacitated and not expected to live. . . . I shall never forget the ride by ambulance from our base to Ely hospital. It was an old Albion ambulance which appeared to be a survivor from World War I. . . . The effect of the solid springs over East Anglian roads was unbearable. . . .'

By April 1941 Joe Lawton was back again on 'ops' starting his stint

---

*Picking up the railway to follow it in to the target. (Ed.)
†Codename for Hitler's invasion plan.

with 75 Squadron at Feltwell, another Norfolk base. 'I was lucky enough to be crewed with Squadron Leader R.P. Widdowson. He had been with the Royal Air Force on the North-West Frontier of India pre-war and, for those times, had had a lot of experience. I believe this fact was to save us all.'

The Hamburg raid on 11 May 1941 was disturbing. 'The sky was still quite light as we set out, avoiding the Frisian Islands and Heligoland, and then heading for the Elbe and the target. We were attacked and hit by what we thought to be a Ju 88. An armour-piercing shell penetrated the armour plate in the turret, and critically wounded the gunner, Peter Cannaway, from Hawks Bay, in the stomach. The co-pilot, Tony Saunders, and I managed to lift him from his turret and lay him on the floor. He was still quite conscious. We gave him an injection of morphine to help him . . . . He died before we could get him back to base. . . .'

Two months later, on 7 July 1941, came a dramatic mission to Munster: 'Tony Saunders had, by now, left our crew and been replaced by Sergeant Jim Ward who came from Wanganui. . . . He was thus the co-pilot with Ben Widdowson on this trip. . . .

The attack was successful, and I was able to take good photographs of the target area.'

It was when the crew of the Wellington were crossing the Zuider Zee on the way home that the incredible incident began. A German fighter attacked from dead astern and inflicted heavy damage to the aircraft – at a cost. Alan Box, Widdowson's rear gunner, had, in turn, hit the attacker who, according to Luftwaffe records, force-landed on the island of Texel in the Frisians. Lawton's account, written some while after the event, describes the drama.

The enemy's fire had cut a fuel line between the starboard engine and the fuselage. The fire which had started became intense, and we prepared to bale out. We tried to douse the flames with liquids we had on board; this proved ineffective. However, as the fire did not seem to be spreading we decided to continue on towards our base at Feltwell.

Jim Ward, the co-pilot, had been watching the fire from his position in the centre of the fuselage, below the astrodome. He felt that he might be able to get out on the wing and, perhaps, tackle the flames. I advised Ben Widdowson of this, and he gave his approval for the attempt. He always used to sit on an old engine cover, and this he offered to Ward. In addition, there was a length of manila rope near the astrodome which was designed to secure the aircraft dinghy in the event of a ditching in the sea. . . .

This rope was tied round Jim's waist, and, with the engine cover under his arm, he climbed out through the open astrodome. I had insisted that he wore his parachute in case the wind force should blow him off the wing. . . . Gradually, he worked his way along the wing to where the flames were concentrated. He pushed the cover into the hole where the fire was, but, unfortunately, the strength of the wind blew it away. . . .

I had been keeping contact with Jim as he worked his way down to the fire, letting out the rope only as far as was necessary. . . . He was getting pretty exhausted by the wind force, and it was essential to maintain the tension on the rope to help him up the fuselage and finally to haul him back through the astrodome and into the aircraft. . . . He was almost done by this time. . . . As we no longer had any intercom working, I went up and advised the pilot that Ward was back on board. . . . By some miracle, the fire died out of its own accord over the North Sea.

As I had given Ben Widdowson a magnetic course to steer back to base before going to help Ward, I had not had another chance to confirm our position. However, we were soon able to obtain a visual as we came up to the English coast. . . . By this time the wireless operator had contacted base and been given a course to steer. . . . Because of our damage, we were instructed to go direct to Newmarket Heath where there was sufficient length of grass to land the aircraft without flaps or brakes. . . .

The pilot landed the aeroplane with the fire engine in attendance. We must have run for at least a mile as there was no means of stopping the Wellington. We eventually ran into some barbed wire defences. . . . It was a relief to get onto the ground. . . .

We left the aircraft at Newmarket and never saw it again. Tremendous damage had been done to it by the night-fighter's cannon fire. . . .

Jim Ward was awarded the Victoria Cross for his extraordinary courage that night, and Ben Widdowson received an immediate DFC. . . . It is fair to say that, but for his great experience, the Wellington would probably have crashed on landing and very likely killed us all. Alan Box got a DFM for his part in shooting down the Me 110 night-fighter.

Ward hated all the publicity which the VC aroused. . . . Ultimately, he prevailed upon someone high up in the air force to let him go back to 'ops'. . . . He was shot down near Hamburg on his second trip. . . . The Luftwaffe buried him with full military honours in Hamburg cemetery. . . .

In my judgement, he should never have been allowed to go back on operations. . . .

A couple of months later, Joe Lawton and his crew were briefed for Berlin. It was 20 September 1941, and almost exactly a year since Joe had been so badly injured over Boulogne. This time, destiny left things rather late.

We took off and set course along our track. . . . Unfortunately our wireless operator did not receive a recall signal, and we went on to Berlin on our own. . . . We had been damaged when we returned to find that fog had closed all the airfields in our group. We did not have enough fuel to go further so we were told to head the aircraft out to sea and bale out.

We landed near Horsham St Faith in Norfolk. It was dark and I did not see the ground before I hit, cracking a couple of vertebrae which has affected me for the rest of my life. . . . I eventually found a farmhouse. . . . As I was carrying a parachute, the farmer, who had opened the window, immediately produced a shotgun and was going to give me both barrels. However, I persuaded him instead to take me to the police station. . . .

L.A. Lawton, St Heliers, Auckland, New Zealand, 1984

Homing for Mum

A short time before Joe Lawton's Berlin experience, 'Popeye' Lucas (Wing Commander F.J. Lucas), another among 75 Squadron's wartime alumni, had a disconcerting start to his second operational tour.

It was the night of 11 June 1941 and the target was Dusseldorf. I don't remember feeling 'superstitious' about the start of a new tour, but there were times on this trip when I thought we were going to provide another statistic. It was probably one of the worst I experienced in over eighty-one night operations over Germany. Afterwards, to my log-book entry, I added the words 'Thirty-four holes in aircraft – a write-off. . . .

I remember it vividly. At the target, all hell was let loose on our first run in. We were thrown all over the place, and my navigator, Dave Florence said, 'It's a dummy run – go round again.' The second run was just as bad, but we got our bombs away before something hit us with a terrific 'whammm', followed by a further 'whumff, whumpp' after which we couldn't close the bomb doors. It was like an inferno, the Wellington was taking hits from all sides, with shell flashes and tracer zipping by, and searchlights probing everywhere. The port motor was struck, and started a fire, which luckily, went out.

Our hydraulics were shot away, and the red light showed the undercarriage was down. I leaned forward to adjust the gyro compass, and at the same instant heard an eerie 'sw-i-i-sh' behind my neck, followed by a rush of cold air. A lump of shrapnel the size of a fist, sliced through where my neck had so lately been, and exited through the other window. Something plucked at my sleeve, and I turned to see what my second pilot wanted, but it was more shrapnel passing through the sleeve of my overall.

Whether the main damage was done on the first two bombing runs, or on the third when we went in for photographs, I never knew, but the effect was cumulative. The exposed undercarriage, and the half-open bomb doors, cut down our airspeed. The petrol tanks had been holed, and the fuel gauges were falling at an alarming rate, and the port motor was barely ticking over. . . .

The Wellington was down to 200 feet as the Dutch coast was crossed. The options then were obvious. The crew voted to a man 'to try to make it home to Mum'. There followed the desperate, agonizing fight back across the North Sea. The East Anglian coast was reached with the port engine virtually seized up and fuel critically low. Then came the devastating advice from base. Divert to Newmarket, fifteen miles away. . . . Feltwell had just been bombed.

With the fuel gauges nudging zero, Popeye Lucas prepared to run straight in for a landing, hoping that their luck would hold. But control at Newmarket wouldn't have it; the orders were positive and direct.

'Please go round again, we have a Stirling coming in on three engines, and it has priority.' 'Lucky bastard,' I retorted, 'we've only got one.' It fell on deaf ears.

Fortunately, I was familiar with the airfield, and could find a place in the dark, well away from the flare path where we could get down – quick. Our Wellington 'floated' interminably until at last, as our remaining engine finally cut, we touched down.

A few minutes later Control came on again: 'You are free to land now.'

As we lounged on our parachutes under the wing of the aircraft, waiting for transport, I reflected upon the variabilities of luck. . . .

For myself, I was 'unlucky' to be taking part in a hazardous enterprise, with no control over my own destiny; but we had been 'lucky' in other ways. Lucky that our bombs were away before we took the big hits in the bomb bay. . . . Lucky that the lump of shrapnel hadn't beheaded me, just as surely as a couple of my luckless ancestors had lost their heads in days gone by. . . . Lucky that some divine providence had willed it that our fuel should last just long enough to get us home, and on the ground. . . .

My second pilot was Tim Williams, of Hawkes Bay, otherwise known as 'Scruffy'. This had been his first trip. He was lying relaxed on the damp grass, his head on his parachute, chewing a blade of grass.

'Gee,' he mused. 'If all the trips are like this one, it won't be so bad. . . .'

Wing Commander F.J. Lucas, Motueka, Nelson, New Zealand, 1984

German Saviour

There were other times when things didn't work out for 75 Squadron. John Dixon, a Royal Air Force sergeant rear gunner from the crags and fells of northwest England, remembers a night in July 1942 when it all went wrong. Fortune, however, dealt him, alone among his comrades, an unexpectedly favourable hand.

Hamburg was the target. Coned, and heavily hit by flak, the skipper, Flying Officer J. Shepherd, and Sergeant J. Winstanley, the bomb-aimer and front gunner, did a grand job getting the bombs away. . . . Sudden, evasive action was taken with a stall-turn down the blinding cone of searchlights. Roaring over the city rooftops, we were caught in a murderous, brilliant barrage of light ack-ack. The front gunner and I got in a few bursts at the searchlights as we sped away. . . .

Our battle-scarred Wimpy, now at tree-top height, took quite a battering as we ran the long gauntlet. . . . But, finally, with our gun turrets out of action, we were overwhelmed and crashed in a meadow near the village of Dose, some ten miles west of Wilhelmshaven. . . .

After getting out of the wreckage in which my right leg had been jammed, I was captured by civilians and handed over to a soldier. He dragged mc away saying that I was to be shot. There was no doubt, by his aggressive manner, that he meant it. He had his rifle with him.

However, another German, Heinrich Dirks,* with real courage, actually wrestled me free and insisted that I was a prisoner of war, and an airman, and had a right to be interrogated by the Luftwaffe. . . . I was then taken to a local pub and from there moved to Wilhelmshaven naval hospital. . . .

From hospital, Dixon was sent first to Dulag Luft, and then to Stalag 8B where he remained until the end of the war. In 1950 he emigrated to New Zealand. He still maintains a correspondence with those who witnessed his sole survival from the destruction of his aircraft and crew.

*John Dixon has added this note. 'Heinrich Dirks was in the Wehrmacht. . . . In 1943, when he was nineteen . . . he went to the Russian Front in an infantry regiment. He was captured and became a POW. According to his sister, their parents never heard from Heinrich . . . Such was the Russians' way. . . .' (Ed.)

95

While I was a POW, I joined with a small group of Kriegies who were interested in literature and writing. . . . I carried some of my poetry home with me. . . .

John Dixon, One Tree Hill, Auckland, New Zealand, 1984

'Autumn'

Stalag 8B, Lamsdorf, 1942*

The soft sound of the cold,
crooning, Silesian wind,
moving the tall, dark trees
beyond a world of wire,
reminds me of the old
and rugged, northern fells.
Of gravel scaurs and screes,
a kettle, singing breeze
above the summer's fire . . .

Again the snarls of war
upon a training ground.
O Wind, your songs are drowned
by loud the battle noise,
a sudden sound of bells . . .
O Time, the simple joys
in days when we were free
to watch the leaves of autumn
fall from an English tree . . .

John Dixon

Lucky Spread

We were on a leaflet raid over northwest Germany early in the war. 102 Squadron was based at Driffield, the old grass airdrome in Yorkshire with a dip in the middle. We were flying in Whitleys and, as the wireless operator, I had to go back in the fuselage, sit or kneel by the flare chute and drop bundles of leaflets which were about the size of a brick. They were done up with a single rubber band, and when they went down the chute and entered the slipstream they scattered on the wind. . . .

After dropping a number of bundles, another crew member – it was usually the second pilot – had to change places with you as there was no oxygen supply back in that position. . . .

By mere chance, instead of kneeling to drop the bundles as I normally did, I sat down and leant back against the side of the fuselage with my legs spread apart for more comfort. . . . There was a loud bang, the aircraft shook, and then I saw that a shell had passed up through the floor and out through the roof. . . .

*See John Dixon's poem, 'Stalag Snowfall' page 260. (Ed.)

If I had been kneeling as usual or sitting with my legs together, my daughter wouldn't be typing this for me today. . . . The shell was either a malfunction or a timed device. Who cares? I do! It was pure chance that it went between my legs.

John H. Moutray, Richmond, British Columbia, 1984

When fortune smiles, take the advantage
Proverb

The Cult of the Reciprocal 2*

Rae Walton, a solicitor by profession, had a war of uncommonly varied experience. From the Territorial Army he was seconded to the Royal Air Force for duty with Army Cooperation Command. But, as he now recounts, in the crisis months of 1941 he was based at St Eval, in Cornwall, engaged in different, and rather more hazardous, work.

A second operational tour was flown with Coastal Command and the long-range Liberators (B-24s) of 503 Squadron, sweeping the shipping lanes off Norway and round the North Cape to Russia. Shot down off Norway, Walton crossed the country to Sweden and eventually found his way back to Britain – and a final tour with Transport Command. Sir Anthony Eden, Lord Mountbatten and other VIPs were among his passengers. The Big-3 conferences also came within his scope.

It was a diverse story, full of strange switches and turns. His time at St Eval still sticks in his mind for one rather singular adventure.

Early in the war, our shipping losses, mostly the result of German submarines operating from the Atlantic harbours of Norway and France, were very serious.

In addition to sweeping the sea routes ahead of convoys to clear them of U-boats, the RAF also bombed the U-boat shipyards, and laid sea mines in their harbours. This was part of the Battle of the Atlantic.

Several squadrons doing this job in 1941 were based at St Eval in Cornwall. They were equipped with Blenheims, Beauforts and Hampdens. I was with No. 53, a Blenheim squadron, and one night we attacked the submarine pens at Brest on the Atlantic Coast of Brittany at the same time as Beaufort aircraft were dropping sea mines in Brest harbour. Each crew was 'de-briefed' on our return. One Beaufort skipper reported how, despite low cloud, mist and heavy flak in the target area, he had eventually found the harbour after a long search. He had successfully dropped his mine at the entrance.

The intelligence officer, recording the report, disclosed that the Beaufort had, in fact, done nothing of the sort. It had been tracked by radar and had flown north instead of south, and the misty harbour it had mined was Liverpool. The crew was shocked to learn this for they quite genuinely believed they had been to Brest.

*See pages 47, 99, 160, 218 and 278.

The cause was simple. The skipper had set a reciprocal course on his compass. Liverpool lay almost on that reciprocal course, and about the same distance from St Eval as Brest. For this error he was severely reprimanded. It was a mistake frequently made – but usually corrected quite quickly.

I never heard of another case with such dire consequences, although I believe the sea mine was traced by the navy before it caused damage.

Rae Walton, Tynemouth, Tyne and Wear, 1984

Editor's note: *There is a piquant aside to this engaging story. The intelligence officer at St Eval, after making the Beaufort captain aware of his error, is said to have added a rider. 'I think I should tell you,' he observed, 'the Royal Navy have reported enemy mine-laying activity at the mouth of the Mersey. The hostile aircraft, they say, was driven off by spirited defence.'*

The captain, still somewhat nonplussed, paused. 'Well', he said, 'I am bound to agree with the "spirited defence".'

St Eval Eskimo

The station intelligence officer at St Eval at the time of the Beaufort incident was Edward Shackleton (Wing Commander E.A.A. Shackleton, afterwards Lord Shackleton of Burley), one of the Royal Air Force's – and, later, Britain's – versatile characters. Rae Walton recalls him. 'I well remember him as one of the two IOs who used to brief us before operations and debrief us after they were over.'

By the end of the war, Eddie Shackleton had reached, via Coastal Command Headquarters (anti U-boat planning staff), the heights of naval and military intelligence at the Air Ministry. It was a prelude to his subsequent appointment to high government office and to a broadly based and distinguished post-war career – Minister of Defence for the Royal Air Force, Lord Privy Seal, Paymaster-General and Leader of the House of Lords in successive Labour Governments. In his industrial and commercial life, Lord Shackleton became the senior executive of the John Lewis Partnership and deputy chairman of the RTZ Corporation. He is a past president of the Royal Geographical Society.

If destiny had earmarked him for entry to the Royal Air Force, it was certainly by a most unusual chance that the intelligence branch claimed his services.

I was about to join the army in 1940 when an acquaintance of mine heard I spoke Eskimo, passed it on to a Squadron Leader Guimaraens (a wine merchant by profession), and I was summoned for interview. A little later I was recruited into RAF Intelligence. A whole group of us arrived at the Air Ministry, and the only 'training' we received was to spend a day amending all the air recognition manuals. The following day I was packed off to RAF St Eval – no square-bashing for intelligence officers! Indeed, I only went on parade once during the whole war and that was to hear Eisenhower's D-Day message.

My posting to Coastal Command was not as silly as appears at first glance. We did, in fact, have a base at Bluey West in Southwest Greenland – which was mainly concerned with ferrying aircraft. Another colleague of mine from Arctic days was the intelligence officer there, the idea, of course, being not only to be able to speak to the Eskimos, but also to bring some expert Arctic knowledge.* In the event, needless to say, I never went near Greenland during the war. At one point I was posted to Iceland, but my station commander (later Air Commodore Revington) sent for me, and asked me why I had been posted. I said, 'Sir, it is probably because I speak Eskimo.' He then asked, 'Do they speak Eskimo in Iceland?' to which I replied, 'No.' He promptly had the posting cancelled, since by then I was heavily involved, both with intelligence-gathering, cross-Channel operations and with anti U-Boat work.

The fact that I spoke Eskimo became rather a joke. One day I was rung up by the command intelligence officer, Wing Commander Jessop, who proceeded to spout some strange language at me. After I said, 'I do not understand you, sir,' he remarked that he always thought I was a phoney and that I did not speak Eskimo at all. I then realized that he was quoting from one of the survival handbooks, and I restored my reputation by commenting that it was West Canadian Eskimo, whereas I only spoke Northwest Eskimo! Perhaps I should add that Eskimo, or Innuit, is virtually the same language all the way from East Greenland to Siberia, but of course there are many variations.

Subsequently I was elected to the House of Commons. My reputation as an Eskimo speaker had followed me there, and the comment was made that I was not expected to be any more unintelligible than other Members of Parliament.

When I first got into Parliament I was sent for by 'Boom' Trenchard† who, after giving me a couple of martinis, said, 'Now, my boy, I have something serious to say to you.' I clicked my heels (I was still in uniform) and said, 'Yes, sir.' Boom said, 'You will support your party (the Labour Party) on all occasions except where the RAF is involved. On those occasions you will support the RAF.' I replied, 'Yes, sir,' and I think I can honestly say I carried out his orders. Certainly, RAF cooperation in the House of Commons, every time the navy tried to steal Coastal Command from us, was very good irrespective of party.

Lord Shackleton, St James's, London, 1984

The Cult of the Reciprocal 3‡

Fifteen or twenty miles down the north Cornish coast, southwest of St Eval, lay the Royal Air Force station at Perranporth. It was a new, wind-swept airfield set on the edge of a steep cliff. 66 (Fighter) Squadron was based there in 1941. The performance of the squadron's long-range Spitfire IIs with a thirty-gallon fixed (non-jettisonable) tank, slung under the star-

*Lord Shackleton's father, Sir Ernest Shackleton, was the great Arctic explorer.
†Marshal of the Royal Air Force Lord Trenchard, the 'father' of the Royal Air Force. (Ed.)
‡See pages 47, 97, 160, 218 and 278.

board wing, was much inferior to the standard aircraft. However, with all the sea there is around the Cornish peninsula and down to the Bay of Biscay, the modification was thought by the planners to be 'a necessary operational requirement'.

There was in the squadron at the time a solidly built, genial and extrovert Royal Australian Air Force character named Roy Riddel (Squadron Leader R.G. Riddel). He was later to win distinction in the Pacific as the aggressive leader of a P-51 Mustang squadron. Dentistry became his post-war profession.

There was a moment in 1941 when Roy must have wondered whether he had a future at all.

Those Spitfire IIs with their blister tanks were awful. . . . There were times on some of those escort jobs that we did when I thought the escorted aircraft were having to throttle back to let us keep up with them. . . . But there was one night when I had reason to be thankful for that extra tank.

I had just finished a long patrol from about Plymouth out to the Scilly Isles and was about to return to base from the western end of the run. For some reason, I set 'red on black'* and started to head still further west out into the Atlantic, bound for America.

I flew on for some while and I only realized what I had done when, suddenly, I woke up to the fact that the 'ops' controller's voice had faded out. It was the moment of truth because I knew I was barely going to have enough fuel to get back. . . .

There was no adrenaline pumping round the body then. . . . Only that cold, clammy, desperate feeling that most of us knew at one time or another. . . .

It was my luck that I realized my mistake with only a minute or two to spare, and made it back to base with the gauges close to zero. . . .

R.G. Riddel, Korora, Coffs Harbour, New South Wales, Australia, 1984

'It Just Came Off in My Hand . . .'

There was another pilot in 66 Squadron during Roy Riddel's time who contributed to the unit's Commonwealth strength. Harry Coldbeck (Squadron Leader H.G. Coldbeck), the New Zealander, may not have set the world alight as a fighter pilot; it was as a photo-reconnaissance exponent in the Mediterranean and Middle East a year later that he came into his own. He took his place alongside Adrian Warburton as one of the natural stand-outs in this field.

However, without a splash or two of fortune he might never have had the chance to shine.

I had qualified for my 'A' licence in New Zealand before the war, so going solo in fifteen minutes at Elementary Flying Training School wasn't a surprise. I was in the air force because I loved flying. . . .

*Air-Force term for flying on the opposite compass course to the one intended. (Ed.)

What we hadn't bargained for was that the Royal New Zealand Air Force would confuse our two courses and send them to the wrong advanced schools. Thus, die-hard aspirants for fighters ended up on Wellingtons and Whitleys, and vice versa. I, a flying-boat enthusiast, finished up on Spitfires!

But when, eventually, I was posted to 66 Squadron I had a bit of good (or bad) luck. Coming back from Brest one day, the throttle of my Spitfire actually came off in my hand. Very disconcerting. I was fortunate to be left with enough boost to give me time to sort out how to control the aircraft, and land it, without a throttle!

H.G. Coldbeck, Remuera, Auckland, New Zealand, 1984

Atlantic Miracle

There occurred on the night of 24 May 1941, in the unyielding North Atlantic, one of the truly great and enduring feats of aviation in World War II. It was achieved by aircraft of 825 Squadron of the Fleet Air Arm, operating from the carrier, Victorious. *Nine torpedo-carrying Swordfish, led by Lieut-Commander Esmonde, sought out and attacked the newly commissioned German battleship,* Bismarck, *pride of Hitler's fleet. This small, but gallant force scored a hit under the bridge, the ship was slowed and the way significantly aided for her subsequent destruction.*

It was the first time that a capital ship had been attacked in mid-ocean by carrier-borne aircraft.

The courage and quality of the sortie against what Churchill called, in a message to Roosevelt, 'a terrific ship, a masterpiece of naval construction', could not in all the circumstances have been surpassed.

Those of the Royal Air Force who were later to see at first hand, and at close quarters, some of the Fleet Air Arm's offensive operations against ships of the Axis powers will never forget the resolve and resource of these aircrews. But, taking everything into account, it would, in retrospect, be hard to accept that there was ever a finer naval air operation – Taranto and Matapan both included – than 825s during the darkness of this daunting Atlantic night.

Fortune may well have favoured – and probably did – these brave aviators; but it was discipline, spirit and training which mattered most – that, and the versatility of their curious, 90-knots-an-hour biplanes which the irreverent called 'Stringbags'.

After the attack, the shadowing force of cruisers, Norfolk *and* Suffolk, *lost radar contact with* Bismarck. *It was a major misfortune at this stage in the chase. The next day, therefore, a rough, uninviting day of poor visibility and low, skudding clouds, 825 Squadron was ordered to fly individual searches to find her.*

One of the aircraft, piloted by Lieutenant Pat Jackson RN (Commander P.B. Jackson RN), with Lieutenant D.A. 'Dapper' Berrill RN, observer, and Leading Airman Sparkes, gunner, making up the three-man crew, swept its designated area to the limit. Then catastrophe! Victorious *couldn't be found on return. 'We were lost in mid-Atlantic.'*

Jackson, down to the last few pints of fuel, had no alternative but to 'ditch'. Just as this dreadful course was about to be taken, Dapper Berrill,

101

Swordfish ditching in the Atlantic

in a billion to one shot, spotted an object in the sea. Jackson takes up the story. Nearly five decades have done nothing to dim its fearful detail.

There, directly below the aircraft, with waves washing over it, was the outline of a ship's lifeboat. We instantly decided to ditch; the perilously low state of our fuel tanks left no other choice. Having dropped a smoke-float to ascertain the wind direction, we made a deck-landing approach into the wind, passing a few feet above the lifeboat and entering the water twenty yards beyond it. By the time we had struggled, drenched and chilly, into our life raft, the aircraft was almost submerged with just the tail showing above the surface. The only other thing visible was the lifeboat, its shape outlined by white, breaking water. We drifted downwind towards it.

The only available tools which resembled balers were our flying boots. With these we baled steadily until at first one, and finally, all three of us could board the lifeboat and shelter from the bitter wind. By now, anxiety and the rough seas had made us all desperately sick; it was some time before we were able to take stock of our bleak surroundings.

The boat came from a Dutch ship, the SS *Ellusa*. There was a grim, soaking bundle amidships which, when opened up, produced not bodies but a sail-bag containing a lug-sail and foresail; sweeps and mast were lashed to the thwarts. There were also a rusty axe and knife, a suit of clothes and trilby hat, a waterlogged tin of fifty cigarettes and a bottle of 1890 Napoleon brandy. The lockers contained ship's hard biscuits and a securely stoppered water beaker. We also had the Verey light pistol and cartridges and navigation equipment and compass rescued from the aircraft.

For two days we sailed, at first eastwards towards Scotland, then, because of a severe easterly gale, westwards towards North America. Once, the boat was completely swamped in the heavy seas, but with frantic baling and the help of a makeshift sea anchor, we stayed afloat. It was about now that we sighted another boat. Everything about it was black, the sail and the figures lining its hull. Only their faces were white, although the eyes showed white in black rings. They were Norwegian, the only survivors from a coal burner in a convoy torpedoed a fortnight before. There were several dead men on the bottom boards. They were heading for Greenland, but had been driven back by gales. They advised that our westward heading would lead to death from cold in the ice off the Labrador coast. Their officer suggested that some of his crew should join us and we should sail northwards in company. My decision to reject this offer was hard, but our boat was lighter and faster and our chances of survival were better alone. We passed over cigarettes and biscuits and went our different ways, ours westward and theirs into oblivion. . . .

The weather continued to alternate between strong and gale-force winds; the violent seas made sleep difficult and the long nights nightmarish. We tried to sleep by watches during the daylight, since it was during the night that we had been swamped by breaking waves. Exhaustion led to fantasies which might have proved fatal had one been alone. The biting cold, and cold, water-soaked biscuit diet, caused severe jaw and toothache, and we all had a great longing for hot food. The brandy we kept for medical purposes only, being too strong for our empty tums.

Boils appeared, and a slowing of the blood circulation in feet and legs. In the case of Sparkes this soon became chronic, perhaps because he wore soaking wet flying boots at all times. (Dapper and I had removed ours in order to move more freely, and because we needed to bale with them.) A deterioration in Sparkes's condition caused us to alter course due north for the nearest landfall, Greenland. Though the possibility of landing near habitation was remote, the chance had to be taken. . . .

Sea birds began to appear, an encouraging sign that land was near, but the foul weather persisted and the sails showed signs of wear. It was a miserable boatload, being driven before a sleet-ridden gale, which eventually sighted a vessel,* passing about a mile distant. Despite our Verey lights, it seemed at first that the ship would pass without the lookouts seeing us, but our last smoke-puff went off with a rather louder 'ponk' than usual and, an answering blast came from the ship's siren. It was a lovely sound, and the sight of her crew as they leapt into our boat to help us aboard was one to remember. . . . †

Commander P.B. Jackson RN (Retd), South Mundham,
Chichester, West Sussex, 1984

*It was the Icelandic ship, *Lagerfoss*, bound for Reykjavik from Halifax, Nova Scotia. Captain Gistlassen was the skipper. He was helpful and hospitable once he knew the survivors weren't German.

†Jackson, Berrill and Sparkes thus reached Reykjavik after 9½ days' sailing. Berrill and Sparkes were in hospital for three weeks, with Sparkes unfortunately being obliged to have his toes amputated. (Ed.)

Never Fear! But *Don't* Volunteer!

David Foster (Lieut-Commander D.R. Foster) was one of the Fleet Air Arm's stars of World War II with a span of land-based and carrier-borne operations which stretched from the Mediterranean and the Western Desert in 1941, to Sumatra and the Pacific in 1945. Success did not stop there, for, with an unusually 'English education' (Stowe and Cambridge) behind him, he rose, in three decades after the war, to the presidency, worldwide, of Colgate-Palmolive, the United States' multinational company.

If there was ever a search for a World War II flyer who, in the face of prolonged risks, appeared to be 'being kept for something', there would be no need to look further than Foster. Two instances, in a catalogue, make the point.

He had reached Egypt by sea in mid-1941 in company with some thirty other FAA pilots and observers, reinforcements bound for squadrons in the carrier, Formidable. *In Fayid he was struck down with illness. He thought at first it was simply sand-fly fever, but when aspirin had no effect he was transferred to hospital close to the Great Bitter Lake and treated for malaria.*

However, when my temperature was supposed to drop it started escalating and paratyphoid was diagnosed. It was eleven weeks before I was on my feet, and at one point, when I dimly recognized the naval chaplain sitting by my bedside, it was touch and go. Later the cause of the typhoid was found to be the body of a dead Egyptian workman who had been pushed into the watertank by his fellow workers!

During the last week or so in hospital, when I could receive visitors, John Wilson* came to see me to say that he had volunteered to go to Malta to join the Fleet Air Arm squadron operating at night from Halfar against enemy shipping. 'Can't you wait for me?' I asked, but he remarked that the doctor had said it would be some time before I was fit to fly again. So I wished John luck and said I might join him one day.

John Wilson never reached Malta. The submarine that was taking him there was sunk with no survivors. . . .

I was released from the hospital to spend two weeks at an army convalescent camp at Al Arish and then a week's leave in Tel Aviv. I arrived back at Dekheila more eager than ever to enter the war. It was not to be; the medical examination showed that my eyesight had suffered (I knew my hair was falling out!), and I was 'grounded' for six months. I was deeply disappointed. . . .

Eventually I was pronounced fit to fly, and promptly asked Tubby Shaw, the CO, if I could join 805 Squadron, as I had flown Fulmars, which was more than most of the squadron had done. He accepted me and said he would speak to Commander Hale on my behalf. I was summoned to appear before Hale, who sympathized with my request, but said that as I had been trained as a torpedo bomber pilot I had to remain one. I was, therefore,

*Foster's close friend since they joined the FAA together in 1940. On arrival in Egypt, and finding no carriers to operate from, the two had volunteered for aircraft testing. . . . They were *always* volunteering for something. (Ed.)

posted to 821 Squadron, a new Albacore squadron being formed by Marine Captain A.C. Newsom.

It was sad to see my friends from 805 Squadron fly off on their way to the Far East, and I wished I had gone with them. With a stop in India enjoying the hospitality of some maharajah, it took three days for them to reach Ceylon. They arrived on a Saturday afternoon.

On the Sunday morning they were 'scrambled' to meet the first Japanese attack on the island. The lumbering Fulmars were no match for the Japanese carrier-based fighters, and over 60 per cent of the squadron was shot down into the sea. Many of the friends I had wished to be with perished in that first encounter, among them Ian White-Smith*. . . .

. . . When I considered my fortunate escapes – from illness, from being able to opt to go with John Wilson to Malta, from flying to Ceylon with the Fulmar squadron and, later in the Desert, from making an abortive attempt to bring an unserviceable Albacore back from a deserted landing ground at night – I decided it was time for me to stop volunteering. . . .

Fate had been kind to me, and I felt that, for the time being, I might have used up my ration of chances. In future, I would accept with a good grace any new assignments that might come my way; but I would not volunteer.†

David R. Foster, Mission Hills, Rancho Mirage,
California, USA, 1984

> There is a tide in the affairs of men,
> Which, taken at the flood, leads on to fortune;
> Omitted, all the voyage of their life
> Is bound in shallows and in miseries.
> On such a full sea are we now afloat;
> And we must take the current when it serves,
> Or lose our ventures.
>
> William Shakespeare (1564–1616)
> *Julius Caesar*, Act IV, Scene III

Greek Tragedy

Jack Hooper (Squadron Leader J.G.M. Hooper), the Rhodesian, and his brother, were both members of 211 Squadron (Blenheims) in Greece in the spring of 1941 when the German forces started rolling down into the country from the north. The squadron, which had been based initially at Menidi, near Athens, was commanded by James Gordon-Finlayson (Air Vice-Marshal J.R. Gordon-Finlayson), known as the Bishop. After flying 100 operational missions, he was awarded the Royal Air Force's first DSO

---

*A friend from their Stowe days. They had travelled out to Egypt together in the convoy. (Ed.)

†The timing was right. Despite other chances and adventures, Foster's operational career for the next four years or so was one of progressive success, culminating, in early 1945, in the brilliant attacks on the oil refineries at Palembang, in eastern Sumatra. (Ed.)

*in the Middle East, before handing over to Squadron Leader Nettleton.
When Nettleton was killed, Squadron Leader Irvine assumed command.*

*The squadron had been moved to Paramythia (translated, it means the
place or valley of fairy tales!), close to the Albanian border, to be in position
for the enemy's advance. Easter Sunday, 13 April, a week after the German
invasion, sticks in Jack Hooper's mind as a 'memorable and dreadful day'.
This is his story.*

Some of the pilots and crews, including my brother and the only other
Rhodesian in the squadron, Jack Cox, had been detached. . . . This meant
that there were seven serviceable, short-nosed Blenheims on the field at
Paramythia that morning. These were ordered to attack military transport
at Prilep, on the Bulgarian border. . . .

I was standing outside the 'ops' tent, being briefed by Squadron Leader
Irvine for the third attack, when he was handed a signal from HQ, ordering
one of the seven of us to be detached to undertake a photographic
reconnaissance of Valona and Durazzo, the two main Albanian ports.

The CO asked if any aircraft was not already bombed up. . . . Mine was
the only one . . . I was, therefore, detailed for the reconnaissance. I
remember there were expressions of sympathy from the others at my ill
luck. There were said to be heavy fighter concentrations around the two
ports.

Off I went on that beautiful, clear afternoon – visibility 100 per cent
and took the photographs of the ports from about 20,000 feet. There was
a considerable amount of shipping in the harbour at Durazzo. No hostile
aircraft, however, appeared anywhere near me, and I returned safely to
Paramythia.

I left at once to take the films to HQ in Athens. It was there that I heard
the dreadful news that not one of the six Blenheims dispatched from
Paramythia on that third raid on motor transport at Prilep had
returned. . . .

The squadron had been jumped by Me 109s just short of the target, and
all six aircraft were shot down. . . . All eighteen crew members, plus Wing
Commander Paddy Coote* from HQ, who had gone as an observer, had
been killed with the exception of Flight Lieutenant Alan Godfrey, who had
baled out successfully from 300 feet, and Sergeant James.

Alan and James were able to bury some of the very good friends we had
lost before struggling back to Larissa where they then got lifts in two
Lysanders which were heading for Athens. . . . Both aircraft were shot
down by 109s as they took off. James was killed, but Alan escaped with
the loss of two fingers of one hand. . . . And so ended 211 Squadron's
operations in Greece. . . .

The Almighty has always been very good to me in my lifetime, but never
more so than on that day in Greece forty-three years ago.

Squadron Leader J.G.M. Hooper, Mandara North, Greendale,
Harare, Zimbabwe, 1984

---

*Paddy Coote had won the Sword of Honour at Cranwell in 1930, beating Douglas Bader
into second place. 'I didn't really mind,' said Bader years afterwards, 'Paddy was a splendid
man, very good all round – at games, at work, at flying, at everything.' (Ed.)

VIP in Peril

The movement of VIPs by air in wartime caused problems and trouble. Their transport had to be shrouded in secrecy. Sometimes it was overdone and led to confusion – and near disasters. Clive Caldwell, then at the start of his fine Desert run, had a disturbing example of it on 21 May 1941 in Cyprus, at the eastern end of the Mediterranean.

... I was leading a section of two Tomahawks, scrambled from Nicosia, to intercept a bogey,* reported by coast-watch. After being airborne for thirty minutes, and now losing height towards base, we sighted a four-engined biplane in green and brown camouflage, but with no identification markings. It was heading at low level towards Nicosia.

Closing the range from directly astern, I was surprised that the target appeared to be unarmed. Holding fire, and pulling away to starboard, I investigated further. There was a not-very-prominent 'crescent and star' emblem on the fuselage and, again, I saw no armament.

As the aircraft continued to head confidently towards Cyprus, despite having a Tomahawk in plain view on either side of it, we stayed this way until it landed at Nicosia. Then we touched down after it.

We were thanked on the tarmac by Anthony Eden, the British foreign secretary, for the 'protective escort' we had provided. He was en route, by Misr Airlines, from Cairo to Teheran, via Cyprus. The aircraft was a DH 86, and the flight had been kept an over-strict secret. ...

When all things were considered, the incident could have resulted in a most unfortunate accident of considerable consequence. It was lucky that it didn't. ...

The Governor of Cyprus, Sir Bernard Battershill, kindly invited me to dinner with Mr Eden that night. Neither of them had any idea of the magnitude of the risk that such secrecy had involved. They were quickly enlightened as to the intent that had brought the Tomahawks behind and alongside that morning. ...

Group Captain C.R. Caldwell, 'The Caldwell Papers',
Sydney, New South Wales, Australia, 1984

'A Flight in Search of God'

The Australians, in the Malta battle of 1942, used to live in an uncharacteristic fear that, one day, when their time on the island was up, 'some f—' base wallah in Cairo' would post them to what, by habit, they called 'the Takoradi Run'. It was the accent and the brash pronunciation which enabled them to accord this trans-African ferry scornful disdain. The syllables were spat out deliberately from the up-turned corner of a deprecating mouth. The prospect of the 'Tacker-rardee Run' became a hideous spectre in their magnificent, fighting lives.

The ferry stretched, unremittingly, for 3500 miles or so, across some of the most desolate terrain on earth. The track ran from Takoradi on the

*Unidentified aircraft.

west coast of Africa, over great areas of the southern Sahara to the Sudan and then, northwards, up the Nile to Cairo and the Middle East. The dangers were plain to see.

For the single-engined fighter pilot, brought up to listen apprehensively for the slightest telltale variation in a motor's throb, it was an effective form of torture. Engine failure and losses went hand in hand. Yet, in 1941 and 1942, when the Axis powers controlled all the important stretches of the northern and southern Mediterranean coastline this was the favoured route for aircraft reinforcements for the Desert.

Lewis Stuart Bevis (Flight Lieutenant L.S. Bevis), from Plaistow, in London's E13 district, was a Royal Air Force flight sergeant when, towards the end of 1941, he was posted to Takoradi. His application to become a night-fighter pilot had been rejected. The story he recounts of one Hurricane flight at the start of his time on the ferry would have been enough to turn most off for good. It is enhanced when seen against the backcloth of three mentions in wartime despatches, a similar number of 'Exceptional' classifications in his flying log book, forty years' holding of a pilot's private licence, and a commercial career in Australia of undeniable worth.

The tale, entitled 'A Flight in Search of God'* was told originally, fully and in detail, in the July 1982 issue of the newsletter of the Royal Aero Club of New South Wales. The editor is indebted to the author and to the club for permission to reproduce this necessarily abridged extract from it.

Takoradi was a strange world after the one in which I had been raised in the East End of London. After a week or two's acclimatization, I was detailed to form part of a ferry group to fly Hurricanes to Egypt. We departed in a flight of six, led by a Bristol Blenheim to navigate us.

The first night was spent in Lagos. The following morning, we lined up for the second leg to Kano in Northern Nigeria, a flight of some 4 hours' duration. In the group with me was another Londoner, Rick. Petrol economy was important and we were instructed to fly at low revs and high boost to achieve this. After about 1½ hours' flying, I developed engine problems with loss of performance. I fell behind the flight and was advised by the leader to make my own way.

However, Rick decided to stay with me. The flight was at 12,000 feet over 10/10ths cloud. I explained to him over the R/T that if I descended below cloud I would not have enough power to regain height. He suggested that he should go down below the cloud and advise me of the terrain. Checking the course on my map, I saw that we could possibly be over mountains up to 5000 feet, so I told him to wait. He did not do so and was found ten days later, dead, having descended into a mountain face.

I continued on, and then decided to try to get below the cloud cover, no longer being in touch with Rick. I broke cloud at about 3000 feet over high ground coming out just above the tree tops to a landscape falling away in front. Being on course, I was able to pick up the Niger river and, in time, landed at Minna where petrol reserves in 4–gallon cans were available.

*The editor warmly acknowledges that George L. Walker of Waramanga, Canberra, himself a civilian pilot, proposed this story in 1984 for inclusion in the collection.

Early the following morning, I went to the strip and started the aircraft. Although the engine was running 'rough', I felt it would get me to Kano.

On reaching Kano, the mechanics inspected the engine and reported several plug failures, due to over-boosting. This grounded me until the following flight came through, three days later.

Joining the flight, we set off for the various stages to take us across the southern Sahara to the Sudan, stopping at Maiduguri, El Geneina, El Fasher and Wadi Seidna, with an overnight stop at El Geneina where the station officer had a reasonably tame lion as a pet.

The flight time from El Geneina to Wadi Seidna was around 7 hours. On arriving, the station officer insisted that we leave, after re-fuelling, for Luxor, a further long flight. We had been flying since 05.45 that morning and were very tired. In spite of our objections we were obliged to leave. The Blenheim now left us to proceed on its way across Arabia to join a squadron in the Far East.

During the flight from El Fasher, I had dropped my maps onto the floor of the Hurricane, intending to recover them at the first landing. But what with being hassled by the station commander at Wadi Seidna, I neglected to do so. However, now being airborne, I thought it would be easy to follow the other five Hurricanes.

After nearly an hour, we ran into a sandstorm, reducing visibility to nil. We got split up and now I was on my own. I made several attempts to land in the desert, pulling away at the last moment from rock-strewn areas. Finally, I noticed a native village with a clear area nearby on which I landed. I was then able to recover the maps. While I was doing this, I was descended upon by a crowd of natives from the nearby village, riding donkeys and camels. While they gathered round, I pointed to place names on the map to establish my position. Abu Ahmed rang a bell and that, apparently, was where I was.

As it was too late now to proceed, the headman brought a rope bed into the centre of the village area and indicated that it was mine for the night. I slept soundly, waking with the dawn. I saw some chickens scratching about and by signs, managed to get three eggs boiled for breakfast. While the natives were obviously friendly, stealing from strangers was, to them, clearly acceptable. I found in the night they had stolen my Verey pistol, my sole defence. When I reached the Hurricane it, too, had been stripped. Gone were the leather gun covers, parachute and other things besides. . . . Rather than argue, I just accepted these Fuzzy Wuzzy tribes, of General Gordon fame, as born robbers.

I started up the motor, surrounded by donkeys and camels. I had checked my fuel and the distance from Abu Ahmed to Luxor, and reckoned I still had enough to get me there. I climbed to 8000 feet and set course.

There is a point, some forty to fifty miles south of Luxor, where a low mountain chain crosses the Nile and cataracts are formed. It was here, while still at some 8000 feet, that the red fuel-warning light came on, telling me I was now very short of petrol. This was a shock; I wondered about the gauges. Looking around, I saw what appeared from high up to be a roadway. However, when I got down to about 1000 feet what had looked a suitable road from higher up was, in fact, a doubtful surface with banking on each side. Committed, I made a good landing, but unfortunately hit a large boulder. This turned the aircraft off the road and onto its back. Although unconscious for a while I was not seriously hurt. Eventually, an Egyptian, an educated engineer working on the Nile, came to help me. He took me to a telephone. After some hours a truck arrived from Luxor with airmen seeing what they could recover from the Hurricane, BN 157.

On reaching Luxor, I was given another Hurricane and joined a flight to Cairo. It was this last section of the route that prompted me to name this story, 'A Flight in Search of God'.

Only those familiar with the desert will know what a khamsin is. The sands are lifted by gale-force winds to heights of 10,000 feet. Flying over a sandstorm of this type gives the impression of being just above the ground – temporarily raised to 10,000 feet.

It was into such a storm that I flew on the last leg of my journey. Once again I became separated from the rest of the flight. I climbed above the sand to 10,000 feet to work out a plan, knowing that I required sufficient fuel reserve to make a precautionary landing if necessary. With this is mind, I decided that the best course was to try to land while I still had petrol in hand. . . .

I let down into the sand level. Immediately, forward vision was reduced to nil. I continued to descend steadily by circling turns, all the while watching the air speed, gyro instruments and altimeter. At around 800 feet, suddenly the colour around me changed from a reddish-brown to grey. This turned out to be the ground. I levelled off, and landed into a 40-m.p.h. wind. I rolled no more than a few hundred yards before coming to a stop.

It was now about 15.00 hours. I tried to get out of the aircraft to look around, but as I was dressed only in shorts and sleeveless shirt, the sand stung too much so I stayed in the cockpit. As the evening drew on, the storm abated as is usual in a khamsin. I took a look around in the dark, returning to the cockpit to try to get some sleep sitting up.

When morning came, the storm began to regain its tempo. However, I had been able to inspect the area. It was a small wadi with soft sand scattered through it. I started the engine and taxied to the far end. Several times the wheels sunk ominously into the sand, making it feel as if the aircraft must go up on its nose. I then realized I would have to prepare a path. The whole day I spent laying flat stones to try to make a firmer surface for take-off. It was tedious, back-breaking work. The temperature was in the 100s. What little water I had in a flask I sipped economically throughout the day. By evening, my confidence was slipping. I knew I was in for another night in the cockpit. I continued to gather stones to prepare for a take-off the following morning. I also knew I was beginning to dehydrate.

By morning I realized the situation was desperate. I had to get off soon. Then another blow struck me. When I pushed the starter button the engine wouldn't turn fast enough to fire. . . . I seemed now almost to lose my power of reason. My mind started to wander back over past years. I thought of my early training – of school, Sunday school and of God. Although I had been brought up strictly in the Church of England, I had in my late teens decided to be an agnostic. I reasoned this was the only way to be free and unencumbered with mythology. Yet, now, in my despair, I sought an answer from God.

110

Sick and weak, I sank in supplication to my knees and began to seek His intervention. As I prayed through burnt lips and swollen tongue, I saw the faces of all those with whom I had argued and discussed religion in far-off days. They seemed to scorn my present weakness. This drove me to my feet and turned me to some action. I summoned the strength to unpack part of the tool kit and removed the engine cowling. I took out several plugs and, using my shirt dipped into the petrol tank, I squeezed fuel directly into the motor. I knew this was my last chance. I psyched myself to reach a point of maximum mental control for this now-critical moment. I removed the copper wire on the throttle, intended only for emergency use, and then I pressed the starter button. The engine turned over and then fired. I knew if it died that would be the end. The tension and suspense were awful.

But the motor had caught properly and the airscrew was spinning. I put down 30 degrees of flap, held the stick back into my lap and opened the throttle wide. The power was surging now, and the aircraft began to roll forward. Slowly, then faster, faster. For the first 200 yards or so it was touch and go. The Hurricane bucked, but with the tail still held down I was airborne, hanging precariously on the prop. Soon I was gathering flying speed. I kept the hood back and climbed into the still, clean air above the storm.

After heading east for some forty minutes, I saw a town on the banks of the Nile with what appeared to be a military barracks and a landing strip beside it. It was Asyut, later to become the site of the largest dam on the Nile. I put down there and was taken to the Egyptian base hospital. The doctors checked me out, I was fed and watered. The next day I proceeded to Kilo 8, my original destination, just outside Cairo.

There is, perhaps, a sequel to this story. I still claim to be agnostic; but a few years ago, while working in my garden, I went to burn some papers. On top was a copy of *Time* magazine. The cover carried a picture of Christ. I could not bring myself to burn it. Instead, I took it back into the house.

Lewis S. Bevis, Lane Cover, New South Wales,
Australia, 1982

Four Tours – with Luck

The South African Air Force's star was now established. The Service's performance in the East African campaign against the Italians was a credit in the balance sheet and further assets were being created, daily, in the Western Desert. The operational effort, which its squadrons and wings were to sustain during the next three and four years – across the Mediterranean into Sicily, and up the length of the Italian mainland and into German airspace – made a vital contribution to the course of the European war.

Those of the Royal Air Force and the United States Army Air Force who served alongside their units, or with their nationals in the mixed squadrons, came to regard them with increasing respect. Like the Rhodesians, with whom they were so closely identified, they brought an aggressive resilience to the task which made them rock-solid and dependable when the chips were down.

Peter Daphne (Major P.P. Daphne), with four operational tours in his log book, was to have as long a run as any of them. He was flying Fairey Battles in East Africa at the beginning and commanding 60, the PR Squadron, with its Mosquitoes, in Italy, towards the end. No one survived that sort of stretch without a grin or two from luck.

13 August 1941 . . . I'm sitting in Fairey Battle, No. 904, on Alamato Satellite Landing Ground, Abyssinia . . . 500-lb bombs are in the bomb bay, and Flight Sergeant Cotton is in the gunner's seat behind me. I'm on my way to Gondar, some 240 miles north-northwest of Addis Ababa, near the source of the Nile and the last Italian stronghold in the East African campaign.

11 Squadron now consists of two Battles and three pilots – the CO, the flight commander and myself. Today, it is my turn to contribute to the discomfort of the Italian garrison. . . . Soon we're in a world of mountains, thickly forested slopes, rocky ravines, tumbling waters and swirling clouds. The compass swings madly as we thread our turbulent way through the jagged peaks and curtains of rain.

At last I see Lake Tana, unexpectedly far to the left, and I pick up a new line on Gondar. Down, down, down to the deck, and there is the airfield – hangar doors open, figures running. . . . Bombs away, and we climb towards the mountains. . . . The clouds and rain thicken. I dare not climb higher into the turbulence above. . . . Water drips into the cockpit. I turn well off course to avoid a partly visible peak ahead. . . . Butterflies flutter in my stomach. . . . Visibility remains very poor. . . .

There are no landmarks, and no comforting radio to guide us home in this world of long grass, marshes and clumps of bush. I circle like a goldfish peering vaguely through its glass bowl. The relief at being free of the mountains is replaced by the chilling realization that we're lost, and that within forty minutes we must land.

Turn left? Turn right? I see a possible forced-landing site, but almost immediately lose it in the murk. We weave through tunnels in the rain, determined to keep visual contact with the ground. Fifteen minutes later, I'm really lost and start disbelieving the various compass headings. I now no longer hope to find our landing ground at Alamato . . . only somewhere where we can make a wheels-up landing from which we can walk away.

A feeling of unwarranted calm now comes over me. Ahead is a rain squall. I turn away from it and catch sight of a strip of open grass, partially surrounded by bush. . . . A gentle turn and we are headed straight for it. . . . The shower curtain is pulled aside and, unbelievably, I see the dirty, whitewashed circle of a landing field. . . .

Quickly, now, before it disappears. . . . Wheels down, flaps down, throttle back . . . bump. . . . A long flying leap . . . bump again. . . . We've landed short. A corner marker flashes past. . . . A smoother run now and we stop. Cockpit canopy open . . . I push myself up and peer out. . . . What on earth is this? A tent shows up under the trees at the far end. I taxi towards it. . . . Wherever can this be?

A truck drives up, and a man in a waterproof cape and mosquito boots gets out . . . It's 'Snake' Snyman! How on earth did *he* get here? A feeling of unreality begins to creep in. . . . Surely, it can't be? But, yes, yes, it is! It's Alamato Satellite Landing Ground, Abyssinia, 13 August 1941.

How we ever found it again, I'll never know!

Major P.P. Daphne, Bonza Bay, East London,
Republic of South Africa, 1984

Life and Death in Balance

Meanwhile fortunes were fluctuating in the Western Desert. For Johnnie Eccles (Colonel J.H. Eccles), then a captain with 21 Squadron of the South African Air Force, 20 November 1941 was a day when fate balanced his life with death.

A column of Rommel's Afrika Korps was advancing on Allied positions at Sidi Rezegh. Nine Maryland bombers from 21 were briefed to attack. Eccles relives the experience.

Crew chat is finished, and as there is another half-hour to 'start up', I move away to sit alone and let my thoughts wander. Yesterday was my wife's birthday, the first we have been apart since our marriage, and I hope things went well with her.

At briefing, we were told there would be fighter cover in the area. But I wonder whether, as on previous occasions, it will miss our particular sector. . . .

Just then the senior equipment officer strolls by. 'Look at Johnnie,' he remarks, 'all pensive . . . Is he worried about the 109s?'

Silly man! Doesn't he realize that any aircrew member with imagination is always worried about enemy fighters. . . .

Take-off is normal. We join up in three vics of three, line astern. As we approach the target at 6000 feet, my upper gunner tells us that enemy fighters are approaching at speed. Our formation accelerates and goes into a shallow dive. Before we reach ground level my No. 2 is hit and goes straight in.

We are also in trouble. . . . I can feel the bullets hitting the armour plating behind my back. I see both engines are on fire. We are at ground level, so there is no hope of survival in a crash-landing.

Over the intercom I tell the crew I will try to gain sufficient height to bale out. There is no response from the two rear gunners. With such accurate shooting and the heat, the possibility of their survival is slim. My observer, whose station is between my feet, is slumped forward. Even when I kick him, he does not respond.

I have been hit in the thigh, and the heat is so intense that the skin of my hands starts peeling back. I try to jettison the cockpit canopy, but the quick release is so stiff I can't do it with my hand. I manage to force it with my head.

Suddenly, all control is gone and the aircraft starts flicking. As I release my straps I am thrown from the cockpit. . . . I fall free and pull the ripcord.

At such a low altitude there seems little chance of the parachute opening

113

in time; but it does – just before I hit the ground with such force that the 3–inch leather belt holding my revolver snaps.

I fall so close to the aircraft that a German patrol which is right there, can't come any closer to help because of the intense heat and exploding ammunition. They indicate that I must crawl out to them. . . .

I was taken to hospital in Bardia, where the bullet was removed from my leg and my hand and face burns treated.

And so began a long spell as a prisoner of war. When I met up with other survivors of that raid, I was told that the whole tail unit of my aircraft parted at 300 feet.

Did that thoughtless remark of the equipment officer affect my luck? If so, was it for better or for worse?

Colonel J.H. Eccles, Lyttelton, Verwoedburg Transvaal,
Republic of South Africa, 1984

Pushed Off at the Pointed End

Painful errors were made in 1940 and 1941 in the name of aircraft reinforcements for Malta and the Middle East. Some of these mistakes were due to lack of planning, others to incompetence, no less. The early land-based flights from southern England, across France and the Mediterranean to North Africa, thence to Malta, Libya and Egypt, were one thing; the carrier-borne operations down the western Mediterranean were something else.

Given a smattering of luck, crews of twin-engined aeroplanes, even of limited experience, were expected to be capable of leading and navigating formations of Hurricanes to a small island 600 or 700 miles distant; but, sadly, this wasn't always so. There were some fearful cock-ups.

However, in 1942 the Royal Air Force, the Royal Navy and the United States Navy got together and put away childish things. The Spitfire formations, which were flown off the carriers at a point north of Algiers, navigated themselves without difficulty over 700 miles of sea to the beleaguered Mediterranean fortress. It was much safer. But before that stage had been reached, some unfortunate lessons had to be learned. Robert McInnes Wilson was an expert witness to one of them.

My first operational flight [editor's italics] is recorded in my log book as follows: '14 June 1941 Hurricane (LR) Z4356 – Self – Solo: HMS *Ark Royal* to Luqa, Malta: 6¼ hours.'

I had been posted straight from CTU to 260 Squadron (Hurricanes) at Drem in East Lothian, where I learnt that they, and 238 Squadron, were due to embark on an aircraft carrier, bound for the Mediterranean, to be flown off to Malta en route to reinforce the RAF in the Middle East.

The CO of 260 assured me that it was all a mistake, and that he would get rid of me for some more experienced pilot, but it did not work out like that, and, in due course, I and forty-seven other pilots went aboard the aircraft carrier, *Victorious*, in Scapa Flow.

In Gibraltar twenty-four aircraft of 260 Squadron, and their pilots, were transferred to *Ark Royal*. The two aircraft carriers then, together, steamed out into the Med, escorted by HMS *Nelson* and sundry other naval units. Somewhere south of the Balearics, four Lockhead Hudsons appeared over the fleet, and each of the four groups of twelve Hurricanes formed up behind the Hudson which was to lead it to Malta. Surprisingly, everybody got off safely – including me, despite some anxious moments. . . .

It was a dismal, wet morning, so the four formations soon lost contact with each other, and as there was complete radio silence, there was plenty of time to brood over the possibilities. . . .

We understood that, with the extra fuel tanks, and provided the prescribed throttle setting and engine revs were maintained, we had ample petrol for an estimated flight of 4½ hours. Three groups got to Malta without incident. My formation, however, was not so lucky.

After 4½ hours I still had lots of petrol. However, when 5 hours had elapsed and the Hudson did a 180–degree turn, I realized we were in trouble.

Because of the radio silence which had to be maintained, there was nothing to do but twiddle with the button on the petrol gauge and the switch for the pumps to the external tanks, and watch the tanks slowly empty. . . . I finally reached the point as, no doubt did the others, when only the gravity tank showed a flicker on the needle.

It was now, after 6 hours' flying, that Malta showed up, miles ahead, like a chunk of bath brick in the sea. About the same time, somebody broke R/T silence to announce that No. 11 (Sergeant Saunders) had baled out.

The rest of us kept churning on, and, miraculously, were still flying normally when we reached Malta. There was no question then of locating Halfar, where we were supposed to land. The pilots of the surviving eleven aircraft all made straight for the circuit at Luqa, in the centre of the island, put their undercarriages and flaps down (we had been well warned that needless belly-landings would be court-martial offences) and proceeded to scramble in as best they could.

I was on the downwind leg when my engine finally cut. Remembering my early instruction, I immediately turned across wind to make sure I would not undershoot.

I had, however, overdone it. I was halfway down the runway, and doing about 100 m.p.h., when I got my wheels on the ground. There was no question of going round again, but my brakes, and an accommodating wall, took care of my problem. . . . Rather to my surprise I was able to walk away from it.

Sergeant McPherson undershot and was killed at the other end of the runway. The others all got down safely, although none had enough petrol left to taxi. . . .

R. McInnes Wilson, Newton Stewart, Wigtownshire,
Scotland, 1984

Editor's note: *McInnes Wilson and Saunders (picked up after baling out) remained in Malta to await transport to take them to Egypt. While there, they were summoned to the AOC's office where evidence was being taken by a Judge Advocate for the court-martial of the Hudson captain.*

The Thorn in Rommel's Side

The losses among the Royal Air Force's Blenheim squadrons in Malta in 1941 were now verging on the catastrophic. Low-level daylight attacks against increasingly heavily defended convoys, plying their way southwards across the Mediterranean in support of Erwin Rommel's Afrika Korps, produced casualties of the most grievous kind. Yet they had to be faced and accepted; the job which the gallant crews were doing was essential – and critical – for the Allies' fortunes in North Africa.

The irony was that, mostly, these units were on short detachments from their bases in 2 Group of Bomber Command in the United Kingdom. There, they had already been lacerated doing much the same daylight job against land and sea targets in northwest Europe. Nevertheless, the disruption which they caused to enemy shipping, with their relatively light 1000-lb bomb loads, was a major factor in the long drawn-out campaign against the Axis forces in North Africa. They were the thorn in Rommel's side.

One statistic should be acknowledged. German records show that in three months – three vital months – from 1 October to 31 December 1941, only 36 per cent of the weapons and materials sent by sea to Rommel from southern Europe actually reached him. It is right, therefore, that some attempt should be made to show the hazards which those who, by destiny, luck, fate, providence, chance or, perhaps, divine intervention, survived this holocaust, were daily facing.

Eric Chandler (Flight Lieutenant E.F. Chandler), who for the last forty years since the war has been a banker in the City of London, was cast in much the same mould as Mike Henry (see page 87, 'Air Gunner's Allergy') as a WOP/AG. His operational entry into that select category of aircrew hung on a chance – and a nerve.

. . . I was called up in September 1939 by the army, who, on discovering I had been accepted as aircrew by the RAF were very glad to get rid of me. . . . Together with 250 other City of London bank clerks, I was sent to Air Service Training at Hamble, near Southampton. . . . After we had taken our wireless exams, we were posted in batches of ten to RAF camps all over England to await a gunnery course. I was sent to Wattisham. This was the home of 110 and 107 (Blenheim) Squadrons. We were attached to the station police and put on guard duties every night. . . . I decided to register a complaint with the 'management'.

I knocked on a door with 'CO' on it. . . . I was met by those steely blue eyes of Basil Embry (Air Chief Marshal Sir Basil Embry)*. . . . I explained that our little band of eight leading aircraftmen were wasting our time doing guard duty, and that we wished to fly in his aeroplanes as WOP/AGs. . . . Having told me to put my hat on and stand to attention, he called in his adjutant. . . . Within two days four of us had gone to 110 Squadron; the other three and myself were sent to 107. . . . I never did go

---

*One of the Royal Air Force's exceptional senior officers and wartime commanders. He never asked a squadron commander to do anything that he wouldn't himself have done – and, indeed, probably had already done half a dozen times. (Ed.)

to a gunnery school, so, strictly speaking, I didn't really qualify as an air gunner despite the intensive training on the squadron. . . .

When, eventually, our posting to a gunnery school came through, there were only three of us still alive. . . .

As Basil and I were both Roman Catholics we used to travel to church every Sunday morning in a 30-cwt lorry; maybe Providence had decided that we should become very good friends. . . .

When my luck finally ran out in 1944, and I was in Ely hospital for twelve months, he went out of his way to visit me and assure me that, come what might, there would always be a place for me on his staff in Brussels.*

An operation on 22 June 1941 by 107 Squadron against a major Italian convoy bound for Tripoli, gives an idea of the horrible consequences of some of these operations. The merchantmen, surrounded by destroyers and flak ships, had been sighted just off the island of Lampedusa. The Blenheims, with inevitable loss, had penetrated the barrage of fire to press home the attack. The 11–second, delayed-action bombs had been released. . . .

A sharp jolt indicated that we also had been hit. I was thrown violently against the side of my turret. An unbelievable pain paralysed my right arm. I ducked down inside the turret to feel my right arm with my left hand, quite expecting to find my right arm had been blown off! At this point I was obviously lucky. The moment I ducked, a snaking line of Bofors tracer played across the aircraft passing through the perspex cover of my turret, where my head and shoulders had been. This brought me to life with a vengeance, determined to fight back. . . . My pilot, Flight Lieutenant L.J. Watkins, had been wounded by a shell, which had torn away the calf of his right leg almost severing the leg from the knee downwards. A machine-gun bullet had also hit him between the legs. The observer, Sergeant Sargent, rushed back to his aid pushing the control column forward to stop the rate of climb before we stalled. . . .

At last we were out of range. . . . A quick conference between the three of us, while the observer applied a tourniquet to the pilot's leg, decided unanimously that we would try and make Malta before the pilot bled to death, or the engines, which were now making very unhealthy noises, packed up.

At this point my radio receiver (our only means of telephonic communication with each other) exploded into my lap, and more holes appeared aft along the fuselage. Elevating the turret again I saw an Italian CR42 fighter curving in for a second attack on what he must have thought to be a crippled, defenceless bomber. I took my time and opened up at almost the precise moment that he recommenced firing at us. At once his nose went up, then, turning over, he slid down into the sea. . . . It must have been almost an hour before I saw the island of Malta rising again out of the sea. . . .

*Embry was then AOC, 2 Group, in the 2nd Tactical Air Force. (Ed.)

Wheels down, we motored straight into Luqa, cutting the engines as we touched the ground. . . . With a burst tyre and damaged wheel, we started to swerve at once ending in a ground spin. . . . By the time we had got the wounded pilot out onto the wing of the aircraft, the party which had been standing by the Watch Office had come rushing up. . . .

There were Atty (Wing Commander O.V.E. Atkinson), the CO, Dr Monroe, A V-M Hugh Pughe Lloyd (Air Chief Marshal Sir Hugh Lloyd), the AOC, and three others. They looked up at us in amazement. . . . The observer was covered in blood, so was the pilot who looked as white as a sheet from lack of blood, while I was thick with sweat, dust and dirt.

The pilot was awarded the DSO (in my view it should have been a VC), the observer, a DFM, and I was duly credited with my first aircraft destroyed.

The pilot recovered, but was never able to fly operationally again. . . . The observer and I had almost a repeat performance later in the year, when we returned with another wounded pilot. We had to drag him out of the cockpit and run with him to clear the aircraft, before it blew up with a 250-lb bomb which had hung up. . . .

When the squadron left Malta for home, we had no serviceable aircraft left to fly. Only seventeen of us remained, and we all managed to get into a Catalina for a night flight to Gib. . . .

When I joined 107 Squadron in 1940, the life expectancy of an air gunner was three weeks. After a while one gets the feeling that it cannot happen to you. . . .

Eric F. Chandler, Kenton, Middlesex, 1984

The best of men cannot suspend their fate
The good die early, the bad die late

Daniel Defoe (1661–1731), who clearly must
have had 2 Group of Bomber Command in mind.

Broom in Bloom

Ivor Broom (Air Marshal Sir Ivor Broom) was a 21-year-old sergeant pilot when he had to tarry, unexpectedly, in Malta in September 1941. He remained to become one of the island's most successful Blenheim captains, surviving four lethal months' operations at the time when the Germans and the Italians were making a maximum effort to get their supply vessels across to North Africa.

After ending the war with a dazzling operational record, and achieving senior rank and command in thirty years after it, he became, on retirement from the Royal Air Force, Controller of National Air Traffic Services and a member of the Civil Aviation Authority.

Broom was never intended to stay in Malta in the first place, but, rather, to proceed to Egypt and then Malaya. It was only by chance that he got caught up in the AOC's quite irregular, buccaneering habits. Air Vice-Marshal Lloyd's losses in aircraft and personnel were so severe, and his replacements relatively so tardy in arriving, that he improvised by 'hijacking' aircraft and crews en route for the East. Many a crew, bound for desert or jungle, found itself ' temporarily retained' for 'necessary detachment' on the island.

The procedure was unorthodox and not to be found in the Air Ministry's rule book. But Hugh Pughe Lloyd could be a defiantly unorthodox commander in the field. He had to be. As an operational AOC, he was in much the same resourceful class — and of similar temperament — to Embry and Keith Park who, by coincidence, was to succeed him almost a year later.

At Lloyd's diktat, Ivor Broom's crew started putting things to the touch, with the customary disregard for the consequences, immediately on arrival on the island.

'After what I had thought was merely a refuelling stop, my crew and I found ourselves on the battle order of 105 Squadron! After we had flown four bombing missions in the next five days, 105 returned to the UK. . . . We, however, were transferred to 107 Squadron. . . .'

The attack, on 11 October 1941, against a convoy making for Tripoli, and its aftermath, gave Broom some reason to wonder whether he might be marching in step with destiny.

I was one of six crews detailed to fly in two sections of three aircraft to find and attack the ships. . . . The leader was a flying officer, the only officer in the formation. I was selected to fly on his right in the first section, and another sergeant pilot, recently out of training, was detailed to fly on his left. After the briefing, the new pilot, detailed to fly on the left of the leader,

Blenheims attacking shipping

asked if I would change places with him in the formation as he found it easier to formate on the right. I readily agreed.

Some two hours after take-off we sighted the small convoy on the horizon, and prepared for our mast-high attack.* On the run in the crew who had changed places with me in the formation was shot down, the aircraft being hit as it passed through the screen of ack-ack in front of the ship it was attacking. I was unharmed, although my aircraft was damaged by anti-aircraft fire. We left two sinking ships, which the second formation deemed unnecessary to attack further – for the price of two young crews in their watery graves. . . .

We continued to sink enemy shipping and, in addition, flew low-level attacks against land targets in North Africa, Southern Italy, Sicily and the Greek Islands. In my four-months' spell, the squadron sank or damaged some 24 ships for the loss of 24 crews. Early in November 1941, a complete formation of three crews failed to return from a mission. We then had no officers left – only sergeant pilots, observers and air gunners.

The next morning, the Air Marshal visited the squadron. He announced that a new squadron commander would arrive in a few days' time, and told me that I was to become a pilot officer immediately. He had recommended me a week or two earlier for a commission, and said that the paperwork would be sorted out later.

I took my sergeant's stripes off my battle dress, put a pilot officer's braid on the tunic, bought an officer's forage cap from Gieves in Malta all for £5, and moved into the officers' mess. My 'official' commissioning came through three weeks later. I doubt whether many young officers' initial commissioning costs were as low as mine at £5! When 107 Squadron left Malta in January 1942, only two of its original pilots were still there and they, with me, were sent back to the UK.

I look back now on those times and wonder what would have happened to the course of my life had Air Vice-Marshal Lloyd not 'hijacked' me at Malta in September 1941. Many of those who went on to Malaya spent most of the war – if they survived – in a Japanese prisoner-of-war camp. I, on the other hand, returned home to marry the girl to whom I have now been married for forty-two years. . . .

What would have happened if my squadron colleague had not asked me to switch places with him in the formation on that fateful day in October 1941? And what, again, would have happened if the loss rate in Malta had been much less than it was and I had not been commissioned there, but had remained a sergeant pilot? Would I have stayed on in the peacetime Royal Air Force and retired as an air marshal?

Were these events, and many others I could relate, really acts of chance? . . . Or is there not a divinity which shapes our ends, rough-hewing them how it will? I believe the latter to be the case. . . .

Air Marshal Sir Ivor Broom, Loudwater, Rickmansworth,
Hertfordshire, 1984

---

*The aim of the formation was to fly as tight down on the water as possible, thus delaying the moment of detection. It was also hoped thereby to take advantage of the ships' guns' inability to depress the angle of fire below deck level. The aircraft then flew on through a defensive curtain of fire to press home the attack. (Ed.)

He either fears his fate too much,
  Or his deserts are small,
That puts it not unto the touch,
  To win or lose it all.

James Graham, Marquis of Montrose
(1612–50)

Blissful Ignorance

Defence had now given way to attack in southern England and in No. 11 Group of Fighter Command the sweeps over northern France and the Low Countries were gathering momentum. Their aim was to entice the Luftwaffe into battle. The Spitfire V was, at the time, well matched with the Messerschmitt 109 F and there was plenty of skirmishing. New personalities were making their mark.

A New Zealander named Johnny Checketts (Wing Commander J.M. Checketts), at twenty-nine, a few years older than the average fighter pilot, had just joined 485, the New Zealand Squadron, at Kenley in Surrey. The time would come when he would be counted among the fine wing leaders in the Command; but, for the moment, guts and application were no substitute for experience. . . .

As a 'sprog' pilot officer, I was flying with 485 on a sortie with Havoc bombers to Le Havre. Our squadron was acting as close escort on the port side. . . . We were in that stupid old formation of three sections of four aircraft in line astern, with No. 4 weaving.

I was tail-end Charlie in Blue Section keeping a good look out behind when I saw two aircraft, which weren't weaving, coming towards us. I thought they had become detached from the squadron and were going to join us. . . .

They were certainly going to join us – but they were 109s and they started firing at me. I turned into the attack and squealed for help. I was scared. I groped for the handle to lower the seat and get down behind the armour plating. I pulled a knob and there was a terrific bang. . . . I looked astern and the Huns had broken off the attack and were diving away. . . .

The action I had taken to lower my seat was not designed for this. . . . I had, in my panic, mistakenly fired the recognition colour* from the signal gun on the starboard side of the fuselage. . . .

I hastened to rejoin the squadron. . . . I don't know how I came to pull that tit because it was on the opposite side from the seat handle.

Did the signal flare scare the Huns off, or was it just chance that I didn't get shot down? I don't know, but the bang I had heard was the noise of the recognition signal being activated. I found this out later, but I was too self-conscious to tell my companions about it. . . .

Wing Commander J.M. Checketts, Christchurch,
New Zealand, 1984

---

*A coloured signal, regularly changed, which could be fired to show trigger-happy gunners and others that an aircraft was 'friendly'. (Ed.)

Wrong Scent

On 21 August 1941 Denis Crowley-Milling (Air Marshal Sir Denis Crowley-Milling), then a young officer in 610 Squadron of the Royal Air Force's Tangmere Wing, put his damaged Spitfire down – neatly, with its wheels up – on a farm near St Omer in northern France. After destroying his radio and other secret items, he then began a walk which, after one blessed, initial break, and with the help of the French Resistance, would ultimately lead him in three decades, to senior status in the Service and, thereafter, to the executive direction of the Royal Air Force Benevolent Fund.

The build-up to the story is important. After school at Malvern, Crowley-Milling joined Rolls-Royce as an apprentice. He got to learn about engines. So, when his squadron, No. 242, the Canadian unit, with the Royal Air Force, got separated from its groundcrews in the shambles of the crumbling Battle of France, he stepped in and serviced its remaining Hurricanes before the evacuation back to England.

He had, moreover, flown No.2 to Douglas Bader in the Duxford Wing throughout the Battle of Britain. So the Me 109 pilot who picked him off that August afternoon in 1941 was entitled, unbeknown to him, to his share of elation. The Germans, however, weren't so pleased when they found that the British victim had given them the slip.

The local farm workers had advised Crowley-Milling of the soldiers' proximity. They had also, unwittingly, offered him a bonus on the side.

I learnt after the war that the Germans had soon arrived with their dogs. But because the farm hands had climbed all over the aircraft and walked round it, the dogs, fortunately, got the wrong scent and set off in completely the wrong direction. . . .

After his initial getaway, Crowley-Milling had kept up a good pace for several hours, dodging potential captors. As darkness fell, he was on the outskirts of a small village. From his hiding place on its periphery, he selected one house which, among all the others, was showing a light. The occupants had forgotten to draw the blackout curtains in one window. This seemed propitious for his cause.

I walked in through the partially opened front door. The house was occupied by a man and two women, one of whom immediately drew the curtain across the window. I stood there in my uniform and explained in my poor French that I was a British pilot, and hungry. . . . I was told to sit down and was given some fried eggs on toast. With the help of an English/French dictionary we began a halting conversation. . . .

The man told me he had a farming friend who, he believed, could help me to contact the French underground organization. (As aircrew we had already had briefings on escape and evasion of capture.) He promised to take me to him in the morning.

That night I slept fully clothed with the window wide open, ready to slip out if necessary. In the morning, the man produced a spare bicycle. He said I was to cycle a short distance behind him, and he would give warning of German patrols.

We eventually arrived at a house where I was questioned closely by two other Frenchmen. I could not understand all the questions, and they seemed rather agitated. Finally, they left me and went into a back room.

After a few minutes one of them came back. It was M. Fillerin who was to help more than thirty aircrew to join the escape route before being arrested on suspicion of being a member of the underground, and put in the notorious Buchenwald concentration camp, from which, happily, he was a survivor. He looked at me and then stubbed two fingers of one hand down into the palm of the other; at the same time he gave the impression of an explosion.

I suddenly realized he was trying to find out whether I recognized the action required to blow up the vital IFF (Identification Friend or Foe) radio on my Spitfire. I said I knew what he meant, and that I had indeed set off the charge (i.e., by pushing down two buttons, alongside one another, at the same moment) and destroyed it. It seemed that, at that point, he had concluded I could be genuine.

It was not until I visited M. Fillerin after the war that I learnt they had decided to shoot me, believing me to be a German posing as a shot-down British airman. The Germans had already used this ruse to uncover French underground helpers, causing some to be arrested – and probably shot.

In my case, I had walked so far from the scene of my force-landing that they had not yet heard about any aircraft or parachute landing in their area. They had, therefore, thought that I must be a German. Fortunately for me (though I was, of course, oblivious to it at the time) M. Fillerin had decided to question me once more. He then gave me the benefit of the doubt.

I was fed, subsequently, into the escape route via Paris and Marseilles, and over the Pyrenees into Spain. Eventually, I was transported back to the UK and was able to rejoin my old squadron.

Air Marshal Sir Denis Crowley-Milling, North Creake,
Fakenham, Norfolk, 1984

Editor's note: *Crowley-Milling did, in fact, have a rough time in a concentration camp in Spain. Malnutrition temporarily affected his eyesight. He soon recovered at home, and later played out the war on fighter bombers of which he became a noted leader.*

A Case of Mistaken Identity

Bernard Dupérier (Colonel Bernard Dupérier) was one among the spirited band of French Air Force pilots who made their way to England after the 1940 collapse, and took their places alongside their British and Allied counterparts in Royal Air Force squadrons. They quickly won the respect of their colleagues.

Dupérier – 'Skip' to many of his British friends – was an experienced pilot who, during the next two and three years, was destined to become an accomplished squadron commander and wing leader. But there were a few moments on the afternoon of 20 July 1941, when he would have offered little for his future chances. An uncharacteristic error in aircraft identification showed how even the most dependable of them could sometimes make mistakes.

242, the squadron to which he had earlier been posted, were operating from Manston on the east Kentish coast. Their task, with their Hurricanes, was to neutralize the enemy's defences during an attack by three Blenheims on an 8000-ton merchantman, with its attendant flak ships, moving a short distance off the French coast opposite Le Touquet. Above, 'Treble Two' Squadron's Spitfires were to provide the cover.

After the attack on the convoy, during which two out of the three Blenheims were lost — just about par for the course at this time — the striking force turned for home. Dupérier who, by design, had been bringing up the rear during the onslaught on the ships, sensed some relief.

I felt that the main part of the operation was now over; my aircraft had not been damaged and so, to conserve fuel, I throttled back. . . . I did not feel it necessary to catch up with the rest of the Hurricanes of 242 which I could see well ahead of me. . . .

I had a last look round and noted the reassuring presence of the Spitfire escort up above. When I saw them diving, I thought that, having not been engaged during the attack, they wanted to have a go at something before returning to base. . . . They were now also at sea level and some hundred yards behind me. . . .

As I was calmly flying straight ahead a few feet above the water, I was concentrating only on my compass. Then, suddenly, I saw on both sides of my aircraft, splashes being thrown up from salvoes of machine-gun and cannon fire. . . . What a catastrophic mistake was mine! A glance in the mirror revealed the terrifying sight of a yellow-nosed Messerschmitt, tens, not hundreds, of yards away, and right on my tail!

What I had taken to be Spitfires of 222 Squadron were . . . 109s!

'Skip' Dupérier was now on his own. . . . At least four 109s against one Hurricane. . . . And his radio was dead, having just had a bullet through it. There was nothing to be done about alerting the rest of the squadron. He was in a tight defensive circle, right down on the deck and still only a few miles off Le Touquet. . . . It was twenty miles back to Manston. Clearly this couldn't go on as he would soon be dangerously low on fuel. . . . And yet, as every fighter pilot would know, the moment he stopped turning into the attacks he would be done. . . .

The one manoeuvre to be avoided at all costs was the reverse turn — to start turning to the right instead of to the left — thus exposing oneself to the enemy's fire. . . . So why, why did I do it? I just don't know. It was as if I had been forced by some outside influence. . . . Whatever it was, I had switched over with lightning speed and reversed my turn. . . . My opponent behind must have been taken completely by surprise for we were now turning in opposite circles. . . . As he passed in front of me at the same level, I instinctively pressed the gun button, registering hits along the fuselage of the 109. . . .

Hugging the water, I fled flat out for Manston. . . . Looking round again, I saw a miraculously empty sea and sky. . . .

How 'Skip' got away with it, he will never know. His action was contrary to the text book, a million to one shot against survival, a recipe for disaster, an invitation to death. Someone must have been about that day to claim for him the one exception to prove the invariable rule.

Back at Manston, his comrades were 'flabbergasted' to see the state of his aircraft. They had given him up for lost.

As we repaired to the crewroom, I found some of my friends in the middle of making an inventory of my belongings and dividing up the flying gear that I wasn't wearing! That, I thought, was a bit quick off the mark!

'But,' one of the pilots said, 'we saw you in a bad way, and when you didn't come back we assumed you had 'bought it'. . . . Besides I could really do with a pair of fur-lined flying boots for high altitudes. . . .'

The logic was irrefutable . . . and we all burst out laughing.

Colonel Bernard Dupérier, Paris, France, 1984

Interlude

'Tim' Woodman (Squadron Leader R.G. Woodman) was numbered, by the end of the war, among the acknowledged exponents of the advanced and sophisticated art of night-fighting and night-intruding deep into enemy territory. There was, however, a brief exchange during 1941 when, at the Royal Air Force station at Drem, hard by North Berwick on the southern shore of the Firth of Forth, he seemed to be pushing his luck too far.

I was with 410 Squadron of the Royal Canadian Air Force and had a French girlfriend at the time. She had escaped from Paris, and had made her way down through France to Lisbon. She had brought her left-hand-drive Citroen with her.

One night we drove down a long track through the woods to the barbed wire and minefield by the shore of the Firth of Forth. It was an out-of-bounds area. A trigger-happy Pole, who spoke no English, came out of the night to the side of the car and challenged us. Y— was petrified. . . . Foreign car, me in grey battledress. . . . Gawd, I thought, how the hell do I get out of this one?

'Jig-a-jig,' I said to him.

'Ah, jeeg-ee-jeeg!' he exclaimed, and buggered off. . . .

Squadron Leader R.G. Woodman, Westbury, Wiltshire, 1984

Laughter in Venice

Wellingtons of 149 Squadron (motto: Forte Noctis), based at Mildenhall in Suffolk, and commanded by Wing Commander 'Speedy' Powell, were detailed on the night of 12/13 January 1941 to bomb the Porto Marghera oil refinery and storage depot in Venice. A secondary target was the oil-

125

storage installation, used by the Italian navy, on a small island in the Venice lagoon.

For Ken Wilson (Flight Lieutenant L.K.S. Wilson), then a 20-year-old Rhodesian pilot officer, and now the chairman of Zimbabwe's largest finance company, this was the last of a series of 'experience raids' designed to blood new aircrew. Captain of the aircraft was Dick Hodgson, and the round-trip was one of some 1500 miles crossing the Swiss Alps twice in the moonlight. ('... Suddenly, the most fantastic sight took our breaths away. To our portside, and towering about 4000 feet above us, were the Jungfrau and the Eiger.... The full moon shining on them in the clear, crisp night turned them into giant stacks of millions of glistening, polished diamonds....')

The mission for Wilson and his mates was one way. What's more, by an unpredictable chance, it ended incongruously, and uniquely, in hilarious laughter. Bomber Command was not to know anything like it.

It was the secondary target that the crew attacked – and blew up. Then, to finish the job off, they did a low-level run across the city dropping bundles of propaganda leaflets as they went. Wilson's recollection remains quite clear.

To my horror, I felt the aircraft shudder violently as if it had hit a cattle grid; bullets burst all round Lofty Harding, the wireless operator, and myself.... Then I heard Dick's voice yell over the intercom, 'We're on fire!' ... Apparently we'd flown right over the only armed naval patrol ship in the lagoon.

We must have still been doing 200 m.p.h. as we hit the water.... I got flung around quite a lot but, apart from bruises, I wasn't knocked out or damaged. It was beyond my comprehension that we escaped injury. The front gunner, Charlie Pummery, was still in his turret. Les Hatherly, the navigator, and Lofty were somewhere behind me, Dick was strapped in his seat and 'Mac' Macanally, likewise, was strapped in the rear gun turret. I dragged myself to my feet and saw the tail unit of 'another' aircraft about 200 yards in front of us and wondered where it had come from. Our engine was blazing furiously. I climbed down and let Charlie out of his turret.... Lofty reached the tip of the port wing and I called out to him to dive in and see how deep it was.

He dived in and then, to our amazement, rose out of the water like a black phoenix, dripping with mud. The areas round his eyes were white, and he looked like a minstrel singer. We all burst into laughter and began to drop, feet first, into the water. Then someone said, 'Where's Mac?' I looked round towards the tail unit. It wasn't there! It was *our* tail unit in front of us. Doubled up with laughter we stumbled over towards it.... I looked at my watch. It was 1.45 a.m....

The 'putt putt' of a low-powered outboard motor brought us momentarily to our senses, and into sight came a 20-foot dinghy-type boat. When he saw us, the helmsman at once swung the boat round and then reversed cautiously towards us. As the crew became visible we became dumb with astonishment. There were about four or five of them and each wore a huge silver fireman's helmet topped with a sort of inverted cornucopia sweeping down to the helmet peak.... We started laughing louder than ever. The boatmen, not unnaturally, were not amused ... We realized they were pointing rather nasty-looking firearms at us.

The crisis was soon over when they saw we were unarmed, and they reversed right up to us. They also suddenly became very – but untranslatably – voluble and friendly, and helped to heave us aboard. I was the last to try and scramble in, but my boots stayed glued in the mud. ...

A grizzled fireman placed a hand under each of my armpits to heave me up, but he suddenly stopped and looked into my 20-year-old face. His face was covered with about three days' growth of beard, and his breath stank of garlic and cheap wine. A look of startled joy appeared in his eyes, and a lascivious grin on his face. '*Ah, un giovonese,*' he said, and promptly placed a juicy kiss on each of my cheeks! 'God,' I thought, 'I'm in for that trouble my mother warned me about at boarding schools!' I slid into the boat and promptly sat firmly on my bottom as we headed for Venice.

We were taken to an island south of Venice on which was a huge old palace, virtually deserted. ... There we were subjected to routine cross-examination. We all stuck to our Red Cross rights – name, rank and number was all we'd give. The officers of the Royal Italian Navy respected these rights, but were convinced we'd been drugged to brave the long journey to attack Italy.

'Why,' they asked, 'if you weren't suffering the after-effects of drugs, were you all screaming with laughter when we captured you?'

We might have told them we were under the influence of the most potent drug in conditions of stress – '*Facetiae Britannicae*' commonly known as the 'British Sense of Humour'. ...

L.K.S. Wilson, Barrowdale, Harare, Zimbabwe, 1984

Beyond Human Bounds

How much can the human frame endure? In the air war, the short answer was 'as much as the mind itself could take'. Some were tougher, mentally, than others, and none more so than the Czechs for whom the Royal Air Force developed so high a regard.

Alois Siska was typical of his countrymen's resolution. He was as good as example as any of the contention that 'fortune favours the brave'. By and large, his luck matched his innate faith. He had been shot down twice already. Now, on 28 December 1941, and during an attack on the docks at Wilhelmshaven, he was to make it three times. His aircraft was hit and caught fire. Eventually, it became uncontrollable and crashed into the North Sea.

The rear gunner perished, but, scarcely credibly, the remaining crew members were able to climb into the aircraft's dinghy. Mid-winter cold and high seas offered them small prospect of survival. After four days of sub-human conditions and false hopes, their resolve had been tested to the limit, and beyond.

On New Year's Day our morale received an uplift. A single seagull flew close to us giving our befuddled brains hope that land was nearby. One of the crew suggested we should try to catch the bird, using its blood to quench our thirst; but, by that time, we were too weak to make the attempt.

Hallucinations then affected the second pilot and, later, he died on my shoulder. Before daybreak on the fifth day, the navigator also died, and daylight disclosed that the wireless operator was unconscious. That left me and the front gunner to discuss our chances of rescue. They seemed remote. Neither of us wanted to be alone with our two dead, and one unconscious companion, so we decided to end our lives using the drugs from the first-aid box.

We hoped that our 'special brew' concocted from a mixture of drugs and seawater would bring us eternal sleep; but the drugs were ineffective and I and my front gunner were wakened on the sixth day by the sound of splashing water. The dinghy was leaking. We were unable to inflate it any more because seawater had put the pump out of commission. . . . Gradually our craft was sinking. . . .

In desperation, we decided to bury the dead crew members thereby reducing the weight and helping to keep it afloat. We tipped the second pilot into the sea, but our fading strength prevented us from doing the same with the navigator.

Suddenly the front gunner cried out he could see land. . . . After a period that seemed endless we were washed up on the Dutch coast, only to be taken prisoner by German troops. . . .

We were taken to a naval hospital in Alkmaar, then to a military hospital in Amsterdam where German doctors decided to amputate my legs. The time spent in the dinghy had left me with frostbite and gangrene. Fate, however, decreed otherwise. The doctors were thwarted, for, as they put me onto the operating table, I had a heart attack, and all thought of amputation was shelved. Different methods of healing my gangrenous legs were used, and they responded in some measure to this treatment.

Six months later I was moved to Germany. . . .

Alois Siska, Zvole u Prahy, Czechoslovakia, 1985

Editor's note: *After spending the next two years in various prison camps, Alois Siska was moved by the Gestapo to Prague in July 1944. He was charged with high treason and espionage against the Third Reich, but the fortuitous attempt on Hitler's life diverted attention and delayed his court-martial in Torgeau. He and eleven other Czech 'criminals' were thus required to wait. Siska 'languished' (his word!) in Colditz before being taken to another camp. . . . But the liberation by US forces saved him and his countrymen from the almost inevitable firing squad. . . . On 15 May 1945 – his thirty-first birthday – he was flown back to Manston, and to two years in hospital, before returning to Czechoslovakia.*

Norge Nightmare

. . . Funny thing, though, all during the war I had a feeling that I would come through alive, but pilot friends of mine who, eventually, were lost, quite openly said they felt the opposite . . .

Conrad Skajoldhammer (Kaptein C. Skajoldhammer), who wrote those words, was a member of the Norwegian Squadron, No. 330, which, in 1941 and 1942 was operating single-engined Northrop N3PB floatplanes on anti-submarine and convoy escort work into the Atlantic from Buda-reyri, in the east of Iceland. An airline captain for much of the past forty years, he recalls one experience which must have tested his confidence to the full.

It was an anti-U-boat patrol, flown on 31 October 1942. Skajoldhammer knew then, just like any other single-engine pilot, that repeatedly long flights over a hostile sea, day after day and week after week, for months on end, produced a form of anxiety neurosis of their own. Only those who had to do it could possibly comprehend what it was like to rest the future on the reliability of one engine and the maintenance of a favourable streak of luck. 330 Squadron's natural concern for the task was not lessened when, one day, their commanding officer, Captain H. Bugge, failed to return from a similar mission. Conrad's apprehension this day can be felt.

... As we flew southwards from our base, the Atlantic weather steadily worsened. We were below a cloud base of 800 feet, with poor forward visibility. Beneath us the waves were rolling large and grey, flecked with streaks of white foam and spray. ...

We were getting close to the southernmost extremity of our sweep, between 300 and 400 miles out into the Atlantic, when, suddenly, and without any warning, the engine cut stone dead. I was flying on a nearly full tank, but immediately switched over to another (there were six on the N3PB), priming the engine and doing everything else to get it going again. ...

We were gradually losing what little height we had, and I knew this small aircraft would have no chance in such enormous waves. This, I thought, was 'it' ... but at about 200 feet, no more, the engine caught again and seemed to start running quite normally. I at once turned for home and tried to gain height. ...

At about 3000 feet, the motor cut again, just as suddenly as the first time. Everything became quiet as we began to glide noiselessly towards the waves. ... We were down to 1500 feet when it picked up once more. ...

I told the crew of two that I had no idea what was wrong, but that I would gain all the height that I could. I really suspected the engine now, and felt that it might, at any moment, snuff out altogether. ... The apprehension, fuelled by one's imagination, was sickening. ...

I cannot remember now how many more times the motor cut on the return flight, but, each time, I drew a bit more on what luck we might have left and got it started. ... Tentatively, we clawed our way upwards until we came out on top of the overcast at some 15,000 feet. But then we faced another hazard – we had no oxygen. The heights at which we normally operated didn't demand it.

I was pretty well drained by this nightmare when, with the weather improving to the north, the mountains of Iceland could be seen in distant outline. ... Could we make it? ... My concern now was to maintain our height for long enough to enable us to do a 'dead-stick' landing in the comparatively still waters of a fjord if the motor finally gave up the ghost.

It was running rougher and rougher all the time, with intermittent coughing and spluttering. . . . The suspense was terrible – just as bad for the crew as it was for me. . . . The lack of oxygen at our height didn't help. . . .

Eventually, as we neared the coastline, the engine cut again, this time for good. Nothing that I did had any effect, but we were close enough now for me to judge that, with the 15,000 feet we still had, I should be able to stretch a 'dead-stick' glide to the first fjord I could find. . . . In the event, I was able to reach not just the coast but our base at Budareyri where we put down. . . .

It was a pale and shaken crew which left the aircraft that day. I had suspected for some time that we might have water in the fuel tanks. In fact, some 11 litres of water were drained off. . . .

Looking back, it was, perhaps, the most agonizing – and yet the most fortunate – experience of its kind that I can remember. We had been fantastically lucky.

Kaptein Conrad Skajoldhammer, Slependen, Norway, 1984

Polish Reprimand!

There weren't many who completed four tours of operational flying in World War II, and those that did drew heavily upon their reserves of luck. John Iverach (Squadron Leader J.A. Iverach), the Canadian navigator, was such a one. He was well into his fourth run of operations when the war in the Far East and Pacific came to an end.

After being trained in Canada on the second course of the Commonwealth Air Training Plan in May 1940, it was to flying boats that he was posted. ('Flying-boat squadrons lacked the excitement of Bomber Command, but there were compensations; for one thing, one lived longer; for another, one got to see more of the world.') Then, in time – and after several months in hospital – DC-3s (Dakotas) and B-24s (Liberators) claimed him in the Far East. Iceland, Russia, Gibraltar, Malta, Egypt, India, Ceylon, Burma, the Cocos Islands, Java, Sumatra and Australia became names in his itinerary.

But nothing was more bizarre or hazardous than the nine months John Iverach spent in 1942, working for Air Ministry intelligence.

I was the squadron navigation officer in 240 Squadron in addition to doing my usual routine flying duties, and I was bored to death. I therefore volunteered for 'two weeks' interesting work' as the job was described.

I was dumbfounded to find what it was – flying with a Heinkel 115, a large, twin-engined floatplane, one of four stolen by the Norwegians from the Germans and flown to Britain. The Royal Air Force had modified them for pick-up and delivery work with secret agents along enemy coastlines. . . .

One trip is inscribed deeply upon Iverach's memory.

In May 1942 we were operating out of Calshot, on the Solent, mainly rendezvousing with fishing boats off the French coast in the Bay of Biscay.

Every time we took to the air we had to file a flight plan forty-eight hours in advance, and submit a revised one on take-off.

On this particular trip, we expected to be returning in the early dawn, and, as a precaution, arrangements were made for another aircraft to meet us in the English Channel and escort us home.

The flight was long but uneventful, until we were approaching the south coast of England, where our escorting aircraft was circling at the appointed place waiting for us. I was somewhat surprised to see what they had sent: a Hampden bomber – of all things – which, at first glance, looked a lot like a German Dornier. But at least *we* knew it was friendly, and we flew off happily with it in formation, heading home to Calshot, which was only about ten or fifteen miles away.

I was busy up in my nose compartment making some final entries in my log, and relieved to have another trip safely behind me, when, suddenly, a half-inch hole appeared in my log, right beside my pencil. At the same instant, one of the slave instruments on the fuselage beside me went whistling past my head, rattling around against the Perspex. I whirled around to see what in hell was happening, just in time to notice a spidery object go spinning off ahead of us. It was our starboard propellor! And then our starboard wing burst into a sheet of flame.

Knut, my Norwegian pilot, shouted into the intercom: 'Dose are bloody Spitfires! Yonny, fire a recognition signal!' As he spoke, he dived the aircraft towards the water below.

I grabbed the Verey pistol and fired – before I realized I had forgotten to change the German recognition signals for our own! Meanwhile, our escort, the 'protecting' Hampden, did the prudent, if not the courageous, thing: its pilot opened up the throttles and took off like a scalded cat.

We got down safely on the calm sea and managed to extinguish the fire, while the two Spitfires made another pass over us, fortunately without firing any more. By then we were only about five miles from the Isle of Wight. We were able to radio for help, and soon had the humiliating experience of being towed into Calshot by a rescue launch, and of listening to the needling of her skipper.

A subsequent court of enquiry revealed that someone in Fighter Command had been tardy in relaying our flight plan to all squadrons in the area, and the last one to be informed was a Polish Spitfire unit. When that squadron's intelligence officer received the information, two of their pilots were already out on patrol. He neglected to have word passed on to them.

When they had spotted what was, unmistakably, a Heinkel 115, they had naturally assumed its companion to be a Dornier, and could hardly wait to get at both!

When asked whether he had taken any disciplinary action over the incident, their CO replied: 'I most certainly did! I confined the two pilots to camp for a week with a reprimand!'

'But why,' parried the investigator, 'did you do that when you knew they had not been told about the Heinkel?'

'Oh,' the CO explained, 'the reprimand was not for attacking. It was for not finishing off the Heinkel, and for letting the other one get away!'

John A. Iverach, Winnipeg, Manitoba, Canada, 1984

Pathos

John Iverach has also chronicled the bravery of one of 240 Squadron's flying-boat crews, operating from Stranraer, on the west coast of Scotland, roundly a year before his Heinkel 115 incident in the English Channel.

In dreadful weather, the crew had answered the call of a stricken ship, torpedoed several hundred miles out in the Atlantic. After locating the ship's lifeboats, dropping supplies and guiding other vessels to the scene, the pilot, Flight Lieutenant Vince Furlong, and his crew, turned for home. But the wind had swung round to the east and now they had to face a 70-knot gale, giving the aircraft a ground speed of no more than 15 knots. . . .

In due course, with fuel almost exhausted, a powered 'ditching' had to be made, well away from land, before the engines finally died. To keep the aircraft from listing hopelessly to starboard in the high seas, the navigator, Pilot Officer Vladimir V. Havlicek ('Dimi' to the crew), a Czech who had escaped from the Nazis to Canada in 1938, climbed out onto the lower port wing, lashed himself to the outer struts, and stayed there during a ghastly Atlantic night. It was an act of almost unbelievable courage.

The next day, by a near miracle, the aircraft drifted onto a beach on the Mull of Kintyre. Dimi was still alive. . . .

Later that day, when the storm had lessened, we flew over to Campbelltown to pick the crew up and bring them back to Stranraer. . . .

It would be nice to say that Dimi, my close friend and room-mate, was duly rewarded for his heroism, but all he ever received was the undying gratitude of his fellow crew members. . . .

His CO neglected to forward Furlong's recommendation. . . .

Ten months later, in December 1941 P/O Havlicek, flying with a new pilot, lost his life when a Catalina sank in a heavy sea in Pembroke Dock, near Milford Haven in Wales, after 'a horrible landing. . . . Without hesitation, Dimi had gone back inside, dragged the unconscious wireless operator forward and pushed him out through the hatch just as the water came rushing in. . . . Dimi was never seen again. . . .'

. . . He used to jot down random thoughts in a very private notebook. In it, I found this strange little verse. It was the last entry, written just before his final trip.

> I wait. For what?
> I wait, and in my waiting lose all sense of time.
> The years go by, though only moments by the sun,
> And seas of time engulf my drowning mind,
> Until one moment, more defined than most,
> Recalls me to the urgent *now*,
> And to the waiting – the endless waiting –
> For what?

John A. Iverach, Winnipeg, Manitoba, Canada, 1984

Editor's note: *It is right to record Iverach's description of 'Dimi' Havlicek.*

'. . . In his native Czechoslovakia, he had been a remarkable, multi-sport athlete. A ruggedly handsome six-footer . . . "Dimi" had represented his country all over the world not only in swimming but also in skiing, soccer and tennis. . . . At thirty-two, his athletic triumphs were only memories – like the fiancée he had left behind, dead in the snow, killed by a hail of Nazi bullets as he escaped across the border in 1938, en route for Canada. . . .'

The 'Impossible' Epic

12 February 1942. Terrific flap today. *Scharnhorst, Gneisenau* and *Prinz Eugen* are out of Brest and heading up towards the North Sea. How they managed to get as far as this without detection is one more mystery of this war . . .

Extract from 217 Squadron's Operations Record Book,
RAF Station, Thorney Island

During Operation 'Donnerkeil-Cerberus' on 12 February 1942, I was faced with the decision whether or not to contact our low-flying fighter escort around the ships, and end radio silence, after a Spitfire pilot, Squadron Leader R.W. Oxspring, had reported the presence of the Fleet over his R/T. I took a very big chance indeed in not breaking the silence and warning the fighters of the discovery of the ships and, therefore, the likelihood of an early attack. But it paid off; we gained a vital hour before the British finally reacted. . . .*

Generalleutnant Adolf Galland, Bonn, Germany, 1984

The undetected departure, in the late evening of 11 February 1942, of the German ships, Scharnhorst *and* Prinz Eugen *from Brest, their dramatic dash through the narrow Straits of Dover in daylight and their subsequent arrival on the thirteenth in their northwest German ports, was one of the most astonishing feats of World War II.*

For the British, who regarded the 22-mile strip of water between Dover and Calais as very much their preserve, it was a humiliation of the most taunting kind. It was like having a stranger walking about in the front garden. The Germans, on the other hand, took an immense and calculated risk, put it to the touch and succeeded, remarkably, against all the odds. It was a brilliant and courageous operation.

It has been claimed – and still is – that the enemy were exceptionally lucky on several counts to achieve this tactical victory. But how much of it can really be attributed to luck?

Edward Chilton (Air Marshal Sir Edward Chilton), a former Commander-in-Chief of Coastal Command and possessing special access to 'persons† and papers', has made, perhaps, the most penetrating study yet undertaken of this incredible story, codenamed 'Fuller'. It has occupied many years. His research and authority are undoubted, his findings histori-

*Had Galland passed instructions to his fighter aircraft, the British listening service would have picked up the messages and the presence of the ships would have been instantly confirmed. (Ed.)

†The Air Marshal was personally well acquainted with the Cs-in-C of the three operational commands primarily concerned – Coastal, Bomber and Fighter. He had many discussions with them – and his friends among their staffs and surviving aircrews – regarding the detail and the background to this affair. (Ed.)

cally important. Here, in this new and specially written assessment of one of the war's great sagas, Chilton makes a notable contribution to the record.

Some years ago, I read that 'Luck in war comes to those, who, by sound planning and preparation, deserve it'. I would say that this would exactly fit the circumstances which envelop the entire story of the so-called 'Channel dash'. . . .

The escape of the two German battle-cruisers together with the heavy cruiser *Prinz Eugen*, from Brest to Germany in February 1942, was an event which shocked Britain. How was it possible for the three ships to pass through an area covered by patrolling aircraft and radar, and how did we fail to bring the enemy to battle when they were eventually located?

What I wish to do is to investigate how we made so many errors, because there must be important reasons for our total failure. In the past, much has been said about the failure of Group Captain Beamish to break R/T silence when he saw the enemy ships at 10.42 on 12 February, approaching the Dover Straits, but I doubt if this had any real effect upon the outcome, for reasons which will later become clear. *This event also deserves attention because it is the only operation of its kind to have been the subject of a judicial enquiry in World War II, but it found no one to blame!** However, a careful reading of the verbatim text shows a strong tendency to 'avoid the issue', and all of the secret information was withheld while other essential evidence was not produced, i.e., the early radar plots.

It is, however, reasonably certain that the enquiry would not have been held if the Prime Minister had been able to tell the House of Commons that both the *Scharnhorst* and the *Gneisenau* had, in fact, been damaged by air-laid mines in the southern North Sea on their way to their home base in the Kiel area. As it was, the reaction of the British press was very hostile, but in Germany, after the initial glow of success, the German naval staff soon saw that while they had won a tactical victory, they had, at the same time, suffered a major strategic defeat, in that we could now withdraw our battleships from North Atlantic convoy service.

Another question that has to be answered is the heavy loss of aircrew and aircraft. How did we manage to lose 17 fighters, 15 bombers, 5 torpedo aircraft and 6 Swordfish T/B aircraft of the Fleet Air Arm? Added to this, many more aircraft were lost in landing accidents owing to the very bad weather. (The Germans lost 17 fighters in combat, but sustained damage to many more in landing accidents due to the weather.)

To lose so many aircraft for no tangible gain is difficult to explain. However, it is clear that lack of effort was not missing at lower levels; the personnel did their very best, but their efforts were either misdirected or not directed at all. To try to unravel the reasons for this 'fiasco', we need to look at the following areas:

1. The set-up in Whitehall
2. The command structure
3. The planning arrangements

*The italics throughout this story are the editor's.

4. The intelligence available
5. The weather forecasting
6. The sources of errors

1. THE SET-UP IN WHITEHALL

Unfortunately, right from the start of the war, there was a lack of understanding between the Admiralty and the Air Ministry about the use of air
power, and it took too long to get matters into the right balance. It is not
my intention to go into all the reasons for this, but the war had suddenly
developed into a vast conflict, quite beyond the thoughts of the service
planners in peacetime, and it was compounded by the financial constraints
of the pre-war governments.

In a nutshell, neither the Royal Navy nor the Royal Air Force were
equipped with the right number of ships or aircraft, armed with the right
weapons, to do the many and varied tasks that were thrust upon them.
Thus it was inevitable that the Air Ministry was unable to meet all the
demands made by the other services, especially the Admiralty. The latter
found it difficult to accept the War Cabinet's policy that Bomber
Command's first task was to bomb Germany! To get things right needed
great skill and tact at the highest levels.

When the 'Channel dash' took place, things were still not right, *but part
of the Admiralty's complaint had been overcome by their being given
'operational control' of the Royal Air Force's Coastal Command.* However,
with this background in mind, it is somewhat surprising to find the
following paragraph in the Admiralty appreciation of 2 February 1942,
which was sent to the Chief of the Air Staff, dealing with the likely departure of the Brest ships: 'Our bombers have shown that we cannot place
much reliance on them to damage the enemy.' I would suggest that this
was very negative thinking on the part of the naval staff and not the way
to produce a positive result. Certainly not the way to galvanize the air staff
into the mood to make sure that the German ships were sunk, come what
may!

*I venture to assert that had 'Bomber' Harris been the C-in-C of Bomber
Command at that time, the ships would have been either sunk or severely
damaged! He would have earmarked two squadrons who would have
known what to do irrespective of the circumstances or the weather, day or
night. They would have trained for the job in the same way as the
Dambuster squadrons were trained later on. He would never have agreed
to earmark some 300 aircraft, the number agreed to by his predecessor
under some pressure from Whitehall.*

2. THE COMMAND STRUCTURE

The naval command structure was quite straightforward; there were flag
officers at Plymouth, Portsmouth, Dover and the Nore. Everything that
went on in their areas was under the control of one commander. In the
'Channel dash', the flag officer at Dover was to play the key role. Unfortunately, things were not so clear cut in so far as the RAF was concerned.

There were three commands involved, Bomber, Fighter and Coastal, and their commanders-in-chief were virtually autonomous within their own spheres. Worse still, with Air Ministry backing, they could not agree to giving the overall control of all the forces involved to C-in-C Coastal Command. Such a state of affairs virtually damned the operation from the start and ruled out a coordinated plan or prior tactical training for the type of operation they had before them.

The best agreement that they could reach was that the Air Officer Commanding No.11 Group (Fighter Command), would cooperate with Vice-Admiral, Dover, in order to provide the necessary fighter cover, while AOC, No.16 Group (Coastal Command), was instructed to see that air attacks on enemy surface ships were coordinated with our own forces. Unfortunately, these arrangements were too loose, and would not stand the test of any surprise movement by the German ships.

3. THE PLANNING ARRANGEMENTS

Soon after the *Scharnhorst* and *Gneisenau* had been located at Brest towards the end of March 1941, discussions were held as to how best to deal with them should they try to return to Germany. It was agreed in Whitehall that any operation must be mainly an air operation as the home fleet was based at Scapa Flow and was already fully committed. In any event, the Admiralty were very reluctant to bring their heavy forces south into an area well studded with mines and close to powerful air forces. However, the Admiralty did undertake to help with light forces from Dover with MTBs and MGBs and possibly some old destroyers from the Nore.

(i) *Lack of Overall Commander*

To cope with this situation, the Air Ministry issued its operational directive to the three commands involved, Bomber, Fighter and Coastal, but the mere issuing of a directive does not get things done when no overall coordinating commander is in charge of the planning. Each command issued its orders, but all were unrelated to each other, and were certainly not on an integrated basis. For example, the vital Channel patrols of Coastal and Fighter Command were not meshed into one foolproof net to prevent the ships from slipping through unobserved. All this was further complicated by the very high degree of secrecy maintained, especially by No.11 Group, which was to play a key role in the operation.

The lack of information and the surprise arrival of the enemy resulted in *the majority of the aircrew involved being unaware of what they were to look for and what they had to attack. Perhaps the worst unnoticed error was in No. 11 Group's operation order of 5 October 1941, which stated that R/T silence was to be maintained, except in an emergency, until the enemy had been engaged!* This unfortunate phrase had been copied from an earlier order which was quite unrelated to the needs of an operation against enemy shipping, when early reporting is vital.

(ii) *Bomber Command's Role*

As regards Bomber Command, there were two roles set for their aircraft; the first was to bomb the ships at Brest as often as possible in the hope of destroying or damaging them, while the second was to sink the ships should they escape from Brest. Later, air mining was added to their role. The first task produced sufficient hits to delay their departure until February 1942. However, it is important to understand that the aircrews of Bomber Command were not trained in the role of attacking ships moving at high speed at sea. Furthermore, our bombers were still lacking the necessary navigation and bombing equipment to attack such targets in poor weather conditions by day or night. Coastal Command was in much the same state because their aircraft radar was rather elementary and unreliable, while their torpedo squadrons were still learning the right technique.

(iii) *Photographic Reconnaissance*

There was one other important requirement, namely, the need for a twice-a-day photographic reconnaissance of Brest, and this started as soon as the ships arrived in the harbour, and was continued up to the time that they left. This was carried out often in very bad weather and at great risk, owing to the heavy defences of AA guns, balloon barrage and fighters. Thus, all the elements of an air plan were in being, but there was a lack of effort to draw them into one coordinated scheme which would concentrate the maximum force at a time and place when the enemy would be at his most vulnerable point, which would be the Dover Straits, if the enemy should go the way that the Admiralty thought most likely.

(iv) *Naval Planning*

Lastly, on the naval side there were two other important planning features. One was undertaken by Flag Officer, Submarines, who tried to keep some submarines outside Brest in order to attack the ships should they emerge, or to report on their departure should they attempt to leave in bad weather. The other was an extensive sea-mining project along the enemy's most likely route. However, at the last minute, Vice-Admiral Ramsey, at Dover, asked for six T/B Swordfish aircraft (Fleet Air Arm) to be moved from Lee-on-Solent to Manston to supplement his slender resources.

4. THE INTELLIGENCE AVAILABLE

Looking back through all the information available to the Admiralty's operational centre, *it is impossible to escape the very strong indication that the ships would attempt to force the Channel 'any time after Tuesday, 10 February'*. This information was passed onto the commands, but for various reasons was not really believed. This was very unfortunate because the Germans had lost their important element of surprise on which they had been counting. *But not enough weight was given to the advice from our agent in Brest (Phillipon) who had already informed us that the Germans would leave Brest in darkness and pass through the Dover Straits in daylight.* Hence, notwithstanding the OIC advice, all the British authorities believed that the Germans would want the cover of darkness for the most dangerous part of their journey, and so would leave Brest in daylight. It is impossible to fault the clear warning given to the naval and air authorities of the likely course of events, but it all hinged on everyone getting adequate warning of the German squadron's departure. Unfortunately, our plans required some hours to come into operation because our attacks had to be coordinated, and there was no overall operational commander in charge to do this.

5. THE WEATHER

On the British side, no special long-range forecasting effort was made. The Cs-in-C made the assumption that 'if the enemy can fly and the ships are at sea', then we will be there, day or night. This was an important error, as the RAF was still some way off being an all-weather air force. An early study of all the factors involved in an operation of this type would have shown that the weather was going to be a major issue, apart from the take-off and landing aspect. It would be vital for successful attacks and for mounting adequate fighter protection. The height of the clouds was also critical for the bombers, since it would not be possible to penetrate the armoured decks of the ships without reasonable height.

Clearly, the Germans knew that the weather was going to be a vital factor for success in their operation, and they appreciated this right from the start of their planning. They set up a naval/air met. team to study the problem, and it was the only time that the two services had cooperated in this field. After the event, we often wondered how the Germans had got the weather so correct; it was just good enough for their fighters to operate, but the low cloud hampered Bomber Command's aircraft and very reduced visibility impeded our torpedo aircraft.

It was not until 1975 that the actual report on this aspect of the 'Channel dash' was located in Germany at the Laarbruch Met. Office, and it turned out to be a classic document because of the remarkable work undertaken and its accuracy when compared with our charts of that period. As the Germans lacked reporting stations in the Atlantic, they used four long-range aircraft and three submarines to send daily weather reports from 5–14 February. This enabled them to get a very accurate picture of the impending weather, and to forecast the front that would move up the Channel on the morning of 12 February, more or less giving all the conditions set out by Vice-Admiral Ciliax, the flag officer commanding the German ships.

6. THE SOURCES OF ERRORS. WAS IT BAD LUCK OR JUST CHANCE?

It is important to appreciate that there had been a long interval between the arrival of the ships in Brest and their departure. Hence, the longer the delay, the greater the possibility that our commanders would tend to attach less urgency to the problem while they had other important tasks in hand. This was especially so in the case of Bomber Command and Coastal Command. Even in the Admiralty, there were those who placed less import-ance on the problem, and some of those who were concerned with it thought that the ships were sure to make the transit of the Channel during the hours of darkness. One might say that this was the airman's best guess, and it was supported by the Admiral at Dover in spite of the advice to the contrary from the naval OIC.

138

(i) Withdrawal of Submarine

It is therefore important to see how chance favoured the enemy. On the evening of 11 February the submarine just outside Brest withdrew without sighting the enemy, hence the logical inference was that the ships could not be making a night transit of the Channel. The next step in the sequence of events was that the Germans intended to sail at 19.30 hours, but were delayed by the nightly Bomber Command raid and so their departure was delayed until 22.45 hours. The photos taken during the raid, when developed that night, showed that the ships were still in Brest, and this information was circulated to all commands, including the Dover Command. This was to have far-reaching consequences which could not have been foreseen at the time.

The next mishap was the failure of the Coastal Command patrols off Brest and along the Channel to spot the ships for various reasons. This was most unfortunate, as the weather was deteriorating and the ships were speeding on their way towards Dover still undetected. Hence, Vice-Admiral Ramsey at Dover was left with the firm impression that the ships were still at Brest.

(ii) Failure of Patrols

To safeguard against this sort of situation, the RAF had arranged a very early PR flight, but the weather was still very bad and the poor pictures obtained were obscured by concentrated smoke over the area where the ships had been; a wise ruse by the Germans, as they knew that this would make it impossible for the British to ascertain if the ships had left or not. Thus, the operational staff at Dover believed that all patrols had been flown normally and no movements had been detected. As a result, they stood down their limited strike force, which had already been depleted by the loss of three MTBs returning from an operation on 8 February.

(iii) 11 Group's Mistakes

However, the first signs of enemy activity were detected by British coastal radar stations between 08.25 and 09.59, registering four plots of enemy aircraft circling in small areas just north of Le Havre. *This information was correctly interpreted in the filter room at Fighter Command as being the start of operation 'Fuller', but, for reasons which are still not clear, the signs were ignored by No.11 Group. It was not until 10.00 that No.11 Group decided to send two Spitfires from Hawkinge to investigate.*

This is where chance could have once more played its hand to our advantage, but it did not turn out that way. One of the Spitfires was piloted by S/Ldr Oxspring, who had not read the operation order 'Fuller', for the simple reason that RAF Station Hawkinge had been omitted from the circulation list, and he was not aware that he was not to use his R/T to report the enemy when seen. He had no special reason to believe that the enemy was so close at hand, as the earlier fighter patrols had not reported anything unusual. Furthermore, he was unaware that he was likely to encounter any other British fighters in the area, so it was a matter of great surprise when he saw a mass of enemy fighters over the German ships, and suddenly spotted two other Spitfires in the middle of the fray.

Spitfire spotting German fleet

(iv) *No Action on Report*

S/Ldr Oxspring reported the ships by R/T to base at 10.35, but for some reason, no action was taken and the record of the transmission later vanished, although it still exists in the German records because they intercepted the transmission and expected immediate attacks to follow. As regards the other two Spitfires, they had come out on a sort of 'private venture', and once again 'chance' came into play. The leading aircraft was flown by Group Captain Beamish from Kenley, the very officer who had issued the fateful No.11 Group instruction restricting the use of R/T. Hence Group Captain Beamish did not report the enemy ships until he landed back at 11.25. One can only guess at the desperate situation the naval commander at Dover found himself in, as he tried to bring his small force back into active status.

(v) *Absence of Co-ordinated Plan*

I will not attempt to catalogue all the mishaps and errors that followed, suffice it to say that all the attempts made to attack the ships came to nothing. The weather was foul, the available forces were limited, *but the main failure was due to the lateness of the alert combined with the absence of a coordinated plan.*

By 13.00 hours, an argument developed between the AOCs No.11 and 16 groups; the latter wanted to delay the air attacks until about 15.00 when a strong force of bombers, fighter-bombers and T/B aircraft (Coastal)

*See Generalleutenant Galland's quotation on page 133. (Ed.)

could be sent to attack the ships covered by a strong force of fighters, but this is where the lack of a well-thought-out plan was felt. It was soon appreciated that the area where the ships would then be was rapidly getting beyond the limit of Fighter Command's radar control. As a result, a series of piecemeal attacks took place, some of which were against our own forces as our destroyers moved down from Harwich.

Chance was even against our destroyers as they were initially given the wrong position of the enemy, and it is just possible that they could have arrived during the period that the *Scharnhorst* was stopped at 14.32 after passing over a mine laid by Bomber Command a few nights before. Some seventeen minutes later she was underway again. The destroyer attacks also failed, as did the bombers that followed. The weather now closed in, and the night drew on. All was not quite ended as the *Gneisenau* hit a mine at 19.55, and the *Scharnhorst* a second mine at 21.34, but the ships finally made it to their bases on the thirteenth. *By luck and good planning, the Germans had succeeded where we had failed.*

CONCLUSION

To conclude, I shall leave the reader with a sort of paradox to consider. After the war, we were to discover that Hitler had firmly instructed Vice-Admiral Ciliax to return his force to Brest should it be discovered before reaching Cherbourg in the early part of its journey. This would have been the worst situation for the British, while the best was that the ships be sunk, and the next best that they should end up in the Kiel area, which they did.

One is reminded of the old saying 'Few things are so uncertain in life as tomorrow', and this is how it proved to be for us in the 'Channel dash'.

Air Marshal Sir Edward Chilton, Henley-on-Thames,
Oxfordshire, 1984

Close Call

There were many providential escapes amid the losses during the two critical days of this Channel operation. Hugh Watlington (Flight Lieutenant H.F. Watlington) of the Royal Canadian Air Force, then a flight sergeant (pilot) with 217 Squadron, detached at St Eval, still recalls vividly his break.

[After briefing], my crew and I were called off the truck just as it was about to depart from the operations block to take us out to the [aircraft] dispersal area. We were then told that, after all, we would not be going on the trip and that a Squadron Leader Thompson would be taking our aircraft instead. . . . Well, he did; and that was the last that anyone ever saw of him. . . .

Hugh Watlington, Hamilton, Bermuda, 1984

From Vian to Survival

The Fleet Air Arm's part in the attack on the German battle-cruisers in the Dover Straits, in which Esmonde and a number of his crew lost their lives in a wonderfully brave, but largely hopeless, assault, is well known. Esmonde's sortie, following upon his leadership of the Bismarck *attack, gained him the posthumous award of the Victoria Cross – and undying fame.*

Out in the Mediterranean, the Royal Navy's flyers were daily matching the courage of their comrades in the Atlantic and home waters. There, Lieut-Commander Frank Hopkins (Admiral Sir Frank Hopkins), who was to carry the Fleet Air Arm's banner in a distinguished and extended operational run, from the United Kingdom to Malta and then, later, to the Pacific, was now feeling the benefit of fortune's occasional tap on his shoulder.

My wartime career was affected by an act of fate which occurred late in 1941. I had then been flying operationally with 826 Squadron (Albacores) for more than eighteen months and badly needed a rest. . . . And so, when I was sent for by Admiral Denis Boyd, who was in charge of naval flyers in the Mediterranean, I thought he would pat me on the back and then send me home to England. I was somewhat disappointed when, instead, he said: 'Frank, I have a wonderful job for you. . . . 830 Squadron, based in Malta, have just lost five aircraft in one sortie including their CO. . . . I want you to go there and take over command. . . .'

I boarded a Royal Air Force Catalina at Alexandria the same evening, bound for Malta, where we were supposed to arrive before daylight the next morning to avoid being caught by Me 109 patrols from Sicily. . . .

I woke to find that it was daylight, and that we were still airborne. By chance, I clambered up to the cockpit and asked the pilot how we were getting on. He said we were a bit late, but there was Malta on our port bow. . . .

He had never been to Malta before, so I was able to tell him that what he could see on our port bow was the German fighter base at Catania, in Sicily, and suggested that he should do a sharp 180-degree turn before someone saw us. . . . We eventually arrived in Malta in one piece on 7 December 1941. That period between December 1941 and July 1942 was a time when we needed all the luck we could get. . . .

One lucky chance probably saved my life on 22 March 1942. A convoy was approaching Malta, escorted by three light cruisers and some destroyers under Admiral Vian, when they were intercepted by major units of the Italian fleet, including a battleship and some heavy cruisers, plus an escort of Me 109s.

Admiral Vian attacked this vastly superior force with his three little cruisers, and I was sent off with *my three available Swordfish* [editor's italics] to attack the Italians with torpedoes. . . .

Halfway to the target we were recalled. . . . On landing, I was told that Admiral Vian had asked for us to be recalled because he thought we might 'confuse the issue'. . . . *Any* other admiral would have welcomed any help he could get, but Vian didn't trust flying machines much . . . or perhaps he was being kind to us because had we carried out the attack I doubt whether any of us could have survived. . . .

Admiral Sir Frank Hopkins, Kingswear, Dartmouth,
Devon, 1984

Polish Delight

At this stage in the war, the fast-growing band of wireless operator/air gunners, having completed their basic wireless training, were being sent in their numbers to operational stations. There, they awaited a posting to an air-wireless and air-gunnery course. The tasks they were given in the meantime were menial, but the luckier ones got the chance to fly.

The experience of Alex Smith (Warrant Officer A.C. Smith), who was later to serve with 162 Squadron's Wellingtons in the Aegean and the eastern Mediterranean before moving on to Transport Command, was a few paces away from the usual run. It was a somewhat unexpected prelude to a career in the City of London Police and – the more so – to the eventual granting of the Freedom of the City of London.

I was dispatched, with another nine 18-year-olds, to RAF Station, Northolt, from where two Polish fighter squadrons were flying daily sweeps over northern France. . . .

The station commander, Group Captain Ford, directed that in the twin interests of improving the camouflage of the airfield and 'digging for victory', we should be employed in ploughing and planting cabbages in the whole area between the perimeter track and the station boundary fence – a very extensive area.

The carrot among the cabbages was that for every 1000 cabbages planted by an individual, that individual would receive in return an hour's flying in the station's Tiger Moth. . . .

We cabbage-planting WOP/AGs under training regarded the Polish pilots, who took us up, with awe. Apart from hammer-stall turns, spins, loops, rolls-off-the-top and other manoeuvres, it was the invariable practice to descend to water level at nearby Ruislip Lido, and then pass through the narrow gap in the trees at the far end before climbing abruptly. . . .

We were always invited and, indeed, encouraged to take hold of the control column, and I incline to think that some of the more interesting aerobatics occurred when each one thought the other had control. . . .

The most memorable flight for me was when, with the squadron leader, we landed, a few minutes' flying time away from Northolt, on an airfield under construction, then wholly unrecognizable as an airfield even in embryo. . . . The short length of runway, so far completed, was dotted with sand heaps, concrete mixers and all the other paraphernalia associated with construction. . . .

We landed, not along the runway, but across the few available yards of it which were sufficiently open to accept the limited wingspan of a Tiger Moth. . . .

It quickly became apparent, however, that once the gentlemen with harsh Celtic accents, who were engaged in the work, had established that we were not in trouble, we were not welcome. . . . The slipstream had blown sand all over them. Between rubbing his eyes, one raised a shovel at us and the gesture could in no way be interpreted as a salute. . . . We were exceptionally lucky to be in a position to rotate the aircraft, smartly, in its own length and then take off again in precisely the opposite direction to our landing. . . .

I remain convinced that our Tiger Moth set three unchallengeable records that day. . . . We had been the first aircraft ever to land at Heathrow, the first ever to take off from there and the one to spend the shortest time there between landing and take-off. . . .

Alex C. Smith, Seahouses, Northumberland, 1984

Phew!

I trained as a wireless operator in Canada, but served as an air gunner in England from 1943 to 1945. . . .

The nearest, I think, I ever came to death was while we were doing our operational training at No.11 OTU at Westcott, six miles northwest of Aylesbury in Buckinghamshire. Working from the satellite airfield at Oakley, we had completed a gunnery and turret exercise, and shoot, at a range near Oxford.

The weather was cold and showery, and when the exercise was finished some of us put the accumulators* onto the truck and climbed aboard. Someone then threw the belts of live ammunition onto the truck, too. They fell across the terminals of the batteries. . . .

There was a sharp burst of fire, and I could actually feel the bullets flying past my ears . . . but I lived!

K.A.J. Bower, Te Puke, New Zealand, 1984

Providential Pick-Up

The South African connection with the Royal Air Force, from pre-war days, had always been strong. Morris, Malan, Hugo, Pattle and others . . . the roll call is impressive. And none shone more brightly, or for longer in wartime, than Piet Hugo (Group Captain P.H. Hugo) from Pampoenport in Cape Province. Yet there was an experience in 1942 which, but for the intervention of the deity, must surely have cut it all short.

It was in the spring of that year, and Hugo had recently taken over command of the Tangmere wing following the loss of his predecessor, Michael Robinson, who had been shot down and killed. It was a tricky time for Fighter Command and 11 Group. The Luftwaffe's Focke-Wulf 190 had established its undoubted superiority over the Spitfire VB. The German pilots knew it, and were full of confidence and aggression. The day of the Spitfire IX had yet to come.

On 27 April Hugo was leading the wing with 340, the Free French Squadron, when, after a fight with the 190s over Gravelines and Dunkirk,

---

*In training, the turrets on the ground were electrically operated. (Ed.)

in which he had given as good as he got, he was obliged to take to his parachute at 3000 feet.

Half a gale was blowing in the Channel, heavy seas were running and Piet had been hard hit in the left shoulder and upper arm by cannon fire. He was in great pain and his left arm was paralysed. Summoning strength and willpower which he didn't think were still there, he deflated his mae west and swam – yes, swam – fifteen yards through the 'mountainous waves' to his dinghy which had been carried away with the parachute pack. . . . The lanyard securing it had been severed. . . .

Two of the wing aircraft had been circling me, but now had to leave because of shortage of fuel. . . . I had had sufficient experience myself of trying to find a dinghy in rough seas to know that it would be a miracle if other searching aircraft ever found me again. . . . Time ceased to mean anything . . . I sat and shivered in violent spasms of shaking in the freezing cold. I must have been in a torpor because I can only dimly remember the bows of a vessel sliding past me and hands hauling me on deck. . . .

. . . I woke up, briefly, in terrible pain to find that I was lying on an operating table. . . . Two doctors were prodding my shoulder. As far as I could gather one was a sewing-on believer, the other a hacking-off fan. . . . When next I came to, I found, with relief, that the hacker-off merchant had obviously lost the day as my arm was stretched above me on a sort of gantry. . . .

It wasn't until Wing Commander Little, bless his kindness, had arranged to bring my wife (we had been married all of nine days) over from Tangmere, that I learnt the real story of my recovery.

A naval gunboat, returning from a patrol off the Dutch islands, had, quite fortuitously and providentially, run across me and picked me up. . . . The Air/Sea Rescue launches had put to sea, but had been forced by the gale to turn back. The Dover-based launch had, in fact, all but capsized as soon as it had cleared the breakwater.

In the years that have passed, people have often congratulated me on my lucky escape. Call it what *you* like. I prefer to think that fate, and some higher destiny, decided that that day was not to be the end of my life.

Group Captain P.H. Hugo, Victoria West, Cape Province, Republic of South Africa, 1984

That power
Which erring men call chance
John Milton (1608–74)

'Home, James, by Staff Car!'

As the fighting in the Western Desert ebbed and flowed, arresting stories were emerging from the squadrons of the Desert Air Force. . . . Here was a mix of all the talents.

Bob Rogers (Lieut-General R.H. Rogers) was beginning a run which, in time, would take him to the summit of the South African Air Force. On the way, there would be command of 40 (Tactical Reconnaissance) Squadron in North Africa and Italy and, with it, the distinction of being the youngest lieutenant-colonel in the Service. On 26 January 1942, however, there was a momentary hiccup in the progression.

I was airborne on an early reconnaissance to establish the whereabouts and strength of the enemy on the southern half of the front. Rommel had attacked a week before from his holding position at El Agheila, and had made rapid progress against light and rather disorganized Allied resistance. . . .

208 Squadron of the Royal Air Force, with which I was then serving, had retired in rapid succession from the landing grounds at Antelat and Msus, and thence to Mechili. . . .

I flew in a southerly sweep to Msus, where I saw an unserviceable Hurricane which we had abandoned there when the squadron left. It was surrounded by German troops, with one sitting in the cockpit. I decided to strafe the aircraft and try to set it alight.

. . . I was hit twice by 37- or 40-mm shells in the engine and the port wing root soon after I had opened fire. Hot oil poured all over me, and in no time I could see very little. I could just imagine what would happen if fire broke out. (Until then I had always flown dressed to keep cool in the hot desert conditions. Subsequently, I decided to cover myself from head to toe, whatever the temperature.)

I levelled off and headed northwest, trying to put as much distance as possible between myself and the airfield I had just attacked. After two or three minutes, the engine seized and I decided to land straight ahead. I could see little with oil covering everything, but by opening the canopy of the Hurricane and looking out sideways, I managed to land successfully.

I was out of the cockpit like a frightened jack rabbit – still scared of the fire risk – to find that I had stopped on the brink of a deep wadi or dried riverbed. I descended to the floor of the wadi and headed north at a brisk pace. I had not gone far when, suddenly, I heard a voice shout, 'Halt, or I fire!' I looked to my left and there, on the opposite side of the wadi, partly obscured by a bush, was the figure of a British officer, pointing a rifle at me. . . . I must have looked a strange sight as I walked towards him, covered in oil.

I identified myself and asked him what he was doing. He was a British major who had been sent out a few days earlier from Corps Headquarters at Msus to reconnoitre possible new landing grounds. . . . Now he was on his way back to Msus to report results! He had with him a staff car and driver, and a scout car and driver.

While sympathizing with me over my misfortune, he nevertheless thanked me warmly for dropping in so opportunely and bringing him up to date! For my part, I was overjoyed at meeting someone with so much transport. . . . I hadn't been relishing the thought of a long walk home. . . .

On checking his petrol supply, we found there was insufficient for our needs, so, despite the risks, we returned to my aircraft, syphoned out the fuel we needed, and then drove home!

We tried, first, to travel north to Derna, but found this impossible, so we decided to head straight for Mechili. We arrived there early the following morning *having passed through both the German and our own lines during the night!* [Editor's italics.]

Many Allied airmen who were shot down behind the enemy lines in the desert managed to walk home . . . but few arrived back in style – by staff car!

Lieut-General R.H. Rogers, Leisure Isle, Knysna,
Republic of South Africa, 1984

The Others Had to Walk

For those who did not enjoy Bob Rogers's luck in getting driven home by staff car, the long trek back on foot to Allied lines was a risky and gruelling affair. Tom Farries, then a 21-year-old leading aircraftman wireless operator, now a bookseller in Dumfries, was one of a group of half a dozen airmen who walked back after being surrounded by German armoured personnel in Benghazi after Rommel's counterattack in late January 1942. Intercepting enemy W/T messages was part of his business.

By the time they started their walk eastwards, across the marshes to the Libyan coast, their little group had swollen to twenty-one escapees. All the 'worldly wealth' they had between them amounted to 'ten cigarettes, a tube of Italian cheese and a Penguin book'.

Lack of food was our immediate and pressing problem. Drinking water out of puddles solved the problem of thirst, but our first relief of hunger came with an encounter with a tribe of Sennussi Arabs, whose chief ordered his wives to prepare a meal of chappatis for us. This first assistance from the Sennussis occurred at the approach to the famous Tochra pass where, with the help of 'George', our Indian medical orderly, who acted as translator, we were warned of German activity in the area, and offered a guide through the village under cover of darkness. While waiting for our Arab guides, we hid in a cluster of gorse bushes, and watched, helpless, as enemy troop lorries drew up and took prisoner another group of British soldiers who were marching towards the main road.

As we progressed, often travelling by night, we were footsore and weary with wet, torn and filthy clothing. Tribes of Sennussi Arabs were our salvation, offering food, shelter and guidance through the worst and most dangerous terrain. By early February the rain was pelting down, and only by great ingenuity did we light a fire for the night's supposed rest. (Using rotten tree roots, a vest and my novel!)

At the Sennussi camp, we succeeded in bartering a wristwatch for a small goat. But in an attempt to barter my cigarette case and pen for a pair of boots, I lost both when the small boy I was negotiating with ran off and failed to reappear. The appalling state of my footwear was temporarily relieved by cutting up an army haversack and strapping it over the remains of my shoes.

A later meeting with other Sennussi Arabs provided me with a pair of boots (albeit two sizes too small) in exchange for my wristwatch. I cut the heels out, and declared that I could walk to Alexandria, if necessary! . . .

An encounter with a herd of goats led to a supreme effort by George and myself to catch and kill one. With a fire lit in a cave, the goat was cut up and cooked, and we drew lots for the kidneys. We then enjoyed a delicious meal and a wonderful night's rest.

After one night of hospitality in the Sennussi village of Fomita, where we were each given a chappati and an egg by the villagers, one of our party celebrated his twenty-first birthday on the remnants of food saved from the night before. On that day, too, we were forced to rob at gunpoint our benefactors of the previous night – a caravan of camels loaded with loot from Allied supplies left behind after the retreat from Derna. We were rewarded for this 'ungentlemanly' behaviour with some tins of bully, dried potatoes, two tins of margarine, two tins of syrup and a tin of biscuits, plus some cigarettes and cigars. Hunger having conquered our self-respect, we proceeded on our way, and stopped at Kersa for a meal.

It was here we met Mohammed Ali, who wanted to reach his family in the Tobruk area. A bargain was struck, with Mohammed agreeing to lead us through the German lines in return for entry to Tobruk and a sack of tea!

With Mohammed's help, we travelled by night and hid by day for four days as we traversed the German-occupied zone, and found ourselves on the morning of 16 February in a small gully over the Tamimi-Mechili track. Two of the group went out to reconnoitre that morning, never to return. They were killed by a South African armoured patrol which had confused airforce blue and Italian uniforms; presumably our men had refused to give a surrender signal.

Driven from our wadi by shells landing only fifty yards away, the remainder of the group ran from the gully. They were only just in time to avoid shells which landed where they had been hiding only minutes before. . . . As we ran for our lives, a South African armoured column appeared over a ridge. And so, waving, shouting and cheering, with tears streaming down our faces, we weary travellers greeted the world again. . . .

T.C. Farries, Dumfries, Scotland, 1984

Caldwell and Waddy

By the end of 1942 Clive Caldwell and John Waddy, the two Australian Desert practitioners, were first and third respectively in the Allies' high-scoring league. They had accounted for 20½ and 15½ enemy aircraft a piece in the theatre. Each had his moments when 'an agency outside the match' seemed to intervene.

Caldwell's experience is difficult to explain.

It was March 1942, and I was flying in the Gazala area, west of Tobruk. The spectacular storm conditions and cloud formations that day seemed familiar. Even as I recognized the setting, I had the feeling that I had lived through this identical experience before – and in the not-too-distant past. Yet I couldn't remember where or when. I was utterly convinced, however, of the sequence that would follow. . . .

Sure enough, just as I had anticipated, the flock of enemy fighters appeared round a cloud column to port. They were right on cue. The ensuing performance was an identical repeat of the earlier action. It was like the re-run of a film, or a dream which had become real. . . .

I felt that, as I had already been given a preview, I knew the outcome. Yet I could change none of it. . . .

I've heard people mention somewhat similar occurrences so perhaps they were not uncommon. However, for me, this was a strange and eerie experience. Nothing like it had ever happened to me before, nor was it ever repeated.

Group Captain C.R. Caldwell, Sydney, New South Wales,
Australia, 1984

Caldwell's mate, Waddy, by his example, certainly couldn't have been accused of lacking resource.

The date was 10 May 1942; I remember it well. We were flying an escort mission in our Kittyhawks (P-40s) for a Boston squadron on a bombing raid on Benghazi harbour. I was leading the top section. . . .

After about an hour, very black smoke started pouring out of the exhaust stacks. The instruments showed oil and cylinder-head temperatures going 'off the clock'. The oil pressure fell away. There was no option but to force land. . . .

Not being keen on wheels-up landings, and knowing the desert pretty well, I decided on a normal, wheels-down landing. It was a success. . . . But I was a long way from home with a long, long walk ahead of me – if I was lucky. . . . I sat in the cockpit trying to unscrew the compass, using a threepenny piece as a screwdriver.

I happened to look up and in the distance saw a ribbon of dust moving in my direction. This could only mean one thing. The Germans had seen me on my way down, and had sent a truck to pick me up. Having no desire to become an uninvited guest of the enemy, I decided to use my aircraft as a taxi as long as it would stand up to the rough desert.

I started the engine up, saw that the temperatures had all cooled down and set off. . . . I was bouncing and banging along, but always heading east – for home. I actually managed to get airborne on a very reduced throttle setting and, flying wheels down just above the sand, I contrived to keep going. . . . At one moment I made it up to about 300 feet, and when the temperatures started rising I found a salt pan and landed again. At least I was now much nearer to base and had avoided the immediate danger of capture.

I waited about half an hour for the temperatures to settle, and then I decided to try to fly the aeroplane again, always aiming to get as far east as possible. I wanted to reduce the amount of walking through enemy territory. Somehow the engine kept turning over with ever-increasing clanging and banging until, just as I reached base, it seized solid. . . .

I was told afterwards I could be heard coming for a long time, and everyone wondered what the noise was until I appeared overhead. . . . It was a strange feeling to see that prop stopped, but I was glad to get out and walk away *among friends*. . . . From then on I had a very special regard for the Allison engine.

So, what do we call it? Chance? Good luck? All I know is that my little green gremlin was working overtime for me that day – just as he did for the rest of the war. . . .

The Hon. John L. Waddy, Cremorne, New South Wales,
Australia, 1984

Saved by the Button

Ken Hunter (Captain A.K. Hunter) was an air gunner in the South African Air Force who became an intelligence/operations officer with the renowned 60 (PR) Squadron, and then, later, with 3 (Light Bomber) Wing. . . . Understandable, therefore, that he should recall fate's attention to one of 60's gunners, Sergeant de Villiers, in March 1942.

The Allied forces were then standing on the Gazala line and 60 Squadron were operating their specially adapted, long-range Martin Marylands, busily photographing large areas of Cyrenaica against its planned reconquest. At the operational height of 21,000 feet and above, the Me 109s and 110s presented a daily threat. . . .

On 8 March Maryland AH 363, with Lieutenant 'Zinkie' English at the controls, was returning after successfully photographing two areas of the Msus neighbourhood of Cyrenaica. At 11.00 hours, east of Tengeder, the aircraft was attacked from astern by a Me 110.

An incendiary shell entered the port side of the aircraft at the bottom gunner/wireless operator's position. It struck the tough, metal release button of de Villiers' parachute harness, penetrated the webbing and clothing beneath, broke the chain of his identity discs and came to rest on his bare chest. . . .

The startled gunner, although burning from shell splinters in his hands and face, continued to operate the lower gun – and his W/T – until he was satisfied the fighter had broken off.

After landing safely, de Villiers was pronounced unhurt save for the splinters and a superficial wound on his chest. . . . Truly, that bullet didn't have his name on it.

A.K. Hunter, Hillcrest, Natal,
Republic of South Africa, 1984

The Magic Carpet

The story of the 'chance' disappearance, in 1942, of a valuable Middle Eastern carpet or rug, and its subsequent recovery, is among the rarer fables of the South African Air Force.

60 Squadron (who else?) were suspected. Their stay in the Lebanon, from where they had been taking survey pictures of the coastline from Port Said to the Turkish border, was ending. Their departure for the Desert was imminent. . . .

When the loss was discovered, the military police throughout North Africa were alerted. At one point, an interrogating officer, pursuing his investigations, was sitting on a couch in the 60 Squadron mess without realizing that its exquisite covering was, in fact, the wanted property.

Glynn Davies (Lieut-Colonel O.G. Davies), 'father' of the squadron and its CO who was to fly two-and-a-half tours of operations before being posted as Senior Air Staff Officer to 2 Wing, with its heavy bombers, is unusually well placed to recount the circumstances. The dateline of his report is 'Beirut, July 1942'.

We were in our favourite haunt – 'the Dug Out' at the Pension Mimosa, presided over by Madame Victoria – and Syd Young, the adjutant, was eyeing covetously the small silk-backed Oriental rug which hung on the wall of the lounge. As the evening wore on he became more and more determined to 'win' it. He confided in me the plan he had devised.

He would organize a game of 'Bok-bok' (High Cockalorum) and make himself anchor man. He would then let the scrum collapse, pull the carpet off the wall, and run off with it to a getaway vehicle.

It almost seemed, however, as if Madame Victoria was aware that something was up. She would not leave us alone, insisting that we all became word perfect in the French version of 'Alouette' she had been teaching us. Syd, meanwhile, was having trouble getting a team to compete with us. Two Irish Guards officers were keen, but only if a team of their fellow officers could be raised. This proved impossible. Finally, a mixture of Fleet Air Arm and RNR accepted our challenge. The game was on. . . .

All went as Syd had planned. We were down first and the scrum collapsed. Syd snatched the carpet off the wall, tucked it under his arm and was out of the door and into the waiting 15-cwt truck before you could say Jack Robinson. But we had reckoned without Madame Victoria! She produced a police whistle from the bosom of her dress, and blew a shrill blast which got the military police there almost before we could get our laggard moving! With no hope of outrunning the police 'jeep' we swung round the corner by the Hotel Normandie, shoved the carpet into the hedge and drove on until caught up by our pursuers. We gave up quietly.

Names, ranks, numbers and units were recorded, but the police were a little put out at not finding the suspected stolen property. When we explained that we had to leave for Cairo early in the morning we were allowed to go. Later, Syd crept out during the few remaining hours of darkness and retrieved the carpet.

The next day we shook the dust of Beirut – reluctantly – from our feet.

It must have been about two weeks later that a dispatch rider arrived at our Desert landing ground from Cairo bearing a heavily sealed envelope. It was addressed 'For the Commanding Officer Only'. The rider handed over the letter only in exchange for a formal, signed receipt. Inside was a full dossier of 'L'Affaire Carpet Magique'. This included a statement by Madame Victoria that 'the carpet was not only of great intrinsic value but of exceptional sentimental value as she had lost her virginity on it as a girl'! It was a master-stroke of psychology! All Syd's pleas fell on deaf ears and the carpet was returned to its rightful home.

Madame Victoria had taken her chance . . . .

Lieut-Colonel O.G. Davies, Tokai, Cape Province,
Republic of South Africa, 1984

P-40 (Kittyhawks) being attacked by Me 109s

Felled by 'Fiffi'

Dick Clifton (Major-General R. Clifton) was a flight commander in 2 Squadron of the SAAF when, around 09.15 on 16 August 1942, the section of four Kittyhawks (P-40s) he was leading during a reconnaissance of the Alamein Line, from the Qattara Depression in the south up to the Mediterranean coastline in the north, was attacked by a Rotte (a pair) of Me 109s from 1 Gruppe of Jadgeswader 27, led by Leutnant Hans-Arnold 'Fiffi' Stahlschmidt from six o'clock high.

Stahlschmidt was then third among the Luftwaffe's highest scorers in the Desert campaign, immediately behind Hans-Joachim Marseille and Werner Schröer.

Clifton turned his section into the attackers, and met the German leader head on. Holding his fire till the last moment, he delayed a fraction too long and the front of his aircraft stopped a volley of 20-mm cannon shells from the German, one of which exploded in the cockpit shattering his left leg and ankle as well as severing the aeroplane's elevator cable.

The aircraft became uncontrollable and Dick Clifton, in great pain, and with his left leg hanging limp and useless, and blood pouring from it, floated down by parachute into the Mediterranean.

I was underwater for only seconds, but broke surface panting and spluttering. . . . The sea, mercifully, was calm, but the low desert dunes seemed a long way off. I struck out for the shore in a slow side stroke on my left side. . . . I recall a momentary impulse to 'hurl in' when my lungs burned with the saltwater I had swallowed and the pain, not only from my leg, but my back as well, seemed overwhelming. My body felt limp and useless . . . *but the fear of death was a stronger emotion* [editor's italics] and the adrenaline this generated forced me to keep going. . . .

My strength, with the loss of blood, and the pain, was fast ebbing away. I had no recollection of how long I had been in the water; time had stood still. . . . Suddenly, I heard a shout in an unmistakable Australian accent, 'You hurt, cobber?' Then strong arms were supporting me. Afterwards came oblivion. . . .

When I came to, I was lying on the warm sand, surrounded by a group of Aussies, most of them stark naked. Someone put a lighted cigarette between my lips, and pointed to another in the circle. 'Hell,' he said, 'you were lucky. So-and-so (mentioning his name) was a life-saver on Sydney beach before the war!'

In no time Clifton was lying on a table in the operating tent. When he saw his leg before it was bandaged on the beach 'it had looked like something on a butcher's chopping block'. Now, as he lay on the operating table, he looked up at the surgeon who was bending over him. 'Please don't hack it off, Doc,' he pleaded.

Shortly before Christmas, at No.2 Military Hospital in Wynberg, the plaster came off for good. It wasn't long before I was walking without a limp . . . and owing my existence to the Sydney life-saver.

Major-General R. Clifton, Knysna, Cape Province,
Republic of South Africa, 1984

Editor's note: *Ten minutes after 'Fiffi' Stahlschmidt had 'knocked off' Dick Clifton, he had gone on to shoot down Lieutenant Trenchard of 5 Squadron, SAAF, in a Tomahawk, who baled out and was taken prisoner. Less than a month later, on 7 September, Stahlschmidt was himself shot down and killed by Flight Lieutenant Curry of 601 (County of London) Squadron. The German had 59 victories to his guns when he fell, from 400 sorties in the Desert.*

In his last letter home he had written prophetically: 'I don't know what fate awaits me. Perhaps things will not go as we hope and pray. . . . But if "it" should happen then I shall know that I have done my duty faithfully. . . .'

The Strength of a Letter

James Sanders went through the operational fire, far away from his New Zealand home. Blenheims, Marylands, Baltimores, Halifaxes. . . . Shipping strikes and reconnaissances by day and night. . . . Western Europe, the Middle East, the Mediterranean and Malta. . . . It was a full war.

And when he writes about it he moves into a different league. One of New Zealand's outstanding journalists and writers – feature stories for the Auckland Herald, sixteen published titles, an artist's ability to illumine his work with brush and pen – it makes an enviable mix. . . .

Providence stepped into Jim Sanders' life in October 1942, and granted him an extended licence. His story, specially extracted from a new manuscript, tears the heart apart.

. . . .I'll tell again of fate.

A certain occasion at Gianaclis comes to mind.

Gianaclis . . . was a Royal Air Force strip on the fringe of the Nile delta. While the British 8th Army gathered itself for the coming storm at El Alamein, 203 Squadron was renewing its strength . . . after being chased out of Burg el Arab by Rommel's eastward drive.

I sat in my tent, writing letters home. The day was warm and the sky was cloudless. Westward, on the edge of the flying field, were the aircraft maintenance tents and from that direction came the rising and falling roars of Pratt and Whitney engines answering to their ground tests.

My flight commander sent a messenger to find me. I was to take Maryland G-George on a test flight, now that her groundcrew had done their repair work on the motors.

'Goddamn,' I complained, 'I'm right in the middle of this letter.'

Sergeant-pilot Brown [not his real name] was close at hand, and he spoke up: 'I'll take her, if you like. I want to build up my flying hours.'

'I don't give a damn who flies the bloody thing, so long as the aircraft is tested,' grumped the flight commander when Brown put the proposition to him.

Brown reappeared soon, lumping his parachute harness and dangling his flying helmet by its intercom cords. He was grinning happily. 'You know,' he said to me, 'I can't get enough of these trips.'

I had just finished my letter when I heard the Maryland being gunned for take-off; and as it tore with full power into the wind and roared overhead, a series of staccato explosions brought us scrambling from our tents to see a stream of vile black smoke trailing from the port engine.

In horror we watched the Maryland continue on, belching more and more fumes and flame, and we waited for the pilot to try and set the machine down and make an escape before the holocaust. But now he was flying over the delta's tangle of palm trees and paddy-field irrigation ditches.

The Maryland was sinking lower and lower with the fire now well out of control. And just before it disappeared from view it turned to port. Brown had probably found a spot to belly-flop the aircraft.

We waited a moment or two in deepening gloom. And soon a ball of smoke, so black and thick that it seemed to be of some solid, evil substance, rose above the spidery, heat-dancing fringe of palms on the skyline. . . .

The smoke rose in a high black pillar and the fire burned for a long time. It was late in the afternoon before one of the trucks brought in the victims. . . .

Demonstrating sublime confidence in their skills and handiwork, four aircraftmen and their sergeant, responsible for the mechanical and general airworthiness of the aeroplane, had begged a joyride of the pilot. All of the six occupants of G-George were shockingly burnt. They were all alive when they were brought back to camp, but through the night the five groundcrew boys died.

I visited Brown when he lay in hospital in Alexandria. He was very ill and his burnt flesh filled the room with the stench of putrefaction. . . .

He asked, softly: 'How are the others?'

'I don't know,' I lied. 'They got out alive, you know.'

'But – they are alive *now*, aren't they?' He begged desperately for my assurances.

'I don't know. Well, yes – yes, I'm sure they are.' I shuffled and stammered. 'But I've been on leave for a week or more. So I'm a bit out of touch. I'm off to Malta soon and I came away from the squadron without really knowing.'

Brown looked at me reproachfully. Although he wanted to hear that the boys had survived the crash, he didn't want to hear a lie or a half-lie. I had wanted to ease his conscience. I had not succeeded with my transparent evasions.

I stood indicted in that hospital room that had the smell of death. If I had flown that test flight it would have been me lying there, swathed in bandages and stinking of the body's corruption. Either way, the groundcrew fellows would probably still be dead. But Brown would have been unharmed and still looking for more flights to bolster up the hour-totals in his log book.

I don't know if Brown survived that crash or, indeed, the war. I went off to Malta and so beyond the ken of the fellows of 203 Squadron and their flying affairs in Egypt.

Fear and death – and luck – went along with me.

James Sanders, Brown's Bay, Auckland, New Zealand, 1984

'The Abandoned Earl'

The stories of Paddy Bandon, 5th Earl and Air Chief Marshal, of Castle Bernard, Bandon, County Cork, now deceased, are many. Only those of the Royal Air Force's Atcherley twins surpass them. Now and then we are lucky enough to be told one at first hand.

. . . I visited the French Club in Suez when I was on a trip to the Canal Zone. As I walked in, I noticed a South African Air Force officer and a Royal Air Force officer sitting on the floor singing air-force ditties. Neither was wearing badges of rank. I knew the SAAF officer as Major Taffy Drew, in peacetime Shell's aviation manager in South Africa.

In walked a uniformed and finely groomed officer who stared, unbelievingly, at Taffy and his friend. He walked over to them. 'I say, you chaps, after six o'clock and improperly dressed! Bad show, what? I suggest you go to your quarters, have a shower, dress and come back when you're decently turned out.'

'And who the hell are you?' enquired Taffy.

'I, sir, am Lieutenant-Colonel Sir Thomas Benson, Baronet.'

'In that case, old boy,' retorted Taffy, 'you're buggered on both counts. This is Group Captain the Earl of Bandon.'

Lieut-Colonel O. G. Davies, Tokai, Cape Province,
Republic of South Africa, 1984

Blinded Ahead

In the spring and summer of 1942, running on into the autumn, the air battle for Malta was being fought to the death. Luck, fate, providence, punctuated the lives of those who survived. The experiences were as varied as the fighting.

It was another beautiful Mediterranean summer's day when my No. 2 and I, from 249 Squadron,* took off from Takali to intercept a raid of Ju 87s covered by a liberal escort of Me 109s. . . .

Our tactics this day were to be different. Instead of meeting the bombers before they began their attacks, and then breaking off to deal with the escort, we were to take the attackers as they reformed northeast of the island to begin their withdrawal to Sicily. . . .

Well placed above the formations as they headed for home, we started our descent. . . . I had decided that the first attack would be from head on. As I dived, the propeller oil seal on my Spitfire broke and, immediately, oil gushed out all over the windscreen and engine cowling. I had no forward visibility, I could only see 90 degrees left and right of the cockpit. . . . I advised ground control that I was aborting. . . .

But the mission wasn't yet over for me. As I was returning to base, wondering what had become of my No. 2, I suddenly saw the Ju 87s on either side of me, and only a few yards away, going in the opposite direction! I then realized that I was in the final moments of flying straight through the flight path of the returning bombers, with their gunners loosing off at me for all they were worth. . . .

Back at Takali, we examined the damage. Several shells had entered the fuselage behind me, and one had passed through the small space between the upper and lower petrol tanks, immediately in front of the cockpit. . . .

I wondered then – and still do – what must have been the thoughts of the German crews as they saw a 'respected' Spitfire closing in on their flight path, flying straight through it, and neither firing nor turning to engage . . . !

O. M. Linton, Ottawa, Ontario, Canada, 1984

Miracle Vision

Frank Jones, another of 249 Squadron's exceptional Canadians, had his moment of inexplicable deliverance.

---

*Described by Christopher Shores, the air historian, as being, in World War II, '*without doubt* (editor's italics) the highest-scoring squadron of the British Commonwealth Air Forces (*Aces High*, Neville Spearman, 1966).

My section of four had climbed to about 25,000 feet south of the island, beautifully positioned up-sun by Group Captain A. B. Woodhall, our wonderful ground controller, to meet the advancing force of Ju 88s with their high cover of Me 109s. . . .

Quickly checking my rear to ensure that no 109s would overtake us in the dive, and seeing my other three Spitfires close behind, I moved in fast from the port quarter against the enemy bombers, opening fire as I closed. My aircraft was hit several times as I passed beneath the attacking force. . . . I flipped over onto my back and headed straight down from 18,000 feet. The stick became sloppy in my hands. I eased back on it to curb the dive, without any response. . . . I tried again and again; I realized then that I had lost control and would have to bale out.

I reached up and grabbed the cable-suspended knob which released the cockpit canopy. . . . One sharp pull and the rubber bobble came away in my hand, leaving the canopy still firmly in place. . . . I was now hurtling earthwards at some 500 m.p.h., unable to get out and with the aircraft out of control. . . .

I called up Woody on the R/T. 'Woody, it's Jonesie here. . . . I've had it. . . . I'm out of control and going in. . . .'

In this moment of extreme, terminal danger, I saw an extraordinary vision before me. Whether it came from the assiduous study I had earlier made on the aircraft, or the lessons I had learnt in ground school, I don't know. But, suddenly, I saw in front of me the image of an open-plan diagram of a Spitfire showing the separate system of bias-trim cables which was apart from the regular elevator controls.

My hand moved automatically to the trimming control which I moved back anti-clockwise. The aircraft started gradually to respond and recover from its dive as the nose was slowly raised. . . . I pulled out at less than 100 feet over the water only to see just above six Me 109s which had obviously followed me down to finish me off. . . .

I called up Woody again and told him of my predicament and position. He came back to say that Laddie Lucas and Raoul Daddo-Langlois, two old buddies of mine in 249, were above me with their No. 2s and would be coming down. . . . The 109s were scattered, and all at once, as so often happened in the air, I was alone. . . . There wasn't an aircraft to be seen. . . .

With careful use of the throttle, and manipulating my elevator trimmers and the aileron (lateral) control I still had, I put the aircraft down between three great bomb craters in the middle of Takali. . . . At that moment the airfield was strafed by more 109s. . . . I leapt out of the cockpit and took cover in one of the bomb craters. I must then have passed out, for the next thing I knew was that the groundcrew who had raced over to me were picking me up and talking. . . .

That miraculous vision I had seen in the cockpit of the separate elevator cable layout had saved my life. . . . The human brain reacts extraordinarily in extreme danger. I still can hardly credit it.

Frank E. Jones, Pender Island, British Columbia, Canada, 1984

The Mystery of the Mosta Bomb

Mosta Church, famous for its unsupported dome — the third largest of its kind in the world — lay about a mile to the north of 249 Squadron's dispersal at Takali, Malta's northernmost airfield. The old Rotunda became a familiar landmark for pilots operating from this much-bombed base.

At 16.40 hours on 9 April 1942, during a Luftwaffe attack on the airfield, and its surrounding facilities, a bomb pierced the dome, fell onto the floor of the church where people were gathered, and failed to explode. It was an extraordinary episode which has become much embellished in the telling. Pure chance it may have been, but he would be a brave man who would deny the Almighty's part in the incident.

Some of 249's groundcrew, who performed heroics in servicing the squadron's aircraft during the height of the battle, were billeted in Mosta no more than a hundred yards away from the church. One of them was James Somerville (Corporal J. Somerville), a redoubtable Scot, and an airframe fitter, who remained in Malta from April 1941 until March 1944. He was a witness to the Mosta bomb affair. As such, his account is important.

I was off duty, lounging on the roof of my billet, enjoying the spring sunshine, when the air-raid alert sounded. . . . Soon the Ju 88s were dropping bombs. . . .

As I rushed from my billet, I saw a woman leave the Rotunda, waving her arms to attract my attention. '*Hafna bombi*,' she said (at least that's what it sounded like), meaning 'big bomb', and pointed to the church. . . . Sure enough, there, on the floor, was a bomb. . . . A glance up at the dome showed the hole through which it had entered. . . .

There were between twenty and thirty Maltese gathered where, in normal times, the altar would have stood. . . . A pick-up truck entered the village square, so I shouted to the blokes who backed the truck up to the high paviour fronting the Rotunda. Between us, we moved the unexploded bomb onto the truck which then drove off in the direction of St Paul's Bay. . . .

Seconds later, as the raid continued, a bomb exploded a little distance away along the Valletta road. A lump of flying metal hit my left thigh and knocked me into the street gutter. . . . As I lay there, I thought how ironic it was to have escaped so many near misses on the airfield at Takali, and then to be felled in a village street. . . .

Soon, a RAF lorry drew up. Phillips, Neale and Smith, other groundcrew, were returning from Gzira where they had picked up a reconditioned Merlin engine. . . . Piling me aboard they took me to Imtarfa hospital. . . .

James Somerville, Armadale, West Lothian, Scotland, 1984

Editor's note: Reports have suggested that the bomb which pierced the dome of Mosta church may have been anything from 500 to 2000 kg. This seems unlikely. A bomb of that size might well have been expected to bring the unsuppported dome down with it. More probable is it that the bomb was the German 50-kg variety, commonly used against airfield targets. . . . Likewise, a 'congregation' of 300 was thought to have been in the church at the time of the incident. Somerville's first-hand witness suggests otherwise.

Torpedo in Store?

Luck extended – for some – from Takali down to Halfar, in the southeast of the island. David Roy, one of the intrepid group of Hurricane pilots who operated from there against all the odds, had, earlier in the year, had an uncomfortable brush with the comparatively fast Ju 88. It ended with a most fortunate escape.

... The opportunity to fire lasted only a second or two, and was answered by a positive stream of fire from the '88' gunners. I was hit in the engine and left alone and silent, with Malta looking like a leaf on the ocean far below.

I lost height at the greatest speed and in the minimum of time, and soon found myself at a few thousand feet over Kalafrana Bay with the hangars of Halfar visible on the higher ground. Having decided on a 'belly' arrival, I crossed the perimeter at a greater speed than that recommended in the training manuals, so that, despite a preliminary 'breaking' in mid-field, I still crashed, at some considerable speed, into a very substantial stone building at the HQ end of the aerodrome.

The noise and dust was tremendous, and this was followed by the usual eery silence, during which two airmen arrived in a rush to investigate my general state of health.

Maltese buildings are, of course, made from the island rock and the blocks are so massive that they are not necessarily held in place by any concrete or mortar. One block appeared to have squashed the Merlin engine into the ground, and another had bent the armour plating behind me like a tin can – so that I was left, bloody but reasonably unbowed, sandwiched between these two giant pieces of masonry. My first question to my rescuers was to enquire the normal purpose of the building to which I had paid such rough attention.

The answer gave me food for thought, and subsequently for considerable gratitude.

'It's the torpedo store room, Sarge,' said the corporal, as he gave me a helping hand from the stricken cockpit. 'But don't worry, we spent all last night moving them to an underground hangar.'

David Roy, Wadhurst, East Sussex, 1984

'Safe' in the Ack-Ack Barrage!

P. Whaley Heppell (Squadron Leader P. W. E. Heppell), 'Nip' to the Royal Air Force and, with Crowley-Milling, Dundas, Johnson, Turner and others, a product of Bader's Tangmere wing in England, was one of those brilliantly mercurial characters (Al Deere was another) to whom some wholly inprobable event always seemed to be happening. He was the joker in 249 Squadron's imposing pack. Few would have guessed, seeing him daily in the thick of the Malta battle, that here, in embryo, was a future chairman of one of Britain's building societies.

... It was 8 April 1942 and, as the massive raid began, I dived in behind the leading Junkers 88 as we entered the heavy anti-aircraft barrage which was being put up over Grand Harbour, Valletta. . . . I knew the Me 109s never ventured into it, and I saw it was the only safe place to attack the bombers. . . .

. . . I recall registering strikes in the wing roots and tail unit of the 88 . . . and the next thing I remember was falling head first towards the harbour sans aircraft.* At about 120 m.p.h. . . . you get a vivid and dreamlike impression that this isn't happening to you. . . . When my parachute opened it seemed that I was on some sky-hook, and not apparently losing height, with bombs falling past, ack-ack exploding and a continuous rattle of machine guns all round. . . .

I crashed into a bomb hole, still conscious but unable to move. I shouted 'I'm British' in case the Maltese attacked me. They seemed to think anyone who was shot down was a Hun, God knows why! I was given a shot of morphia by an MO and taken to Imtarfa hospital. Shortly afterwards I was on the operating table about to have the gashes in my head and legs sewn up. . . .

. . . Three times the lights went out (effects of the bombing) just as I was about to be anaesthetized. . . . The third time I went off to sleep on the table before the pentathol was injected. . . .

I woke up about noon the next day to find that I was black, green and blue all over. My muscles had been so badly damaged by the shell blast which had disintegrated my Spitfire that it was a week before I could sit up in bed without assistance.

The only part of the aircraft which was found, was the tail, which would have fallen like a leaf. It was recovered from Sliema cemetery!

P. Whaley Heppell, Guyzance Bridge, Morpeth,
Northumberland, 1984

The Cult of the Reciprocal 4†

. . . 'Jumbo' Gracie (Wing Commander E. J. Gracie) was some character. . . . After taking off from the United States Navy's aircraft carrier, *Wasp*, north of Algiers [at 05.45 on 20 April 1942] to lead a group of Spitfires to Malta some 700 miles away, he started heading, with the other aircraft formating on him, on a reciprocal course back to Gibraltar. . . . The carrier had passed through the Gibraltar Straits on the previous day. . . .

Despite the strict radio silence, some observant sergeant pilot in the formation called him up on the R/T. 'Say, Red Leader, when are you setting course for the island?'

Back in Malta, 'Jumbo' had to tell the story against himself. . . .

P. Whaley Heppell, Guyzance Bridge, Morpeth,
Northumberland, 1984

Editor's note: *Squadron Leader Lord David Douglas-Hamilton who led his own 603 (City of Edinburgh) Squadron off* Wasp *that day, later gave*

---

*Heppell received a direct hit from our own flak. (Ed.)
†See pages 47, 97, 99, 218 and 278.

the gaffe expression. Had Gracie ended up in Gibraltar instead of Malta he would have put up, he wrote, 'an imperial black'. Source: Lord James Douglas-Hamilton, David's nephew, Member of Parliament and author of The Air Battle for Malta (Mainstream Publishing, Edinburgh, 1981).

Italian Blooding

On 13 August 1942 a 22-year-old second lieutenant of the Regia Aeronautica, deployed temporarily with his squadron on the island of Pantelleria, took part in his first air battle over the critical, eastbound Malta convoy. The merchantmen, surrounded by their heavy naval escort, were fighting a forbidding passage through the Mediterranean 'narrows' to the island. They were taking a fearful pounding. In the air above, much of hell was breaking loose.

Lieutenant Francesco Cavalera (Generale Francesco Cavalera), a newly joined Macchi 202c pilot of the 51st Wing at Gela in Sicily, was at the start of a spectacular military career. Beginning as a cadet at the Accademia Aeronautica, he was to rise, in the next thirty-six years, via squadron and wing commands, to the summit of the Italian Air Force and, finally, to the office of the Chief of the Defence Staff. It was the first time that an air-force officer had occupied the post.

His opening story, written with engaging modesty in the third person, shows how, from the start, fortune was striding out with him along the forward path. It was so often the way with destiny's 'chosen sons'.

The young lieutenant had been the last to be posted to the squadron. By the time he reported for duty the numbers were already complete. . . . Thirteen pilots, thirteen machines − nothing left over for the junior pilot to fly. When the squadron had deployed to Sicily he had had to follow on from Rome by train. But there was time on the way to pass a few hours in his home town; time there to see again the girl he had left behind; time to lose his heart. . . .

So he arrived at the airfield at Gela a week after the others. During that week there had been many battles, over the Mediterranean and over Malta. Of the six lieutenants on the squadron, five had not returned to base. . . . Five out of six in just one week!

Cavalera's first encounter followed the pattern which was all too familiar to the old hands in their first days with a squadron. The mission was to accompany a formation of Italian Stukas (Ju 87s) sent to attack the warships escorting the convoy. The job was not only to provide top cover for the bombers, but also for the fighters which were giving the attacking force close support.

. . . The young lieutenant had no time for what was going on below. He had to stick to his leader, and at the same time keep scanning the skies across on the starboard side of the wing. . . .

So he was not conscious of the Stuka attacks on the convoy, nor of where their bombs were bursting, nor was he aware of the manoeuvres of

161

the escort formation as they threw themselves against a wall of anti-aircraft fire coming up from the warships below. . . .

Up ahead, there appeared some fighters, undoubtedly enemy. Spitfires? Hurricanes? He had studied for months for this moment, poring over films and photos, but now, faced with the real thing, it was quite a different matter. He saw tracer coming from his leader's gun ports, burying themselves in the flanks of the aircraft in front, and many of his fellows were similarly engaged.

The lieutenant was not in a position to open fire. Nor was he expected to. In any case, he preferred it this way. He would not have found it easy to shoot to kill – even against the enemy. He had acquired the feeling that all airmen, from whatever part of the world, were somehow all members of the same family, aloof from the petty squabbles of ordinary men. It was an ideal to cherish and to live up to. . . .

But now all the combats seemed, for the moment, to be over, the tangling and skirmishing was at an end. . . . He was on his own. His leader had disappeared, and, with him, all the rest of the formation. . . .

The young lieutenant frantically looked about him. What on earth should he do? If he flew back on his own he would look like a coward who had fled from the battle.

He could already picture the face of the Capo Calotta,* the most senior lieutenant in the mess, who could censure, chide, lampoon, and even order you to buy drinks for the rest of the mess if he thought you had shown insufficient respect for the wing and its hallowed traditions. . . .

The lieutenant searched the sky above the convoy and scanned every aircraft. All of them seemed to be carrying the RAF roundel. It did not occur to him that, being alone, he was an easy target, a 'sitting duck', for any of the British fighters. A glance at the fuel gauge brought him back to reality. His remaining fuel was diminishing rapidly and it began to seem unlikely that he could ever get back to base. His instinct for survival took the upper hand, and feeling like a dog with its tail between its legs he turned onto a heading which he thought would take him back towards Pantelleria.

Soon, with the fuel gauge close to zero, he crossed the coast. Breathing a sigh of relief, he positioned himself for the landing. Hardly had he touched down when the engine hesitated, then stopped dead. Before the aircraft had come to rest, he was surrounded by his fellows. All speaking at the same time.

'Where were you hiding?'

'Did you think you could sink that convoy single-handed?'

'Don't you know we've been back for half an hour?'

'Were you trying to be the big fighter ace?'

'We had almost given you up for lost,' said the Colonel. . . . And peering

---

*'Capo Calotta' – this appointment did not exist in the Royal Air Force. In the Regia Aeronautica, however, he was, in effect, the 'senior' junior officer in charge of the 'junior' junior officers. The position still exists in the Italian Air Force, and carries with it considerable powers and respect. (Ed.)

round his shoulder as he spoke was the grinning face of the Capo Calotta. . . .'

Postscript: *During the Regia Aeronautica's attacks on the 'August convoy', there occurred one of those chance incidents which demonstrated the humanity which existed between the opposing sides in the air war. Francesco Cavalera remembers the story well.*

Captain Antonia Cumbat was the leader of a flight of Stukas. He had been forced to abandon his aircraft, followed by his crewman, and – fortunately – by his dinghy. But their safe bale-out was of small consolation. They were a tiny dot in the vast expanse of sea, and Cumbat remembered how relatively few pilots, in his position, were ever found and rescued.

The hours slipped away and, with them, his hopes. Then, just at sunset, a German rescue seaplane appeared on the horizon. It came closer and closer, then passed by and flew off into the distance. It had not seen them. Almost at that moment a Bristol Beaufighter appeared above them. They had been discovered, but by the enemy!

The Beaufighter pilot had also seen the German aircraft and set off to follow it. Surely he would not attack a rescue aircraft? On the other hand, one sometimes heard that these aircraft took advantage of their immunity to fly more warlike missions. . . .

Cumbat saw the Beaufighter catch up with the German aircraft, then pull in front of it, forcing it to change direction. When the floatplane was redirected onto the right course, the Beaufighter pilot then led it back towards the dinghy. Only when the seaplane had alighted beside the Stuka crew, and taken them on board, did the Beaufighter leave the scene, rocking his wings in salute as he departed. . . .

After the war, Cumbat tried, with the help of the Royal Air Force's Air Historical Branch in London, to trace the British pilot. He succeeded, only to learn that this gallant man, holder of the Distinguished Flying Cross, had, later, been killed in action.

Generale Francesco Cavalera, Rome, Italy, 1984

I have learned
To look on nature, not as in the hour
Of thoughtless youth; but hearing often-times
The still, sad music of humanity.

William Wordsworth (1770–1850)

The Biter Bit

If Providence had granted Francesco Cavalera a reprieve from his formative trials, so also did it reserve a moment of compassion for Roderick Smith (Squadron Leader R. I. A. Smith), the Vancouver lawyer, who, before the war's end, was to command, with conspicuous success, the Royal Canadian Air Force's 401 Squadron during the Allied drive through northwest Europe.

His brother, Jerrold, also operating from Malta, had recently been posted as missing, believed killed. Jerry had earlier made history by becoming the first man to land a Spitfire on the flight deck of an aircraft carrier (US Navy's Wasp, 9 May 1942) without tailhooks.

Rod Smith, quickly avenging his brother's loss, had just been promoted to command a flight in 126 Squadron at Luqa. Now, on this fifteenth day of October, he was to survive an experience which, eight times out of ten, would have proved mortal.

One of the last Axis raids on Malta had been delivered. The attackers, with throttles wide open and noses down, were beating it back to Sicily, and home. Rod, from well above, sighted two yellow-nosed Me 109s right down on the water, travelling flat out. Coming out of a fast dive with his mate, Prosser Hanks (Group Captain P. P. Hanks), he concentrated on the left hand of the two Messerschmitts, both of which seemed to be pulling away with excess speed. . . . A burst over the top of the 109 would, he thought, make it turn and offer the chance to engage. But now his guardian angel seemed to have other ideas.

For some reason I glanced down at my left wing and happened to see a small bullet hole in it just a few feet from me. I assumed I had picked it up earlier, when we were sparring with the 109s high up. I then fired a few more rounds over the top of the 109 in front of me, but still he would not turn. . . . I looked again at the bullet hole in my left wing, and saw a second one about a foot from it. It took a long second for me to realize that there must be a 109 behind. . . .

I broke violently to the left and upwards. In an instant things began to happen. Exploding balls of fire making sharp cracking bangs appeared on the left side of my engine. The aircraft shook as if poked from behind by long metal rods. The cockpit filled with the smell of cordite. The engine oil pressure dropped to nothing. The oil temperature shot upwards. But the engine kept going without missing a beat. Over my left shoulder I saw the yellow nose of a 109 about 100 yards behind me and closing in. Puffs of smoke were billowing from its guns and being blown back over it. It came so close it almost touched me as it passed behind. . . .

As soon as I was pointing back to Malta, I straightened out and climbed at full power. We had been told that if a Rolls-Royce Merlin engine ever lost its oil pressure you should flog it, not nurse it. To my great relief I reached 600 feet and then 1000. The engine kept delivering full power. I marvelled how it could do this with no oil pressure. I switched the R/T over to emergency and called 'Mayday! Mayday! Mayday!', the oral SOS. Immediately, the Malta controller responded. 'Keep transmitting,' he said, 'we've got you!' Soon I was at 2000 feet and Malta looked closer.

To my wonderment and admiration the engine kept going till I reached 3800 feet and was almost at the coast of Malta. By then, acrid smoke was pouring through the cockpit and the power was failing. I baled out and was rescued from the sea.

I could never ask for greater luck than I had on that October morning when two bullets, timed and spaced by chance, gently warned me not to linger.

R. I. A. Smith, Vancouver, British Columbia, 1985

The Absolute Terror of It

By the end of 1942 the Harris stamp had been engraved deeply into the character and operational pattern of Bomber Command. The climactic years of the great night offensive, 1943 and 1944, lay ahead. Already, some of the individuals, who would give operational expression to Harris's tactics and strategy in the closing years of the war, were beginning to emerge.

Among the navigators, Ben Bennett (Squadron Leader T. Bennett), who was later to star with 617 Squadron at Woodhall Spa, was now making his way with 49 Squadron at Scampton.

The naked honesty of his account of his personal feelings during the attack on Duisburg, the inland port at the apex of the industrial Ruhr, on 8–9 September 1942 – his sixth trip – tells much of the hideous ordeals which Harris's crews were, nightly, having to endure . . . and of the large parcel of luck they needed if they were to survive the length of even a single operational tour.

There was a shock at the briefing.

As a 'sprog'* crew we were somewhat disconcerted with the special orders we were given that night. We would be ten minutes behind all other aircraft on the operation. Our aircraft would carry a special camera, fitted with an open shutter. This would start to operate when the bomb doors opened, and continue until the magazine was exhausted. It was hoped that the exposed film would record continuous traces of the fires caused by the raid, and allow an early assessment of the operation's effectiveness.

I was a sergeant navigator at the time, and it was the first occasion (but certainly not the last) that I felt a silent, intense anger at a bomber crew being asked to add to the normal perils of an operation through the 'good idea' of some 'faceless wonder' in higher authority. I would have thought a great deal more of these 'strategists' if they had undertaken to accompany the luckless crew and discover, at first hand, the efficacy of their suggestions, instead of sitting, comfortably and safely, awaiting the results of their experiments. . . .

The flight to the target, after picking up the enemy beacon near the Dutch-German border (an orbiting point for the Luftwaffe's night-fighters from which they were vectored to targets and areas by their ground controllers) was uncharacteristically muted.

We could see the Duisburg area burning ahead, but the defences were strangely quiet . . . .

But then, as the bombing run began the blue beam of the master searchlight found and held our Lancaster. It was followed at once by other probing fingers of light. . . . We were held fast in a cone of searchlights. . . . I crouched at my navigation table, throat dry and parched. Although I was wearing my flying helmet, with its padded earpieces, and had an oxygen mask clamped across my face, I could hear a sound like hail drumming on the sides of the fuselage. I knew, without looking out, that heavy shells were bursting all around us, pattering the aircraft with shrapnel. . . .

*Inexperienced. (Ed.)

Now came the fear . . . and the terror – until an innate faith took control.

I felt the bitter bile rise in the back of my throat. My heart and pulses pounded under the mounting stress of the greatest fear I had ever experienced. The frantic gyrations of the aircraft were giving us a helter-skelter ride planned in hell! Time and again, I felt myself leave my seat, and the navigation instruments on my table rose with me, as the Lancaster plunged earthwards in a sickening dive . . . only to find myself pinned down on the chart table, as now the aircraft clawed for altitude. . . .

These experiences added to my absolute terror until I felt that, in some way, I was detached from humanity and mankind . . . that no one in the whole universe had the slightest care for me. I felt so totally alone that I shivered as if being blasted by the lowest temperature that could be measured. There was an emptiness within me that almost choked me with its volume. . . .

In a flashing, blasphemous moment, I felt that I knew what had wrung the cry '*Eli! Eli! Lama sabachthani*?' from the soul of the Christ as he hung upon the cross. To this day, I am not sure that I did not shout aloud with terror. . . .

Then, a buoyant calm seemed to come to sooth away all my hysteria, all my unspeakable fear. It was almost as if someone had whispered a reminder to me that my wife, my mother, the great East End padré friend of my life – all these, and others, were praying for my safety every night and that my faith required me to believe that their prayers would be heard in heaven. We were still bathed in the full, awesome glare of the searchlights, but now I could sit calmly and await the inevitability of what, I felt, must surely come. . . .

Watching the application of my friends in the cockpit . . . the resolution of the wireless operator . . . and appreciating that, throughout the horrendous experience, neither gunner had made any comment on the intercom as each devoted himself to the search for enemy fighters, I thought to myself, what a fine company to go with. I was still placidly resigned to what I regarded as the inevitable end of this nightmare. . . .

Without warning, inky blackness now replaced the blinding light in which we seemed to have lived for an eternity. The roar of our four Merlins was a deep-throated song of triumph in the lonely night sky. . . . We had shaken free from that cone of death and now night, dear, dark, blessed night had lovingly embraced us in her protective, concealing cloak. . . . Providence gave me another sight of the German fighter beacon allowing me to adjust accurately the rough course I had already given the pilot to the coast. . . .

Very soon we were heading for home and safety, and for touchdown at Scampton at 04.55 hours, a shaken but thankful 'sprog' crew.

. . . Of course, examination showed that the whole film had been fogged out by the blinding light of the searchlight, an obvious outcome to the experiment which anyone with fair operational experience could readily have foreseen. . . .

There is a footnote to this graphic, human story.

. . . The terror which seized me in those few minutes – for that is all that it was – is as real to me now as it was over forty years ago. But I was never again to plumb such depths during any of my further fifty-six bomber operations. . . . The experience brought me a reassurance and a belief that, beyond the gamut of human fear and terror, there lies an infinite calm and peace – a majestic tranquillity which enables us to face the last enemy without flinching. . . .

I like to think that that benign peace which touched me momentarily on that autumn night more than four decades ago, was also the last emotion of so many of my dear friends and comrades who flew out but who were not destined to return. . . .

Squadron Leader T. Bennett, Westcliffe-on-Sea, Essex, 1984

A Bomber Pilot's Prayer

Sit with me, Anger, be my guide,
Be second pilot at my side,
Give me my straight, true course to steer
Through the dark labyrinth of fear.

But, Pity, be not absent when
My bombs go hurtling down, Be with me then
That I may not insensate be
Nor outcast from humanity.

Anonymous

Japanese Zero crashing

Pacific Turning Point

The great central-ocean air battle for Midway Island, now numbered among the historic naval engagements of all time, was fought out between 3–6 June 1942. It turned the course of the Pacific war for the United States, and left the stricken Imperial Navy to withdraw, deprived for ever of four of its major aircraft carriers – Akagi, and her sister ship Kaga, as well as Soryu and Hiryu.

Iyozo Fujita (Major Iyozo Fujita) was an officer of the Hiryu, and one of the Japanese navy's most successful fighter pilots. He finished the war with 42 enemy aircraft destroyed or damaged, and was a lucky survivor of the island battle. He lived to become, in peace, a pilot and an executive of Japanese Air Lines. DC 4s, 6s, 7s and 8s, and then the Boeing 747, were a far cry from his days with the Zero in the Indian Ocean and Pacific theatres.

Fujita is one of a handful of veterans of the attack on Pearl Harbor on 7 December 1941, who survived to operate at Midway, Rabaul and Guadalcanal, and who was still operational at the end of the war. Now president of the Japanese Zero Pilots' Association, he remembers his Midway experience for its impact upon his life and the extraordinary luck it brought. . . .

I had spotted an enemy torpedo aircraft approaching our carrier. After turning into it and firing a good burst, my own aircraft was hit in the engine and the oil feed by a shell which seemed to come from the direction of the carrier. . . . With fire spreading and the cockpit filled with smoke, I had no worthwhile alternative but to bale out, despite being at no more than 600 feet at the time. . . .

I hit the water a split-second after the parachute had opened. It was a tremendous shock. Had the 'chute opened a fraction of a second later, I would have been commemorated at Yasukuni Shrine. . . .

I went down under the water and then, assisted by my life jacket, floated to the surface, only to see the cruiser, *Zintsu*, passing me by, going at full speed. . . . On the horizon I could see three black columns of smoke where I knew our fleet to be. I started to swim in that direction. My mind went back to my training days at the naval academy at Etajima and the long distances we used to swim between 7 a.m. and 8 p.m. Sometimes we would not return to the shore until twilight.

But the distance now was much greater, perhaps twenty miles. I guessed it would take me all of twenty-four hours to make it – if I could. . . . I began to think about the danger of sharks. . . . I remembered being told that sharks will not attack anything larger than themselves, so I unwrapped the muffler round my neck and let it trail behind me in the water.

The cold was intense. The day temperature around Midway in June was high, but the water remained very cold. . . . I felt I must put my muffler back around my neck at least to give me some idea of warmth. If the sharks attacked, why, that was destiny; there was nothing I could do about it. My toes and feet, hands and fingers were quite numb with the cold. I began to wonder whether the distance was going to be too much. Hunger and fatigue seemed to be making me drowsy.... It would be so easy to die like this....

A Type 96 seaplane flew overhead. I summoned the strength to lift myself and wave, but it did not notice. My hopes were falling fast; after seven or eight hours in the water I was getting near the end of the road.

Then, as I rode up on a big wave, I got a better view and caught sight of the carrier, *Akagi;* it looked to be about two miles or so away. I couldn't be sure how far. It was still burning after the attacks, but seemed to be making some way. As I swam closer I could see there was a destroyer attending it. It turned out to be the *Nowaki;* eventually a look-out spotted me; I thought I saw a machine gun being aimed at me.... When they realised I was an officer of the carrier, *Soryu*, a rope ladder was lowered and willing hands stretched out to haul my exhausted body aboard....

I recall seeing two former classmates of mine from the naval academy, and then being given food and dry clothing. After that I must have passed out, for I could remember nothing more for quite a time.

In the end, I was sent back to an air base in Japan for a while before being transferred to the carrier, *Hiyo* converted from the merchantman, *Kashiwabara-Maru*. When she was damaged by fire, we were sent to Rabaul; then from our bases on Bouganville and Buin we attacked Guadalcanal, some 300 miles distant....

I had now come to realize that I had survived the ordeal of Midway because it was my destiny that I should. I saw there was a destiny in life, and that's what had guided me.... It was God's will that had shaped my destiny.... That is what Midway, and other wartime escapes meant to me.... It was upon this concept that my life's philosophy was built.

... There were many uncomfortable situations to cope with after the war, but I was able to deal with them because I could now see that this was my destiny....

Iyozo Fujita, Zero Fighter Pilots' Association,
Tachikawa-Shi, Tokyo, Japan 1984

The editor is indebted to Henry Sakaida, the Research editor of the US aviation journal, *Fighter Pilots in Aerial Combat*, Mission Viejo, California, for his advice and assistance in preparing the translation of the foregoing text. Thanks are also due to Jiro Yoshida, director of the Zero Fighter Pilots' Association and administrator of Japan-American Cultural Exchange, an organization developing student programmes with the UK and USA, for his help in stimulating this contribution.

How Saburo Made It

The early Zero pilots we met were exceptionally good, with a fine aeroplane to fly. One day, one of them did an upward roll right in front of me just as I was on the point of stall.... Rather like thumbing your nose at a guy ...

Squadron Commander, Roy Riddel, Royal Australian Air Force

On 7 August 1942 US marines were landing on the island of Guadalcanal in the Solomons. Over Tulagi, to the north of Guadalcanal, Petty Officer

169

First-Class Saburo Sakai (Lieutenant S. Sakai (jg)), of the Tainan Kokutai,
Japan's answer to Johnnie Johnson, Joachim Marseille, Pat Pattle, Dick
Bong and Clive Caldwell, all rolled into one, had become unwittingly
involved with Douglas Dauntless SBD dive-bombers. Fire from their
gunners had inflicted upon him serious bodily harm.

Bullet fragments became embedded in his skull; he was blinded in the
right eye and the vision of his left was impaired. Shrapnel had hit him in
the back, chest and thigh. And ahead of him lay a 4½-hour flight across
water. His trusted Zero's engine was still good, but the fuel factor was
going to be critical. His chances, in all the circumstances, were poor, to
say the least. Something more than flying and fighting ability was required.
Henry Sakaida, a student of Saburo's wartime career, picks up the narrative.

Sakai was losing blood fast and was fighting to retain consciousness. As
he began to weaken with the blood loss and the agony of his injuries, a
vision came to him. It was accompanied by a familiar voice which was
saying: 'Saburo, Saburo, keep awake, keep awake! Shame on you if you
allow your guard to drop! You must fight to live. . . . You must keep
fighting!'

As he listened to this admonition, the vision of his mother appeared
before him, scolding him as she used to do sometimes when he was young.

She was stern, but motherly and persuasive, determined that her message
should penetrate her son's fading consciousness. 'Saburo,' she kept
repeating, 'you must fight! You must fight for your life and your honour.'

As she spoke, Sakai felt that she was compelling him to head his aircraft
in the direction of her choice, willing him to fly the compass course that
she – not he – desired. . . .

It was sufficient to help him retain his purpose and control, until at last,
to the jubilation of his comrades, he reached Rabaul and touched down
with his fuel almost spent. . . .

Sakaida has added a rider to Saburo's extraordinary experience.

After being sent back to Japan for further hospitalization and surgical
attention, Sakai returned once more to operations, but now with one
eye! . . .

On 5 July 1944 he was ordered to fly a kamikaze mission from Iwo Jima
[in the Bonin Islands, some 800 miles eastwards from Okinawa]. Fate
intervened, and Sakai's flight was intercepted by the enemy's Grumman
Hellcats, leaving him no choice but to abort.

In worsening weather, and with his two wingmen tucked in tight with
him, Saburo's problem was now to locate and regain his base. As he
searched over the great expanse of sea and his anxieties began to mount,
he saw again, just as he had done two years before, the vision of his
mother. . . . This time there was no admonition, only the direction to fly
was conveyed. . . . Following her guidance, Sakai and his comrades made
their way home. . . .

Henry Sakaida, Mission Viejo, California, USA, 1984

Skidding for Dear Life

When we came back [to Australia] from the UK in 1942, we formed two squadrons of Kittyhawks (P-40s), 75 and 76. 75 had been in Port Moresby [southeast New Guinea] earlier and had really been decimated. . . .

It was generally accepted then that the Zero could out-climb and out-turn the Kitty, particularly the E-type we had at that time. The idea, therefore, was to have a standing patrol high up over the base [Port Moresby] when the enemy arrived with their bombers and fighters from Lae. . . .

On one occasion, we didn't make the height and got jumped by the Zeros. There were about ten of us. . . . I was flying another bloke's aircraft. I had flown it before and I knew it always swung strongly to the left. . . . The chap who usually flew it was a delightful character, but he must have had a very strong right leg!*

. . . When we were bounced, we lost four aircraft and pilots straight away. . . . One Zero then fastened onto me, so I did what any law-abiding hero would do in a Kitty – I dived. . . . The aircraft got going down at about 500 m.p.h. and was skidding to the left at some similar speed. . . .

Large holes, and some smaller ones, started to appear in the starboard wing, and, as we discovered later, lots more in the tail area – all accompanied by the usual noise and smell. After this, the aeroplane would only turn to the left. . . . The Jap pilot must have felt very frustrated. . . . †

When I eventually landed at base, Lex Winten, the man who usually flew the aircraft, came out of the flight tent. 'Christ, Riddel,' he said, 'look what you've done to my plane.' I thought he might have been pleased to see me back.

I have often wondered since, what would have happened that day had I been flying my own aircraft, which dived more or less in a straight line. . . . I don't think I would have been given another forty-odd years!

R. G. Riddel, Korora, Coffs harbour, New South Wales,
Australia, 1984

Homing to Safety

Guy Townsend (Brigadier General Guy M. Townsend) was serving with the United States 13th Air Force when, towards the end of 1942, he was based at Tontouta, on New Caledonia, in the South Pacific. He was then a second lieutenant, flying B-17s, on his way to completing 450 combat hours in the Pacific theatre. He was to finish the war as a major with the 16th Bombardment Wing, equipped with B-29s.

There was one tortuous incident which occurred during Townsend's time at Tontouta. It exposes as well as any description the chances and hazards

---

*Great pressure would have been needed on the right rudder bar to correct the swing to the left.
†With the aircraft skidding to the left, the Zero's fire would effectively have been aimed right. Deliberate skidding either to left or right was an old evasive ploy. (Ed.)

which accompanied the operations in this area, and shows something of the Americans' flair for improvisation.

General Townsend recounted the story to Dr James C. Hasdorff in the course of a recorded interview at Everett, Washington, on 12–13 July 1982, for the United States Air Force Oral History Programme, conducted under the aegis of the USAF Historical Research Center, Maxwell Air Force Base, Alabama. The editor is indebted to Dr Richard Kohn, Chief of the Office of Air Force History, for permission to take the following extract from the exchanges. Townsend is speaking:

Tontouta is in the mountains [of New Caledonia] and has a river that runs by it. It was a pretty tricky place to get into, particularly in bad weather. . . . We had worked out a procedure so you could get into that place when the weather was real bad. . . .

There was a freighter torpedoed out on a reef off the island there. If you went over this freighter, which was about seventy miles north of Noumea, and took up a certain heading, you could hit the mouth of the river. [After this], we just worked out a low visibility approach and timed it very precisely [to lead you] onto the runway. . . .

We worked this thing out, and about three or four weeks later, we were up in the mess hall one day when we were having a horrible storm. (This was the fall of 1942.) It was a typhoon coming through there – a hurricane or tropical storm.

The base commander, Major Cook, came over and said to me, 'Lieutenant, you know, Colonel Caldara is trying to get in here, and he can't make it. I want you to go down to the tower.' So we jumped in our jeep and ran down to the control tower. This was a tent up on top of the hill. There was a staff sergeant operator on the radio. I could hear Colonel Caldara speaking on it when I walked in. The sergeant was white. He just handed me the microphone.

When the Colonel quit talking, I said, 'Colonel, what is your position?' He said, 'Is that you, Townsend?' I said, 'Yes, sir.' He said, 'We are down here at Noumea, and we are circling this reef, and we are going to go to Fiji.'

I said, 'Sir, how much fuel do you have?' So he told me, and you really didn't have to think very long to know he wasn't going to get to Fiji. He said that he wanted me to alert the navy, and so forth and so on. I said, 'Sir, can you see the reef?' He said, 'Yes, I can see the reef.' I said, 'Head north on the reef.' I noted my watch, and he said, 'Okay.'

He headed up north on the reef, and I was timing him. I said, 'Sir, when you get to the old ship out there – when you see that old freighter, let me know.' So he did. I turned him to the heading and gave him an air speed, and told him to tell me when he saw the mouth of the river. He saw the mouth of the river. Then I vectored him up the river and got him in off the end of the runway.

It was about ten miles up to the end of the runway. There was a 9000-foot mountain right on his left-hand side. 'Turn south now, turn right to 210 degrees.' He came back and said, 'You mean left.' I said, 'No, sir, right – right to 210.'

I didn't tell him there was a 9000-foot mountain right on his left-hand wing tip. . . . I knew he was lined up on the runway, although he was about eight miles out. Right at that time, lightning struck the tower. It burned my hand, but not badly, and it knocked the radio out.

The sergeant dived under the table and hooked up another radio and handed me another microphone. Of course, Caldara was screaming and hollering because he hadn't heard from me for about thirty seconds.

I had timed this thing, and about that time it started raining just horribly again. So, I let him down to 200 feet – just strictly on my watch. He said, 'I can't see a thing.' I looked at my watch again and knew he was right off the end of the runway, so I told him to start a 200-foot-per-minute descent at the end of forty-five seconds.

'Cut your power, Colonel, and land; pull back on the stick.' He did, and he didn't see the runway until he was on it. He rolled out, and it was raining so hard that he could not see to taxi off the runway. He stopped the airplane right at the tower, still on the runway. We all got in our jeep and drove out there, and they were standing under the wing there like a bunch of drowned rats. Caldara jumped out of the airplane, came running over and threw both arms around my neck. . . .

The back door of the aircraft opened up and out came General Harmon, Admiral Halsey, Admiral Nimitz, General Twining, and General Jamison. He had the whole command of the South Pacific on board, and he also had General Frank Everest.

When they came out there they said to the Colonel: 'Gee, Smokey, that is the damndest thing we ever saw in our lives! How in the world did you get in here in weather like that?'

He said, 'Hell, I don't know. Talk to this lieutenant here.' They said, 'Gee, we didn't know you had GCA (ground-controlled approach)* at Tontouta.' He said, 'We don't, but we've got this lieutenant.'

The Colonel turned around to me and he said, 'How long have you been a second lieutenant?' I said, 'Sir, since May.' He said, 'That's long enough. You're a first lieutenant right now. . . .'

*Bad weather and low-visibility landing aid. (Ed.)

Luck Goes with Numbers
1943–1944

The build-up of the Allied air effort in the Atlantic, across the European continent and in the Far East and Pacific theatres now mounted to new peaks. The output of aircraft from the factories, and the flow of air and ground personnel from the training centres in Britain and the Commonwealth and from the United States, swelled to the point of saturation. As the size and weight of activity multiplied so did the strange machinations of fate and fortune.

Of the tens of thousands of surviving airmen who helped to sustain the advance, worldwide, during 1943 and 1944 there were few who hadn't, at the end of the day, some extraordinary tale of chance to relate.

One among them was Derek Bielby, a Coastal Command pilot, operating against the Atlantic U-boats. He recalls the experience of a Polish crew of No. 304 Squadron, from Chivenor near Barnstaple, in north Devon, one black night in the Bay of Biscay in the winter of 1943. It proved again the rugged durability of the Wellington aircraft.

Polski Contact

The night-aircraft of Coastal Command were navigated, in those days, by dead reckoning. The method depended on the constant measuring of drift* by taking back bearings on flame floats dropped overboard. These devices ignited on contact with the sea.

As drift-taking took place with monotonous frequency, the sea was often dotted far and wide with the flame-float pattern of other aircraft of 19 Group flying parallel courses in the saturation search for surfaced U-boats. Indeed, on a moonless night with a heavy overcast, it appeared as though the heavens and the sea had changed places.

Flying one night in such conditions, the captain of one of 304's Wellingtons was suddenly puzzled to see four glowing red dots just in front of him. Equally suddenly the apparition vanished, and the aircraft shuddered with the stupefying shock of hard contact. Baffled by the swiftness of the phenomenon, the captain realized that there had been a collision of some sort, and though the aircraft vibrated uncharacteristically, it was manageable and still flew. As the patrol was reaching its limit, the pilot at once

*The variation in an aircraft's intended track over land and sea due to winds. (Ed.)

174

turned for home and the long, lonely haul over six hundred miles of hostile sea.

It was only after the aircraft had been safely parked and the engines shut down that the groundcrew discovered that the Wellington's fin and rudder were missing. And when a Coastal Command Liberator returned to its 19 Group base the same morning after an all-night Biscay sortie, minus the outer part of a wing, the realization of what had actually happened gradually dawned.

The patrolling Polish pilot had seen the red-hot exhausts of the four-engined Liberator as it closed on a collision course. Inches only must have averted the sudden and total loss of both aircrews and aircraft. Chance had, yet again, played a fateful hand. . . .

Derek Bielby, Stokesley, North Yorkshire, 1984

'Getting Your Own Back'

The more mundane and pressing needs of the human anatomy sometimes caused problems — and hazards — in the air. But they had to be solved — somehow. The old hand had his answers for nature's irrepressible demands. The embryo captain of aircraft often had something to learn.

Early in 1943, at the age of nineteen years, I was flying Whitleys from RAF Station, St Eval, Cornwall, doing anti-U-boat sweeps over the Bay of Biscay as part of an operational detachment from No. 10 OTU. We did not carry a second pilot but I had been trying, without noticeable success, to teach my bomb-aimer — a rotund Yorkshireman called Sergeant Braithwaite — to at least keep the aircraft straight and level.

After some four hours of creeping line-ahead searches at about 400 feet, I became aware — with increasing urgency — that my bladder was at about its limit of extension. I asked myself the futile question: Why had I not 'gone' before take-off. It did not help.

The only 'facilities' available in the Whitley were the 'Elsan' chemical lavatory, which was positioned near the rear gun-turret, a very long crawl down the narrow coffin-like fuselage. However, I decided to chance it and, after climbing to 1500 feet, I got out of the pilot's seat, holding onto the control column with one hand, while Sergeant Braithwaite scrambled breathily into my place. He then appeared to freeze like a gargoyle, with the wings of the stick clenched tightly in his hands. After a few minutes of rather impatient instruction, I set off on the long crawl to the rear of the aircraft. It is not always easy, inside a dark fuselage, with no openings or windows, to know what is going on in the cockpit, but I had hardly got halfway to the 'Elsan' when I realized that all was not well. This was because I found myself becoming glued to the portside of the aircraft, which made me think that, for reasons best known to Braithwaite, we were turning starboard fairly steeply. Cursing and bursting, I scrambled back to the cockpit to find that, indeed, we were heading rapidly for the sea in a starboard spiral with my bomb-aimer still clinging, rigidly, to the control column.

After putting things right — which was not difficult for a pilot — I tried again. This time I got some two-thirds of the way down the fuselage before having to return. And this time I got Braithwaite out of my seat and resumed the flying myself.

I consulted the rest of the crew. There was some discussion amidst ill-concealed merriment in which I did not join. Eventually someone came up with the bright idea of filling a French letter. Someone else produced a Durex from his field-dressing pocket and, after much fumbling with clothing, I put it on. Oh, the exquisite relief!

Thereafter, the only problem was the disposal of the Christmas-pudding-sized heavy balloon. No problem, I thought (although that was not our 1943 idiom). I eased back the sliding window on my left-hand side, and manoeuvred the full balloon towards the open space. Unfortunately, I foolishly omitted to tie a knot in its neck, with the result that, as soon as it hit the slipstream, there was a whoosh! and it all emptied back into the cockpit, directly into my face.

As I pondered damply on whether I would dry out during the next three hours of our patrol, I heard Sergeant Braithwaite's voice in my earphones. 'Ee, Skipper,' he said, 'tha' might call that getting your own back!'

His Honour Judge Alan Coulthard, St John's Wood,
London, 1984

Editor's note: Editorial licence, and a proper desire to cover the field over which luck held sway in the lives of young and virile aircrew, prompts the addition of this rider to the Judge's Biscay experience. As Flight Lieutenant A.G.W. Coulthard, of the Royal Air Force's Bomber Command, and, after the war, a 1st Officer with British Overseas Airways before being called to the Bar, he had an eye for the unusual.

'Arriving on my squadron – No. 77, Bomber Command – at RAF Station, Elvington, Yorkshire, in 1943, I had to take my crew to see the station medical officer for what we regarded as the usual pep talk. The MO turned out to be a charming young man – and very Irish.

'After his medical homily about the perils of venereal disease – with particular reference to the young ladies we might meet in the City of York – he ended his talk as follows: "Now dawn't forget, chaps, one goirl's as loikely to have 'ut as the next one – if not more so!" '

Jockey Club Suspension

The Judge wasn't alone among those aircrew who had to rely on a little (each-way) luck to save them from nature's calls. Horrie Wright (Warrant Officer Noel H. Wright), the Australian wireless operator/air gunner, now 'a licensed Rails Bookmaker with the Australian Jockey Club, a coin dealer and a Fellow of the Royal Numismatic Society of London', who flew with Bomber Command, had his share of it. He and his crew were undergoing their operational training at No. 17 OTU at Silverstone, in Northampton-shire, now the site of the famous motor-racing circuit.

One summer's evening, while flying on a pleasant cross-country navigational exercise in a 'semi-obsolete' Wellington, I had occasion to have to relieve my bladder. Ninety-nine per cent of these aircraft had no hatch covers. To reach the rear of the aeroplane, where the 'Elsan' can was located, I had to cross over the open hatch. As I went to step past it, the kite lurched violently, due possibly to turbulence, and I fell sideways towards it. I instinctively grabbed for something – *anything* – to save myself, not least because my parachute was neatly stored in the correct position under my seat in the wireless operator's compartment.

By a million to one chance, my searching fingers clutched the electric cable which ran the full length of the inside fuselage. Although this was fastened with light metal clips, two or three of which broke away, the cable miraculously held. There was I, for perhaps twenty seconds or so – it seemed like an hour – holding on with a strength born of desperation. One quarter of my body was inside the kite and three-quarters of it outside being pulled with terrific force by the slipstream. Down below, in the English summer twilight, was a picture postcard scene with the beautiful green countryside and neat hedgerows looking so peaceful. . . .

The rest of my crew were, of course, oblivious to my predicament, and here I was resigned to enter the Pearly Gates (if that's where WOP/AGs went).

Another one million to one chance now occurred. The old Wellington hit some more turbulence and, due to the whip-like effect of the cable, I was catapulted upwards and all of a sudden I found myself sitting inside the hatch! I still had a vice-like grip on the cable, but I was at the extreme limit of my strength, with my heart pounding like a base drum inside my chest. I was unable to speak or listen out on the radio for about the next quarter of an hour. . . .

To this day, I can still picture the lovely English countryside down below and how peaceful it all looked. . . .

Noel H. Wright, Punchbowl, New South Wales, Australia, 1984

Fate's Choice

These were stern and demanding times for the aircrews of Bomber Command, as radar and other scientific developments – on both sides – reached new levels of effectiveness. Don Charlwood, the author, lived through this period as a navigator of the Royal Australian Air Force. His No Moon Tonight *(Angus & Robertson, 1956; Goodall Publications, 1984) provides, at first hand, the most moving insight yet written into the individual minds of a Lancaster crew as its members steeled themselves to endure the unrelenting ordeal of an operational tour. He knew all about the fickleness of fate.*

In January 1943 our pilot and engineer reported trouble with our Lancaster's port inner engine. As the squadron was operating at high pressure, a thorough overhaul was deferred.

On 13 January an outside crew came to the squadron. They were from 12 Squadron; we were 103, based at Elsham Wolds, a few miles from Brigg. The battle order for the night showed our crew to be taking Lancaster

L London; the strangers were to take our B beer. Despite its shortcomings, it was unthinkable that we be separated from our own aircraft; besides, we had twice had shaky dos when flying L and wanted nothing further to do with it. Our skipper protested to the wing commander.

Probably the wing commander believed he was giving our crew the better aircraft. He assented readily enough to our request. Thus, at 17.00 hours, we lined up for take-off in familiar B beer, carrying a 4000-lb bomb plus ten cans of incendiaries.

I turn to our pilot's diary: 'On take-off I noticed an unusually big swing to port; corrected it as best I could and hauled her off the deck at 120 m.p.h. The rear gunner called up to say that bags of smoke were pouring from the port inner. A moment later the motor caught on fire. Doug (engineer) feathered it immediately. We weren't a hundred feet off the deck, indicated airspeed less than 120. I levelled out and built the speed up for the climb. . . .'

Fortunately our aerodrome was fairly high and it happened that take-off was over a valley. In Brigg, the fire brigade saw our trouble and quickly turned out to shadow us. By a superb piece of flying, and close cooperation from the flight engineer, our pilot nursed B to a safe altitude. The fire brigade were astonished to see us vanish in the direction of the coast. Soon afterwards we dropped our bombs into the North Sea. A con. rod, that had passed through the sump of our port inner engine was found on the runway.

Some hours after our safe return, we learned that the crew of strangers in L London had failed to return from the operation. At first we expressed feelings of guilt over their fate, but then it struck us that had they taken B without knowledge of its faults, their fate would almost certainly have been the same. And B's bomb load might well have exploded on one of those Lincolnshire villages we knew so well.

Don Charlwood, Templestowe, Victoria, Australia, 1984

Silk and Panic

Don Simpson, the Canadian educationalist, became, by the war's end, one of the Royal Canadian Air Force's well-tried and decorated navigators. 426 Squadron, based at Dishforth, near Ripon in Yorkshire, a 6 Group unit in Bomber Command, claimed his services. The start for him, as for many others who achieved later success, was inauspicious; it was also astonishingly lucky. His original Wellington crew had been lost on a suicidal daylight mission into Germany – an operation which the previous extraction of two badly infected wisdom teeth, followed by a 'dry socket', had coincidentally compelled him to miss.

Then, on one February night in 1943, Don and his new crew were briefed to attack the German navy's U-boat pens at Lorient, on the Atlantic seaboard, in western France. Their captain, a Royal Air Force pilot, was experienced, having already survived one operational tour; but he had subsequently been shot down over England at night by an intruding Junkers 88 while he was instructing at an operational training unit. The incident had left its traces. Understandably, he was exceptionally jumpy – as Simpson now recalls.

. . . During a steep turn off the target, our aircraft gave a sharp jump and started to vibrate vigorously. 'What's happened?' shouted the skipper into his mike.

'I think we've been hit by flak,' returned Rolly, the Polish Canadian wireless operator, sitting at his set, just in front of me. . . .

To my consternation, the next message from the skipper was: 'Abandon aircraft. Everyone bale out!' I peered at the altimeter in Rolly's compartment. It recorded a steady 12,000 feet, only 500 feet below the height we had just bombed at. . . .

'Skip,' I said on the intercom, 'why bale out? We've only lost 500 feet and that was probably from the tight turn off the target.'

'Bale out, I say,' came the answer. 'I can't hold this aircraft much longer. It's going to fly apart.'

'Nonsense,' said I, 'Wimpys don't fly apart.' 'Bale out,' he retorted. 'It's an order.' The voice was hysterical.

So this is the way it happens, I thought to myself, as I reached down to pull out my navigator's parachute from beneath me. . . .

For Simpson, there was now a shattering discovery.

Imagine my chagrin when all I got, as I stretched down, was an armful of silk and shroud lines looking like a bowl of spaghetti. 'Nav here, Phil,' I said, just as the second dicky* climbed over my back to reach the emergency escape hatch in the rear fuselage, 'I can't bale out. My parachute is open!'

'It doesn't matter,' came the reply. 'Bale out.' Meanwhile Rolly, all sympathy, put a brave face on it. 'I'll try to help you, Don, to put it on.' 'Never mind, Rolly,' I said, 'I'd just as soon take my chances in the kite. . . .'

At this moment of gloom, a strong, commanding voice came on the intercom. It was our rear gunner, 'Hardrock' Davidson. 'For Christ's sake, Phil, settle down! These people down there are damned unfriendly. . . .'

Strangely, Phil *did* settle down. He rescinded the order, we rescued the second dicky who, by this time, was sitting with his feet dangling out of the escape hatch, ready to jump, and I gave Phil a course for Hurn, the nearest English base. . . . At the French coast, he decided to try to make it – which we did. . . . Next morning, we found that the only damage was 1½-feet square of aircraft skin which had lifted, causing a turbulence that hit the tail plane and set off the vibration. . . .

So my open 'chute had saved the aircraft – and all our crew from a long sojourn in prison camp. . . .

D.W. Simpson, Ottawa, Ontario, Canada, 1985

Fluctuating Forecasts

Unexpected and fortuitous changes in weather conditions were constantly affecting operational decisions – and chances. Every aircrew member knew

*Second pilot. (Ed.)

well the emotional extremes (usually discreetly concealed) which they aroused. George Bain, Canadian television commentator and, for many years, columnist of the *Toronto Globe* and *Mail*, caught the sentiments exactly in a verse he wrote at Topcliffe in Yorkshire, in 1943, when he was serving as a pilot with the Royal Canadian Air Force's 424 Squadron, in 6 Group, Bomber Command. Thirty-six operations against the enemy had exposed to him all the human sensations. The editor gratefully acknowledges the poet's permission to reproduce these lines which were published in *Wings Ahead*, London, 1943 in 'Oscar, the Bard's' column.

> I'm keen, very keen, and I'm anxious to fly,
> The weather's not fit? Not a bit? My, oh my!
> Eight to ten tenths of the blackest of cloud?
> It's horrible, fiendish, it can't be allowed.
> And here I was all set for a night on the Ruhr,
> But now I stay home – very sad to be sure.
> A whole evening free and there's nothing to do,
> Except for the Bull and a pint – maybe two,
> Or that book in the mess that I've only half read,
> Perhaps, for a change, going early to bed,
> Or a picture in town and a restaurant meal.
> (How much would I rather a jaunt over Kiel)
> I really don't care very much for the rest,
> I'd much prefer Hamburg, or Bremen, or Brest.
> The weather is clearing? We may even fly?
> Impossible! Stupid! Why, look at the sky.
> The front has passed over you're sorry to find?
> Well, what about me – my God, what a bind!
> I've a date, I feel ill, my kite is U/S.
> My aunt has just died. My nerves are a mess.
> Gotta have time off; just one evening free.
> Not very keen? Why – who d'ya mean? ME?

> George Bain, University of King's College,
> Halifax, Nova Scotia, Canada, 1984

A Floating Tiger

The accomplished stars of the various Commands could always point to the moments when luck gave them a nudge and whispered 'pass'. Ross Stanford (Flight Lieutenant R. M. Stanford), who moved from 467 (RAAF) Squadron to swell the Australian strength in 617, can point to a couple of them which could have turned out differently.

My first flying in England was done at No. 22 EFTS at Cambridge on Tiger Moths. One calm night in February 1943, I had been doing circuits and landings for an hour and a half. On what turned out to be the last landing that night I came in as usual, but the Tiger would not stall onto the ground. About halfway along the flare-path I finally touched down. I quickly ran through the rest of the flare-path, and then careered on into the darkness wondering whatever I was going to run into.

When I thought my speed was down enough to turn, I veered right until finally the port wing ran into something quite solid and the aircraft stopped. This turned out to be an air-raid shelter, but, fortunately, the sides were banked up with soil.

After some time another Aussie pilot found me, and was most relieved to find that he did not have to pull a dead airman from a wreckage.

On reporting to flying control I found out I was exonerated from blame, as a wind had come up and my last landing had actually been downwind.

I will never forget the fright that experience gave me. . . .

A guiding hand was resting again on Ross Stanford's shoulder later that year, soon after he and his crew had joined 467 Squadron at Waddington, near Lincoln.

A lot of aerodromes in England were hampered by flocks of plover settling and feeding near the runways. Waddington was one of them. On 16 December I was taking off on a night-flying test, and was airborne at ten feet when a flock of these birds also became airborne right in front of me.

Many were killed by the propellers of the aircraft, but one hit the front windscreen and came right through and hit the left ear of my flying helmet.

I consider this to be my luckiest escape from death [editor's italics]. If the bird had hit me full in the face I would have been blinded and feel sure I would then have lost control of the aircraft and crashed. . . .

R. M. Stanford, Fulham Gardens, South Australia, 1984

Spectre!

Date: 14 February 1943 Take off: 18.54 hrs.
Target: Milan, Italy. Time on target: 22.41 hrs. Height: 12,000 feet
Aircraft: Lancaster Mk III ED 495 of 9 Squadron, Bomber Command
Base: RAF Station, Waddington, Lincolnshire

As we neared Milan, we could see anti-aircraft fire and searchlights, and we knew it would soon be our turn. . . . Now Jimmy Geach, the bomb-aimer, was in charge as he called out directions on the intercom to Jim Verran. His calm voice was saying 'Left – left. . . . Right a bit. . . . Steady . . .' as we started the most dangerous part of any bombing raid – the straight and level bombing run which had to be held for another twenty seconds or so after the bombs had gone, waiting for the photo-flash to go off. . . .

. . . At that point, my job, as wireless operator, was to stand on the step ahead of the main spar and put my head up into the astro hatch . . . to assist the gunners in keeping a look-out for fighters. . . .

For some inexplicable reason, I did something I had never done before: I looked directly above me and got the shock of my life. In the glow from the searchlights and target I saw another Lancaster thirty feet above us on exactly the same heading and, like us, his bomb doors were open! The 4000-lb bomb looked enormous, and I knew it could be released at any second. I yelled into my microphone 'Hard-a-port!' Somewhere I had read that it was a natural reaction of pilots to go to port; anyway, our crew was well-trained and Jim stood ED 495 on its wing tip, and we went round again to do another bombing run. . . .

This drastic evasive action added to the normal tension one always felt over any target, and being on our wing tip we momentarily got an unusually good view of Milan! Someone said, 'What the hell's going on?' and I answered, 'Ask me when we get back to base.' Someone else said, 'Anyone for the can?'

Jimmy Verran knew this brief conversation would release tension, and, being a fine crew, it was business as usual a few seconds later. . . .

John H. Moutray, Richmond, British Columbia, 1984

The Deil Looks After His Ain?

. . . The manning of the Pathfinders had actually failed during the first six months [from 15 August 1942]. . . . But from March 1943 we took care of our own manning. . . . I became Don Bennett's horse thief and found that groups (other than 4 Group) were not bothering to earmark good crews for the Pathfinders. Some even used PFF as a dumping place for crews. . . . All this had to change.

Group Captain T. G. Mahaddie, extract from his lecture,
'The Bombing Years', delivered in Winnipeg, Manitoba,
on 5 November 1982

Hamish Mahaddie, the incorrigible Scot, with an unchallengeable Service base to work from, became one of the 'keys' on Bennett's HQ Staff at 8 Group, Bomber Command's Pathfinder Force. He remained there until the war's end. There was, however, one target-making night early in February 1943, when Hamish must have wondered whether there was likely to be a future at all.

. . . Of all my 'chances', this was the one which stands out stark, and oh! so real, from all the others. It was the attack on Köln (Cologne) on the night of 2 February 1943, when the Stirling we were flying went out 'C' Charlie and came back 'C' Colander with 174 cannon shells peppering its fuselage, received micro-seconds after our bombs had gone. . . .

Four of the crew were wounded. I was only 'pinked' through my parachute, but our wireless operator had three fingers shot off while he was 'tinselling'*. . . . The worst aspect was that the ailerons, which provided the lateral control, had been severed. So, simultaneously with the bursts of cannon shells, and without any warning from the gunners, I began a violent diving turn to starboard. After reaching an alarming altitude, with no apparent ability to counteract it, I realized that effective lateral control had gone. . . .

As we were diving under full power, I made to grab the throttles. Somehow – and this was providential – I caught hold of the two port throttles. This had the immediate effect of bringing the wings level. . . . I could then trim the aircraft out of the dive to regain the 10,000 feet we had now lost.

*Interfering with German ground control. (Ed.)

Shells had passed on either side of my seat; the instruments were a mess. There was a horizon of sorts, but the thing that puzzled me was the Pole star. . . . What had happened to the Pole star – and to Tommy (Flight Lieutenant F. D. J. Thompson), the nav? I asked which side the Pole should be on, and received the deservedly caustic reply: 'On the *right* – unless you're flying to Munich!'

. . . All this had happened in a matter of seconds. Meanwhile, Jock Stewart (Flight Sergeant C. Stewart), the flight engineer, had crawled into the root of the wing to try to establish where the aileron cables had been cut, but almost at once he had to be brought back to tend the wounds of the WT/Op, Eddy Edwards. . . .

By a cunning and crafty use of the throttles I was still persuading the four Rolls-Royce Merlins to get us back on course. . . . As it happened, it was indeed fortuitous that I flew my 'reciprocal' to the south, because we didn't then have to re-enter the Köln defences. . . . But no sooner had Jock managed to rejoin the two severed ends of the aileron cable than the gunners warned me that we were being stalked by a fighter. When, halfway back to the coast, it attacked, my ham-fisted evasion tactics destroyed Jock's handiwork and I was back again to having to juggle with the engines to maintain control. . . .

Back at base, after surviving the anxious sea crossing, Hamish felt 'an overwhelming sense of relief'. With the wounded now in safe hands, he could reflect upon the night's chances. . . .

I never could understand why the fighter went for the fuselage, normally they always aimed for the petrol tanks in the wings. . . . And had the pilot's attack come only seconds earlier, he could well have had the Big Bang with the full bomb-load – but so, too, would his aircraft have gone Bang with 'C' Colander. . . . It was only later, much later, I discovered that, with the armour-piercing shell embedded in my parachute, I had . . . a stain on my pants no bigger than the size of a sixpence. . . .

Maybe it all followed the ancient Scots maxim: 'The deil looks after his ain!'

Group Captain T. G. Mahaddie, Downwind, Craigweil,
West Sussex, 1984

Lost Fish

There was still plenty of hard fighting ahead before Africa was finally redeemed in May 1943, and the way paved for the later invasion of southern Europe. The Mediterranean fates were keeping a few cards up their sleeve before calling it a day. They played one of them in darkness on 17 January for the benefit of Charles Grant, navigator of No. 39 Squadron, and the rest of the crew of a torpedo-carrying Beaufort, based at Luqa in Malta.

We took off at 18.47 hours to find and attack a convoy of four merchant vessels, escorted by four destroyers, in the Sicilian Channel. . . . Our first run in, after locating the ships, was abortive – we discovered too late that the target we were attacking was a destroyer and not one of the four supply vessels. . . .

At that moment the moon escaped from the clouds and left us silhouetted against it. Immediately, there was intense ack-ack from the whole convoy and its escort. The gunner was wounded in the leg and, as we were later to discover, our engine nacelles and fuselage were holed. . . .

Hugh Watlington (Flight Lieutenant H. F. Watlington) our Bermudian pilot with the Royal Canadian Air Force, was just turning to make a second attack when our WT/Op shouted that the torpedo had gone. 'Nonsense,' said Hugh (or something stronger), 'I haven't even pressed the tit.' A torch was passed to the WT/Op and, sure enough as he shone it into the bomb bay, it was confirmed that our tin-fish was no longer there!

Three and a half hours after take-off we got back to Malta (purely on my DR, I may say – our wireless and navigational devices were all U/S!) The groundcrew at once saw that the steel hawser which held the torpedo in place had been severed by the flak, and was hanging in two pieces at the sides of the bomb bay. If the shrapnel had hit the nose of the torpedo, instead of the steel hauser which secured it, it could have exploded the 300-400 lb of TNT in the warhead.

As far as we know this was the only occasion on which a torpedo was shot away from under an aircraft and the crew and the aeroplane survived. . . .

Charles M. Grant, Edinburgh, Scotland, 1984

On a Wheel and a Flare

Some of the Air/Sea Rescue operations in the Mediterranean were outstanding in their quality and daring. Between October 1941 and April 1944 the Royal Air Force's High Speed Launch, No. 128, based at Kalafrana, in Malta, made 106 successful rescues – 79 Allied and 27 enemy – some of them undertaken unescorted, as far as 180 miles out from the island, deep in enemy-dominated waters.

L. G. Head (Flight Sergeant L. G. Head), a member of the crew of HSL 128, has included the story of an exceptionally fortunate rescue of a German airman in a privately circulated record he has compiled, 'Royal Air Force Air Sea Rescue, Malta, 1941 to 1944 High Speed Launch 128'.

A Wellington had sighted flares on the sea, 55 miles 213 degrees from Delimara Point, at 04.30 hours on 12 June 1943. HSL 128 had been called out, aided by a Swordfish of the Fleet Air Arm from Halfar. After a protracted search of an area well covered by enemy aircraft, things looked hopeless. The Swordfish had headed away to the southwest, and the launch, now quite alone, had been recalled. Head's diary entry records a sudden and unexpectedly favourable turn.

Turned away from search area and set course for Malta. At 14.45 hours, after travelling a few miles sighted man ahead sitting on an aircraft wheel. He was a German Ju 88 pilot, Horst Gerhard, and he had been out on a mine-laying operation when his plane crashed in the sea. He was uninjured, and pointed out a possible spot where another of the crew might be. A

184

search was made and the body of one of his crewmates discovered. This second man had drowned, and was buried at sea.

Gerhard could speak fluent English, and said he had been on holiday in the United Kingdom on many occasions pre-war as his uncle was a professor at Edinburgh University. On relieving him of his wet clothes, Gerhard was found to be wearing an elaborate gold and enamel decoration round his neck. This had been awarded to him for service as a bomber pilot in the German Condor Legion which had taken part in the Spanish Civil War.

Gerhard had sat on his wheel all morning watching the launch searching for him and at one time, 10.13 hours, had fired off his last distress flare. This was the smoke seen by the launch crew at that time. *As he had lost his distress flare pistol Gerhard had held the flare in his bare hand, and fired it by pointing his automatic revolver and firing at the percussion point at the base of the cartridge. Needless to say a somewhat risky and despairing operation.* The launch after effecting the rescue returned to base at 18.02 hours.

The Swordfish aircraft finally returned to Malta some days later, and the pilot had a most extraordinary tale to tell. After flying over the launch at midday during the search, his radio and engine began to give trouble. He was unable to contact the launch, so made for the nearest land, which was the Italian-occupied island of Lampedusa. The Swordfish touched down successfully on the enemy landing strip during a massive American bombing raid and the crew dived into the nearest shelter. The Italians . . . had had enough of war, and surrendered the island and garrison to the Swordfish crew. The Italians repaired the plane, and eventually the Swordfish flew to North Africa bearing a written surrender document. Some difficulty was experienced by the crew in persuading the Allied military that their story was in fact true, but eventually they were believed and the Allies occupied the island.

This is thought to be the only occasion when an island has surrendered to an aircraft. . . .

L. G. Head, Stokenchurch, Buckinghamshire, 1985

When every morning brought a noble chance
And every chance brought out a noble knight
Alfred, Lord Tennyson (1809–1892)

Tenuous Contact

The cooperation between the sea and air forces in the years of the Mediterranean war was always close and usually (for the Allies) effective. It needed to be. In waters closely surveyed by the Axis powers' land-based aircraft, the one was normally heavily dependent upon the other for survival.

David Souter (Lieut-Commander D. C. Souter) who, forty-odd years later was to become high sheriff of Tyne & Wear, saw much of it at first hand as an officer in Motor Torpedo Boats. There was an unmistakable identity of spirit – twinkle, if you like – between the crews who manned the MTBs and the aircraft.

In Alexandria, we used to liaise with the RAF to see what, respectively, we looked like from the air and from the sea.

I was standing one day behind the pilot of a Beaufighter making a dummy machine-gun attack down a line of 3 MTBs in line ahead. The leading boat was soon in the pilot's sight, and although it took sharp avoiding action, the pilot easily and disappointingly, by a flick of his wings, quickly had the boat again in his sight. I reckon she would have been a goner unless the aircraft had been shot down first.

But as we disengaged, the aircraft gave a high-powered thump which caused me to hit my nose on the top of the pilot's armour-plated seat. I asked him what that was. 'Oh,' he said, 'I think it would just be the tail wheel touching the sea!'

And then again. . . .

During an eastwest Malta convoy, three MTBs were towed by merchant ships in order to sink the Italian fleet when it appeared two days later, after which we would enter Malta harbour fully covered by the Royal Air Force, with VCs on our breasts.

In the event, the weather was too bad and our tows were released. One boat, commanded by Bobby Allan, later Lord Allan, was damaged and was slowly filling with water. He disappeared in the darkness, but, later, having seen a Verey light away to starboard, I steered my boat towards it.

On arrival only Allan's forecastle was above water. We launched our rubber dinghy and pulled his crew over. They were all in the water hanging on. I asked them why the hell they didn't get in. 'We're looking after our cases of whisky and gin,' they said.

In fact, we were lucky because the ship towing my boat, MV *Bhutan*, was subsequently sunk by enemy aircraft. As we had great difficulty in disposing of the wire tow, and had to cut it under the water with a hacksaw (my No. 1 did that), we might well have been dragged under or kept stationary as a wreck-marking MTB. . . .

Finally. . . .

Early in 1943 there was an MTB, commanded by Lieutenant Ross Campbell, Royal Canadian Navy Volunteer Reserve, which was making an overnight passage alone from about Derna [in Libya] to Malta. Campbell had been warned that the island was often shrouded in mist in the early morning. . . .

As his ETA approached, there was no sign of the island – nor until much later, when they proceeded down the swept approach channel, waving as they went to the crew of a small vessel, flying the red, white and green flag.

The coxswain, a regular rating, told Campbell that Valletta had changed a bit since last he was there, which prompted Campbell to wonder whether he was approaching the right place. . . . It turned out to be Italian-held Pantelleria and, although it was broad daylight, he was able to withdraw.

On his way back he ran out of petrol, so three MTBs were sent out with petrol in 4-gallon drums to resuscitate him, together with the Royal Air Force's available air cover.

On arrival, he was sent for by Vice-Admiral, Malta, one Sir Arthur

Power, and given the biggest dressing down of the war. At the end the Admiral asked him if he had any idea what his folly had cost in terms of air and sea effort. 'No, sir,' Campbell replied, 'but whatever it is, just dock it off my pay.'

After the war, Campbell represented Canada as her ambassador, I think, in Rome. . . .

D. C. Souter, Newcastle-upon-Tyne, Northumberland, 1984

Under the Stars and Stripes

Ford Porter (Major Ford D. Porter, Jr, USAF, Retd), from Chicago, had twenty-seven years' service with the USAAF and the USAF, having transferred in wartime from the Royal Canadian Air Force to the USAAF. After night-fighting in North Africa, he returned to the UK and the US 8th Air Force to fly C-47s in support of the Third US Army in the advance through northwest Europe and across the Rhine into Germany. Reconnaissance Mosquitoes also came within his remit.

In all Ford's service, there was one experience in North Africa in 1943 which remains fastened upon his mind.

I was flying with the 414th Squadron and had landed my Beaufighter at Tafaroui Air base, Oran, Algeria, after a night-fighter sortie. It was just after first light, and my radar observer and I decided on a quick trip into Oran. The sun was beginning to rise, and, as we rounded a bend, I had suddenly to stop the weapon-carrier which we were driving. I was hit hard emotionally – really shaken.

There, right ahead of us in the clear early morning light, was a war cemetery and in it were hundreds of crosses, row upon row of them, under the protection of the American flag. I recalled the lines I had read, repeated and memorized in my youth:

> In Flanders fields the poppies blow
> Between the crosses, row on row*

Now I was confronted with the reality of the couplet. As a Yankee combat pilot, I had seen the resting place of my fellow Americans. I shall never forget that scene and the impact which, by sudden chance, it made on me. . . .

Major Ford D. Porter, Jr, USAF (Retd), East Hagbourne,
Didcot, Oxfordshire, 1984

Acquitted?

Early in 1943, 255 and 600 Squadrons – night-fighter Beaufighters – shared the same airfield in North Africa. The commanding officer of 600 Squadron was Wing Commander 'Paddy' Green (Wing Commander C. P. Green). His reputation among the members of 255 was that of an extremely tough,

*John Macrae (1872–1918).

187

'no-nonsense', dedicated pilot and commanding officer – a man who did not suffer fools gladly and regarded almost any mistake as sheer and unforgiveable incompetence.

One of the 255 Squadron pilots was Flying Officer Bob Sprag, a burly, red-haired South African with a robust 'couldn't care less' approach to all things in life. It would be difficult to find two characters more different than those of Bob Sprag and the commanding officer of 600 Squadron!

One night Bob Sprag was vectored onto an unidentified aircraft – not showing the 'IFF'* identification. His navigator got an AI† contact, and brought Bob up behind the aircraft which Bob identified as a Ju 88. He was well aware – as were all Beaufighter pilots – that it was very easy from certain angles in the dark to confuse a Ju 88 with a Beaufighter. But he decided this was a Ju 88 and opened fire. The Ju 88 reacted incredibly quickly and skilfully and got out of his fire.

Bob had difficulty in keeping in contact and was then surprised, as he followed the aircraft, to see it fire the Verey light 'colours of the day'. However, a quick check by Bob's navigator showed that these were *not* the correct colours of the day. The combination of IFF and firing false colours confirmed in Bob's mind that this was not only a skilful Ju 88 pilot but a cunning one as well! He managed to close near enough to get in another quick burst, and saw strikes on the Ju 88. But as the Ju 88 swung across him with evasive action he was horrified to realize that it was, quite unmistakedly, another Beaufighter!

He returned to base and bluntly told the intelligence officer that he had had a go at some fool in a 'Beau' who hadn't shown the IFF *and* had fired the wrong colours of the day. He was at once told that he had tried – unsuccessfully – to shoot down the commanding officer of 600 Squadron who had already landed, unhurt, in his damaged Beaufighter in a none-too-pleased state of mind.

In due course an enquiry was held at Headquarters. It was decided that Bob Sprag was by no means entirely to blame, having been misled by the lack of IFF and the wrong 'colours of the day'.

A good ending to the tale might have been for Bob and Paddy to have been seen having a drink together that evening. In fact, the conclusion was a very short reaction by Paddy Green. As they left the enquiry he turned to Bob Sprag and without a trace of ill-feeling – but with his normal dedication to perfection – said, 'Sprag, you're a bloody bad pilot. You should be ashamed that I'm still alive to talk to you. From where you came up behind me you should have destroyed my 'Beau' with your first shot! The wrong identification is forgiveable: bad shooting isn't!'

The Hon. Mr Justice Drake, Harpenden, Hertfordshire, 1984

The Judge adds another (and probably unique) example of 255 Squadron's Tunisian chances.

One of our crews, a Norwegian pair called Bjorn and Bugge, had an early success in shooting down a Cant Z 1007 (bis)‡, and there were the usual

---

*Identification Friend or Foe.
†Airborne radar for detecting enemy aircraft. (Ed.)
‡Italian floatplane. (Ed.)

celebrations in the mess the next night. Because they were Norwegian, the press thought it a good story and wrote a small piece about them. A few days later, they were astounded (and dismayed) to be posted back to England as a result of a minor diplomatic row. It transpired that Norway had never declared war on Italy (only on Germany)!

Encounter in St Firmin

Close and valued friendships were being formed among the diverse nationalities which made up the Allied air forces, and particularly between the British and their comrades from subjugated Europe. The daily facing of mortal danger provided common and unifying ground.

Richard Gayner, a member of the Auxiliary Air Force, with a successful run of operations to show – France and the Battle of Britain, then night-fighting in England and North Africa – can point to a fortuitous meeting which demonstrated how durable these wartime relationships proved to be.

I was posted to 153 Squadron, Beaufighters, at Reghaia, Algeria, in 1943. We were part of 336 Wing which also contained a torpedo 'Beau' squadron, a flight of high-altitude Spitfires and two French fighter squadrons equipped with the beautiful, but deadly, Airocobra (P-39). An understandable distaste for Service rations led the French squadrons to keep a large flock of sheep in the care of several Moroccan shepherds.

Among the operations staff was André Letellier who became a firm friend until I was posted to Malta in 1944.* I did not think of André again until 1954, when I was driving with my family to the South of France. Some fifty miles southeast of Grenoble, on the N85, lunchtime was fast coming up and I spotted a minor road sign pointing towards the Alps and to St Firmin.

We stopped in the village, and were lucky enough to find a table in the crowded hotel dining room. During lunch, I became uneasily aware of a man, a good many tables away, who seemed to be staring at me. . . . Hard to imagine why anyone should do so, seeing that I had but one friend among fifty million Frenchmen.

In the end I walked over. It was André, of course, who told me that whenever he drove south from Dunkirk, where he lived, to join his Marseillaise wife on holiday, he always stopped at St Firmin, his favourite village in the whole of France. . . .

Only two or three years later, one of those ghastly black-bordered envelopes arrived, postmarked Dunkirk. . . . André Letellier, of course.

Will any reader calculate the odds against our meeting in St Firmin?

Richard Gayner, Henley, Oxfordshire, 1984

*To command Royal Air Force Station, Luqa. (Ed.)

Plymouth Ho!

The first half of 1943 was a time of great importance for la belle France. Admiral Darlan had been assassinated on the previous Christmas Eve. General Giraud was in command of the Free French in North Africa, and, in London, General de Gaulle was generally recognized as the leader of the Free French in Europe. It was known that the two generals did not entirely see eye to eye, and, for that reason, General de Gaulle went only twice to Algiers in early 1943; once immediately after he had flown out to the Casablanca conference in January, and again shortly after the final defeat of the Afrika Korps in May.

RAF, Lyneham in Wiltshire was the recognized point of departure for VIP passengers, and so to Lyneham he came on both occasions. On one of these – and at this distance in time I cannot be certain which – I was the flying control officer on duty for his flight. The weather report over the Bay of Biscay was reasonable, but a cold front was sweeping across southwest England, bringing rain, 100 per cent low cloud, strong winds and poor visibility. It was with some relief that I watched the General's Liberator disappear safely into the evening gloom, en route for Portreath in north Cornwall where it was due to cross the coast.

Meteorology was not an exact science in 1943. (To digress, I remember once arriving on duty at the control tower in bright morning sunlight, only to find that the met. reports showed Lyneham to be shrouded in thick fog since dawn. Investigation disclosed that the decorators had been at work in the met. office, and had whitewashed over the window through which the observations were made.) On the occasion of General de Gaulle's departure, the forecast wind was from the northwest. In fact, by take-off time, it had veered to the north, inexorably pushing the Liberator off course southwards. It was not long before the Royal Observer Corps reported that it was heading straight for the Plymouth balloon barrage.

Consternation! Wireless silence was mandatory for outgoing aircraft because of the proximity of Occupied France. Nevertheless, we broadcast on every conceivable frequency instructions to the aircraft to turn northwards. There was no result. There was no time to haul down the balloons. The best we could do was to concentrate every available searchlight in and around Plymouth onto them, in the hope that, even through the cloud, they would be seen and avoided.

The aircraft flew straight on. It passed through the balloon barrage several thousand feet below the balloons themselves. For five agonizing minutes we waited to hear if it had struck a wire. At last – and it felt like five hours – the report came that the Liberator was through safely and heading out to sea.

Had it been otherwise, might we have seen General Giraud as the first post-war President of France?

His Honour Judge Brian Galpin, Sunningdale, Berkshire, 1984

... And then the Jeep Stalled

Command in the Desert or Italy of 24 Squadron, the South African Air Force's light-bomber unit, carried a clear-cut responsibility. It was regarded as a standard-setter in an aggressively efficient Service, and it had the reputation of never having had an indifferent CO.... Cecil Margo was cast in the line of its distinguished incumbents.

Early in the afternoon of 25 March 1943 at Zuara, the squadron's advanced landing ground in the Western Desert, a B25 squadron of the US Army Air Force passed overhead at 500 feet. They were obviously returning from an army close-support mission. Significantly, there appeared to be two aircraft short. One of them, trailing fuel, opened its bomb doors and jettisoned a 1000-lb bomb. It fell among our Bostons, lined up near the runway threshold for that night's operations, but did not detonate.

One hour's delay fuse? Move! Trucks were manned and pilots and ground crews drove in mad haste to the aircraft, started up and taxied them to safety....

The area was cleared. The hour was up. Let's wait another hour. Still no bang. That damned bomb had to be moved or detonated to avoid interference with the night's operations. Captain 'Pop' Lewis, ex-Royal Flying Corps and now the squadron's armaments officer, took over. Picks and shovels were produced and furious digging exposed part of the bomb, lying at an angle fairly near the surface. Pop read hurriedly from some manual. 'Can't remove the fuse – it is probably the booby-trap type.' He cleaned the exposed steel casing, taped a slab of gun-cotton to it, and cut a short length of fusing, one end of which he pushed into the gun-cotton.

'Pop,' I ventured, 'surely that fuse is too short.' 'More than adequate,' he explained. 'It says here it burns very slowly.' He added, 'You keep the jeep running. I'll light the fuse, and we'll drive to the shelter of that old German half-track over there. There'll be plenty of time.'

I started the jeep. Pop disappeared into the hole as he bent to light the fuse. He emerged suddenly like an arrow from a bow. The message was clear – the fuse was too short. Cock-up number one. He flung himself into the jeep. We were three yards from the bomb. The jeep stalled. Cock-up number two. There was an eye-searing flash and enormous pressure on the eardrums. I thought I saw a huge fragment of shrapnel flying into the far distance, but my vision was too affected to be sure.

I turned to 'Pop' Lewis. He was still there, but the old German half-track, which was to have been our shelter, had vanished with the explosion.

The Hon. Mr Justice Cecil Margo, Lower Houghton,
Johannesburg, Republic of South Africa, 1985

Nearly Hammered

Ray Armstrong (Lieut-General R. F. Armstrong) is numbered among a select few who flew a tour of operations in the Western Desert and then, eight years later, another with the United Nations in Korea, commanding a squadron in each theatre.

It was against such a background of operational experience, together with a specialist knowledge of armaments and weaponry — and a spell at the Imperial Defence College in London — that the General rose to become Chief of Staff of the South African Defence Force. But he wouldn't have reached the summit had not luck intervened on his side during operations to break through the southern part of Tunisia on 26 March 1943.

Flying in close support of the 8th Army's advancing troops, he had briefed his pilots in 2 Squadron of the 7th (SAAF) Wing to pick enemy gun emplacements, slit trenches and other suitable targets, and attack in pairs. . . . Eventually, Ray had himself run out of ammunition in all save one of his Kittyhawk's six .5-calibre machine guns.

I attacked my last target with one gun firing . . . and as I did so a fairly large-calibre bullet came through the edge of my front windscreen and passed between my left arm and chest, and through the cushion behind my back, setting it alight. It continued on through the metal back of my seat and up against the armour plate behind. . . .

My left arm was bleeding profusely . . . and the cockpit was filled with smoke. I now swung my aircraft towards the advancing New Zealand troops, at the same time climbing in case I had to bale out. However, shortly after passing over the troops I saw, away to my left front, a large EPIP tent with a red cross on its roof. I turned towards it and was delighted to see, alongside it, a casualty evacuation airstrip on which I landed.

I climbed out of my aircraft, removed the burning cushion and was surprised to find that the strap of parachute harness, behind my left shoulder, had been burnt through. . . . The New Zealand medical personnel were most helpful and pretty impressed by my lucky let off. They dressed my superficial wounds, gave me an injection and a cup of tea, and invited me to stay the night. . . . I declined their kind offer as I was anxious to find out how my colleagues had fared.

I landed back at Hazbub . . . as the sun was setting, and was thankful to discover that my squadron had lost nobody although eight out of our eleven aircraft had been hit by ground fire. Several of my pilots had had close shaves. . . . Unfortunately, both Nos 4 and 5 Squadrons had suffered casualties. . . .

The Desert Air Force had, however, provided good support and, by the end of the next day, the 8th Army had won a resounding victory at the Battle of El Hamma. . . .

Lieut-General R. F. Armstrong, Glenwood Village,
Lynwood Glen, Pretoria, Republic of South Africa, 1984

A Farewell to North Africa*

North Africa skies are a paler blue than Canada's azure dome,
And there isn't the same full zest of life as in our own Canadian
home:
You can't go sailing on crystal lakes or tramp through fresh forests
green
And the soft, sweet sprinkle of April rain is something that's never
seen.
You suffer from heat in the scorching day and a raw, damp cold at
night,
While the glisten of snow on an evergreen bough would be a heart-
cheering sight.
You're pestered by insects and covered with dust and the towns have
the stench of the dead,
And there aren't any shady, grassy spots beside laughing brooks for
your head.
You've hated it all from the moment you came and wanted to leave
it behind,
For birds and the blossoms and meadows you've known and eyes
that were loving and kind.
Well, it's all over now, and the moment has come to bid this broad
country goodbye
Yet I cannot but wonder if some of us won't, in our hearts, find the
ghost of a sigh
For whenever you've lived in a place for awhile, despite all its
hardships and pain,
When the time to depart comes there's always regret that you never
will see it again.

Squadron Leader L. H. W. Metzler,
424 Squadron, Royal Canadian Air Force

Warren Metzler was killed in action in Europe in the summer of 1944.

Self-Sufficient

... The story ... concerns Air Vice-Marshal G. B. Beardsworth who, on finding he was responsible for administering a signals unit based in the Seychelles, decided to visit it. When there, he chanced to enquire the purpose of the unit; the NCO in charge explained that its sole duty was to give homing bearings to the flying-boat that brought them their rations.

(Rather like the armament factory, which I recall in 1940 produced just enough guns to defend itself against air attack.)

Air Chief Marshal Sir Theodore McEvoy, Rowledge,
Farnham, Surrey, 1984

*Reproduced by kind permission of the Wartime Pilots' and Observers' Association of Winnipeg, Manitoba who included it in their 4th Commonwealth Wartime Aircrew Reunion Souvenir Programme, 6–9 September 1984.

On Instruments in the 400

I had a shock one dismal afternoon [at North Weald] when a Beaufighter crept in to land while the airfield was closed due to severe bad weather. The intrepid pilot ... [was] ... Diana Barnato ... [of] ... the Air Transport Auxiliary. Looking very beautiful in her immaculate uniform, she ran a comb through her hair before climbing out ... to tell me she was short of fuel and had had a very rough flight through thunderstorms. ... I discovered later ... that her Beaufighter had no ... radio or navigational aids. ... They were an exceptional group of pilots in the ATA and Diana was one of the very best

Group Captain W. G. G. Duncan Smith (*Spitfire into Battle*, John Murray, London, 1981)

The girls of the Air Transport Auxiliary were, indeed, an engagingly courageous lot, delivering single-, twin- and four-engined aircraft to the squadrons, often in sub-standard weather. They had their casualties. An earlier experience of Diana Barnato's was as alarming – and as providentially fortunate – as any.

The ATA had decided that recruits, such as I, should not be taught to fly on instruments. ... And as we sometimes did several different deliveries in different types of aircraft in a day, it wouldn't have been practical to carry a radio and have to waste time tuning in and testing before each flight. ...

However, it was when the weather turned sour that things went wrong.
I had been taken out in London the night before by some 601 Squadron pilots. ... In the 400,* 'Little Max' (so-called by us to distinguish him from his famous father, Lord Beaverbrook)† and Billy Clyde had drawn a lot of diagrams on the tablecloth and lectured me on what to do if I ever got into cloud. ...

'Straighten the aircraft up, first,' said Max, 'and *think*. You usually go into cloud sideways.'

'Always watch your safety height,' said Billy, 'get back onto your original course, then turn slowly and gently – a steady Rate 1 turn – back onto your reciprocal heading, and retrace your steps. Leave your throttle setting where it was when you entered the cloud, and let down in as shallow a dive as possible. ...'

The instruction was as timely as it was salutary. Next day, Diana had to deliver a Spitfire IX BS148 from Hanworth to Cosford. It was one of those exceptional days when the dew point‡ had risen dramatically. With the variation in temperature, the whole of Central England was shrouded in cloud, much of it right down on the deck. After setting out 'in lovely sunshine', Diana flew straight into the muck as she headed northwest over the Cotswolds. The options were now few. ...

I couldn't bale out because I was wearing a skirt! The wartime black stockings were a bit short and left off just above my knees; my wartime panties (made out of silk from old parachutes) didn't come down to meet

---

*Exclusive nightclub in Leicester Square.
†Squadron Leader (then) The Hon. Max Aitken, CO of 601 in the Battle of Britain.
‡Moisture content in the air.

the stockings, so there was a large gap of *me* in between. . . . And, anyway, the 'chute straps chafed the insides of my legs. . . .

But I had, I knew, passed Little Rissington on the way up. That was 750 feet above sea level and was, presumably, still in sunshine. . . . I would turn on my gyro compass as Max and Billy had said and try to put down there. I would give myself a break-off height of 800 feet – madness only having 50 feet to spare, but I knew no better then. . . .

The altimeter began to fall alarmingly to 600 feet. At that moment I broke cloud at tree-top level. The trees flashed by with the cloud just resting on the tops, and the rain pelting down. . . .

Then, momentarily, I caught a glimpse of an aircraft on a small stretch of grass. Little Rissington, I thought, and turned tightly, keeping the little grass bolt-hole in view. It looked more like a pond than a landing ground as the rain cascaded down. . . .

I landed, splosh! And at once I wondered whether the Spitfire would go up on its nose. But I skidded through the puddles and eventually came safely to rest. A tall RAF man came out of a Nissen hut with a camouflaged rain cape held aloft over his head. As he came up to the aircraft, I got out onto the wing – and my knees collapsed. . . .

'I say, Miss, you must be good on instruments.' I didn't want to disillusion him, nor did I want to ask where I was and give the game away that I had been lost. Just then I saw a large notice board. 'RAF Station, Windrush. Navigation and Blind-Flying Establishment. Altitude 560 feet.' My knees began to give way again. . . .

I was glad of the mug of steaming tea which the RAF man brought me. . . .

Diana Barnato Walker, Horne Grange, Horne, Surrey, 1984

Innocent WAAF

. . . My wife served in the WAAF as a clerk (SD) on radar, and was stationed at one time in a large country house at Sopley in Hampshire. One day, for reasons which matter not, she had to cycle to the nearby RAF aerodrome at Hurn. The weather was appalling. The rain was really heavy, and, head down and wearing one of those cumbersome gas capes, she pedalled through the storm.

Suddenly, she became aware of a jeep overtaking her with an illuminated sign on the back 'Follow me'. She did so and eventually, when the jeep stopped, she dismounted and was marched up to the control tower. There, with water dripping onto the floor from her cape, and her hair soaking wet, she was torn off a monumental strip by the duty officer.

She had been cycling along the main runway. . . .

His Honour Judge C. Raymond Dean, QC, Boston Spa,
Lincolnshire, 1984

Scuppered

The squadron leader chief flying instructor (name, address and wartime base supplied) thought he had the perfect answer to counter *under*confident student pilots. . . . The Tiger Moth had a control column in the instructor's cockpit which could be removed when the aircraft was flown solo.

To show his confidence in the pupil, the squadron leader's trick was to remove his stick and throw it over the side leaving the ball firmly in the student pilot's court. The practice was well known to pupils, so one bright lad took a spare stick with him. When the CFI's stick was thrown over the side, it was at once joined by the pupil's spare one. It was with difficulty that the instructor restrained himself from following them down.

On landing, the squadron leader's fingers were found to have been lacerated by thrusting them into the empty socket left by his stick.

H. Robert Harriss, Eaglescliffe, Stockton,
Cleveland, 1984

Saved – by the Spin of a Coin

By this stage of the war, the accident-prone characters had mostly made their mark. The marvel was how some of them kept coming back for more. They were like corks; nothing would keep them down. Jack Meakin (Wing Commander H. J. W. Meakin) took more punishment than most, and yet he was going as strongly at the end as at the start. . . .

Fairey Battles and then Blenheims in 2 Group (he went from pilot officer to squadron leader in a month in 82 Squadron), then Venturas and low-level Beaufighters in 1943 and, finally, in 1944, wing commander flying of 138 Wing's Mosquitoes, in 2nd TAF*. . . . It was a relentless progression, interrupted, momentarily, when, on baling out of a Blenheim, (hit by our own flak), he lost most of the fingers of his right hand to a propeller. The deficiency was quickly rectified by means of a specially manufactured steel hook, secured to the wrist by a leather strap.

Mark it, Jack had started early.

At fourteen, I purchased for £12 a Humber motor cycle. On my very first day, I was stopped for carrying my brother, Peter,† on the back without a regulation pillion seat. I was fined £10 and disqualified for a year!

A providential deliverance came early in May 1943, at Methwold in Norfolk. He had just been posted to command No. 464 (Australian) Squadron equipped with 'dreadful Ventura aircraft'. . . .

I had only been on the station a few days when, on 3 May, orders came through from Command to bomb a powerstation on the northwest outskirts of Amsterdam. I tossed a coin with Len Trent, the leader that day of 487, the New Zealand Squadron, as to which of the two squadrons should go. He won, and ten of his eleven aircraft were shot down, mainly

*2nd Tactical Air Force.
†Peter Meakin, killed while a cadet at Cranwell, low-flying a Siskin. (Ed.)

by fighters*.... Len survived as a POW, and was awarded the Victoria Cross....

Wing Commander H. J. W. Meakin, Chisipite, Harare,
Zimbabwe, 1984

The Mentors

The majority of the outstanding squadron commanders and wing leaders, who rose to the top in the second half of World War II, found a mentor on the way up. Nine times out of ten, the accomplished exponents of the bombing, fighting, reconnaissance, strike or ground-attack art could all point to some exceptional character and say: 'See him? He was my man – I learnt it all from him. He was the one who taught me all I ever knew.' The association was usually as fortuitous as it was fortunate.

1. BROADHURST

Take Karel (Charles) Mrazek (Group Captain K. Mrazek), the Czech, who led his country's wing in Fighter Command with a balance and an ability given to few. Harry Broadhurst (Air Chief Marshal Sir Harry Broadhurst), the incomparable 'Broady', who dominated the commands he was given, became his idol when 313, Charles's squadron, was posted to Hornchurch.

He was about thirty-six years old, which meant he was about five years older than I.... His welcome to the station was friendly but not excessively 'matey'. He did not know much about us; we were the first Allied squadron to come under his command. It was not clear whether he was pleased or dismayed. He did not know what he could expect of us, and I, in turn, did not know what to expect of him.... Here we were, trying to assess one another....

He did not promise anything – only that we could expect hard work ahead of us; he said he expected military discipline from the whole squadron both on the ground and in the air. I assured him of that, and thus ended my, or rather my squadron's welcome to Hornchurch....

He flew with us on nearly all the sorties over France, always leading the wing. I even suspect that when we did not receive an operation order from Command or No. 11 Group, he planned a sortie himself in which the wing might get the chance to provoke the Germans into taking to the air....

What impressed me most was the way Broady led the wing. He always had it controlled. One day, when we were the top cover, we were just about due to turn back to Calais from St Omer, when Broady called me to draw my attention to 'Huns' above us, and pointed out that one of my own aircraft was straggling behind. I had already seen ME 109s above but, looking behind and to the right, I noticed my Blue 4 some way behind the rest. It was a new member of my squadron, Hlousek. I slowed the squadron down and called to him to catch up....

*In fact it was the result, largely, of a dreadful mess-up by the Operations staff at 11 Group, Fighter Command. (Ed.)

I admired Broady who, from down below at 10,000 feet, could always keep an eye on the whole formation as well as watching for the enemy. . . . And so he imparted to me one lesson after another and I became a diligent student, trying all the time to model myself on him. . . .

One evening in the local pub Broady said to me: 'You know Charlie, I feel quite safe down below when I have you "Butchers" above.' 'Butcher' was the call sign of 313 Squadron. That gave me a warmer feeling than the glass of whisky which had just been poured out. . . .

Group Captain Broadhurst was simply a great and natural commander, not only in the air but also on the ground. He had a friendly and humane approach to all his subordinates. However, when it was necessary, he could be very firm and uncompromising. In personal contact, he was sociable and approachable. In his presence, his airmen, even those of much lower rank, never felt inferior, or overlooked. He knew how to appreciate mastery of the air and in battle.

I salute you, dear Broady. You made my time at Hornchurch unforgettable and you gave me great experience. I enjoyed your company and admired your skilful leadership. It was my special luck that I was given the chance to serve under you. . . .

Group Captain Karel Mrazek, Jablonec, Czechoslovakia, 1985

2. GIBSON

John Searby's (Air Commodore J. Searby) leadership of the historic Peenemunde raid* on the night of 17/18 August 1943, in which he acted as the Pathfinders' Master Bomber, remaining over the target for some forty-five minutes until the last attacking aircraft had turned for home, makes one of the epic tales of World War II. He has told it himself (Peenemunde: Great Raids No. 1, The Nutshell Press, Chippenham) with a clarity which lays bare the precision with which the onslaught was planned.

Here, in a personal reflection, he remembers the luck which brought him, at one man's summary diktat, under Guy Gibson's (Wing Commander Guy Gibson, VC) wing in the critical – and impressionable – early phase of his operational run with Bomber Command. He had just completed an enforced spell on the exacting South and North Atlantic Ferry. In terms of airmanship and navigation, Searby was, by then, already widely experienced.

I first met Guy Gibson in the autumn of 1942 – on posting as a flight commander to No. 106 (B) Squadron, stationed at Syerston. The brief interview with my squadron commander was not of the happiest. He had lost three good crews on the previous night over Cologne, was short of sleep, and a bit on edge.

In reply to his question about my past history, I said I had recently come off the Atlantic Ferry, following which I had done a few Wellington sorties but nothing of any consequence. He heard me out, obviously not interested,

---

*The German top secret V1 and V2 experimental rocket base on the Baltic coast. The attack was a major setback for the development programme in which the Germans were the pioneers. (Ed.)

and impatient for me to finish. He walked over to the window with his back to me, hands thrust deeply into the patch pockets of his service dress jacket (a habit he had) and then spat out: 'Atlantic Ferry! . . . you can forget all that. *This is the real thing.*'

I said nothing, and, for good measure, he threw in this one . . . 'And anyone who doesn't like it can get out.' I began to dislike him; but I saw the letters to next-of-kin lying on his desk awaiting signature and made allowance for his mood. Later, I learned that writing these letters was always his first priority. Even though he had been flying himself on the previous night, he went early to his office and discharged this painful duty.

As I went through the day, I asked myself more than once, just how I had contrived to get myself into this situation, but, of course, it was none of my own doing. A small man, wearing the rank badges of a wing commander, who sat in an office in Adastral House (part of the Air Ministry), had done it all. I only saw him once, and never again afterwards, and yet he had spun the wheel which had sent me to Syerston – the end of a twisting path which had begun in Montreal, wriggled down through the West Indies to Brazil, West Africa and back to the headquarters of the North Atlantic Ferry Organization in Canada. It was a tortuous route, not wholly enjoyable, and bearing its own hazards, though as nothing by comparison with what I was about to experience.

Gibson was truthful if somewhat blunt. We became good friends, and a few months later I succeeded him when he left to raise the Dams Squadron. . . .

. . . I owe much to his leadership and humanity. We can all learn, and I learned from him. Later, in the Pathfinder Force,* under Bennett, where the task was the more demanding, I still borrowed much from Guy. If one could only contrive to combine the technical skills with the leadership necessary to exploit them.

Now, in my dotage, I realize that . . . he was right when he cut me down to size, leaving no doubt as to what the future held. Bomber Command was a great leveller and nobody thought too much of himself. There were no 'aces'. The long and, at times, sordid struggle changed those who survived.

To quote one writer: 'In the beginning they stood poised, tensile, with a wide-eyed eagerness for their first take-off. At the end, it was all too clear they had suffered a loss-rate never before borne by a military force of comparable size in the history of the world.'†

Air Commodore J. Searby, Brandon, Suffolk 1984

'The Night I Died'

. . . I rapidly came to the factual conclusion that . . . I did not expect to survive a tour of thirty operational bombing sorties. . . . It was, perhaps, a rare flash of realism which I accepted then dismissed from my mind. . . . I

*John Searby commanded 83 (PFF) Squadron.
†*The Lost Command*, Alastair Revie.

can now only regard my survival as 'living on borrowed time' and an unexpected bonus.

'The Night I Died' is an example of coming to terms with the possibility of 'death, probably in one of its least pleasant forms'.

> The spiteful, vicious flak rose thick and fast
> Across the angry sky. The slow symmetry
> Of tracer shells accelerated past
> My turret. A kaleidoscopic geometry.
>
> The clouds, target tinged, reflected red and green.
> The merging colours spun madly round and round.
> A blood red arterial mist obscured this scene
> Of sickening vortex before we hit the ground.
>
>   . . . The night I died.

'The Night I Died' is taken from The Moon Shines Bright, *a collection of war poems, written by Sergeant Jim Brookbank between 1944 and 1946 while serving as a bomb-aimer with IX Squadron, Bomber Command. The proceeds from the sale of this work, which has been privately published, are devoted to the upkeep of IX Squadron's Memorial and Museum, which stands in Bardney village, some eight miles east of Lincoln, and to the Royal Air Force Benevolent Fund and the Leonard Cheshire Foundation.*

The Ice-Cream Man Obliges

Leadership of the wing at North Weald, 11 Group's station near Epping in Essex, was one of Fighter Command's coveted jobs. Kaj Birksted (Colonel K. Birksted), the Dane, was in command of it for much of 1943. By the end of his time, he had established himself as one of the outstanding all-round wing leaders of World War II.

The experience is still etched deep on his mind – and so, too, is an exchange which occurred after he had taken over from the New Zealander, Jamie Jameson (Air Commodore P. G. Jameson), another able fighter leader. Italy was then on the point of abandoning the struggle.

Jamie had fought with 46 Squadron in the snow, ice and thaw of northern Norway in 1940. Although not trained for carrier landings, the squadron had landed its Hurricanes on the flight deck of *Glorious without tailhooks* in the Norwegian sea when evacuation became necessary. Almost at once, the carrier was sunk by German surface ships. There were few survivors. By a stroke of luck, Jamie, who, with Cross* and five others, had drifted for three days and two nights in a life raft in heavy and frigid seas, was sighted and picked up by a British vessel.

Despite his ordeal, he persisted in his determination to be allowed to return to operational flying. In the end, he succeeded and by an extraordinary coincidence he became, some 2½ years after his awful experience in Norway, the leader of the Norwegian wing at North Weald.

---

*Squadron Leader K.B.B. 'Bing' Cross (Air Chief Marshal Sir Kenneth Cross).

The squadrons were a magnificent lot — groundcrews as well as pilots — indomitable, cheerful and dedicated to the liberation, at any cost, of their beloved and beautiful country from the German occupiers. Many had escaped from Norway in unbelievably imaginative and daring fashion. They were second to none as testified by an official Fighter Command document listing them among the six top-scoring squadrons in the Command in 1943. Indeed, one *was* the top scorer — and this with minimal losses, a point of particular importance when replacement pilots were scarce. . . .

When Birksted, who had commanded 331 Squadron, followed Pat Jameson, he retained the New Zealander's call sign, Mahjong — 'a Maori term for a chieftain'. He had a high regard for the North Weald ground controllers and his relationship with them was close and friendly, as it was with their operational staff. . . .

One day, early in September, during a massive air operation over France, the easily recognizable voice of the North Weald controller was heard over the RT. 'Mahjong leader! The Ice-Cream Man is no longer making ice cream. Out.'

The whole wing then knew that Italy had capitulated to the Allies.

Colonel K. Birksted, Hampstead, London, 1984

Strangers in the Night

With all the sophisticated radar equipment which the Allies could now employ, night-intruding by our fighters was becoming an important factor in support of Bomber Command's offensive. It made the Luftwaffe crews, bent on stalking our bombers, feel very uneasy.

No crew had more experience of the role — or stuck at it longer (they were night-fighting together either defensively or offensively for four years) — than the 'old firm' of White and Allen (Air Commodore H. E. White and Flight Lieutenant M. S. Allen) of 141 Squadron. They were a brilliantly irreverent pair, collecting between them a remarkable six DFCs — three apiece — a most unusual tally.

The Peenemunde attack on 17/18 August 1943 (see 'The Mentors: 2. Gibson', on page 198) provided Harry White and Mike Allen with a thoroughly interesting 'mix'.

Four lines of yellow tracer streaked over our canopy, and almost simultaneously we heard the rattle of cannons. There was a shout from the navigator: 'Some bastard's firing at us.'

'I know,' I said. I had already pushed everything — stick, rudder, throttles — into the 'bottom right-hand corner'. As night-intruders, 141 Squadron's remit that night was for one flight to escort the Lancasters out as far as the limited range of our Beaufighters would allow. Our other flight was, later, to meet the returning bombers as deep into Germany as possible and escort them home. Our targets were the enemy night-fighters which ranged along the bombers' route.

Mike Allen and I were approaching Hamburg at about 16,000 feet on a clear but very dark night. Mike had picked up a contact on his radar.

Normally we would know from the type of contact whether it was hostile or not. This time we did not. I suppose, looking back, that was why I was less alert than I should have been. I presumed it would be 'one of ours'.

Using our radar we closed rapidly from two to three miles, and had to lose height to put our target slightly above so I could identify it visually against the rather lighter sky. Going 'downhill' we had built up a fair overtaking speed. . . . At 500 feet I realized this shape was a Messerschmitt 110, a twin-engined German night-fighter.

I swore. I was closing too fast to open fire. I eased back the throttles. I dare not snap them shut. If I did there would be sheets of flame from our exhaust. We would be seen. To help lose speed I turned hard to port and then back to starboard. It was at that precise instant that we became the target. The ME 110 must have seen this Beaufighter slip out from underneath him and then, slowing down, turn to port and starboard in front of him. A gift. . . .

If it hadn't been for that momentary glimpse of four lines of tracer streaking past, I would not have had that split-second lead which I needed to get the hell out of it. If he hadn't used tracer – and only some German night-fighters did – he would have had time to correct his aim before I knew I was being attacked. He would then, perhaps, have written this story – not me.

Chastened, breathing deeply, but having evaded, we climbed back to our operating height. Neither Mike nor I was in a mood to let matters rest.

Twenty minutes later, using our radar, we were closing slowly on a known enemy aircraft. Even at full throttle it took an age. Our opponent was obviously on his way towards our returning stream of bombers. Mike read off the range: '1500 feet . . . 1200 feet . . . 1000 feet'. . . . It looked like another ME 110 . . . '900 feet'. . . . It *was* an ME 110. . . . 'Still 900 feet'. . . . And again, 'Still 900 feet.'

Even at full throttle we couldn't close the range further. I took aim. Nine hundred feet is not ideal on a dark night. I opened fire with our four cannons and six machine guns. There were strikes, like fireworks; flecks of flame; flashes; the Messerschmitt dived steeply. . . . It might have been destroyed, but we couldn't be sure.

We climbed to our operating height again, and reset course to meet our returning bombers. On we went eastwards. Shortly, there was another enemy radar contact.

'It's a Junkers 88, Mike.'

My navigator grunted and looked up from his radar. 'Fix him properly,' he said. 'Don't bugger about this time.'

Slowly I closed to 700 feet. I took careful aim and gave him everything. . . . The fire flashed through the fuselage and engulfed the port engine. The Ju 88 was well alight. . . . It spiralled down shedding pieces of burning aircraft. Minutes later, it blew up as it hit the ground. . . .

With fuel now critical, we set course for base. . . . We had made a hash of one attack, and had only survived to make two successful attacks that same night because our attacker had – by chance – been armed with visible tracer ammunition. . . . For Mike and I that tracer had been the difference between life and death. . . .

Forty years later, Martin Middlebrook, researching his book on the

Peenemunde raid, found and interviewed a pilot of a Messerschmitt 110 who had been attacked and shot down at the precise time and place of our second encounter on 17/18 August 1943. He had been burned and had baled out. . . .

And so the real score that night was 1 Beaufighter frightened; 1 Messerschmitt 110 and 1 Junkers 88 both destroyed. One up; two down.

Air Commodore H. E. White, Hartlip, Sittingbourne, Kent, 1984

'Smudge'

'Smudge' was a rather Special 102 Squadron dog, based at Pocklington in Yorkshire. His owner was H. L. Mackay (Flight Lieutenant H. L. Mackay), an Australian air gunner, with an extensive operational record with 2, 3 and 4 Groups of Bomber Command. The animal was 'very much a "Heinz" job with a mixture of sheepdog in him'. He had been given to Mac by a Suffolk farmer named Smith (hence 'Smudge'), who farmed land near Stradishall. 'The dog had the distinction of flying with us on an operation. Nobody knew he was on board until we were over the North Sea. He was the only undecorated member of the crew which was captained by "Millie" Millson (Wing Commander A. E. Millson).'

Smudge, bless him, was 'about eighteen months old' when, on 3 November 1943, this strange incident occurred.

When I got back to my room, the dog was ecstatically happy and excited,

'Smudge', the dog

jumping up and down, wagging his tail and barking. I had not known him behave like that before.... When I finally turned in, he refused to get off the bed.

Some hours later, when Johnnie, my batman, brought me my cup of tea, I asked him if he knew why Smudge had been so excited when I returned from ops.

'It was very peculiar, sir,' Johnnie replied. 'I brought him his grub as usual last evening just on eight o'clock, and he started to wade into it straightaway. Suddenly, he stopped, growled and started to prowl round the room. He went on growling and barking. Then he lay down with his paws on his head, and started moaning as if he was in pain.

'I couldn't make it out so I thought I had better stay with him. I sat down and had one of your cigarettes, sir. After about half an hour, he suddenly jumped up, barked, wagged his tail and went back and cleaned up his plate. Queer, sir, wasn't it? I wonder what it was....'

'Johnnie,' I said, 'strange things do indeed happen.' I then recounted to him the events of the previous night's ops.

At eight o'clock, when we were over Dusseldorf, three incendiary bombs were dropped on our Halifax from an aircraft above us. We thought it was a Stirling.... One of them passed right through from starboard to port without doing any damage. The other two became jammed in the bomb doors....

By the time we had been able to get things sorted out and the flames had been got under control, we were pretty sure we would make it back to base. By then it was just about 8.30. It was a dicey affair.... We were very lucky to get away with it....

H. L. Mackay, Roleystone, Western Australia, 1984

Editor's note: *Tragedy followed. Two weeks after this incident with the dog, Mackay was asked by the BBC to broadcast about it. While Mac was in London, Smudge went missing from Pocklington. He was never found despite nationwide publicity. Letters of sympathy poured in for the owner. There was one from a German, Frau Koeppler, 'written in fine old German script. Her dog had been killed that night in Dusseldorf.' The letter reached Mackay in 1946 in Kenya.*

'Not My Destiny to Be Killed...'

David Shannon (Squadron Leader D. J. Shannon)* survived two continuous and critical bombing years, first, with 106 Squadron and thereafter with 617. He emerged, at the end, as one of the air war's elite. Looking back at these years – and at the subsequent times when he was flying the trunk routes with Transport Command – he realizes now that it was obviously 'not my destiny to be killed in an aeroplane'.

Chance took a hand early on when our course, flying Whitleys at OTU, at Kinloss, proved to be the first from which crews were sent to squadrons

*See 'One of the Vertebrae', page 40. (Ed.)

in 5 Group which were re-equipping with Lancasters. On my first night solo in a Whitley, doing circuits and bumps, I had an engine cut at about 200 feet, just after take-off. I did a great wide right-hand circuit and got back on the runway. The comment of my flying instructor, back in the crew room, was forthright: 'We never expected to see you back in here; coffins don't fly so well on one engine!'

From Kinloss, I was posted to No. 106 Squadron where W/Cdr Guy Gibson had recently been appointed to command. After conversion onto Lancasters, we were ready for the slaughter. I was lucky to join a squadron with such high morale, and to find a Canadian navigator, Danny Walker, who stayed with me for over two years. However, it was here that I soon learned that friendships had a habit of being quickly lost by non-returns from operations. Empty seats around the table in the mess told their stories.

Having stretched my first tour to thirty-six operations I was told I was to have a rest as an instructor at an OTU. This did not suit my ideas of war. I had seen too many good chaps returning to operations from such a posting, only to go missing on the first or second trip of the second tour. I therefore volunteered for Pathfinders, and was accepted by No. 83 Squadron in No. 8 Group. I hadn't been at Wyton for more than forty-eight hours when I received a telephone call from Guy Gibson, asking if I would like to join him again as he was forming a special squadron. If so, he would send an aircraft to pick me up the next day. I accepted with alacrity. Fate again.

No. 617 Squadron and the Dams raid have become part of history, but not a day goes by without my giving thanks that I am one of the survivors of the original squadron. After having been called off my run on the Möhne (the Dam wall had collapsed just before the release point of my bomb), we then went on to a successful attack on the Eder Dam. We lost nearly half the squadron that night so who is to say fate wasn't with me?

Later, there was a night when we were taking off to attack the Saumur Tunnel with a 12,000-lb deep-penetration bomb slung in the bomb bay. Two engines cut just at the critical point before lift off, and we went slewing across the airfield. I thank God for the Lancaster undercarriage which stood the strain. We came to rest with my bomb-aimer peering over the earth wall surrounding the bomb dump. His remark, 'That was a close one, Skipper – thank God we weren't fused,' remains a masterpiece. Len Sumpter always was and still is a stalwart chap.

The Dortmund-Ems canal was another raid where chance took a hand. In mid-September 1943 a small force of eight aircraft from our squadron was briefed to try and breach the canal at a point where, if the raid was successful, this very important German waterway would be drained. It was another of Barnes Wallis's excellent ideas.

On the first night, we had just got beyond the Wash and over the North Sea when we were recalled. The met. aircraft had reported fog over the target area. Turning onto our reciprocal course to return home, David Maltby, the leader of my formation in which I was flying No. 2, dipped a wing into the sea and crashed with a tremendous explosion. We circled the spot for some three hours until rescue vessels arrived on the scene, but all to no avail. David was to have been best man at my wedding on 21 September.

The next night we tried again; eight aircraft took off, no met. reports were received, so we proceeded on our way. But met. had boobed, as the fog was forming very fast as we approached the target area. The light flak was severe, and at low level in the fog I had one near-miss collision, scraping some trees while getting low enough to let one of our aircraft shoot above me. We had seen three aircraft shot down, but all we got was an odd glimpse of the canal, insufficient to line up a bombing run.

After about an hour of circling there was a slight shift in the fog – enough to let us make a hurried run and then bomb. Unfortunately, the 12,000-pounder dropped on the wrong bank of the canal and only caused slight damage. Only two of the eight aircraft which took off returned from the raid, and one of them had returned early after being unable to find the target. We lost many of our invited wedding guests that night. . . . Ann and I missed a lot of close and dear friends at our wedding reception.

In retrospect, one can see now how one's wartime service blends into a whole. All survivors know they are lucky. I certainly was, but again let us thank our stars for the outcome. Defeat was too awful to contemplate. It was this thought, and the spirit which was there, that kept one going. . . .

Squadron Leader David J. Shannon, Dulwich, London, 1984

The Challenging Atlantic Run

People think nothing nowadays of flying from Europe to the United States or from Kennedy to Heathrow; they take it in their stride – except, perhaps, the jetlag and the boredom of it. Forty years and more ago, the Atlantic Ferry, flown at comparatively low altitudes, and often on two piston engines, was a very different matter. It could be a hazardous affair.

John Searby (see 'The Mentors: 2. Gibson, page 198) knew all about it. Two brief reflections, the first, on the southern crossing, and the second, on the north, are sufficient to expose the dangers.

. . . Next day, in Miami, Florida, we were rounded up by a civilian and taken to the US Army Air Corps base to join a motley crowd of American civilian pilots. . . . It was a fantastic situation; our colleagues had been recruited from crop-dusting, barn-storming, bush-whacking soldiers of fortune, with the odd ex-airline pilot among them. With the exception of the airline men, none had flown out of sight of land, and our mission was one of getting a number of transport aircraft from Miami to Lagos, in West Africa. These aircraft [Lockheed Lodestars and Douglas Dakotas] had been loaned to Britain, and their role was to be in support of the 8th Army fighting in North Africa. The only problem was that of delivering them over a route, never previously flown, taking in some dubious airfields in South America.

There were no radio aids; maps were available as far as Belem in the mouth of the Amazon, and although we were told the navy at Trinidad would provide Atlantic Charts, these were not forthcoming and I had recourse to squared paper and the meridianal parts taken from Inman's tables. Bubble sextants were borrowed from a variety of sources, including Pan American Airways and the University of Miami. As to weather forecasting . . . well, there wasn't any after leaving Trinidad, but a five-year chart of the prevailing winds over the South Atlantic proved valuable. The Intertropical Front, stationary all the year round, hung over the Guianas and was reckoned worthy of note, producing monsoon-like conditions. . . .

Not all were happy with the prospect, and during the next few days some left. Those who stayed were tough, self-reliant individuals who didn't baulk at the uncertainties, including the possible hand-refuelling of aircraft from 50-gallon drums, weather, rough gravel landing strips, bugs and the long haul over seventeen hundred miles of ocean. . . .

The aircraft were good, but the idea of navigating by the stars had them puzzled. Great interest was shown in our handling of the bubble sextants and the relevant mathematical tables. Some saw it as a kind of wizardry, and the co-pilot of my own aircraft never ceased to be astonished at the ease with which I picked up a nice little three-star fix over the ocean. In clear weather the stars shone with great brilliance on the Atlantic crossing and at Natal, in Southern Brazil, I was treated to the never-to-be-forgotten spectacle of the Southern Cross. . . .

On take-off from Natal the aircraft proved sluggish and very tail-heavy; the gravel strip ran close to a hangar and, for a moment, I had my doubts about making it. Slowly it climbed into the darkening sky, and settled down at eight thousand feet over the sea.

After an hour or so . . . I got a whiff of petrol, and looked back to see Hank, our co-pilot, in the act of pouring petrol from a 4-gallon drum into the big cabin tank which had been specially fitted to increase endurance. To my horror I observed a cigar in his mouth – which, fortunately, was not alight; he had a habit always of chewing one, but it gave me a jolt. Grinning hugely, he carried on topping up the tank . . . and the mystery of our being tail-heavy at take-off was solved. Hank had deemed it necessary to ensure against running out of fuel, and had packed the tiny toilet compartment in the tail with 4-gallon drums, keeping this matter secret. . . .

I qualified in Montreal to fly Hudsons from Gander in Newfoundland, to Prestwick in Ayrshire, on the North Atlantic run – a very different cup of tea from the smooth southern crossings. This was late September and the weather was the enemy, battling through strong fronts with icing conditions, flying the Great Circle with a strip of plywood on my lap holding the relevant portion of the North Atlantic Chart, and taking my sights through the Perspex windscreen. The only radio aid to navigation was the solitary Barra Head beacon, and the wireless operator took our bearings whenever he could pick it up – which was very seldom The true aids lay overhead – the stars and the planets – all, by now, old friends on whom one could safely rely. . . .

One feels very much alone in the middle of all that sea by night. The autumn and winter are the bad times – or used to be before the jet age – and one gets a feel for weather. The seat of one's pants can be of the greatest use sometimes. . . .

I have seen the approach of the great 'fronts', the steady build-up of the forces of nature massing ahead of me, and faced the old, old question familiar to the long-distance flyer: do I go down or do I battle through – I can't climb any higher? I take out the electric torch, stuck into the top of my flying boot, and examine the leading edges of the wings to see the first layers of rime ice forming and growing steadily. . . . A decision must be made. . . .

This is old stuff – laughable in these days; but the satisfaction and sense of achievement when one broke cloud to see the flat Ayrshire coastline, with that beautiful long runway at Prestwick, after twelve-and-a-half hours without leaving one's seat, and the gas tanks knocking on empty, left no more to be said. . . .

Air Commodore J. Searby, Brandon, Suffolk, 1985

Dropping on Thick Ice

Alexander Bowie, himself an experienced navigator with 231 Squadron on the Atlantic Ferry, has added this story to the chances of these operations. It is taken from Per Ardua Ad Astra: A Story of the Atlantic Air Ferry, *by Air Commodore Griffith Powell, a privately circulated work, 'produced during Air Vice-Marshal George Beamish's* time in charge of 45 Group of Transport Command'. Alex Bowie 'can personally vouch for' this incredible mid-winter escape.*

It occurred at Dorval, Montreal, involved one of the ferry's senior pilots, and was claimed by the author to be 'probably unique in aviation history'.

A Boston aircraft was on test with Captain J. S. Gerow as pilot, and Mr H. Griffiths as technical assistant, when part of the cockpit flooring became dislodged. Mr Griffiths fell through to the extent of hanging at arm's length below the aircraft.

This occurred at 4000 feet in bitter winter weather, and Captain Gerow quickly realized that the only chance of helping Griffiths was to fly very low over frozen Lake St Louis with the hope that a glancing landing blow, even at high speed, might save his assistant's life.

He therefore circled the aircraft as low over the lake as possible without hitting the propellors. . . . When Griffiths was unable to hang on any longer, he let go and miraculously survived to the extent that he was able to walk ashore. . . .

Alexander Bowie, Edinburgh, Scotland, 1984

Luck Sat in a Chair

Superstition and luck – the two elements were so often mixed in an airman's sensitive mind. Frantisek Fajtl, the successful Czechoslovak author, who, in wartime, enjoyed the distinction of being the first of his countrymen to command a British squadron – No. 122 (Spitfires) at Hornchurch – demonstrates the point by personal experience.

. . . I was in a hurry to get to my favourite chair for the briefing. However, 'my' chair had already been taken by a member of 64 Squadron. I was too

---

*Air Marshal Sir George Beamish.

embarrassed to tell the occupant that 'my' chair was my lucky charm. I sat elsewhere and felt uneasy. As the intelligence officer unveiled the target map, I heard a voice behind me: 'Hell, it's Lille again. . . .'

Halfway across the Channel I remembered 'my' chair and what its 'loss' meant, but I drove away my apprehension by convincing myself that the operation would go well; as the CO of 122, I concentrated on leading my squadron.

As the Bostons, which we were covering, bombed and turned for home, we were attacked by German fighters. In the melee, my aircraft was hit; I had to dive away to escape my pursuers. When I levelled off right down on the deck, my Spitfire was on fire and smoke was filling the cockpit. Then the motor quit and I had no alternative but to land straight ahead.

Fate smiled. . . . There was a flat field right in front, and I landed the aircraft in it, wheels up. The moisture in the ground quelled the fire underneath. I ran quickly away, fortunately electing to head south. Soon I came across an old woman working in a field with a teenage boy. 'Are there Germans about here?' I asked. 'Over there,' she replied, pointing to a large building in the direction from whence I had come.

I moved fast. Our intelligence officers had always advised us to get as far away as possible from a crashed aircraft, and never to enter the nearest inhabited place. I ran on as far as I could and then lay down in a ditch to rest. 'Find something better than this,' my brain dictated.

Avoiding another village, and scouring the terrain, I came upon a stream. I sank down into the water on my back. Only my nose protruded through the surface so I wouldn't suffocate. . . . This dodge probably saved my life, as the inevitable search party, with sniffer dogs, lost my trail. . . .

Frantisek Fajtl, Praha, Czechoslovakia, 1984

Editor's note: Helped first, by a Pole and then by a French lawyer, as well as by the underground, Frankie Fajtl made it to the south and over the Pyrenees into Spain. There, with three other British comrades, he was arrested and slapped into 'three flea-infested prisons and then a concentration camp called Miranda de Ebro. . . .' Three months or so after being shot down, he was back in England. He arrived on his thirtieth birthday and was soon back flying again.

Return to Go

The fatalists who contend that 'it's all in the Book' and there's little we can do to change it, could well cite the case of Michael Beetham (Marshal of the Royal Air Force Sir Michael Beetham), the last Chief of the Air Staff to have flown operationally in World War II. If that, indeed, is their contention then surely they will concede that, on the night of Wednesday, 29 December 1943, the fates were having to work overtime to keep the future marshal in business.

. . . 50 Squadron, Skellingthorpe, just outside Lincoln and in the heart of 5 Group country. 'Ops' are on tonight and briefing is at 14.00 hours.

Fifteen crews from the squadron, so more than a hundred of us crowd into the Nissen-hutted briefing room.

The squadron commander pulls back the curtain over the map and reveals the target – Berlin. We swallow a little. For me and my crew it is only our seventh trip, and this will be our fourth to the 'Big City'; the Battle of Berlin is clearly on. Seven hundred Lancasters and Halifaxes from the Command will attack in five waves, all phased through the target in twenty minutes to saturate the defences. Mosquitoes will carry out diversionary attacks on Magdeburg and Leipzig. We are to feint towards Leipzig, and then turn north to Berlin at the last minute.

The met. man tells us there will be heavy cloud over most of Germany, widespread fog and poor visibility. Hopefully this will restrict their fighters. Our bases are forecast to be fine for return. That is a relief, for on our last trip to Berlin we returned to fog-bound bases, and only got down in Yorkshire with difficulty.

Out to aircraft dispersal at 16.00 hours for a final check of everything. We have our brand-new Lancaster VN/B with the latest paddle-bladed propellers, air-tested this morning and this is our first trip in it.

Take-off at 17.00 hours. All fifteen aircraft taxi out in turn, and there is a good crowd as usual beside the runway controller's caravan to see us off. . . .

Three-and-a-quarter hours to the target. We climb to cross the Dutch coast at 19,000 feet, and then gradually get to maximum height around 20/21,000 feet. Our route is north of the Ruhr, and then southeast past Osnabruck and Hanover towards Leipzig. . . . A sharp turn north twenty miles short of Leipzig with the diversionary aircraft heading straight on – hopefully the fighter controllers will be deceived.

The final run up north to Berlin. We are in the third wave. Much more activity now with searchlights trying to penetrate the cloud and pick up the bombers ahead of us. Plenty of flak as we approach the target, but not really close. No sign of fighters. Some turbulence from the slipstream of other bombers – always a bit disconcerting.

Wanganui marker flares ahead going down on time. We will be bombing blind. The markers are well concentrated, and a good glow of fires started by the aircraft attacking ahead of us shows through the cloud. . . .

Straight and level now with two minutes to go and bomb doors open. Bomb-aimer calls 'bombs gone' on the middle of the markers. We feel the 4000-lb 'cookie' go, and then the canisters of incendiaries – always a relief to have them away and the bomb doors closed again. We fly right across Berlin and out well to the north before turning for home. Navigator says 4 hours to go. . . . A long haul to the Dutch coast; we eventually cross, but don't relax – you can get caught by fighters over the North Sea. The weather clears and we get safely down at Skellingthorpe at half past midnight.

At de-briefing we report a quiet and uneventful trip – for Berlin. Just one aircraft lost on our squadron – not bad for such a tough target and looks like it has been a good attack. And so to our bacon and eggs and bed at 02.00 hours.

Next morning I report to the flight at 10.00 hrs to see whether 'ops' are on that night.

Flight Commander says 'So you had a quiet trip last night?' 'Yes,' I reply. 'Fairly uneventful.' 'Come with me,' he says. We drive out to the flight dispersal and to my aircraft. . . . Two of my groundcrew are on the top of the starboard wing. *I am staggered to see a large hole through the starboard wing outer fuel tank – a clear gash through it.* 'What have you done to our new aircraft?' asks my corporal airframe fitter. 'We are going to have to change the wing.' We have collected an incendiary from another Lancaster above us over the target – the outline is clearly visible through the wing. 'Didn't you really feel anything over the target?' queries the flight commander. 'No,' I say. 'Some usual turbulence from the slipstream of other aircraft, and some flak, but not close enough to worry.'

I thank my lucky stars *we always use the outer wing fuel first so the tank would have been empty and purged with nitrogen* (editor's italics) well before the target – and I wonder how close had been the rest of the bomb load.

Marshal of the Royal Air Force Sir Michael Beetham,
South Creake, Fakenham, Norfolk, 1984

'I Have a Dream . . .'

Those who believe there were outward and visible signs of divine intervention in the air war could well cite two experiences of Nick Knilans (Major Hubert C. Knilans) of the United States Army Air Force, a peacetime dairy farmer from Delevan, Wisconsin, who had travelled up to Canada before Pearl Harbor to join the RCAF.

The first occurred on 23 September 1943, when Knilans was captaining a Lancaster of 619 Squadron,* based at Woodhall Spa, during an operation to Mannheim. The target was attacked from 20,000 feet at 21.50 hours and take-off had been at twilight. The vision was seen on the outward flight.

The upper sky before me was still somewhat lighted. A figure of a woman, several thousand feet above slowly emerged into my startled view. I recognized this vision as that of a girl I had loved very much. She had died six years before at the age of nineteen. I had kissed her goodbye one evening, and a short while later her father had telephoned me to say she was dead from pneumonia, unsuspected until it was too late. I had been one of the pall bearers. . . .

Now, she had a slight smile on her lips as I flew towards her. . . . The vision soon vanished into the darkening sky. I said nothing to the crew then or later. I did not know whether she had appeared to reassure me that she would keep me from harm, or that she was welcoming me into her world of the hereafter. I certainly hoped it wouldn't be the latter. . . . Maybe, I thought, someone was trying to point, for me, a way. . . .

---

*Nick Knilans eventually joined 617, Leonard Cheshire's squadron, also based at Woodhall Spa, on 14 January 1944. He had transferred from the RCAF to the USAAF, but continued to fly with the Royal Air Force. (Ed.)

It was two months later, on 26/27 November, that the next intervention became manifest. Nick's Lancaster was one of sixteen aircraft which the squadron had put up that night for an onslaught on Berlin. Heavily attacked on the outward flight, first, by a Ju 88 (which was shot down) and, then, by a Me 110, the Lancaster lost an engine some 250 miles short of the target and suffered damage to the tail assembly. Many captains would, at that point – and justifiably, have jettisoned the 4000-lb 'cookie' and the 3000-lb of incendiaries, and pushed off home.

Knilans, on the other hand, pressed on on three engines, losing height down to 13,000 feet, bombing from that level and getting a good photograph in the process. This was the seventeenth of the fifty-three missions he was ultimately to fly, and it earned him (unusually) the immediate award of the DSO.

It was on the run-in to the target that Nick experienced the sensation which was later to change the course of his life.

. . . As we approached Berlin out of the darkness, the streets and the buildings began to take shape. From our height, with the flares above us and hundreds of searchlights below, the scene became increasingly clear. It was a vivid and dramatic moment. Blockbusters, looking like 50-gallon oil drums, were tumbling down past us from the bombers above. Amid all the buffeting and noise of the light and heavy ack-ack, my 18-year-old flight engineer, Ken Ryall (Sergeant Ken Ryall), spoke up. 'Should we pray, Skipper?'

'No,' I replied, 'not while we are about to kill more old men, women and children down there.'

But then I was overtaken by a thought, by a dream, if you like, that if I survived this trip and the rest of the war, I would try to do some type of public service – to try, as it were, to balance my personal books. . . . Good deeds and actions versus destruction. . . .

After the war, I changed my career from farming to teaching, and this is the work I have followed for the community for the past quarter of a century until my retirement. I guess that experience on the approach to Berlin told me where my destiny lay. . . .

Hubert C. 'Nick' Knilans, New Auburn, Wisconsin, USA, 1984

'Night Bombers'

Eastward they climb
Black shapes against the grey
Of falling dusk,
Gone with the nodding day
From English fields.
Not theirs the sudden glow
  of triumph
That their fighter brothers know,
Only to fly through cloud,
Through storm, through night.
Unerring, and to keep

Their purpose bright,
Nor turn until
Their dreadful duty done,
Westward they climb
To race the awakened sun.

Anonymous

This verse is taken from *Verse from the Turret: An Air Gunners' Anthology*, edited and compiled by Squadron Leader W. R. Rainford, ex–38 Squadron, who has kindly given permission for its reproduction. Proceeds from this collection of poems go to the Royal Air Force Bomber Command Museum at Hendon.

The CO's Name on the Bullet

Why should a leader's aircraft stop a volley of cannon shells that had really been intended for his inexperienced No. 2? Jack te Kloot (Squadron Leader J. te Kloot), the Australian sheep farmer from Queensland, who took over 249 Squadron at Grottaglie during the Italian campaign, and made such a success of leading it through much of the Balkans fighting, could well pose the question.

As a new and junior pilot in 229 Squadron, flying No. 2 to his CO, he witnessed, at first hand, a classic example of the point. It happened just before the Sicilian landings in July 1943. The B-25 (Mitchell) bombers for which 229, with their Spitfire IXs, were flying high cover, had just dropped their bombs on the airfield at Biscari, near Gela, in southeast Sicily, and were turning for home.

As we came out of the turn, someone reported over the R/T 'Bandits at six o'clock, above.' Our CO, Squadron Leader White, gave the order 'Break left 180 degrees.' I followed him round, keeping station behind him.

The next thing I knew, his aircraft had exploded right in front of me. We had been jumped by a second wave of FW 190s which also appeared to come from above and behind. Their leader, with his excess speed, had overshot me in the dive and his cannon shells had pumped into the CO's Spitfire instead of mine. . . .

A glance to the right, and there was another 190 beside me; it was only a wing's span away. I can still see the German pilot's face, his white helmet and oxygen mask. . . . I looked in my rear mirror and there was another 190 on my tail, closing from above. . . . With the throttle jammed through the gate, I turned as tight as I could into the German who seemed to drop below. Just then three cannon shells from the other 190 penetrated my wing; fortunately, they were outboard of the ammunition trays and did not explode. . . .

With my engine roaring and the airframe shuddering, I held my Spitfire in a tight spiral. Suddenly, I realized the trees were only just below me. There was now no other aircraft in sight. I had no idea where I was except that the mountains of Sicily were very close, and I had a course home to

Malta written on my sleeve. I felt I had been engaged for a long time and must be running short of fuel. I didn't understand, in my inexperience, that the combat had only lasted a few minutes. It had seemed like an age. . . .

I pressed the fuel indicator button and saw the needle registering half full. I thought it must be sticking. In my panic, I banged it with my knuckle and destroyed both the glass and the needle! Now I had no idea what fuel was left, nor could I remember our take-off time and thus how long I had been airborne. . . . Just then I looked up and saw an aircraft coming straight towards me. It was one of 185 Squadron's Spitfires. Both a bit shaken, we joined up and flew back to base together.

The CO was later reported killed. His fate was that, by pure chance, his aircraft had taken the shells that must have been intended for mine. . . .

Why should it have been him when, really, by all the rules, it ought to have been me? It was my extraordinary luck to escape that 'bounce' by the 190s and then live to see the war out. It was his unlikely misfortune to perish. Beyond this, the fates had been kind to me. By wriggling out of my desperate predicament when I was so 'green' and, therefore, so vulnerable I had been allowed to learn, in those few minutes, many of the lessons which were to serve me so well in the future. . . .

Squadron Leader J. te Kloot, Longreach,
Queensland, Australia, 1984

Yugoslav Sequel

There is a memorable sequel to add to te Kloot's story. When the Queensland farmer took over command of 249 at Grottaglie, in the heel of Italy, his close friend and fellow-Australian, 'Shortie' Beatson (Flight Lieutenant John Beatson), a dairy farmer in Victoria until his death in October 1984, was just completing a fine operational run with the squadron and about to go off on a rest. Flight commander of 'A' Flight, he had been involved, on 16 December 1943, four months after te Kloot's fracas over Sicily, in a 'bombing and straffing mission' across the Adriatic to Yugoslavia. During it, his No. 2, Flight Sergeant Docherty, was hit by ground fire and seen to force land – successfully – some miles inland from the Albanian coast. He was observed to destroy his aircraft.

Beatson, who fortunately recorded this note of the incident only a few weeks before he died, at once set about organizing a rescue operation for his No 2. The Royal Air Force Walrus, an amphibian used for Air/Sea Rescue, was unserviceable, so, instead, an Italian Cant seaplane, with a Regia Aeronautica crew (Italy had by now capitulated and its airmen were flying with the Allies) was dispatched with a Spitfire escort from 249. 'Shortie' was leading the fighters.

The operation was unsuccessful because the Italians weren't keen on flying too close to the enemy-held coast. They kept shying off to the north. I flew in front of them, waggled my wings, fired a burst across their nose and almost yelled at the pilot through his window, but he wouldn't go in to the shore. I got so furious I thought quite seriously of shooting the Cant down into the water. . . .

After sending one of our Spits back with the seaplane, my No. 2 and I flew on to try to find Docherty. We spotted him, nicely holed up in some scrubby land; he was waving. . . .

Just then, two ME 109s appeared. I turned into them and was promptly shot down by a third. . . . The times I had said to new pilots who came to my flight, 'If you see two 109s always look for a third.' I had forgotten the advice!

I was lucky enough to be able to bale out, my parachute opening no higher than 300 feet. I came down in the water only a few hundred yards from the shore; after resting a while, I started swimming inland aiming to try to meet up with 'Doc'. . . . Then I saw three Spits overhead, and soon a Walrus landed to pick me up.

As it taxied up to me one of the crew, Flight Sergeant Pickles, grabbed me and started to haul me up the side. Just then a German machine-gun post opened up from the shore. A bullet passed smartly between me and my rescuer, hitting him in the fleshy part of his upper arm. It was the arm that was holding me, and he never let go! I can still see the look on Pickles' face as we came under fire!

Hearing all the excitement over the R/T, the wing commander flying at Grottaglie, 'Timber' Woods (Wing Commander E. N. Woods), and the CO of 126 Squadron, 'Bowie' Debenham (Squadron Leader K. B. L. Debenham) got into a couple of aircraft, slipped across the sea to Yugoslavia, and under cover of the hills laid off behind the German fighter base waiting for enemy aircraft to land. . . . It was an old trick we used to play. We never saw either of them again.

The tally wasn't in our favour – Docherty was a POW (probably) and we'd lost his aircraft; my aeroplane had gone, and 'Timber' and 'Deb' hadn't returned. . . .

Next day, we went over again with the Walrus on the off chance that we might find 'Doc'. The 'Wally' landed and started taxiing towards the shore, but it got stuck on a sandbank; and there was 'Doc', who had seen us, waiting on the shore, waving. He didn't seem to have his mae west, and he had never learnt to swim. There was nothing to be done. It was all the Walrus could do to free itself – and take off. Poor 'Doc' had to be left on the shore. . . . It was a hard ending.

There was, however, one consolation. As we turned for home with the Walrus, four Me 109s dived down on us from about 8000 feet. But they hadn't seen 126's [Spitfire] IXs above them. It was quite a dogfight. All four of the 109s were shot down.

John Beatson, Agnes Via Toora, Victoria, Australia, 1984

Misfortunes come on wings and depart on foot
Proverb

Bucking the Trend

Andy Black (Flight Lieutenant Andrew M. Black) was an experienced and decorated wireless operator in a Halifax crew of 10 Squadron, Bomber Command based at Melbourne, in Yorkshire. A Scot, and a pre-war stock-

broker's clerk in Glasgow, he emigrated to Canada in 1947 and spent the next quarter of a century serving the Federal Government.

Two reflections from his operational days demonstrate as clearly as any examples could do the disparity which existed in the judgement of commanding officers. Some had exceptional perspicacity and under-standing, others should never have been appointed to their office in the first place. For a member of aircrew with problems, it was pure luck what quality of commander he might be dealing with.

Andy Black's pilot and captain was George Vinish, 'a tall gentle and quiet Canadian from a small town, Wakaw, Saskatchewan, whose parents were immigrants from Rumania. I admired him greatly.' It was on a trip to Hamburg that an embarrassing incident arose. Markers and searchlights ahead confirmed the proximity of the target.

Suddenly, the silence on the intercom was broken by our skipper. 'Guys,' he said, 'I have this weird feeling – something is urging me not to take us over the target tonight.'

There was a shocked silence, and then our senior crew member, Flying Officer Kitchen, the navigator, piped up, 'Nonsense, George, we've got a job to do. Let's get on and do it and get home.'

But George came back. 'I don't know, fellers, what it is. Call it a premon-ition, if you like. Whatever it is it feels pretty powerful. . . .'

With that, the aircraft began banking and turning to port, while the pilot asked for a course westwards for Flamborough Head. The bomb-aimer was instructed to jettison the bomb-load in the North Sea.

This was our fifth operational sortie, and we all knew the kind of reception we could expect back at base when the story was told. But nothing that any of us said swayed George from his determination to turn back. His mind was made up. . . .

When it all came out at the de-briefing, the crew was at once stood down and George was ordered to see the medical officer first thing in the morning. The upshot was that we were off for two weeks while the pilot was ordered a complete rest.

Eventually, we all went back on 'ops' together as a complete crew and finished our tour of thirty-one operations. George was a particularly successful and capable captain, bringing back some excellent photographs of the attacks. It must have required great courage to do what he did. His decision to abort couldn't have come easily.

I feel pretty certain now that whatever induced our pilot to turn back, in all probability saved our lives. . . . Where we were certainly lucky was in having in Squadron Leader A. D. Frank a fine and understanding flight commander in charge of 'A' Flight. Things could have been very different with someone else. . . .

Andy Black's other recollection is of a very different character. Berlin had been attacked, a good picture obtained and the crew's twenty-second operation was, thankfully, behind. The following day the squadron was stood down. In the evening, the bomb-aimer, Sergeant Bob Walker, took a trip into York where he attended a dinner party.

Halfway through the dinner, Bob looked at his watch and remarked that 'in about half an hour' Berliners would be startled by a loud explosion from one of our timed, delayed-action bombs. . . .

Unbeknown to Bob, an intelligence officer, who was also at the dinner, heard his remark and reported him to his CO for careless talk. As a result, Bob was relieved of his duties and put under arrest pending court-martial. . . .

Our crew went on and completed its tour, but Bob, who was severely reprimanded, had to join another. On their second mission they were shot down and posted as 'missing believed killed in action'.

Question? Had Bob Walker not been court-martialled, would he have survived? Or, again, if he was destined to die, would the rest of his original crew have perished with him? Who can say?*

Andrew M. Black, London, Ontario, Canada, 1984

Crashing for Luck

Nobby Blundell (Sergeant H. M. Blundell) is the historian of 463 and 467 (RAAF) squadrons. As he looks now at the record, he wonders whether it was his luck to have crashed in the middle of the war while he was visiting his old squadron, No. 456 (Beaufighters) at Valley in the Isle of Anglesey.

As a qualified motor mechanic as well as a wheat farmer in Weethalle, New South Wales, pre-war, it wasn't surprising that, on joining the air force, I should be trained as an engine fitter. It was as a Fitter II E that I travelled to England with 456.

But after a while, I decided to remuster for aircrew training as a flight engineer. It was while I was on the course at Warmwell in Dorset, that I went back to Valley to see the squadron. During the visit I was on a short trip as a passenger, and the aircraft in which I was flying crashed. I was in hospital for some weeks, and when I recovered I was declared unfit for operational duties. . . .

Nobby was eventually promoted to be a trusted, sergeant engine fitter of 'B' Flight of 463 Squadron at Waddington, and there he stayed from 1943 until the end of the war, interspersed with a trip to Russia in 1944 at the time of the attacks on the Tirpitz *in northern Norway.*

The three aircraft (Lancasters) that I was responsible for in the flight were lettered JO P, JO R and JO Z. *During the two years or so with the squadron, I lost from those three aeroplanes, fourteen Lancasters – an average of just over four replacements per aircraft. JO P was, in fact, replaced six times. In all, 101 aircrew were lost from those three aircraft in that time.* [Editor's italics.]

---

*No one can say. What we *can* declare is that it was a great pity the intelligence officer, who reported Bob Walker to his CO, wasn't thereafter asked to do a tour sitting in the rear turret of a Halifax. (Ed.)

I sometimes wonder whether I should be here today if I hadn't crashed that time at Valley. . . .

H. M. Blundell, Trinity Beach, Cairns,
Queensland, Australia, 1984

The Cult of the Reciprocal 5*

John Nedwich was the bomb-aimer (air bomber) of a Lancaster of 467 Squadron during the attack on Berlin on the night of 15/16 February 1944. It was his fifteenth operation. Later, he was to transfer to the Pathfinder Force.

We had dropped our bombs and were on our predetermined course leaving the target area.

A little while later, I saw, from the nose of the aircraft, that Polaris was on our port side when it should have been on the starboard side.

I broke intercom silence and pointed this out. The pilot then found that he had been flying 'red on black'.

Had I not spoken up at that time, I wouldn't be here now. . . .

J. W. Nedwich, Dover Heights, New South Wales,
Australia, 1984

They say there's a Lancaster leaving Berlin
Bound for old Blighty's shore
Heavily laden with terrified men
Bound for the land they adore

From the Bomber Command song

Navigational Differences

I. THE NIGHT OF THE GREAT WIND

The possession of a first-rate and punctilious navigator in a crew was an asset of incalculable value in the balance sheet. Doug Bancroft (Flying Officer B. D. Bancroft), who spent thirty post-war years in the printing industry in Adelaide, eventually founding his own business, had a jewel in his crew in 158 Squadron at Lissett, Yorkshire in 1944.

It was by sheer chance that I had personally selected Alwyn Fripp (Flight Sergeant A. Fripp) of the RAAF as my navigator at OTU at Abingdon. I was taken with his quiet, steady attitude, his dedication to accuracy and the constant cross-checking of his work. . . .

That the confidence was well placed showed up in the Berlin attack on the night of 24/25 March 1944, in which were the most unsettling circumstances of the Great Wind.

*See pages 47, 97, 99, 160 and 278.

218

The met. report at briefing advised good weather conditions all the way with little cloud, and winds expected to be only light and variable.

However, on reaching the enemy coast the navigator advised me that *we had drifted over fifty miles south of our flight-plan track, and that he had calculated a wind velocity of 100 m.p.h. from the north, and that ETA* on target would be 22.52 hours (some fifteen minutes late)*. [Editor's italics.] The wireless operator, Sergeant Leonard Dwan, was instructed immediately to advise group control of the wind velocity and direction, and the navigator to give me a new course directly to the northern side of the target area in an endeavour to recover some of the time. We arrived some ten minutes late, and I could see that the bomber stream was widely scattered no doubt because, as was revealed later, quite a large number of crews were adhering to the met. forecast winds. *I witnessed several unfortunate mid-air collisions, many of which would have been caused by aircraft which had gone wide of or to the south of the target area turning back directly into the main stream entering the target area from the north.* [Editor's italics.]

After the bombing, the potentially hazardous effects of the wind variation was seen again on the homeward run.

Adhering to Alwyn Fripp's wind velocity and directional calculations we were able to maintain the original flight-plan tracks back to base, although when north of Osnabruck we could see that many aircraft had again drifted well to the south, were caught in heavily defended areas and were being shot down by the defences. In all, seventy-two Bomber Command aircraft failed to return from the operation. . . .

B. D. Bancroft, Modbury, South Australia, 1984

2. ICELAND – WICK: SAVED BY A MINUTE!

There was the other side of the navigational coin.

Before the RAF established a base in Iceland, a small detachment of three Coastal Command Whitleys and crews was sent to Wick to carry out anti-U-boat patrols between the British Isles and Iceland. At that time this area was the major route for U-boats going from Germany to the Atlantic. Our main watch from the aircraft was by radar, and so we did not depend on good visibility.

We were returning to Wick from a patrol to Iceland flying at less than 1000 feet in cloud. It was possible to see the sea below us from time to time where the cloud thinned, but there was no visibility ahead. We should have made landfall on the eastern part of the north coast of Scotland, having passed about fifty miles north of Cape Wrath where the hills were 1000–2000 feet high. I was piloting at the time, having been given the course to fly by my navigator. I did not query it at the time, but as time went by I began to feel more and more uncomfortable. The sea was flat and there could not be much wind. The course seemed to me to be more southeasterly than I would have expected. What started as a niggling doubt became, after some twenty minutes or so, unbearable, and I said to my

*Estimated time of arrival. (Ed.)

219

navigator, 'Are you sure this is right?' There was a pause of a minute or so, and then he said, 'My God! I have forgotten the variation.' So we had been flying 14 degrees off course.* I immediately made a sharp turn to the north to enable him to work out our proper course.

In due course we landed at Wick and reported to the ops room. 'You must be the aircraft that turned just off Cape Wrath,' said the operations officer. It then transpired that we had turned when we were two to three miles from Cape Wrath. If we had maintained our original course for another minute we would have flown into the side of the mountain. Saved by a minute!

The Rt Hon. Lord Justice Waller, Kingsley Green,
Haslemere, Surrey, 1984

3. THIRTY SECONDS WAS THE SPUR

For Charles Barry (Captain C. H. H. Barry), senior flight commander of 60 (PR) Squadron, South African Air Force, and his navigator, Lieutenant G. R. Jeffreys, it boiled down to selecting a course and a prayer.

It was one of those days when your instinct told you it wasn't going to be healthy flying. Something in the air. Not enemy aircraft or flak. The weather at base. It looked unpromising. But met. assured us it wouldn't deteriorate. So my observer Geoff Jeffreys and I took off from San Severo (opposite the spur in Italy) in our Mk XVI Mosquito for a mapping job in the Po Valley.

The target weather was good, Geoff's guidance on the runs was excellent, as usual, and we turned for home an hour or so later, confident of a successful job. At 27,000 feet over the Adriatic, just east of Ancona, we entered thick cloud and began descending. I called up 'Commander', the superbly efficient area control unit near Termoli, and asked for a plotted return to base.

Geoff and I relaxed. All seemed well, as a check every five minutes revealed. We just stooged on in the murk, losing height as directed, flying the plotted course, warned that the cloud stretched down to ground level. Then the VHF went dead. . . .

I had levelled out at 500 feet above the sea, but we hadn't the foggiest – apt word, that – idea of exactly where we were. If we turned to starboard we would cross the coast and fly into the Apennines; if we stayed on our present course, we would fly into the spur of Italy.

'We'll have to take a chance,' said Geoff after we had examined all switches and channels to confirm the VHF was powerless. 'Turn on to 240 degrees and pray.' We did both. . . .

After about half a minute the cloud suddenly broke. About 500 feet below us was the choppy surface of the sea with the coastline coming up. On our port side, so close you could have touched it, was the Gargano

---

*Put simply, aircraft were navigated by reference to *magnetic* north, not true north, to compensate for the magnetic 'drag' from the North Pole. This required the addition of so many degrees to the course, dependent upon the latitude. In Sir George Waller's example, the navigator had forgotten to add on the small matter of 14 degrees – some oversight! (Ed.)

Peninsula, the spur of Italy. Another half-minute on our former course and we would have flown straight into it. . . .

C. H. H. Barry, Johannesburg,
Republic of South Africa, 1984

Passed for British

And so vanished . . . our able leader who, fired by the thought of Czechoslovakia in her agony, and backed by a glowing record of three years with the RAF, inspired our men. With his determination, ruthless efficiency . . . charm and utter disregard for [his] personal safety . . . he raised the squadron . . . in four months . . . from a rabble of bewildered frustration to the keen and efficient fighting force it is today. . . . We shall miss him . . .

Thus the Operational Record Book (RAF Form 540) of 198 Squadron, the low-attack, Typhoon unit, based at Manston in 11 Group of Fighter Command. The lament was for its CO, Jiři Maňák (Squadron Leader J. Maňák), another of the talented Czechs serving with the Royal Air Force, who joined his countryman, Frantisek Fajtl (see 'Luck Sat in a Chair, page 208), in the rare distinction of being a Czechoslovak commander of a British squadron.

Maňák was the only Czech in 198, the rest of the pilot strength being composed of two Australians, eight Canadians and some eight Englishmen – 'all young and eager to fight'. An unusually effective command of the English language was an attribute in his office – and, as we shall see, in captivity.

Maňák had been hit by groundfire during a 'train-busting' operation over Holland on 28 August 1943. Struggling back to the coast, the Sabre engine of his Typhoon then seized. 'I had no choice but to ditch straight ahead against the high waves.'

Miraculously, he survived.* 'The aircraft went right under, deep down into the sea. . . . I released the compressed air into my mae west and that shot me up to the surface. . . .'

Unfortunately, a 40 m.p.h. gale blew Jiři and his dinghy onto the Dutch island of Walcheren, and into captivity.

I was taken to Dulag, an interrogation camp for airmen near Frankfurt. I had to undress completely, and every crevice of my body was examined. Buttons which contained compasses were removed, but the compass I was holding in my hand was never discovered! Battledress linings revealed maps of France, Belgium and Holland. . . .

Next morning a German officer came in, and his first sentence was spoken in Czech which I pretended not to understand. . . . I gave my name as James, instead of Jiři, and I left the accents off my surname, Manak, thinking of 'Mick' Mannock of the First World War. That, with my rank, number and religion was all I gave. . . .

*The chances of ditching a Typhoon successfully were rated worse than with any other fighter aircraft. (Ed.)

Then one day in came a young German officer, who said he was a fighter pilot and had been shot down during the Battle of Britain; he had hurt his spine and could not fly any more. He kept coming in for several days, giving me cigarettes and trying to draw me in conversation, but I was cautious. On one occasion he even brought with him a young German airman, supposedly his nephew, who was said to be spending his leave at his home. His job had been to monitor our R/T frequency. . . . He said he recognized my voice, and even described some of our trips and radio conversations before I was shot down. . . . Then the Battle of Britain officer asserted that I must provide information about our Typhoons, otherwise they had orders to hand me over to the Gestapo. I countered by saying that, for me, it would be better to be handled by the Gestapo than be court-martialled after the war for revealing military secrets.

Then suddenly, there was a change. . . . He came in one morning with an interrogation form which contained my number, rank, name and religion. I signed it and was given a POW number for Stalag Luft 3 (No. 2378). I was thereupon released from interrogation. . . .

Much later, Maňák learnt the reason for this change of heart. There had been a cross-channel operation designed by the Allies to entice the Luftwaffe into battle. As a result, a number of new prisoners had arrived at Dulag. These were given priority for immediate interrogation.

My interrogator, showing the compassion of one fighter pilot for another, terminated my questioning in deference to more instantly pressing work. Thus, out of fifty-one Czech airmen who were prisoners, I was the only one who passed as British. In 1944 many of the others were handed over to the Gestapo in Prague, court-martialled as traitors of the Third Reich and sentenced to death. Only the early end of the war saved them.

All our families were in concentration camps. My father was sent to Buchenwald on the first day of the war. Early in 1942 he was again questioned about my escape from Czechoslovakia. In September of that year, he, my mother, my two brothers and my two sisters were all sent to the concentration camp at Svatobořice. Thus, my family spent, in aggregate, nearly twenty-one years in German concentration camps. . . .

It was our special luck that we were all able to meet again in the summer of 1945 in 'free' Czechoslovakia. . . .

Jiři Maňák, Praha, Czechoslovakia, 1984

My Affair with a Mosquito

Few aviators can have been in the flying business longer – or with more piloting involvement – that Karel Ranoszek (Wing Commander G. K. Ranoszek), one of the most versatile of Poland's airmen. He served four air forces in war. He gained his 'wings' in the Polish Air Force in 1931, and stayed with it until the blitzkreig *and tragedy of 1939. He picked up the reins again with the French Air Force, and, when France succumbed, he moved on to England and to the Royal Air Force – with no English word in his vocabulary and no possessions save the suit he was wearing.*

222

To complete the quadrilateral, he spent an operational period during the second half of the war seconded to the United States Army Air Force in Britain. Now, fifty-four years on from his first 'solo' in Poland, Karel still holds a pilot's licence, flying a Piper twin Comanche in South Africa 'because its behaviour is nearest to the Mosquito'.

There was an operation on 1 September 1944 (Ranoszek was then commanding 307, the Polish night-fighter squadron at Church Fenton), a night-intruder to the Luftwaffe's night-training establishment near Stettin on the Baltic, which tested sharply his apparently liberal supply of luck. Fate fired two barrels at him that night.

First, it was, exceptionally, a night 'when the Luftwaffe had stopped all flying to simplify identification procedures for the German ack-ack batteries. For them anything flying was hostile.' Thus, there were no targets for the Polskis.

Then, second, as they turned for home after a fruitless search, Ranoszek's navigator/radar operator was taken ill — 'really sick' — and was unable to take any further interest.

North of Kiel, we ran slap over a German flak ship which the navigator would normally have picked up on the AI (radar) screeen and I could easily have avoided. . . . I felt the Mark XII Mosquito being repeatedly hit amid the searchlight beams and coloured tracers. All hell had broken loose. . . .

But the Mosquito kept flying 'although in a somewhat wobbly fashion'. It was on the run into Coltishall, the forward base near the Norfolk coast, that damage became manifest.

As I lowered the flaps on the approach, the aircraft banked over to the left and nearly turned over onto its back. A quick retraction of the flaps saved us and I landed successfully without them at a very high speed. . . .

After taxiing in and switching off 'all was quiet except for some gentle hissing and gurgling in the pipes'. The sick navigator was given immediate attention, and then one of the groundcrew, shining a torch underneath the wing, shouted out: 'Jesus bloody Christ! Come and look at this, sir.'

The mess was unbelievable. A big shell had gone through the port wing, missing the main fuel tank by inches. The flap on that side only had a few ribs left. We finished counting the bulletholes in the aircraft at 300. But neither my navigator nor I had even a scratch — a clear case of 'more luck than brains'.

The aeroplane was a write-off, and another was sent to take us back to base. I doubt whether anything but a Mosquito could have stood up to that kind of punishment and still got us back. . . . That's why I love the Mosquito.

Wing Commander G. K. Ranoszek, Kensington,
Johannesburg, Republic of South Africa, 1984

Operation Pulpit

The Reverend Rodney J. Pope, vicar of the United Benefice of Great Saling and Little (Bardfield) Saling, at Braintree in Essex, was a sergeant bomb-aimer with XV Squadron (Lancasters), based at Mildenhall in Suffolk. He completed an operational tour in December 1944, was granted a commission and, in 1946, left the Service to take Holy Orders.

Two 'chances' during his time with the squadron – each very different in character from the other – add variety to this collection and weight to the vicar's contention that 'almost always what appear to be chance happenings at the time can, on retrospective reflection, be seen to fit into the general plan of life. . . .

The first was during his crew's original operation.

According to our navigator, we were muddled up with another crew, so our first sortie was a ten-hour night operation to Stettin (a bit much for new boys!). Worse was to follow; the compass system became U/S soon after take-off, and we had to rely entirely on the pilot's compass. . . . Somehow we neared our destination without too much difficulty. . . . Unfortunately, however, the navigator was not quite sure of our exact position, and due entirely to inexperience I decided that we were far too early, so it was agreed that we should do a dog-leg to lose a little time . . . only to find that the target was a great deal further away than I had imagined. So it was that we found ourselves over it about twenty minutes after everybody else had left for home!

The cloud base was low, and lowering, so we set course for home deciding that the best plan would be to keep under cloud cover: the next indication we had of our exact position was when we crossed the English coast. The cloud was low, and it was raining hard, but we rejoiced with exceeding great joy that we had successfully made landfall.

There was a story going round that our log was displayed in the navigation section under the caption, 'The crew which should not be here!' True or false, we certainly learned much that night which was to benefit us through the coming months.

As to the second 'chance', we might, perhaps, hazard the guess that the circumstances of Rodney Pope's first sermon, preached as he neared the end of his operational tour, were no less deranging than the reception he and his crew had received over Stettin, twenty minutes after the rest of the attacking force had left. 'Suitable' ordination candidates in the forces occasionally helped out in local parishes.

One Sunday evening, in October 1944, I was assisting the vicar of Mildenhall at St Peter's [West Row] when, suddenly, in the middle of the service, he came over to me and said, 'It is getting dark and I have no lights on the car – can you carry on and preach the sermon?!'

With that the incumbent departed, and the truth suddenly dawned – I was committed to preach a sermon for which I had no notes, was utterly unprepared, and in which art I had no experience or training at all.

In due time I arrived in the pulpit, the content of my address has long been forgotten both by me, and I am sure by anyone else who may have been there; but it could not have been too unsatisfactory as I was often asked to repeat the exercise at both St Peter's and St John's [Beck Row].

On reflection, I wonder what might have been the bishop's reaction to this extremely unorthodox behaviour. I suspect not very favourable, but, then, the war years produced many oddities and irregularities!

The Reverend Rodney J. Pope, Great Saling, Braintree, Essex, 1984

Editor's note: A remembrance service is held annually at Mildenhall for those members of XV, 149 and 622 squadrons who gave their lives while serving at this base. Rodney Pope arranges it, and each year a hymn is sung which he composed. 'They seem to like it so we use it . . . set to the tune of "O Valiant Hearts". . . .'

'Hymn Of Remembrance'

O God, our Father, hear our humble prayer
For those we loved who rest within thy care;
Give them the fullness of thy joy and peace,
Where life, and love, and praise shall never cease.

They gave their lives that others might be free—
Count what they gave as offered unto thee—
And, as at Calvary, Love saved through thy son,
So may they share the victory he has won.

When we remember them before thy throne,
Grant that our hearts with them may be as one;
Their prayers may aid us in this world of strife,
Still bound by friendship on the path of life.

Love, hope, and faith, and sacrament we share—
With them ourselves committing to thy care—
O bring us all to thy eternal light,
Out of the darkness of this mortal night.

May we no more be called to take the sword:
Teach us to trust the power of thy Word:
So that the victory, hardly fought and won,
May found the Kingdom of Our Lord, thy Son.

Rodney J. Pope, Air Bomber XV Squadron

The Rising Price of Berlin

By 1944 the cost of the onslaught on Berlin had become very high. Judge G. G. A. Whitehead (Flight Lieutenant G. G. A. Whitehead) and his Halifax crew from 76 Squadron, based at Holme upon Spalding Moor, fifteen miles southeast of York, had an unattractive sample of it on 21 January.

. . . As the bombs left the bomb bay there was an almighty crack as we were hit in the nose by flak. The bomb-aimer, Flying Officer Don Morris, was killed instantly and the wireless operator, Flight Sergeant Stokes, was badly wounded. There was a large hole in the port side of the nose, involving the navigator's compartment, and all his instruments, charts etc., were sucked out of it.

There was some damage in my department, the worst of which was to both compasses, which were completely inoperable. One engine failed, and the aircraft was difficult to control, but we turned westwards and I told the navigator that I would keep Polaris in the starboard cockpit window, and although that would involve flying over more enemy territory than was healthy, provided our luck held we might make the shorter sea crossing to UK. There was 10/10th cloud below, and Polaris was our only navigational aid.

We held on like this for ages, gradually losing height. Fuel was a problem. . . . Although we had plenty on board, the flight engineer reported that he was unable to use the starboard tanks because of damage to the fuel-cock mechanism. Both port engines began to overheat. I saw the clouds ahead were breaking, and I told the crew that if there was land below they should be prepared to 'get out and walk'. I instructed them to prepare Stokes, the wounded WOP, for a static-line parachute exit if I deemed it necessary to give the order.

We were at 3000 feet when we reached the break in the cloud, but it was not possible to identify anything on the ground. I adopted the 'I am lost' procedure by calling 'Hallo Darky' on the radio several times, but got no reply. . . . We were down to the last half pint of our useable fuel, so I gave the order to bale out. All the survivors got out and landed safely. My exit was 'hairy' because the aircraft had a mind of its own and wanted to do aerobatics as soon as I let go of the controls, but I made it and it passed me on the way down!

We had hoped that the land might have been Suffolk or Essex, but on the way down I realized there were no coal mines in these counties. I landed in the back garden of a miner's cottage in Lens, in northeastern France! It was only when I got back to UK some 3½ months later that I found out the reason. Our forecast wind was from 270 degrees; during the evening it had unexpectedly veered round to due north, thus forcing us south of our intended track.

Of the crew of eight (we had a second pilot), the bomb-aimer was killed, the second pilot, wireless operator, flight engineer and mid-upper gunner were captured and became POWs; the navigator and rear gunner were given shelter by a farmer in the Pas de Calais, and were liberated by the Canadian Second Army in June 1944. I began walking and arrived in Gibraltar on 2 May 1944. I was in the UK two days later. . . .

His Honour Judge G. G. A. Whitehead, Boston,
Lincolnshire, 1984

By Chauffeur to Prison

Some still cannot comprehend the chivalry which existed between the Luftwaffe's fighter pilots and leaders and their British and American counterparts. When the ruthless cut and thrust of battle was put behind, there was an identity of interest and spirit which transcended normal enmities. Like fishermen, fighter pilots quickly found common cause.

Wolf Falck (Oberst Wolfgang Falck) personified these relationships. A compelling and strongly independent character, his ability as a night-fighter leader was confirmed by the record. In peace, his perceptive intellect, courtesy and charm – and his humour – provided the base for represen-tation of the United States' McDonnell Douglas Aircraft Corporation in Germany. There is an experience which he tells at first hand that exposes these wartime truths.

It occurred when Wolf was based with his night-fighter wing at Deelen, near Arnhem, in Holland. He was flying his Me 110 back to the airfield one sunny day after a duty visit to Hamburg, when ground control reported a high-flying photographic-reconnaissance aircraft (assumed to be a Spitfire) heading back to England from the Hamburg area. He was invited to shoot it down.

Falck gave chase, but the advantage of height, position and speed lay with the opposition. In due course, the commander of Night Fighter Wing No. 1 returned to base. As he approached for landing, he was astonished to see a Spitfire, on its belly, at the far end of the runway. . . .

I met the British pilot, depressed and dejected, in our crewroom. I made him welcome and told him that I expected his was the aircraft I had been chasing from Hamburg. . . . How was it, I asked, that he had come to land at Deelen on a lovely, clear summer's day?

The squadron leader, a kind, medium-sized, extremely nice man, whose name I cannot, unfortunately, now remember, told me he had completed his mission and was heading, well-content, for home. . . . Gradually he had been overcome with drowsiness; he couldn't concentrate, had lost interest and had begun to feel utterly depressed. His true senses had deserted him.

Seeing an aerodrome right under him, he did what any pilot in such a state would try to do, he let down and landed. It wasn't until he had touched down, run along the runway and got some good air into his lungs that he began to recover. Then, to his dismay, he recognized the Me 110s and the German signs around the airfield. But it was too late to try to open up and take off. Instead, he lifted the undercarriage lever to prevent making us a present of an operational Spitfire. . . . But such was the quality of British workmanship that we had no difficulty in making the aircraft fully airworthy again. . . .

The explanation? It was quickly found there had been a leak in the Spitfire's oxygen supply. The squadron leader had been starved of oxygen at altitude, and had virtually passed out.* But now, Wolfgang Falck was determined

---

*'Altitude sickness' was well known to pilots. (Ed.)

to facilitate his passage into captivity. Rather than hand the British PRU*
pilot over to the 'authorities' (the correct procedure), he took a character-
istically unorthodox – and, for him, risky – course.

I instructed my technical officer to fly the squadron leader to Frankfurt in
my Me 110 and then take him to the prisoner-of-war camp at Oberursel.
My 'guest' was certainly baffled when I told him my plan. . . . So, later
that afternoon, armed with cigarettes and chocolate, and seen off by the
officers on my staff, he flew off, southeast, to Frankfurt in Me 110 'G9 +
GA'. . . .

A couple of hours later, the telephone rang in my office. The squadron
leader was on the line confirming his safe arrival at Oberursel after a
'marvellous flight' which, he said, had enhanced his admiration for the Me
110. He wanted to thank me for our attentions at Deelen, and for delivering
him from the more conventional forms of prisoner-of-war transport. . . .

Unfortunately, I have never heard from him again. I hope so much that
he is still alive. I would be so pleased if we could re-establish contact
in rather more propitious circumstances, and consolidate our friendship.
Perhaps he, or a friend, will read these lines. I would be so happy if we
could meet!†

Oberst Wolfgang Falck, St Ulrich, Tirol, Austria, 1985

Fortunate Flak

The German night-fighters, attacking British bombers, had problems. One
was their own flak. Ken Climie (Squadron Leader J. K. Climie), a New
Zealand structural engineer from Paraparaumu Beach until his retirement,
bore expert witness to it on 27 April 1944.

He was then on his second tour with No. 75 (NZ) Squadron and his
fiftieth operation – this time in a Lancaster Mk III to Friedrichshaven –
when fate stepped in during the routine run up to the target.

I followed the bomb-aimer's '. . . left left – left left – left left – steady –
right – steady – steady – steady – bombs gone'.

And then, someone said, 'Christ, Skipper, didn't you hear Morgan?' (He
was our rear gunner.)

During the bombing run, Morgan, in his usual, unperturbed voice, had
come on the intercom: 'Fighter dead astern, slightly below, coming in to
attack. Prepare to dive port – go.' But I had heard nothing, and so did
nothing but follow the bomb-aimer's directions. We were a sitting duck.

By chance, a split second after the rear gunner had said 'go' there was
a heavy, flak burst between us and the fighter. Apparently the burst was
closer to the fighter than to us, causing it to dive vertically out of sight. At
the time we all trusted that his dive would carry him into the inferno
below. . . .

J. K. Climie, Paraparaumu Beach, New Zealand, 1984

*Photographic-reconnaissance unit. (Ed.)
†If the squadron leader *is* still alive and reads this, the editor will gladly put him in touch
with his old 'benefactor' if he will make contact.

Ju 88 attacking Lancaster

Grounded Chances

Unpredictable chances were being reported on the ground as well as in the air. Two examples which occurred during the fighting after the Normandy landings in 1944, make the point.

1. BLINDED VICTORY

In the autumn of 1944, No. 2 Canadian Army moved rapidly along the northern coast of France and Belgium to liberate the port of Antwerp. The army bypassed Dunkirk containing a German garrison, which, apart from denying the port to the Allies may have harboured those who preferred to remain there rather than to return to face the rigours of the Fatherland and the disadvantage of defeat. This garrison was provisioned at night by Heinkel 111 aircraft flying from Germany, dropping their loads and returning without landing.

Among the Allied forces containing the garrison was 146 Light Anti-Aircraft Regiment RA (commanded by Lieut-Colonel J. P. Widgery, later to become Lord Chief Justice of England) and which included 86 Light Anti-Aircraft Battery RA and also 283 Light Anti-Aircraft Battery RA (The 'Rough Riders'). In December 1944 I was temporarily in command of 'A' Troop of 86 Battery and our six 40-mm Bofors guns were deployed on a ridge to the southwest of Dunkirk. We were then operational only at night, working in conjunction with searchlights. A modest chance of success had been achieved, I believe, by confusing the Heinkel crews into dropping

229

their loads onto ground occupied by the Allies – by the simple device of firing Verey lights similar or identical to those fired by the German garrison to identify their position.

One very foggy night a Heinkel flew immediately over our guns – whether through the confusion perpetrated by us or by bad piloting will never be known. The familiar drone of the Heinkel was clearly heard: it was exceedingly low. We were all determined to shoot it down as it would have been an easy target, especially as the searchlights were tracking it, aided by radar. But we could see nothing, except the beam of searchlights in the dense fog. Not a gun was fired.

Suddenly the Heinkel engines opened up to full power, and we realized that the pilot was diving to get out of the blinding glare of the searchlights – but too late and too low. In seconds the Heinkel crashed into the ground. . . . All the crew were killed.

This may well be a unique occasion of an aircraft being 'shot down' by searchlights alone!

His Honour Judge M. J. Anwyl-Davies, QC,
Southwark, London, 1984

2. THEY ACCEPTED THEIR CAPTORS' SURRENDER

Gerry McMahon (Wing Commander G. McMahon), an Irish-Scottish Geordie from Newcastle-upon-Tyne, and, after thirty years' service with the Royal Air Force, a security manager in industry, certainly opted for variety in war. Armourer, and an original member of the Bomb Disposal Squadron, he volunteered to remuster as an air gunner in 1941. A year later, he had completed his tour of thirty-three operations with 97 Squadron in 5 Group of Bomber Command.

There followed, in the last two years of the war, a spell with 620, 196 and 513 Squadrons of 38 Group, working with the Special Air Services and the 6th Airborne Division, on secret-dropping missions in western Europe. On 'D' Day of the Normandy landings – 6 June 1944 – the Stirling, in which McMahon and the rest of his crew were towing a glider, was shot down. The Canadian pilot, Flight Lieutenant Gordon Thring, performed heroics in manipulating the blazing aircraft into a wheat field.

Taken into custody by a pair of 'well-armed Germans', the crew was ordered to march to new positions during the following night. They were also required to carry with them a 16-stone wounded soldier.

The man seemed to weigh a ton, so, to get a rest, we kept calling out 'Holtz!', in turn, in the dark. This brought the entire company to a standstill and caused the officer in charge to come over each time and see whatever was happening. Finding a damaged motorcycle, we put the wounded soldier on the saddle, but, somehow, going downhill, we lost control. After the man and the bike had been pulled out of the ditch, the officer decided to let his own men take care of the wounded.

Next day, the officer brought us champagne (he said the water was polluted!), sausage and bread and we rested in a deserted château. Two days later, RAF ground-attack Typhoons came over and reduced the three-storey building to rubble. During the attack, we shared the slit trenches in the grounds with our captors. Their morale was now getting very low.

The same afternoon, the German officer in charge of the company sent for me and Gordon Thring, as we were the only officers in the crew. Obviously highly embarrassed, he said to us: 'I wish to surrender myself, and my forty men, to you!'

You could have knocked us down with a feather! Gordon and I went into a huddle and decided to accept the surrender. We insisted, however, that they must all march, fully armed, with our crew and give themselves up to the first Allied force that we found.

En route, another party of Germans, thinking this was a reinforcing group for their own troops, joined the column. They were a hand-picked bunch of snipers, so it was with some relief that we suddenly found ourselves surrounded by a force of Canadians.

I shouted out the facts, and after getting a receipt from the Canadians for one German officer and sixty-one soldiers, they arranged for us to be returned to England in a Royal Navy destroyer. . . .

Thus ended one of the war's quickest escapes – shot down, captured and returned all in four days. . . . All this, and sixty-two German prisoners in our logbooks, too!

Wing Commander G. McMahon, Stevenage, Hertfordshire, 1984

Bovril for a Boyo

Bruce Lawless (Flight Lieutenant F. B. Lawless) was an experienced Tempest pilot from Christchurch, New Zealand, flying with 486 (NZ) Squadron from Newchurch, by Romney Marsh, in Kent, at the time of the Normandy landings. He later joined his compatriot, Group Captain Desmond Scott, with the strikingly successful 123 Wing at Merville in France, and, by the end of the war, he had been decorated both by Britain and the United States.

Bruce claims 10 June 1944 was a day when fortune wore a smile – and then a frown. . . .

We were flying a routine cross-Channel patrol when my engine failed at about 6000 feet. We had been told it was inadvisable to try to ditch a Tempest in the sea as the scoop in front of the engine could make it tricky. The Typhoon, similarly, had trouble (see 'Passed for British', page 221).

I tried to bale out, but couldn't remove the hood with the [release] toggle. After struggling to no avail, there was no option but to ditch and hope. Luckily, when I hit the water, the hood flew off, so I quickly hopped into my dinghy and set sail for Folkestone. . . .

After a while, a Royal Navy destroyer came by and at once started manoeuvring alongside. Good, I thought, there'll be a few free drinks in the wardroom. Alas! a Royal Air Force air/sea rescue launch, which had put out from Dover, beat the navy to it – and all I got was a cup of Bovril!

This was the first Tempest to be ditched in the sea, so I was ordered to go to London to tell the world about it. . . .

F. B. Lawless, Point Clear, St Osyth, Essex, 1984

231

'Spike' and 'Fred'

Desmond Scott (Group Captain D. J. Scott) was, by any test, one of the Allies' really great operational leaders of the air war. Ground attack and close support for the armies was his business, and, first, Hurricanes and, then, Typhoons were his tools. He flew three, aggressively hard tours of duty and took a lot out of himself to do it, for Scottie, behind a block of granite, was capable of deep emotion. Losses affected him severely. He knew he was lucky still to be 'in play' at the end.

He had been brought up in the country in his native New Zealand, surrounded by animals. As a thoroughgoing countryman, he had a way with them and could read their minds; and they, in their turn, always looked as if they had the measure of his. They accorded him affection and respect.

'Fred' was already in residence when I took command of 486 (NZ) Squadron. A small, chocolate and white, short-haired, long-tailed mongrel, he treated our squadron dispersal as if he was the landlord. After falling over him a couple of times I had to remind his owner, Arthur 'Spike' Umbers, that, although I was very fond of dogs, I preferred to risk my neck against the enemy, and his dog should be made aware of it.

After my sharp reprimand, 'Fred' must have got the message for, thereafter, he kept well clear of me and always looked on me with suspicion. . . .

I posted Umbers off operations in the autumn of 1943, and didn't see him or his dog again until some twelve months later. By this time I was commanding 123 Wing – four squadrons of rocket-firing Typhoons then based at Gilze Rijen in Holland. While leading a low-attack mission on the German border town of Wesel, I was hit by flak and . . . [was lucky to] . . . force-land on Volkel airfield. The first person to meet me was Umbers. He was now back on operations commanding 486 Squadron. . . . As he drove me from my aircraft towards the squadron dispersal, I saw 'Fred' standing in the snow near the doorway, his eyes focused on our arrival. He showed no sign of affection or indeed recognition . . . and quickly disappeared into the warmth of the hut. . . .

Umbers offered to drive me back to Gilze Rijen and I gladly accepted, for that morning I had received the startling news that the Germans were gathering their forces for an assault across the Maas. This breakthrough was aimed at Antwerp, and I preferred to be back in command of my wing as soon as possible. . . . Gilze Rijen was in a direct line between the Maas and Antwerp.

We had much to talk about during our drive. Most of the boys who had flown Typhoons with us at Tangmere had been killed or were prisoners of war. . . . As the jeep hummed along the Dutch highway and the dark trees of evening melted into night, our conversation became interspersed with long periods of silence. I was still contemplating what might have been my own fate a few hours earlier over Wesel when I felt a cold muzzle at the back of my neck, and a warm tongue briefly licked my ear. A moment of canine affection that may well have been a message of farewell. . . .

I begged Umbers to stay the night, but he had an early morning show to lead and was taking off next afternoon for England to visit his wife and new-born baby. After dropping me off at Gilze Rijen, 'Spike' and his dog set off on their return to Volkel. I never saw either again. Umbers was killed next morning – shot down by flak while attacking barges on the Dortmund-Ems Canal. I mourned his loss. We had shared many a tight spot together. . . . I shed a tear, too, for his little dog. A faithful camp follower who had given his squadron everything he had – a mongrel dog who played his own important part during a crucial stage in the history of a war-torn world. . . .

Group Captain D. J. Scott, Christchurch,
New Zealand, 1984

Why the Dutch Farmers Had to Run

Mosquitoes of 2 Group, in the 2nd Tactical Air Force, headed by Air Vice-Marshal Basil Embry (Air Chief Marshall Sir Basil Embry), a tiger of a field commander, were now ranging by day and by night all over western Europe and Scandinavia, 'rubbing out' pinpoint, precision targets at a low level. Casualties, mainly from groundfire, were heavy.

Dick Sugden (W. R. Sugden), of 464 Squadron at Hunsdon in Hertford-shire, who, since 1940, had had a basinful of operational flying – in the Middle East as well as from the UK – ran into trouble one Saturday afternoon in 1944 during the attack on the Hazmeyer Electrical Equipment factory at Hengelo in Holland. . . .

The navigation officer, Flight Lieutenant Webb, folded up his file, smiled and said: 'It's a very good route, chaps, there should be hardly any flak. . . .' As we pushed out of the briefing room, I exchanged glances with 'Bunny' Bridger, my navigator. We had heard that one before. . . .

True to form, as they were following the railway line into Hengelo, and to the target, Dick spotted a German flak train drawn up in a siding.

As we opened our bomb doors, everything opened up as well; there was no chance of dodging the wall of tracer. I jabbed my bomb-release button several times to make sure the bombs had all gone, and turned for home.

It was then that Bridger said, 'Our starboard wing's on fire.' Monaghan, flying on my right, also noisily confirmed this on the R/T. I tried to feather the prop, no good; then the fire extinguisher, also no good. The wing was now well alight; there was nothing for it but to get down before it folded up. As we were flying right on the deck there was not much chance to pick and choose, but, fortunately, Holland is nice and flat. I shouted to Bridger to hold tight, and tried to lose some speed, but we must still have been doing about 200 m.p.h. when we touched down. It was a very noisy 'landing run' as we slithered and swerved for half a mile, shedding bits and pieces on the way.

Poor old Bridger was thrown clear (he broke his legs), and I managed to cut myself free of the tangle of wires and harness with a 'Boy Scout' knife which I carried. Some kind Dutch farmers picked us up, and ran like mad towards their house. When I looked back I saw the reason for their speed. Our 'Mossie' was burning fiercely, and scattered amongst the wreckage were three obscene-looking bombs.

The release gear must have been hit before I pressed the bomb-return button. *If I had known* three of the bombs were still aboard I would never have attempted a crash-landing, but would have climbed fast to give us a chance of baling out. With our bulk, and that tiny door, I don't think we'd have made it before the wing broke up. . . .

W. R. Sugden, Ruwa, Zimbabwe, 1984

Catching the Bug

Hitler's 'secret weapons' – the V-1 flying bomb, alias the 'Doodlebug', and the V-2 rocket – were now coming unpleasantly into play. It wasn't until the anti-aircraft guns, with their sophisticated gun-laying equipment, were ranged along the southeast coast of Kent that the defences began to master the V-1.

For the fighter aircraft, however, they provided a fast, but predictable target. The experience of Tony Liskutin (Squadron Leader M. A. Liskutin), one of the Royal Air Force's able Czechs, was both fortunate – and bizarre. The date was 8 July 1944.

Immediately after getting airborne on an air test, I saw, by chance, a flying bomb crossing over Dover on its way towards London. My new Spitfire IXA, MK-670 DU-V, accelerated easily to about 300 knots, and the interception occurred above the main road between Ashford and Maidstone.

It was quickly getting dark and becoming difficult to judge the distance behind this glowing jet-pipe. My height over the high ground of the Quarry Hills was under 500 feet. When I thought I was about 250 yards behind the infernal machine, I took careful aim and fired a one-second burst from my cannons. . . .

It happened, literally, in a flash. I did not even see the strikes before flying right into the fireball – and out the other side. Fifteen minutes later I landed back at Lympne. My aircraft wasn't seriously damaged, but something had happened to my self-assurance.

Between pressing the firing button and entering the fireball . . . I had a momentary sensation that I was looking at the V-1, and my Spitfire, from some 500 yards away to the left. It was quite clear, despite the darkness, and I must have been a good deal closer than 250 yards from my target.

The incident does not make any sense. It had occurred very briefly, probably in less than a second. But why was the vision so vivid, and why do I keep remembering it still?

People claim to have seen flying saucers. Was it something like that? Or was it just a quirk of my imagination? Obviously, I shall never know the answer. . . .

Squadron Leader M. A. Liskutin, Fareham, Hampshire, 1985

Nuremberg

The story of the attack on Nuremberg on the night of 30/31 March 1944 – Bomber Command's single, most devastating reverse of the war – is now history. The bald figures expose the extent of the calamity. 55 out of the 781 aircraft dispatched aborted. Of the remaining 726, 95 did not come back. Another 10 were written off on return.

Did luck affect the outcome? How far did fate or chance come into it? In the context of this collection, there are three interesting submissions to offer. The first is an extract from a short letter written on 9 November 1979, thirty-five years after the event, by Marshal of the Royal Air Force Sir Arthur Harris, Bomber Command's C-in-C at the time of the raid, to Air Commodore Henry Probert, head of the Royal Air Force's Air Historical Branch. Thanks are due to the Air Commodore for permission to quote.

The letter asked for a suitable reply to be sent to a schoolboy who had written to the Marshal about Nuremberg. Harris's manuscript aside is revealing.

I think this lad deserves all the help and encouragement we can give him . . . [but] . . . I'm sorry he wants to specialize on Nuremberg – *the one real disaster, and we were lucky not to have had a dozen* (editor's italics). . . .

Next is a comment by 'Tim' Woodman (Squadron Leader R. G. Woodman), *a widely experienced and successful night-fighter and intruder pilot from 169 Squadron in 100 Group of Bomber Command.*

When the intelligence officer revealed details of the raid on the map . . . I was appalled. I said that if the bombers took the route indicated, there would probably be disastrous losses, possibly reaching the 70s – which had already occurred. I had discovered on the night of 24 February, just over a month before, one of the German night-fighter beacons, indicated by a low-powered searchlight. It was southwest of Mannheim.

As I nosed up to it in my Mosquito at 20,000 feet, I obtained a number of AI [radar] contacts of German night-fighters orbiting it, awaiting instructions from ground control as to the whereabouts of the bomber force which was on its way to Augsburg. . . . I selected one of the contacts and shot down a Ju 88. . . .

The Resistance had subsequently sent us a captured map from a German night-fighter which gave the positions of all such beacons. Now Bomber Command were sending their main force right between two of them. . . . We voiced our views to Group. Air Commodore 'Rory' Chisholm (Air Commodore R. A. Chisholm), the senior air staff officer,* passed them on to Command. . . . No change.

Then I asked that two of us should go ahead of the bomber force . . . and get stuck into the German night-fighters before the bombers arrived. . . . Again Bomber Command refused. Instead, I was ordered to fly across the head of the bomber stream as it climbed into Germany, and take up a patrol ten miles to the south of its flank. . . . Idiotic and stupid beyond

---

*Chisholm was himself an accomplished night-fighter pilot. (Ed.)

reason – comparable to a destroyer taking up patrol alongside a convoy. . . .
I resolved that, come what might, I would head for one of those beacons
when I got into Germany. . . .

*In fact, Woodman's Mosquito developed engine trouble – serious trouble
– en route but, typically, he pressed on. In Royal Air Force jargon, he was
'a press-on type'.*

I was late arriving and the bombers were ahead of me as they flew east. . . .
*I crossed through the stream which was some fifty miles wide instead of
the expected five.* . . . They were already being shot down. The Germans
couldn't go wrong. The massed night-fighters around the beacons pounced,
calling in others like the Munich wings. We counted forty-two bombers
shot down from that point to Nuremberg. . . . Then my engine caught fire
again, and I came back on one. . . .

Squadron Leader R. G. Woodman, Westbury, Wiltshire, 1984

*One other expert view can be introduced. It comes from Gerry South
(Group Captain G. J. South), one of a select number of pilots who flew
three, repeat three, tours with the Pathfinder Force.*

I suppose the chance in our trip to Nuremberg that night was that we had
no navigational problems, were not intercepted by night-fighters nor were
we damaged by flak. On an operation when ninety-five bombers were lost
– and ten more by crashes after returning to England – luck must have
been on our side.

   . . . But how much was pure chance and how much due to the good
work of the groundcrew who produced an aircraft in a perfect state for
operations? And again, ill luck was, perhaps, countered by accurate
navigation. . . . Our little Yorkshire radar operator, Norman Kaye, was
a real expert . . . and the accuracy of track-keeping was largely due to
him. . . .

   This skill enabled us, as a Pathfinder crew, to be selected as openers of
an attack. On the Nuremberg raid we were 'Primary Blind Markers' and
so at the head of the stream. . . . This was usually considered to be a good
position as the enemy might not, by then, have had time to assess the
nature, strength and location of the attack.

   Then, beyond all this, I had had the good fortune, when I joined 7
Squadron, to take over a 'headless' crew – their captain having left after
completing his third tour. They were seasoned, well-trained and
disciplined. . . . It could easily have been my lot to have been given inexperienced or inattentive crew members. . . . I'm glad to say all this crew survived
the war. . . .

*A good start on operations – no matter what the role – counted for much.
In this, Gerry South was, by his own admission, lucky, going initially
'with two RCAF chums' to 405, the fine Canadian Pathfinder Squadron,
equipped with Halifax Mk II aircraft, and internationally based with
British, American, Australian and New Zealand representation in it. The
first trip for each of these three newcomers as captain, was Berlin.*

When the time came to start up and take off, the two starboard motors of my aircraft flatly refused to 'catch'. . . . Time went by and I was so 'green' that things got beyond the point where we were able to transfer to the spare aircraft. *This was the only occasion in my three tours with Pathfinders when we failed, as a crew, to take off and complete an operation as briefed.* (Editor's italics.)

My two Canadian friends, however, were both shot down on that Berlin trip, one crew never being heard of again. . . .

The fault in our motors was traced to some random electrical problem. My crew then were old-timers in the squadron, and were not as sanguine as I was about Berlin sorties. . . . I often wondered whether one of them was responsible for our abortive mission – most un-Pathfinderlike behaviour . . . but the slight, persistent doubt remains.

The flight engineer, the crew member most likely to know the real answer, went missing with another pilot about three months later. . . .

Group Captain G. J. South, Woking, Surrey, 1985

'Tis all a Chequer-board of Nights and Days
Where Destiny with Men for Pieces plays:
Hither and thither moves, and mates, and slays,
And one by one back in the Closet lays.

Edward Fitzgerald (1809–83), *Omar Khyyám*

But Was It Really LMF?

How big a factor was LMF – Lack of Moral Fibre – on operations? There was much less of it than some would have us believe. During the worst of the night-bombing offensive against Germany – in 1943 and 1944 – less than half of one per cent of all aircrew involved were affected by it. But the judgement of commanding officers in the matter was often crucial. Some were much harder – and less understanding – than others. For a potential victim, it was sometimes a matter of luck what kind of a character he had to confront.

Stephen Puskas (Flying Officer S. Puskas), a decorated Canadian Halifax captain from No. 429 (Bison) Squadron, at Leeming in Yorkshire, who flew thirty-nine operations with Bomber Command in 1944, introduces an interesting slant on the issue. He chanced to be a first-hand witness to a strange incident.

His crew were all young – between 19 and 21 – with the exception of the flight engineer, Jack Phillips, who was thirty-three, and they had already had to ditch in the sea on the night of 10/11 March off the east coast of Scotland with their aircraft on fire. Their rear gunner, Flight Sergeant Wilf – (name supplied) from British Columbia, had had a particularly disturbing time getting out of his turret and into the crew's dinghy. By temperament, he was described as 'naturally highly strung and excitable'.

Just over a fortnight, and a second operation, later, on the night of 26/27 March, the crew took part in the attack on the Krupps factory at Essen, in the Ruhr. It was clearly 'a shaky do'. After bombing the target successfully, the crew were subjected, for nearly an hour, to a relentless succession

237

of attacks by three and, perhaps, more German night-fighters while Puskas went through the full repertoire of evasive tactics. The running battle continued for much of the way back to the North Sea. It was incredible that, despite their persistence, the attackers were apparently unable to inflict serious damage upon the aircraft. Credit for this went substantially to the pilot, but Wilf, hammering away in his rear turret, and Alvin Williams, the mid-upper, had plainly proved a thorn in the assailants' side. One fighter was seen to break up and plummet earthwards, and another was thought to have suffered a similar fate. It had been one hell of a battle. . . .

Let the captain pick up the story.

The groundcrew were jubilant, proud of what their kite and aircrew had come through. They inspected the Hally for possible damage and made plans for repairs, promising to have the aircraft ready for the next operation. The armourer informed me that we were almost out of ammunition. . . .

All the while, Wilf stood off to one side by himself, and was very silent. We tried to involve him in our chatter, but to no avail. He said this was 'it', and that was his last trip. I was sure he would change his mind after some sleep.

That morning we had an appointment to see the station commander, Group Captain Bryant, who wanted to hear about our trip. After we had finished our story, he hinted that some sort of recognition might be forthcoming, but, to his dismay, our rear gunner told him what he could do with his recognition. That was Wilf's last trip, and nothing was going to change his mind. Needless to say, this unexpected response upset the station commander, and he made it quite clear that flight sergeants do not talk to group captains that way.

Wilf must have done a lot of soul-searching to come up with this decision, and displayed a lot of nerve to stick with it. He could have accepted his recognition and fudged his way through a tour of duty, going sick and getting away with it. But no, he was honest and didn't hesitate to reflect his feelings. . . .

I am sure the earlier ditching experience was the beginning of his uneasy mind. . . . I have always felt ashamed of what 'the organization' did to Wilf. They could have been more understanding and compassionate, instead of sending him home LMF. Everyone has a breaking point, and the limit varies with each individual.

The United States Army Air Force had a 'Flak House', a rest home, for those airmen who felt the strain and needed professional help. Not the RCAF. You were either in, fit to fly, or out. One or the other.

Our rear gunner was posted off the station without delay. Alvin Williams agreed to take over the rear-gunner position. We picked up a new mid-upper and went on to finish our tour.

Stephen Puskas, Waterdown, Ontario, Canada, 1984

Editor's note: *The author of this story, in his humanity and understanding, has tried to keep in touch with his former gunner. In 1983 when he was in Vancouver, Stephen Puskas saw Wilf again for the first time since the Essen trip in March 1944.*

'He came to my hotel to see me. . . . I knew he wanted to unburden his thoughts and feelings. . . . He remembers vividly the trip which terminated his Service career. He told me there was a certain amount of harassment from "the organization" as he was processed down the line towards the back door. . . . It has left him·somewhat bitter. . . .'

'The Gunners Song'*

At night we fly to Hamburg,
To Berlin or the Ruhr,
Another trip, another 'Op'
Will I ever end this tour?
Another flare, another fight,
Another airman dies,
The pungent air's our battlefield,
Our blood has stained the skies.
And it was just three months ago
When I was young and green,
While now they call us veterans
Though my age is just nineteen.
Still, I'll just go on flying
And sing the gunners' song;
I guess my turn has got to come
How long, O Lord, how long?

Victor Cavendish,
ex–88, 106 and 83 Squadrons

Prophetic

Coming events cast their shadows before them
Proverb

There were many instances in wartime of a chance event or experience affecting the future course of a man's career. Judge Eric McLellan's example was far removed from the usual run. The incident occurred in the latter part of 1944 when he was serving as the signals officer of a B-24 (Liberator) wing in Italy, an appointment he had held for some eighteen months.

Casualties had been quite shocking, and there had inevitably been some failures of nerve, though these were remarkably few and of a sort which could be dealt with by bundling the unfortunate character concerned out of the way.

At this point a case turned up which could not be handled so conveniently. One of the wireless operators on the way to Ploesti, had

*Taken from *Verse from the Turret: An Air Gunners' Anthology*, See 'Night Bombers', page 212.

caused his aircraft to turn back by reporting damage to the radio system which appeared to admit no explanation but deliberate damage.

It was already on my plate in one capacity, but it soon turned up in another and still more disconcerting guise. I was walking back to lunch at the mess a few days later, when I fell in with the group captain. I knew him very well and flew, when I did, as a member of his crew. He had a very grave face. He said, 'They've charged your chap with failing to do his utmost in the face of the enemy. That's a capital charge. You must defend him.'

I had never been in a court of law in any capacity whatever, and had no idea how to set about my task. However, I had two great advantages. The first was a thorough knowledge of air signals and equipment, which no legal prosecutor could possibly match. The second was an entire freedom from any professional legal inhibitions of etiquette or indeed anything else. (Editor's italics.)

If my client is still in the land of the living he will, I am sure, agree that his story had little in the way of anything to add verisimilitude to an otherwise bald and unconvincing narrative.

So I set about polishing his narrative in a way no professional could have done. The prosecution expert was an old friend, who wanted blood on his hands no more than I should have if our roles had been reversed; the other members of his crew were prepared to be almost tiresomely helpful. The whole feeling of the court was with me. Nevertheless, it was touch and go. For he was not charged with cowardice, and he had undoubtedly behaved in a very odd way.

In those days a court-martial sat from beginning to end. It was about midnight in a room lit only by unshaded bulbs that I rose to make my final speech for my client's life. No doubt it was worse for him. But it remains in my mind with probing searchlights, 10/10ths cloud and circling a runway with a crash on it and petrol running out, as one of the recollections one would rather forget.

I sat down. The court closed. After an age we came back and they acquitted on the major charge, though there was inevitably a reprimand.

A few days later I was walking to the mess for lunch and fell in with the group captain. He said he was pleased. I said I was mighty relieved. He said, 'I wasn't thinking about him. I was thinking about you. This is what you are cut out for.' A little later I decided he was right.

His Honour Judge E. B. McLellan, Catherington,
Hampshire, 1984

Norge 'Luck'

Johan Christie (Major-General Johan K. Christie), the Norwegian flight commander of 35 Squadron in the Pathfinder Force, flew forty-eight marking operations with his crew. In a note which he made at the time, he was in no doubt about the part that luck played in the selection, build-up – and success – of the team.

Considering that all my crew have been brought together by chance, by

240

what amounts to a sheer gamble, I think I have been exceedingly lucky. The amazing thing is that, after some time, *all* crews think very highly of each other. There are, I believe, three main reasons for this:

1. All people become nicer, better human beings, when their lives are in danger.

2. The whole crew know the situation, they know that all are dependent upon each other. Because of this they try very hard to do their best and this, in turn, is recognized and appreciated by every crew member.

3. The crew learn about one another, about each one's special ways – of talking, of behaviour, about his knowledge and his qualities. This way they develop confidence in one another.

I think my crew got a shock when they discovered what sort of a pilot I was. . . . I had had four or five different instructors; they all seemed to agree with me there was little hope of ever converting me into a useful pilot. On one occasion I went to my flight commander and asked him to tell me straightly whether he thought I would ever be any asset to the war effort, or whether it would not be just as well to pack up right away and go back to office work. I found it rather pointless to kill off a promising crew. . . .

He answered that he believed things would be OK, and otherwise gave the impression that he thought this was a normal case of 'Lack of Moral Fibre'.

One can see what a gamble it has been – that's why I say I have been so lucky. . . .*

Major-General Johan K. Christie, Hjellum, Norway, 1984

Taxiing Trouble

Aeroplanes taxiing on the ground . . . flying boats taxiing on the water – in each case the utmost vigilance and respect was demanded of the pilot. Accidents and mistakes, which could easily happen, were regarded as heinous – and costly – by commanding officers. They were usually pilot-induced and due to carelessness or overconfidence. They could also be highly dangerous. For the transgressor, the penalty normally fitted the crime. But lucky near misses also abounded; two can be cited.

I. ON LAND

Peter Firkins, the Australian author, who, at eighteen, flew a tour of operations from Binbrook, twenty miles northeast of Lincoln, sitting in the rear gun turret of one of 460 (RAAF) Squadron's Lancasters, had a tortuous experience which he would probably prefer to forget. It happened on 25 March 1944, two nights after a shaker of a trip to Bremen. The crew had

---

*Johan Christie's was one of the highly regarded crews in PFF. It required something more than luck to achieve this. In fact, Christie was a punctilious, meticulous captain who thought things through and planned everything down to the last detail. (Ed.)

then returned on two portside engines, with the flight engineer reporting as they approached for an emergency landing, 'We're out of fuel, Skipper, you'll have to go straight in.'

The motors died as the aircraft rolled down the runway. 'We were a fairly irreverent crew, but we did feel that some guiding hand had been directing us during the longest two and a half hours of our lives. . . .'

Now it was Hanover.

We taxied out of our dispersal in the half-light of early evening, which is often a difficult time to distinguish silhouettes. We were just turning onto the perimeter track, when I caught sight of a Lancaster bearing down upon us, its two churning port engines coming into line somewhere about the position of my rear turret.

I yelled 'Look out' over the intercom, and had visions of two full bomb-loads going up, so swung my turret to the beam to beat a hasty retreat, only to jam my rather bulky frame in the small door.

The two aircraft came to a grinding halt, the two engines of the other Lancaster severing our fuselage a few yards behind my turret. Keith Bennett, the pilot, unable to raise me on the intercom, climbed out of the escape hatch above the cockpit and came running down the top of the fuselage to see if he had an extinct rear gunner, only to discover a jammed one. To make matters worse, the Lancaster with which we had collided was a flight commander's and his ill humour took some considerable time to assuage. . . .

All Bomber Command aircrews were superstitious and this, we knew, was our thirteenth operation in twenty-four days. We were all pretty tired although we didn't particularly realize it at the time. But we believed that fate had once again taken a hand. Had we gone on the raid we might, in all likelihood, have 'bought it'. . . .

Peter Firkins, City Beach, Western Australia, 1984

2. ON WATER

Taxiing a flying boat on water introduced additional dimensions and hazards which were never present on land. Sea, wind and current all came into play. Moving a boat from A to B was a very different task from nipping a single-engined fighter out of dispersal, along a perimeter track and out onto field or runway for a squadron or wing take-off.

Hector Monro (Air Commodore Sir Hector Monro, MP) who, in a life of public service and private business, has known ministerial office and the presidency of the Scottish Rugby Football Union, had, by the end of the war, become a proved flying-boat captain. Even so, there was a September evening in 1944 when, but for some providential intervention, he could easily have ended up on the mat.

The trauma occurred at Killadeas, on Lough Erne, in Northern Ireland. He was converting from Catalinas onto Sunderland IIIs and training a new crew, none of whom had any experience of Catalinas and very little of Sunderlands. He had been asked to move a Catalina up the Lough to the slipway. Conventional thinking would have suggested a tow behind a dinghy or launch.

... Overconfidence or foolhardiness, however, encouraged me to say we would taxi along ... and save considerable time. It was quite a task showing the crew what they had to do ... especially explaining to the flight engineer, Bill May, how to start the twin Wasps from his isolated position in the tower.

... Eventually we started the engines and were off, with myself climbing about the boat giving directions and leaving Eddie Edmonds, my second pilot at the controls. He had started as a corporal pilot before the war, had over 3500 hours as a flying instructor, and was desperate to get onto an operational squadron.

Flying boats weathercock quickly into a moderate wind, and as we taxied across wind through the rows of moored boats, I was quite happy that when we were about fifty yards off the jetty she would swing to starboard into wind and coast up to the buoy another 200 yards ahead. ...

Maybe it was Ireland. Maybe it was bad luck, but suddenly the wind died completely. Our speed increased and the Catalina just would not turn into a non-existent wind. As the jetty approached, I rapidly opened up the port engine until the throttle was right through the gate. With a crescendo of noise and spray she came round, lifting the port-wing top float over the jetty by six inches or so.

We made the buoy with a chastened captain covered in sweat. I had been within six inches of a court-martial or worse, though the crew were impressed and spoke of 'cutting it fine'.

But my everlasting thanks go to the marine-craft section, the only witnesses of a near disaster. Never a word to anyone, and certainly not the station commander, Group Captain John Barraclough, now Air Chief Marshal Sir John Barraclough, and a fellow Honorary Air Commodore in the Royal Auxiliary Air Force!

Air Commodore Sir Hector Monro, MP, Kirtlebridge, Dumfriesshire, 1984

Spotter Extraordinary

The army's tiny 'spotter' aircraft performed wonders for their military masters, landing on a dime or a sixpence in minute fields or narrow clearings. Their pilots reported vital information primarily for the army's (and sometimes the navy's) guns, achieving their mission often in the face of vigorous defence. If anyone needed luck, they did.

The British called them Air O P Squadrons. Their Auster aircraft, 'unarmed, unarmoured and very slow', were expertly serviced by Royal Air Force personnel and their pilots were all army gunner officers. One of the leading exponents of this role was Alec Hill (Major G. A. Hill) the CO of 662 Squadron, in peacetime a London stockbroker and international golfer. His squadron's support of General Horrocks' XXX Corps (Brian Horrocks used to fly reconnaissances with Hill – they made an interesting pair) in the great drive up through France to Brussels and beyond, became a feature of this specialized and hazardous work. The 11th Armoured Division, the 50th and the Guards Armoured, all came under 662's purview. It was a measure of these operations that they won Hill a rare DSO.

It was when XXX Corps entered Brussels on 4 September 1944, that the CO of 662 Squadron enjoyed one or two unexpected breaks. After the astonishing speed of the advance since early June, what was now badly needed was a good landing ground for airborne supplies, particularly petrol. Fortuitously, Hill knew Brussels Evere from pre-war days. Was this former civilian airport still in enemy hands and was it suitable? It was his job to find out.

I drove quickly to the flight with the Guards Armoured Division, borrowed an aircraft and flew gently forward over the housetops of Brussels until I came to Evere. All was peace and quiet. The hangars seemed to be almost totally destroyed, but otherwise there appeared to be no damage. . . .

I landed, wrote a message to Corps Headquarters, saying that Evere was deserted and capable of taking any aircraft they liked. I then flew back over the headquarters and dropped my note in a message bag. I ordered four of our aircraft and a certain amount of transport to come to the airport, hopped into my jeep and drove back to Evere.

. . . The four Austers came flying in over the housetops. Then, suddenly, all hell broke loose. The air was filled with black puffs and a deafening noise. The four Austers were caught in a barrage of AA fire. I sat in my jeep unable to do anything and could not believe that they could avoid being blown to bits. God, however, was on our side. Three of the planes managed to land and taxied at racing speed behind a badly smashed hangar. The fourth, which had been hit in the wings, flew off westwards. The enemy guns now turned on the airport itself and made matters very unpleasant. . . . They had not risked giving themselves away to one miserable little aircraft when I had done the reconnaissance; they were waiting for bigger fish. . . .

The three pilots who had landed, and myself, were sheltering behind a hangar wondering what to do next, when out of the few comparatively undamanged buildings strolled, I repeat, strolled an immaculately dressed Belgian from the civilian airline, Sabena, whose aerodrome it was. He said, 'I am afraid you are having rather a bad time.' The Germans, he added, had five 88s dug in 1100 yards up the road – 'But do not worry,' he said, 'they are very bad shots!' . . .

I got through to Corps HQ from the wireless truck and said we were in a mess, could we have some help, please, and as quick as possible. XXX Corps conjured up some armoured cars and sent a company of Guards to see what could be done about the German 88s.

Shortly after, to our horror, the RAF, who had now received my very first message before all the trouble had started, arrived in an Anson, presumably to check whether my statement about the capacity of the airport was correct. The Anson flew slowly round once and all was quiet. Then it lowered its flaps and the barrage started all over again. The RAF pilot whipped up his flaps and, by the grace of God, flew off unscathed. . . .

By nightfall the Guards had captured the German guns and this invaluable, undamaged (as far as the surface was concerned) airfield was now in British hands.

Next day DC-3 Dakota transport aircraft were landing at the rate of thirty an hour, bringing up supplies of all sorts for the army. It was wonderful to see this happening, on what 662 AOP Squadron now referred to as its 'own airport', blithely disregarding the fact that had it not been for the armoured cars and the Guards Division we wouldn't have lasted very long....

I have always felt that had XXX Corps, with its tail so high and the enemy in a state of demoralization, been allowed to go on it might have reached Germany on its own! I imagine, however, that logistically this was impossible....

G. Alec Hill, Sandwich, Kent, 1984

Bold resolution is the favourite of Providence
Proverb

What Price Arnhem?

Heavy risks were taken in the Battle of Arnhem.... Had we been more fortunate in the weather, which turned against us at critical moments and restricted our mastery in the air, it is probable that we should have succeeded ...

Winston S. Churchill, The Second World War: Vol IV,
Triumph and Tragedy (Cassell, 1954)

Montgomery's Arnhem operation, called Market Garden, got off to a bad start. Ill-conceived, and doomed to fail before it began, it was an operation that depended ... on the weather. The planning was not carried out by the commanders on the spot, but was handled by a combined headquarters in England, which was like trying to conduct an orchestra from across the Channel ...

Group Captain D. J. Scott, RNZAF, Commander of 123
(Typhoon) Wing, Typhoon Pilot. (Secker & Warburg, 1982)

It [the failure of the Allied Air Forces to fly two sorties on the first day of the operation] completely mucked the whole thing up because only half the original force was able to go for their objectives ...

Major-General John D. Frost, whose 600 heroic
paratroopers held the north-end of Arnhem Bridge
against superior German numbers for four days,
quoted in the Daily Telegraph, 21 September 1984

... Air Vice-Marshal Hollinghurst (Air Chief Marshal Sir Leslie Hollinghurst) wanted to fly the two sorties, but was overruled.* Had there been two sorties on that first day, much of the peril subsequently experienced by both the RAF and the USAAF would not have been there.... The air battle had been won over France so completely that it ought not to have been too difficult to maintain air superiority over southern Holland.... The weather was perfect on 'D' Day of the operation....

The appalling fact is that even at this stage of the war, I had no means whatever of calling for air support, nor was there any at Brigade level. I do not believe there was any even at Division.... (Editor's italics.) (See ' "Joubie," The South African', page 303).

Major-General John D. Frost, correspondence with
the editor, 9 October 1984

*By Lieut-General L.H. Brereton, US Commander of the 1st Allied Airborne Army (Ed.)

What, then, of the performance of the Royal Air Force's fighters during the Arnhem operation? How strong was their resolve to see things through? Maurice Perdrizet (General Maurice T. Perdrizet) reflects upon a supporting operation which he led with 345 (Free French) Squadron's Spitfires based at Deanland, near Lewes in Sussex, and provides a first-hand answer. It happened on 19 September, a day when destiny, providence and luck joined forces, resolved to see these intrepid Frenchmen safely through.

Extract from the daily record of RAF activity: 'Seventeen Spitfire squadrons were detailed to escort a wave of DC-3s and gliders to Arnhem. A single squadron, No. 345 (FAF), partially accomplished the mission. (Visibility: 100 yards; ceiling: 10/10ths cloud at 200 feet.)'

The Arnhem adventure is in its third day and seems to be running into difficulty. . . . The wing has been able to put up one or two shows a day up till now, but the morning has been very damp and misty and it is still barely possible to see the control tower, a hundred yards away, through the fog. . . .

At around 15.00 hours, the telephone rings. The duty officer picks up the receiver and almost at once puts it down. 'Briefing!' he shouts. . . .

The paratroops are clearly now in a desperate situation and must, at all costs, be resupplied. The DC-3s and gliders are about to take off and our three squadrons, forming the escort, are to follow at short intervals. . . .

As we take off and head northeast towards Manston in tight formation, the ceiling is down to 300 feet and visibility, in the heavy rain, is steadily deteriorating. Crossing the coast and heading out across the North Sea, we plunge into fog, but the twelve aircraft tuck in tight keeping solid formation. . . .

The leader of the squadron ahead of us announces that he is turning back; almost at once the controller asks me about my intentions. 'We'll have a try,' I say. Immediately there is a shout over the R/T: 'Lagos! Look out ahead.' There is just time to pull up sharply and pass over the top of the DC-3s and gliders which have also turned for home.

We cross the coast at Ostend and set course across Belgium. But now the controller calls again. 'We're still trying,' I reply. Soon it is obvious that there will be no improvement in the conditions and there is plainly no point in going on. We turn slowly and smoothly, keeping the squadron together, and start heading back towards Manston. . . .

. . . Suddenly, just ahead, there are chimneys and factories and houses, hundreds of houses . . . and now the flak and clouds of tracer, firing at point-blank range from all sides. It's Dunkirk! We have come out four miles too far west. As all twelve aircraft dive towards the sea, the port's 88-mm guns keep up their barrage and shells throw up spouts of water around our wing tips. We have not seen this before – heavy ack-ack firing very accurately on a dead flat trajectory. . . . These last few seconds have seemed like an eternity.

We head for base, and now I call the leaders of the three sections; every one of them is still there. . . . As the twelve Spitfires skim the treetops and weave a way along railway lines and rivers, only the Lord knows how we have contrived to make it safely home. . . .

But we had, at least, had a try. . . .*

General Maurice T. Perdrizet, Crest, France, 1984

Bad Luck, Good Luck

Life will always be unequal; but in terms of chances in war it was more unequal for some than for others. Capitaine Jean Calmel (Général J. Calmel), who survived one of the roughest periods of the bombing offensive against Germany to become, before his retirement from the Service, Vice-Chief of the Air Staff of the French Air Force, saw tragic evidence of it when he was flying with 346, the 4 Group, Free French Halifax Squadron, based at Elvington, southeast of York, in the autumn of 1944.

Bomber Command's two French squadrons, 346 and 347, suffered some cruel casualties. 'In the eleven months from June 1944, to 8 May 1945, they flew, between them, 2500 sorties, dropping 10,000 tons of bombs. But, during the period, the losses amounted to 79 per cent of the original aircraft strength and 48 per cent of the original aircrew strength, killed or missing.'

On 10 September Calmel, soon to win a 'gong' for his gallant efforts, had just landed from a daylight attack on a V-1 (flying-bomb) site at Octeville in northern France. It was dusk and he was taxiing in to dispersal.

Lancaster with bomb exploding

*This is General Perdrizet's specially adapted version of the story which appeared in *Silence en Vol*, published by Jean Accart in 1947.

Immediately behind him, the squadron commander, Lieut-Colonel Venot, was touching down. Suddenly, there was a violent explosion which sent shockwaves reverberating across the airfield. Unbeknown to Venot and his crew, a 200-kilo bomb had hung up and fallen to the ground with the landing impact. Flames quickly enveloped the aircraft and, with it, the crew. Miraculously, Venot, semi-conscious from the blast, 'had managed to lift the cockpit canopy and jumped four or five metres to the ground, just as the flames were licking his face and hands. . . .

'The remainder of the crew, stunned by the explosion, were unable to get out. Only little Biaggi, the rear gunner, recovered consciousness. . . . He was screaming, imprisoned in his turret. . . . We could do nothing. Helplessly, I wept at the loss of Kipferle, Coupeau, Finale and Biaggi. . . . I had loved them like brothers. . . .'

Venot, alone, survived – later to become a general. A few weeks afterwards, fate pursued a different course. Calmel, returning with his crew from a night operation, was diverted to a United States Army Air Force base in East Anglia. Anxious to impress the Americans with the standard of French airmanship, he followed all the accepted procedures to the letter, parking his aircraft tidily with the rest of the squadron on an unused runway. B-24s (Liberators) were occupying all the dispersal areas.

. . . Carefully, I cut the engines and went through the standard 'stop' procedures, one of which was to leave the bomb doors open on parking. . . . While I operated the levers with Roux, my flight mechanic, the crew climbed down from the aircraft, soon to be surrounded by a group of interested and helpful American crews.

. . . As the bomb doors opened I heard a sinister sound of crumpling metal followed by a dull thud. . . . I knew instantly what had happened. . . . I shut my eyes. A bomb which, like Venot's, had hung up, had now fallen to the ground and would explode any moment.

Agonizing seconds passed, but nothing happened! I dared to look up and there was everyone, fleeing in all directions away from the aircraft like a flock of sparrows, or throwing themselves to the ground behind any available shelter. . . . I did not feel very comfortable with my 'egg' underneath, only a few metres away. . . .

I breathed again and, followed by the loyal Roux, assumed an air of indifference, as we got down and began to inspect the bomb which had rolled harmlessly against a wheel. . . . Luckily, it had fallen quite flat without striking its fuse. . . .

Général J. Calmel, Paris, France, 1984

Anglo-American Miracle

A great change took place in the air war in 1944, and hastened its end. The daylight offensive, which had got under way in 1943 mainly with B-17 Fortresses, of the United States 8th Air Force, assisted by the 15th Air Force based in Italy, against precision industrial targets in Germany and central Europe, represented an altogether new dimension in the European

*campaign. Like an unseen hook to the jaw, it rocked the Luftwaffe back
onto its heels.*

*This revolution – for that's what it was – was made possible by the
United States' development of the long-range, single-engined fighter and,
in particular, the P-51B Mustang, powered by the Rolls-Royce Merlin 66
engine. It meant that there wasn't a target in Germany which couldn't be
reached by escorted B-17s.*

*The installation of Rolls-Royce's latest two-speed, two-stage, super-
charged Merlin, to be manufactured eventually under licence in the United
States by Continental and Packard, turned the P-51 into one of the great
aircraft success stories of World War II.*

*Luck and coincidence, plus a good dollop of expertise, brought it all
about, and Ronald Harker, the senior liaison test pilot of Rolls-Royce,
whose name was for years synonymous with the Derby-based firm, was
the first to see the aeroplane's potential.*

*By chance, he had come to know Ian Campbell-Orde (Wing Commander
Ian Campbell-Orde) – 'The General' – from their pre-war days together
in the Auxiliary Air Force. And Campbell-Orde was now commanding the
Air Fighting Development Unit at Duxford. A Mustang, with the US Allison
engine in it, had been sent to AFDU for assessment. 'The General' had
flown it and concluded that Harker should do likewise. He, therefore,
telephoned him at Derby on 29 April 1942, and the next day at Duxford
one of the most brilliant concepts of the air war was born.*

As I flew the aeroplane, I felt it had a number of desirable features which
the current fighters lacked. I was impressed by its fuel capacity . . . which
was three times as much as the Spitfire. . . . I liked the .5-calibre, heavy-
machine guns mounted close inboard in the wings . . . the high rate of roll
and, perhaps, most important of all, its low drag which gave it a very
noticeable increase in top speed over both British and German contemporary fighters. . . . One saw immediately the possibility of the Mustang as
an air superiority and long-range penetration fighter – if only it could be
fitted with our latest . . . Merlin. If this was successful, it could be the
answer to both the Me 109 and the Focke-Wulf 190, thus providing
qualities that the Spitfire [and other US and British fighters] lacked. . . .

I went to see Hives [Lord Hives, chairman of Rolls-Royce], having
previously asked our performance people to calculate what the [improved]
performance was likely to be with the Merlin. The answer had come back
that it would be 50 m.p.h. faster, and the rate of climb would be much
quicker, also with greatly extended range.

I summoned all the enthusiasm and conviction I could muster, told Hives
what a splendid aircraft the Mustang was, and how it was badly needed
in the RAF and could we have one at Hucknall [Rolls-Royce's test airfield]
to do a Merlin conversion? He saw the point, and there and then telephoned
Air Marshal Sir Wilfred Freeman at the Air Ministry, recommending that
he authorize three Mustangs to be sent to Hucknall for this purpose. . . .

The first Merlin installation was completed and flown on 13 October
1942, the work of conversion having started in August. My initial flight at
Duxford had been on 30 April, so we had moved fast once the go-ahead
had been given. . . .

The good news of the Merlin Mustang's vastly improved performance spread like wildfire and was conveyed to Washington. . . . Large orders were placed. . . . Extra factories were built, and production was to rise to 500 per month. In all, over 15,000 Mustangs were produced. The aeroplane became indispensable in the Pacific where long range was an absolute necessity. . . .

Had Harker, at Rolls-Royce, and Campbell-Orde, at Duxford, not been in their respective places at that juncture – and friends from their Auxiliary Air Force days, each with a regard for the other – the course of the conflict might well have been different. Such are the chances that friendships and contacts bring in war – and peace.*

R. W. Harker, Knightsbridge, London, 1984

Providential End

On 30 May 1944 Dick Alexander (Major R. L. Alexander) – 'Dixie' to one and all – was flying a new P-51 Mustang, with the 2nd Squadron of the 52nd Fighter Group from Magna airport, south of Termoli in Italy. The B-24s the squadron was escorting were to attack targets at Wels and Linz, 100 miles or so west of Vienna. A flight commander, and one of the early Eagle Squadron pilots, 'Dixie' had gone up to Canada from the United States in 1940 and joined the RCAF. After three hard operational years, he was now one of the most experienced fighter leaders in the USAAF to which he had transferred. He had 157 missions behind him.

Now, flying long sweeps to Ploesti and into Austria, Bavaria and lower Germany in a new aeroplane, far superior to anything the Germans could boast, we were encountering the air opposition we all looked forward to. I was thirty years of age, my health was excellent, I was feeling seasoned and confident. I felt I had arrived. . . .

Just before the target was reached, the B-24s were attacked head on by a section of aggressive Me 109s which then pulled up and prepared for a second pass. But when 'Dixie' took his P-51s into them, they spiralled down to get away. Alexander followed one of the 109s right down to the rugged, mountainous terrain below. . . .

. . . He then dropped down into a valley, and as we flew into it I fired three successive bursts from about 200 yards. We were on the deck, and I observed strikes on his port wing and cockpit area. He made a gentle turn, and simply flew into the side of the mountain. . . .

I started to pull up and my engine coughed a couple of times and then started to splutter. . . . I did all I could to make the motor respond, without success. . . . I managed to get 300 or 400 feet over the hills. I did not have

---

*A detailed story of the development of the P-51 is to be found in Ronnie Harker's books *Rolls-Royce: From the Wings 1925–1971* (Oxford Illustrated Press, 1976) and *The Engines Were Rolls-Royce* (Macmillan Publishing Co. Inc, New York, 1979).

the height to bale out, and I knew that crashing into the wooded, hilly area could be disastrous. And then, as I pushed the nose down to keep from stalling, I spotted two small clearings directly in front of me. They proved to be two small pastures, each no larger than a good-sized football field, divided by a little creek. . . . I aimed at the first, hit hard, bounced once over the creek . . . and wound up in the trees at the far end. . . .

I scrambled out of the aircraft and saw several bulletholes along the lower part of the engine cowling, telling me where I had been hit. . . . I checked my maps and escape packet, placed the fire canister over the wing tank, pulled the pin, and started walking. . . .

That evening, I heard later, the squadron received a call from the B-24 group at Foggia, enquiring if we had lost one of our pilots. The crew of one of the 24s had admitted to hitting me, and seeing me go in.

Chance, fate, karma – call it what you like. Certainly an overeager B-24 gunner accomplished something that the Germans had never been able to do. My flying career was ended, and I was about to spend the remainder of the war as a POW. And yet, from what had seemed to be an impossible position, fate had provided me with a little patch of ground (probably the only one for many, many miles) to ensure me a longer life. I have mulled this over many times, and can only reach one conclusion: I was not intended to fly any more, nor was I intended to die. . . .

Dick Alexander, Piper City, Illinois, USA, 1984

The Luck of the Draw

. . . I later learned that 82 per cent of our class had washed out or been killed before completing their training at Maytag Field. Only 18 per cent graduated hoping to become the world's hottest fighter pilots.

And every one of them was assigned to fly a B-24.

Captain J. D. Fleming, United States Army Air Force

Pink Elephant*

Jim Fleming (Captain J. D. Fleming), now a businessman in Atlanta, Georgia, and a deacon of the Baptist Church, was a navigator in a B-24 crew of the Squadron operating, in 1944, with the 450th (H) Bombardment Group of 15th United States' Army Air Force from bases in North Africa and Italy. Their missions had ranged widely to strongly defended targets in Rumania, Hungary, Austria and southern Germany. Unexpectedly, the crew were detailed for a special assignment to the United Kingdom. Its outcome must have left the survivors wondering what other tricks fate might still have left to play.

'You gonna jump?'
'Damn right I'm gonna jump. Let's go, men!'

---

*Jim Fleming, who completed fifty-one missions, has specially adapted this story from his book, *With Wings As Eagles* (Perry Communications Inc., Atlanta, Georgia.)

They followed me out onto the catwalk. We looked at the British country-side below, through the open bomb-bay doors.

'Don't look high enough to me,' Darby ventured.

'We're not gettin' any higher,' I said. 'Follow me.' I crammed a hard-boiled egg into my mouth and we all baled out. . . .

Our . . . top-secret mission to England was so secret that even the pilot could only tell me that we had been ordered to report to 'some joker in Whitehall'.

We had flown all night in the ancient, war-weary Liberator, still painted desert pink and battle-scarred from its final combat mission, the ill-fated, low-level raid on Ploesti. Coming up from Casablanca, we had used up our fuel dodging German patrols over the Bay of Biscay and circling over the British Isles seeking a break in the undercast. I thought about the two soldiers who had wanted to bum a ride with us from Casablanca to England. I had played the horse's ass and put them off the plane because they had no parachutes.

The break in the clouds was right over the RAF fighter base at Fairwood Common. We circled, and as we tried to line up with the short runway, the fuel pressure on all four engines dropped to zero. . . .

I had closed out my navigator's log and peeled my breakfast egg, thinking everything in the garden was lovely. Now, at just over 300 feet, up jumped the devil. Thank God I had rehearsed this scenario in my mind a hundred times. I snapped on my chest pack, hit the bomb-bay door lever and headed for the catwalk, motioning the others to follow.

Now I was falling upside down, wondering why the RAF was firing tracers at us. (They were red flares, intended to guide us into the field.) My 'chute opened ten feet above some telephone wires. I tugged on my left riser cords, desperately trying to save the family jewels. It worked brilliantly, except that I slammed into the ground with the 'chute half collapsed.

The British Home Guard were quickly to the rescue:

'Lemme help yer, sir. Hurt yerself?'

'Did everyone get out?'

'Yus, sir, all four brollies opened and the kite pranged in the 'edge.' As my brain was translating this into American language, there was an exuberant shout from young Darby, sprawled on the ground nearby:

'I made it! I'm in England!'

The Home Guardsman towered above him:

'Not bloody likely, young man. Yer in *Wales!*'

I looked up again and there were two beautiful young ladies – a WAAF opening the ambulance door for me, and a smiling NAAFI lady holding out a cup and asking, 'Tea, anyone?'

My pilot, Harvey Helmberger, gave up his chance to bale out so he could hold the plane steady for the rest of the crew. When the old Pink Elephant smashed into the ground he was thrown through the windshield, but later fully recovered. The crew chief, who was not a flyer, refused the order to follow me and died of injuries sustained in the crash. The Pink Elephant was a pile of junk metal.

The 500-lb top turret broke loose on impact, and crashed through the flight deck, exactly where the two hitchhiking soldiers from Casablanca would have been had I not been such a horse's ass. And though my leg was injured, the hard-boiled egg had saved me from breaking all my teeth when I landed with the collapsed 'chute.

The commanding officer of Fairwood Common, Sandy Johnstone (Air Vice-Marshal A. V. R. Johnstone), and all his people were most gracious, and treated us royally even though we had dropped in unannounced. . . .

The joker in Whitehall never did reveal the top secret to us. Perhaps, I should have gone back to Italy and asked my old Italian barber, or his 9-year-old grandson, The Little Kid, what it was . . . for *they* had told me, twenty-four hours before the order was issued, that we were going to England. . . .

J. D. Fleming, Atlanta, Georgia, USA, 1984

Deliverance by Tattoo

Before Ron Lamb (Warrant Officer R. Lamb) became a fighter pilot in the Royal Air Force, he was a young Army Territorial, serving as a trooper with the Duke of Lancaster's Yeomanry. 'One night in Aldershot in 1939, I got rather tight with some companions and was persuaded to have a tattoo on my right forearm. When I awoke the next morning, there it was! The Rose of Lancaster topped off by a fine-looking Union Jack. . . .'

Four years later, in August 1944, Lamb was based in Italy with 32 Squadron. One day, while attacking enemy locomotives in northern Greece, his Spitfire was hit in the coolant tank by groundfire and he baled out. He landed in the Pindus mountains and was soon in the hands of the ELAS partisans.

The leader strode up to me and thrust a Luger pistol in my face. '*Sprechen Sie Deutsch?*' he asked. Shaking my head I pointed to my right arm and said, 'RAF – English.' Several of the other partisans pointed and nodded. . . . The Union Jack tattooed on my arm had certainly saved my life, because later that day I was taken to a village where I was questioned by an English-speaking partisan leader. He told me that the partisans who found me, having seen my aircraft crash in flames and the second Spitfire flying around, assumed that I was a German pilot. Their leader wanted to shoot me on the spot!'

R. Lamb, Sale, Cheshire, 1984

Saved by the Damage

John Pratt (Flight Lieutenant J. Pratt), of 225 Squadron, was flying a tactical reconnaissance one morning in the Rome/Anzio area during the Italian campaign. His Spitfire IX received a direct hit in the cockpit from light flak while he was at 4500 feet near Velletri, on the edge of the Anzio bridgehead.

My immediate reaction was to bale out. Fortuitously, I was prevented from doing this by the damage to the hood; the canopy was jammed tight. Had

I been able to get out, I would not have survived; I had been wounded in many places and was losing blood too fast.

Time was running out . . . . The only place to land was on the bridgehead airstrip near the coast. I hadn't the strength now to lower the undercarriage so I made a wheels-up landing, coming to a grinding halt – fortuitously again – close to a US Field Dressing station. The instant attention I was given saved me. . . .

I remember little after this except that, having been operated on, I was later evacuated by sea to the RAF hospital in Naples. After a few days' convalescence at Sorrento, I was able to rejoin the squadron . . . fortunate, indeed, to be alive.

John Pratt, Ruwa, Zimbabwe, 1984

First-Degree Murder

As new pilots and crews continued to be fed into the squadrons to make good the still sizeable losses, their inexperience was manifested in several ways, not least in their 'trigger-happiness' and in their sub-standard aircraft recognition. Cases of mistaken identity were by no means rare (see 'Acquitted?', page 187 and 'Providential End', page 250).

John Hodgkinson, a dentist from Orange, New South Wales, witnessed a most regrettable example of it in November 1944, during his time in northern Italy with 3 Squadron of the Royal Australian Air Force.

The squadron had been out of operations for a while converting from P-40s, Kittyhawks, to P-51s, Mustangs, but, now, six of us were detailed to act as high cover for a Special Duties, RAF Lysander which was to land and deposit, in broad daylight, two exceptionally brave and well-decorated [DSO & MC & bar apiece] army officers, deep inside Austria.

On the way north, we encountered formations of B-17s and P-51s returning to Bari, in southern Italy, after a USAAF bombing raid to Germany. A P-51 pilot pulled out of the formation, nearly collided with us on the way in, and shot the Lysander down, killing all on board.

This was fate at its worst. . . .

J. A. T. Hodgkinson, Orange, New South Wales, Australia, 1984

Editor's note: *In a lighter vein, John Hodgkinson was operating with 239 wing one day when the USAAF's aircraft from Bari were out on another bombing raid to Germany. An all-negro figher squadron was in the party, working on the same R/T frequency as John's 3 Squadron. There had obviously been quite a skirmish with the enemy. By chance, John heard one of the pilots, Rastus, separated and clearly in some difficulty, call out to his No. 2, George. 'George,' he said, 'come on up here 'cause ah's got a 109 on mah tail.'*

George, plainly no respecter of No. 1s, came back, cool as you like. 'Rastus,' he retorted, 'what do you think Uncle Sam's payin' you for?'

Holed Up with a Bomb

Humour was never far away, even in the critical moments of the air war. Extreme tension and laughter often marched arm in arm. The South African Air Force's Bob Rogers (Lieut-General R. H. Rogers) (see 'Home James, by Staff Car, page 145), now moving fast up the operational ladder, tells of the extraordinary escape of an NCO in his (40) Squadron at Forli, some fifty miles southeast of Bologna and twenty miles inland from Italy's Adriatic coast.

It was right at the end of 1944, at a time when 7 Wing of the SAAF was operating its Spitfires vigorously in a fighter-bomber role with a 500-lb bomb slung under the aircraft's belly. . . . The chance of a hang-up in the air – with the bomb subsequently coming adrift on landing – struck cold at the heart. . . .

On one occasion a 40 Squadron maintenance crew was working on one of our Spitfires dispersed near the runway, when four 7 Wing Spits joined the circuit. It soon became evident that No. 4 in the section had a hang-up. All work then stopped as everyone carefully monitored the aircraft's approach to land.

All went well until touchdown, and then the bomb parted company with the aircraft and came bouncing down the runway in the direction of 40 Squadron's dispersal.

With one accord the 'erks'* scattered, one of the NCOs making a beeline for a nearby bomb crater. Glancing back over his shoulder he saw that the bomb was gaining on him so, from a great distance, he dived into the crater, to land, with a splash and a thud, in the icy mud and slush at the bottom. He was followed almost immediately by a second thud beside him.

'Thank God we made it,' he said, turning to see who had joined him. And there, looking coldly at him, was the bomb!

I was told later that the NCO's exit from the crater was even more spectacular than his arrival. Fortunately, the bomb failed to explode. . . .

Lieut-General R. H. Rogers, Leisure Isle, Knysna,
Republic of South Africa, 1984

Our Soviet 'Allies'

The mining of specific stretches of the Danube at very low levels by night – a most dangerous operation – was undertaken during the summer of 1944 and resulted, eventually, in a massive disruption of the oil flow from Rumania up to Vienna. Jack van Eyssen (Major J. van Eyssen), flying one of 31 (SAAF) Squadron's B-24s, completed a particularly successful sortie on the night of 30/31 July. He has provided a picture of the hazards.

We circled left, lost height and speed and headed upstream above the water *while my radio altimeter, set for thirty feet, showed green. Then it flashed yellow then red indicating that we had reached and dipped below thirty*

---

*Airmen – groundcrews. (Ed.)

feet. [Editor's italics.] Slight backward pressure on the control column and we reached and stayed in yellow while our speed settled at 190 m.p.h. The bomb-aimer called 'ready to drop – One' and the second pilot came in with 'two three drop – two three drop – two three drop etc.,' until all six mines had splashed into the river at pre-determined 3–second intervals, which spaced them about 300 yards apart. Then all hell was let loose as fourteen guns on either side of the river opened fire on us, and lit the sky with tracers. Our aircraft shuddered as all our gunners returned the fire raking enemy gun emplacements. . . .'

These fellows earned the decorations which came their way. . . .

Van Eyssen, today the honorary colonel of 31 Squadron, was shot down in the early hours of 14 August, not on a mining operation but during one of the tragic supply-dropping missions to Warsaw, at the time of the Polish uprising. He and others of his crew baled out some twenty-four kilometres southeast of the capital. It wasn't long before he found his way to Moscow, there to become the 'guest' of the British Military Mission. Unexpectedly, and by some dubious chance, he was called to the Kremlin by the admiral in charge of the British naval contingent, who led him to a conference hall where 'upwards of twenty Russian naval officers were already seated. . . . The mining of the Danube was to be an item on the agenda. . . .'

The short description which follows reveals the nature of our Russian 'allies'. . . . It quickly became apparent to the 31 Squadron captain that this wasn't to be a conference, but an interrogation and he was the one to be questioned.

The Russian officer at the head of the table was at least an admiral of the fleet, and he called the shots through an interpreter. Initially he put 'bread-and-butter' questions. . . . Then he warmed to his point by asking how, where, when, from what height, and how many mines I had dropped into the Danube. Then came the 64,000–dollar question. How did the mines work? To this I answered, 'I don't know.' When my answer was translated my interrogator flew into a rage while all others glared at me as if I was the devil himself. . . .

The message coming through seemed to be that we were allies fighting the worst tyrant in history, and here I was purposely withholding vital information when, after all, Russia had borne the brunt of the war. My anger rose, and when I did have the opportunity to speak I briefly explained that the mines were 'top secret' and that I was only paid to transport and drop them, not to design, build or maintain them.

Back in the admiral's office I blurted: 'What the hell was all that about?' He replied with a grin: 'You see, the Russians have overrun Bucharest and an area to the west of it. Your mines are still active and are blowing up Russian shipping!' 'That,' I said, 'is the best news I've heard in months, sir.'

His rejoinder was explicit. 'I agree, but don't quote me!'

Colonel J. L. van Eyssen, Waverley, Johannesburg,
Republic of South Africa, 1984

Attack Torpedoed

Meanwhile, away up in northern Norway, close to the North Cape, the German navy's only battleship, Tirpitz, *the largest in the world, was lying in Kaa Fjord, still undergoing repairs after the navy's previous, audacious attacks upon her. Until she was finally disposed of, the danger to our Arctic convoys, and those in the Atlantic, would remain.*

In August 1944 the Fleet Air Arm was to launch its third 'and final' onslaught on the capital ship. Codenamed 'Goodwood', the operation was to involve some '200 aircraft from five carriers – Indefatigable, Formidable, Furious, Nabob *and* Trumpeter . . .'.

Jeff Powell (Commander Jeffrey W. Powell, RN), then a lieutenant and senior observer of 846, a mine-laying Avenger Squadron, with extensive operational experience behind him in the Western Desert, the Mediterranean and elsewhere, thought well of the concept. It had been planned for weeks in meticulous detail; the carriers had been at sea 'for some days before sailing . . . practising taking off [and] forming into a single formation of about 150 aircraft, all below 300 feet. . . .'

There were no illusions. ' . . . Those of us in the Avenger Squadron realized that such a low-level attack in daylight would be pretty hazardous, with casualties likely to be very heavy, but we thought it a very effective plan. . . .'

Then came one of those chance happenings, which fate seemed to keep in reserve for inconvenient moments, and which were inseparable from the vicissitudes of war.

. . . We were in position at the launch point on 22 August. . . . That evening *Trumpeter* and *Nabob* withdrew to westward to refuel their frigates and *unfortunately ran into U-354 outward bound from Narvik. She torpedoed* Nabob *and badly damaged her, then torpedoed the frigate* Bickerton *which sank.* [Editor's italics.] The hit on *Nabob*'s stern produced a 50-foot hole and precluded her taking any further part in the operation. Many of her crew were transferred to the escorting frigates who, with *Trumpeter*, were ordered by the C-in-C to escort *Nabob* back to Scapa Flow.

So that chance torpedo hit on *Nabob* put paid to the mining Avenger involvement in Operation Goodwood and left some very frustrated aircrews in both ships as they sailed back to UK. Admittedly they had a lucky deliverance from what would have been a very hazardous strike, but the really bad luck was missing the opportunity for a well-planned and rehearsed attack in which, hopefully, the mining would have given the Fleet Air Arm a chance to sink *Tirpitz* by attacking her from below, where she had no armour protection.

Two days later on 24 August, *Indefatigable, Formidable* and *Furious* carried out the heaviest dive-bombing/strafing attack of all, and achieved two hits through very effective smoke screens. *One 1600-lb bomb which had penetrated eight decks unfortunately failed to explode!* [Editor's italics.] That was the last FAA attack on *Tirpitz*. . . .

Commander J. W. Powell, RN, Newport, Saffron Walden,
Essex, 1984

Suddenly, the Wind Stopped

Two New Zealanders – among a number of others – tried to break from Stalag Luft III at Sagan, some ninety kilometres southeast of Berlin, in 1944, the tragic year of the Great Escape. Through ill luck both failed; yet, each in his failure, was dealt a survivor's hand.

1. JACK RAE

Jack Rae (Flying Officer J. D. Rae) was one among the small group of exceptional New Zealand fighter pilots who won special glory in World War II. His performances with 249 Squadron in the Malta battle in 1942, and, before and after it, with 485 in 11 Group of Fighter Command, 'made' him. His eye was well in, with 13 enemy aircraft confirmed destroyed, when, on 22 August 1943, over northern France, the motor of his Spitfire called it a day and he became a prisoner.

The plan which he and his Canadian mate, Jack Probert, had hatched to take them out of captivity (and, hopefully, into the cockpit of an unguarded German aircraft) had been approved by 'Big X' (Squadron Leader Roger Bushell), the camp's escape leader. It demanded, for its success, 'a dark and stormy night and a nerve-wracking crawl of 140 yards from Hut 119, under the traversing sweep of the searchlights and the cover of the armed guards, until the wire was cut. . . . It also required a painstakingly created camouflage of sheets which encased each of us completely. . . .'

The conditions seemed largely to have been satisfied when, unpredictably, there came the first of two bad breaks.

With heart pounding, we had covered only about ten yards. . . . Then, horror of horrors! the wind suddenly dropped, the clouds disappeared and it turned into a calm, freezing cold, moonlight night. . . . All we could do was to go forward . . . moving only inch by inch . . . and trying to keep the dreadful scraping noise as low as possible. . . . We knew that in about two hours the guard with the very large German shepherd dog, named Heidrich, would be making his routine round of the compound. . . .

. . . Still we crept on and on. . . . Amazingly, we passed in front of the sentry tower and now Jack was ready with the wire cutters. . . . The first wires were cut, leaving only about three to go. It was then that chance struck us another cruel blow. They had just changed guards and the new one, either because he was a fitness freak or was freezing cold, decided to start jog-trotting, back and forth, along the full length of the wire. . . . Every time Jack's cutters came out he seemed to be coming at us again. . . .

Time was running out and dawn was now very close. . . . Jack made a quick cut at the wire, the movement was seen – and all hell was let loose. . . . The sentry up in the tower was just about having a fit, trying to grab the machine gun, the searchlight and his rifle all at the same time. . . . We stood up, hands raised, looking like a pair of ghosts in our camouflage. . . .

Lady Luck had dealt us a hard blow – or had she? Shortly after this came the Great Escape. We might have drawn a number to join in the

258

break. Of the seventy-eight who escaped, fifty were shot by the SS, on the orders of Hitler and the Gestapo, after being recaptured. . . .

J. D. Rae, Keri Keri, Bay of Islands, New Zealand, 1984

2. LEN TRENT, VC

In nearly thirty years of remarkable service, in war and in peace, Len Trent (Group Captain L. H. Trent, VC) experienced an amalgam of luck – good and bad – such as few could have equalled in a lifetime. Two incidents during the war probably looked at the time to have been just about the worst that fate could offer. Yet, in retrospect, each could be argued to have been a providential deliverance.

Len had been shot down over Holland on 3 May 1943, and taken prisoner in the most unfortunate circumstances which were not of his making (see 'Saved – by the Spin of a Coin', page 196). Yet he was probably lucky to have got away with his life.

Nearly a year later, on the night of 24/25 March 1944, when the Germans rumbled the Great Escape from Stalag Luft III while it was in progress, the New Zealander was next to break from the tunnel named 'Harry'. Nos 1–78 had all gone through. His number – 79 – was the next out.

. . . The relatively slow build up of unseen, but very real, danger finally got to me and I could feel my heart pounding so hard that it was actually knocking the wind out of my lungs. . . . The jackboots stopped, and except for the sighing of the breeze in the pine trees above, everything went very quiet. . . . My God, I thought, as I lay flattened on the ground, the guard must hear my heart thudding on it. . . .

I discovered later that the guard had not seen me, but was only a pace short of the exit hole, fumbling with his trousers and about to have a pee, when he noticed the movement – or heard the noise – of No. 80, Bob McBride, behind me, arriving at the top of the ladder. . . .

I heard a grunt, followed instantly by the action of the bolt of the guard's rifle and the crack of the first shot. . . . I fairly bounced to my feet with my hands in the air. '*Nicht schiessen, Posten,*' I shouted. '*Nicht schiessen!*' (Don't shoot, sentry. Don't shoot!) I was relieved to see the guard raise the rifle towards the treetops and fire the second round. . . .

The rest of the saga – the three weeks' solitary confinement; the news of the abhorrent murder of fifty of the seventy-eight escapees (including Roger Bushell, the architect of the escape); the terrible, inhuman, forced march of prisoners from Sagan to Trenthorst – there were still another twelve months of personal hardship and privation to endure. But, four decades later, Len Trent could see the picture in perspective.

. . . As for me, and the chance drawing of No. 79 out of 500, it was probably the luckiest ticket of my life. As I lay flattened on the frozen ground cursing my luck, while the guard, quite by accident, wandered to the very edge of the tunnel's exit thus preventing my escape, I could see only my stark misfortune. . . .

I have since come to realize that my guardian angel was certainly taking care of me that night. . . . Had I been recaptured away from the immediate vicinity of the camp, I would have been taken with all the other escapees to the Gestapo headquarters and, most probably, ended up as ashes in an urn beside Roger Bushell's. . . .

Group Captain L. H. Trent, VC, Leigh, North Auckland,
New Zealand, 1984

'Stalag Snowfall'

Stalag 8B, Lamsdorf, 1944*

Snow falling
whirling and swirling.
No calling
of birds.
Soft words
drifting over
the hush of morning . . .
Suddenly excited
voices of men, sounding
more like boys,
hoping soon to be rounding
the clean, cold whiteness
into the brightness
of shining snowballs.
Hurling or curling
balls of beauty;
glittering grenades
of Silcsian snow

John Dixon

He Wanted to Fly with His Friends

Few of the Luftwaffe's combat leaders had amassed the aviation experience which Wolfgang Späte (Major W. Späte) was able to bring to the air fighting over Germany and western Europe in 1944 and 1945. He had begun flying gliders in 1927 when he was sixteen, and by the late 1930s he had developed into one of the country's most successful, competitive glider pilots. He had, moreover, built and flown his own glider.

The transition in due course to the leadership of a unit named Erpro-bungs-Kommando 16, which was engaged in the operational development of the rocket-propelled Messerschmitt 163, designed by Dr Alexander Lippisch and built by Messerschmitt pre-war, was easily understood. Spate had already flown the 163 by 1942 and two years later, in May 1944, he flew it on its first operational sortie.

*See John Dixon's poem, 'Autumn', page 96. (Ed.)

260

Me 163 and B-17s (Flying Fortresses)

When this futuristic aeroplane went into squadron service with the Luftwaffe in 1944, it was to Wolf Späte that command of Jagdgeschwader 400 – the Me 163 Jagdgeschwader – was given. JG 400 was composed of 2 Gruppen (wings) of 3 or 4 Staffeln (squadrons). One gruppe was operating from Brandis, near Leipzig, and the other at Stargard, near Stettin.

From February 1945 until the end of the war, Späte was operating with Jagdgeschwader 7, with its jet-propelled Messerschmitt 262s. His total of 99 confirmed kills at the close included 4 B-17s and 1 B-24 shot down in the 262. (Those who knew Späte's leading and flying believe that his actual total was closer to 120.)

It makes a striking record, particularly when account is taken of the six months' spell from May until October 1944 when he was commanding IV Gruppe of JG 54 with the conventional Focke-Wulf 190 A8. His own – and his pilots' – chances of surviving the catastrophic losses which beset the Luftwaffe's squadrons at this time, must have seemed slim. . . .

. . . After fourteen days [of commanding the gruppe] 26 out my 80 pilots had died. Statistically, the last one of us to go could have expected to have survived, at the most, six weeks. Altogether, in three weeks, we lost 42 pilots, a large part of our flying strength. . . .

Späte cites a moving example of a young lieutenant, Detlef Jung, only son of a wealthy father whose industrial interests could certainly have ensured that his son be classified as being on essential work and, therefore, exempt from military service. But Detlef was deaf to his father's pleading. He came, fresh from combat school, to 16 Stafel in IV Gruppe. The kommandeur, because of the special circumstances, tried to shield him from the more dangerous operations.

. . . The next day, our unit would be leading the whole formation. As I had led it often on previous occasions, I handed over, in the normal course of things, to a subordinate who had a reputation on the Eastern Front for experiencing 'engine failures'. I thought that when he had 100 aircraft behind him, the responsibility would exercise his mind and force him to keep going. . . .

I was wrong. . . . Five minutes after take-off he was back with the usual complaint – 'engine failure'. A young officer took over, and led the formation. . . . The staffeln returned in ones and twos, broken up by the superiority of a better-equipped enemy. . . . Six of our pilots were lost – including Jung. . . . He did not *have* to fly, but he was determined to go with his friends. His body was found hanging from his parachute; he had been shot while baling out. . . . Two more of the dead pilots had received similar wounds. . . . I did not sleep much that night for Detlef had become like a young brother to me. . . .

. . . Next day it was my turn to lead. . . . There was [the usual] tough opposition. . . . Suddenly, a single-engined aircraft pulled up steeply out of a dive, just ahead. I opened fire . . . from eighty metres. The Spitfire was obviously hit. . . . I dived away down to the deck where I always felt safest. Beeken, my No. 2, stuck right with me. Together we swung away and turned for home.

. . . A parachute hung in the air. I could tell at once it wasn't German. . . . Now I could take my revenge for Detlef Jung. But should I? Should I?. . . .

Such are the chance decisions – and fortunes – of war.*

Wolfgang Späte, Edewecht, Germany, 1984

A Historic Act of War

Ben Drew (Major Urban L. Drew), from Detroit, Michigan, was a 20-year-old 1st Lieutenant in the 8th United States' Air Force, when, on 7 October 1944, flying a P-51D Mustang named 'Miss Detroit', he became the first Allied airman to shoot down two of the Luftwaffe's newest Me 262 jet fighters in a single mission. It was, in the circumstances of the early exchanges between jet and propeller-driven aircraft, a historic act of war, tinged, here and there, with a streak or two of luck.

Drew, whose base was at Little Walden, near Saffron Walden in Essex, was on a deep-penetration, escort mission with the B-17s of the 8th's 1st Bombardment Division to targets in Czechoslovakia. Running fights had developed between US and German aircraft all along the route. By the time the 375th Fighter Squadron, which Ben was leading that day, had

---

*Wolfgang Späte has taken this specially condensed story from his book, *Der Streng Geheime Vogel*, published in Germany in 1983. (Ed.)

reached the Osnabruck area they had already lost three pilots, including the leader's No. 4 man.

As they passed over the jet airfield at Achmer, at around 15,000 feet, Drew saw two Me 262s taxiing out for take-off. Rolling his P-51 onto its back, he took his flight down in a 480 m.p.h. vertical power dive, pulling out at 1000 feet to pick off, first, one and, then, the other fighter soon after each had become airborne.

The two German aircraft, piloted by Leutnant Kobert, who was killed in the attack, and Oberleutnant Bley, who baled out safely but perished later the same month in another operation, were from the celebrated and newly formed jet unit, Kommando Nowotny. Their's were the Kommando's first recorded Me 262 losses.

Fortunately for Drew, one of the German Air Force's outstanding pilots and leaders, Major Georg Peter Eder,* was on the ground at Achmer at the time of the engagement. He would have been leading the Kommando on the interception but for a 'flame out' in his No. 2 engine before take-off. By a rare and happy coincidence, and following exchanges between the United States and German Air Forces, Ben and Georg Eder were able to make contact nearly thirty-nine years after the event. . . .

Drew, now an aircraft broker and consultant, who divides his time between South Africa, the United Kingdon and the United States, is the first to admit the luck which surrounds this episode.

My wing man, Lieutenant Robert McCandliss, was shot down by ground fire that day almost immediately after my attack on the 262s at Achmer. Fortunately, he baled out successfully and was taken prisoner. But he wasn't, of course, there, to confirm the destruction of the two 262s, when I landed back at Little Walden.

Worse, when the intelligence boys went to extract the film from the camera in my P-51, they found that the new colour cartridge which had been fitted had jammed, and not a single foot of film had been exposed. . . .

However, General James Doolittle, commanding the 8th Air Force, having heard the account of the mission and the evidence, awarded me the two victories. . . . It was naturally a real disappointment at the time to know that, because of the lack of the gun-camera film and a supporting statement from my wing man, the recommendation for an award was denied. . . .

Luckily for me, all came right in the end. When contact was made with Georg Eder, he was able to confirm the loss of the two Me 262s that day back in October 1944. He had seen it all happen. What's more, he recognizes that had his own jet not become unserviceable just before take-off, it might well have been his aircraft rather than those of his two squadron mates which caught the shells from my P-51. This was *his* chance.

It was as a result of Georg's witness, and the correlating evidence which had additionally been secured, that the awards and decorations section of

*Georg Eder had an astonishing record. He is *credited* with 96 aircraft destroyed of which 42 were B-17s and 6 were B-24s; 22 were shot down while flying the Me 262. He was himself shot down 17 times, being wounded on 14 occasions. . . . How's that for luck? (Ed.)

the US Air Force, felt able to renew the original recommendation for an award. . . . This was *my* chance and honour. . . .

Urban L. Drew, Missoula, Montana, USA, 1985

Editor's note: *The award of the United States Air Force Cross, the second-highest decoration for gallantry in the face of the enemy, was conferred upon Major Drew by Verne Orr, Secretary of the US Air Force, in Washington, on 12 May 1983, thirty-eight years and eight months after the deed that won it. It made a fitting epilogue to a martial feat of arms.*

Gambling the Last Throw
1945

Victory was now assured, but still the dice were being well shaken and rolled. The outcome of each personal lottery was just as unpredictable in 1945 as it had been in 1939. Loss was as likely to come up as survival with the result resting in the palm of an invisible hand. Fate played some of its foulest tricks in the last weeks and days of battle. Many whose earlier fortunes had made them seem impregnable against assault now perished cruelly at the last encounter. Others, like the prisoners, whose future had appeared so bleak, presently saw the first light of a real dawn. But right up to the final throw, none could be sure which way luck would turn.

The Swings and Roundabouts of High Command

Reputations in the high commands had, by now, been made and the leaders were assured of their place in history. Some had, indeed, reached the summit by way of the misfortunes of others. Perhaps they had always been destined to rise just as their less fortunate counterparts were fated to fall. Whatever the reasons, the chances which lined the route to high command make, in retrospect, a fascinating study in the course of war.

Henry Probert (Air Commodore H. A. Probert), head of the Royal Air Force's Air Historical Branch at the Ministry of Defence in London, is better placed than others to assess the consequences. He looks back now at the picture in all its prophetic and extraordinary relief.

The loss of a high commander through some military accident has always been a risk of war, and one need do no more than recall the death in 1916 of Lord Kitchener, Chief of the Imperial General Staff, aboard HMS *Hampshire*, to appreciate the incalculable consequences. In World War II the advent of the aeroplane as the most rapid means of transport added a further dimension to these risks, and a mere two months before it began had come a signal warning. On 28 June 1939 a DH86B of No. 24 Squadron piloted by Wing Commander D. F. Anderson took off from Biggin Hill conveying several distinguished passengers to Belfast for celebrations to mark the opening of its new airport at Sydenham. Running into bad weather over the Irish Sea they were compelled to turn back, and eventually found themselves over the hills of northwest England where they crash-landed at Kirby-in-Furness. By remarkable good fortune nobody was killed, but at risk had been Sir Kingsley Wood, Secretary-of-State for Air; Air Marshall Sir Christopher Courtney, Air Officer Commanding-in-Chief, Reserve Command; and Air Vice-Marshal Sholto Douglas, Assistant Chief of the Air Staff – all destined to play key roles during the war.

While it could so easily have been much worse, for Courtney the injury he sustained cost him the post of C-in-C, Fighter Command, which he was about to take over from Sir Hugh Dowding. So Dowding stayed at Stanmore to become the victor of the Battle of Britain, and in due course Courtney went to the Air Ministry as Air Member for Supply and Organization, the post in which he served for the rest of the war with great distinction but no chance of glory. Far younger than Dowding and a man of much more open personality, his style of leadership would have been very different, as might well have been his conduct of the battle itself, and thereafter he could hardly have done other than remain in high operational posts, with the opportunity of becoming one of the greatest of the RAF's wartime commanders. All we can do today is speculate on what might have happened had his kneecap remained intact.

Nor can we do more than speculate on the likely consequences in January 1942, had the pilot of the Boeing Clipper bringing the Prime Minister back to England from the Washington Conference not decided to change course. In Volume 3 of his memoirs Churchill himself vividly describes how the aircraft had been flying through mist for ten hours when Sir Charles Portal, after consulting the captain, told him they were immediately going to turn north. As Churchill was subsequently informed, had they held their original course for a further five or six minutes he, Portal, Pound and Beaverbrook would have been over the German gun batteries in Brest. But fortune had favoured them.

NAVIGATIONAL ERRORS

It was not always so. On 20 November 1940, a Wellington aircraft of No. 214 Squadron, Serial T2873, took off from Stradishall [ten miles southeast of Newmarket in Suffolk] en route for Malta and thence the Middle East. On board, in addition to Squadron Leader Samuels and his crew of three, were two passengers, one of them the 51-year-old Air Vice-Marshal Owen Boyd, previously AOC, Balloon Command, and now about to become deputy to the Commander-in-Chief, RAF, Middle East, Sir Arthur Longmore. After calling at Gibraltar, the aircraft set course for Malta, but owing to errors in navigation ran short of fuel and was forced, instead, to land in Sicily. Although the Italians were later to claim that the aircraft (described by them as three-engined) had been intercepted by their fighters north of Cape Bon and compelled to land in Sicily, there is no evidence to support this; Italian prisoners interrogated soon afterwards in Malta merely stated that the Wellington had force-landed south of Noto with engine trouble and that the crew had then burned it completely. All were taken prisoner, and Boyd was freed soon after Italy surrendered in 1943.

A substitute was, of course, urgently required in the Middle East where Longmore had been pressing, ever since August, for someone to share the increasing load, and the choice fell upon the then Director-General of Research and Development in the Air Ministry, who wisely decided to fly out by the less direct but much safer route through Takoradi. His name was Arthur Tedder. As he points out in his own memoirs (*Without Prejudice*) Longmore had in fact originally asked for him to be sent, but the Prime Minister – who in those early days of the war took a close interest in the more senior military appointments – had refused to agree. But now chance stepped in, and Tedder was on his way to a leading role in the air war over the Western Desert, eventually to the key position of deputy to General Eisenhower for Operation Overlord, and finally to the desk of the Chief of the Air Staff. Bearing in mind Churchill's initial doubts about his abilities, could he still have become one of the RAF's most distinguished wartime leaders without that error of navigation, or would he have remained one of the backroom boys whose contribution would forever go largely unrecognized?

GOTT'S LOSS

Strangly enough, it was the loss of one of Tedder's aircraft, Bristol Bombay LS 814 of No. 216 Squadron, that occasioned another crucial switch in high command. On 7 August 1942 this aircraft was ready to carry out a routine casualty evacuation flight in the Western Desert from Burg el Arab to landing ground 90 when, with twelve wounded soldiers already on board, the captain was ordered to wait for three other passengers, one of them Lieutenant-General 'Strafer' Gott. According to the Official History, Gott, who had just been appointed to command of the 8th Army, was – unknown to Air Headquarters, Western Desert – going to Cairo on leave; the Operations Record Book for No. 216 Squadron, on the other hand, speaks of him returning there for a conference with Churchill. Whatever the purpose, he found himself aboard an aircraft which, owing to an overheating engine, was flying at 500 feet rather than the 100 feet that was usual in the forward area. The pilot, Flight Lieutenant James, believes that they did fly at 100 feet, but the contemporary documents are quite specific that they were higher than this and thus more vulnerable to German fighters. By unfortunate coincidence, the ORB states, a number of Me 109s on intruder patrols were being driven westwards by RAF fighters and crossed the path of the Bombay. Attacking from astern, they riddled the petrol tank, thus causing petrol to pour through the inside of the aircraft. Soon after the pilot had touched down in a very skilful forced-landing the Bombay was again attacked and set on fire. The medical orderly escaped uninjured through the hatch, followed by four others, including the pilot; two of these were seriously injured, and with Gott and all the others on board having been killed almost instantly, the pilot – himself injured – set out alone to seek help. It was 2½ miles before he found it.

General Gott, who had commanded first 7th Armoured Division and then 13 Corps in the long North African Campaign, had more experience of the desert than any other senior commander, but he himself felt he had been there too long and would have welcomed a change of scene. General Brooke, Chief of the Imperial General Staff, realized this and had urged the appointment of General Montgomery, but Churchill had overruled him.

Gott would lead the 8th Army for the forthcoming Alamein Battle, while Montgomery would command the British Land Forces in Operation Torch, the invasion of French North Africa. Now, once again, chance had thwarted Churchill's wishes, and he was compelled to accept the officer originally proposed. Had Montgomery not been placed in command of the 8th Army and become the victor of El Alamein, could he still have become the leader of the Allied Land Forces for Overlord and subsequently Chief of the Imperial General Staff? It is idle to speculate, but certainly much hung on the chance shooting down of that Bombay.

CHANCE WAS THE FACTOR

But was it chance? The pilot, who still reflects on this strange event, does not understand why the Germans continued to attack the aircraft after it had been forced down. To him it seemed as though they were making a determined attempt to destroy it and its occupants, which suggests that they might have known the identity of the senior passenger. While it seems unlikely that there could have been an intelligence leak given the timescale involved, the possibility cannot be entirely discounted; on balance, however, one is inclined to conclude that chance was indeed the determining factor.

Perhaps Gott was a fateful name. It was on 3 May 1943 that Navigator Captain J. H. Gott of the United States Army Air Force boarded Liberator 123728 at Bovingdon [near Hemel Hempstead in Hertfordshire] along with fourteen other crew and passengers. They were bound for Iceland, via Prestwick, where they were to receive a full weather briefing before proceeding further. Instead of landing there as instructed, however, they decided to fly on, and as they approached Iceland, making for Meeks Field, the weather deteriorated rapidly and they were unable to make radio contact. Flying low along the southern coast they spotted the RAF base at Kaldadarnes, where Gott fired a double red flare, but failed to see the return signal telling them to land. They continued westwards and then turned north along the west coast in the hope of swinging into Meeks, but with visibility almost nil and radio reception impossible they decided to turn back to Kaldadarnes. While retracing their course they lost sight of the coastline, drifted in over the land and struck a hillside. Only the tail gunner survived to tell the story of how fourteen men met their deaths, including General Frank Andrews, one of the Army's most distinguished airman-generals.*

GREAT USAAF CAPTAIN

One of the 'great captains' of the United States Army Air Force, General Andrews had been appointed a few months earlier to succeed General Eisenhower as European Theatre Commander in charge of all American forces in Europe. For an airman this was an unique distinction, whose

*Details of the crash are contained in *Forged in Fire* by De Witt S. Copp (Doubleday). This volume and its predecessor *Five Great Captains* also contain much information about Andrews' career.

significance may be further demonstrated by the fact that his post was filled after his death first by General Devers, and later once again by General Eisenhower when he returned to Northwest Europe as Supreme Commander for Overlord. While it would probably be going too far to suggest that Andrews might himself have become Supreme Commander he was a man who had already headed GHQ Air Force, the United States Army's aerial combat arm, had held the joint-command of the ground and air forces in the Caribbean Theatre and had then been Commander of all United States forces in the Middle East. One of the USAAF's greatest airmen, very highly regarded by General Marshall, the Chief of Staff, and particularly well thought of, too, by the British leadership, he must surely have held a very senior post of some kind during the final phases of the war. At whose expense we shall never know.

LEIGH-MALLORY'S ROUTE

To conclude this cautionary tale for high commanders, we move on to 14 November 1944, when at 09.07 hours York aircraft MW126 took off from Northolt on the first leg of its flight to India. On board was Air Chief Marshal Sir Trafford Leigh-Mallory, en route, with his wife, to take up his new post as Commander of the Allied Air Forces in Southeast Asia. The pilot, Squadron Leader Lancaster, possessed much experience of flying Sunderlands in Coastal Command, and had recently been selected as Leigh-Mallory's personal pilot for his tour in the Far East. When it was decided to use a York aircraft for the outward journey and then in the theatre itself, time was already short, for Admiral Lord Louis Mountbatten was anxious to have his new air commander arrive as soon as possible. Consequently, Lancaster was unable to complete a full course at the operational training unit, and the special conversion course laid on for him by No. 511 Squadron at Lyneham gave him a mere 9 hours 40 minutes' flying time. Much as the experienced pilots there wanted him to undertake at least one trip as second pilot as far as Algiers – and as Lancaster himself wanted to do – there was simply no opportunity.

The route chosen for the flight to Naples, the first port of call, was the standard one via Cherbourg, Poitiers, Toulouse, Marseilles and Corsica, and for the flight across France the forecast was for cloud with heavy icing. As far as is known, Lancaster intended to fly over the top at 17,000 feet, yet when sighted at 10.00 hours by a Dakota in appalling weather conditions somewhere between Granville and Laval he was at a mere 1500 feet. The pilot of the Dakota decided to turn back, but the York flew on. Later that day, Naples reported it overdue.

Continuing bad weather made an effective aerial search impracticable before the seventeenth, but then intensive operations were mounted along the route, particularly over the Massif Central and towards the Pyrenees. All were to no avail and the subsequent court of enquiry concluded that the aircraft had either crashed in the Bay of Biscay, flown into the Pyrenees, or been shot down by German defences over Western France or the Channel Islands.

Strangely, in retrospect, nobody seems to have thought of the aircraft drifting off track to the east, which is what actually happened. Shortly after midday it was heard flying northwards near the little village of Rivier d'Allemont, some sixteen miles east of Grenoble in the French Alps, followed by an explosion. The appalling weather made it impossible to send out a search party, and although the local gendarmerie were informed, the fact that an unidentified aircraft had crashed in the Alps was not relayed to those who were looking for the York in Central France. It was not until 4 June 1945 after the winter snows had melted, that a local farmer discovered the completely smashed and partly burned wreckage at a height of 6500 feet near the top of the mountain. The crew's watches had stopped at 12.35, 2½ hours after the last sighting, and the consensus among the investigators was that the aircraft, flying south, had hit the mountain top with its tail and somersaulted into the snow. This evidence conflicts with the recollections of those who heard the aircraft just before the accident, and nobody will ever know precisely what happened to Leigh-Mallory's aircraft in the 2½ hours it took to cover the 400 miles between its last-known position and the mountain side where it crashed. Thus departed the most senior member of the Royal Air Force to be killed during World War II; he and his wife and their companions are buried in the tiny churchyard of Rivier d'Allemont, set amid the splendours of the Alps that claimed them – just as the greatest mountain of them all had, some years before, claimed his brother in another of the unsolved mysteries of our time.

So it was that, through chance, a further very senior RAF officer was enabled to set the seal upon his own career. Leigh-Mallory, who before his appointment to the Far East had been the Air Commander-in-Chief of the Allied Expeditionary Air Force for Operation Overlord, had begun the war as Air Officer Commanding, No. 12 Group, Fighter Command. It was here, during the Battle of Britain, that his advocacy of 'The Big Wing' had brought him into dispute with Keith Park, the AOC of No. 11 Group. The merits of this controversy do not concern us here; suffice it to say that while Leigh-Mallory took over 11 Group afterwards and then moved on to become AOC-in-C, Fighter Command, Park – who was widely thought to have deserved higher operational command – was sent to a training post. While subsequently he went to Malta as AOC, and then became AOC-in-C, Middle East, in January 1944, it seemed to many that he had been left aside from the centre of the action. It was the events of 14 November 1944 that gave him his opportunity, for in February 1945 he took up the post formerly destined for Leigh-Mallory, a post in which he would direct the Allied Air Forces in Southeast Asia at the climax of the war against Japan.

Is there a moral here? Let us be content with the thought that the successful commander needs luck on his side – all the training, all the skill, all the experience, all the personal qualities will avail nothing in the face of ill fortune, and the best plans in the world can fail if they leave out of account the element of chance.

Air Commodore H. A. Probert, Air Historical Branch (RAF),
Ministry of Defence, London, 1984

Messerschmitt Moments

If strange chances had studded the path to top commands, so, too, on operations, were the crews reporting bizarre events. Bill Davies (Flight Lieutenant William I. Davies), for one, then a navigator with 156 (Pathfinder) Squadron, based at Upwood in Huntingdonshire, and for many years since a Toronto real-estate broker, recounts an experience from his Bomber Command days which defies rational thought.

It happened early in 1945 when his crew in Lancaster, 'T' for Tommy, well on their way at the time to a total of forty-three operations, were passing south of Heligoland after a deep-penetration raid into Germany. The wireless operator, Warrant Officer J. T. Barnes, later to become Lord Mayor of Northampton, was manning a Fishpond, *codename for a radar device designed to warn of approaching enemy fighters. Picking up telltale 'blips' on the screen, Barnes gave the alert. Davies recalls the subsequent play.*

We knew there was a German night-fighter squadron on Heligoland . . . and, sure enough, two Me 110s were seen and identified immediately behind us. They carried out curve of pursuit attacks on us for maybe twenty minutes, and all the time we were following the normal corkscrewing evasion procedure. Extraordinarily, neither of the two enemy aircraft opened fire. . . .

Naturally, we didn't open fire either, but watched this strange tactic continue for what seemed like an eternity. I well remember getting out from under the blackout navigation compartment curtain and seeing the two 110s without difficulty. Not once did they open fire, and, of course, we were fully aware that had they done so our chances of not being hit many times were slim indeed. Again and again they performed their curve of pursuit procedures to a running commentary from our mid-upper gunner. . . .

After numerous attacks without firing the two aircraft suddenly disappeared and we landed back at base. I find it very difficult to believe they had no ammunition, or that they couldn't get a bead on us owing to our corkscrewing tactics. We all thought at the time it was an act of God. . . .

William I. Davies, Toronto, Ontario, Canada 1984

Presumed Killed

Alex McQuilkin (Sergeant Alexander McQuilkin) was a flight engineer flying from Lissett in Yorkshire, when, on 7 February 1945, his squadron, No. 158, of 4 Group, Bomber Command, was briefed for an attack on Goch, some thirty miles northwest of Duisburg. The crew had been brought down to 4000 feet because of the difficulty in identifying the target. The raid was then called off, but 'as we turned for home there was a violent explosion and the nose section forward of the pilot cockpit was missing completely . . .'.

I turned to help our Australian skipper, Jack Beeson (Flight Lieutenant J.

L. Beeson), who was struggling to maintain control. . . . He waved me away and gave the order to bale out. . . . Four members of the crew, the pilot, navigator, bomb-aimer and our Australian wireless operator/air gunner, were all killed. . . .

Despite a badly damaged ankle and frostbite, McQuilkin evaded capture for four days and nights before being caught. After receiving hospital treatment, first in Wesel and then in Munster, he and nine other prisoners were put on a train to Frankfurt.

The ten of us and our two German guards were in the front compartment when fighter bombers attacked and put some 300 cannon shells into the engine. . . . Another prisoner and I were forced to remove the fire from the fire box. Eventually, we reached the interrogation centre on foot and while in solitary confinement I was interrogated every day for a week. . . .

After forced marches to Nuremberg and Moosburg, our camp was liberated by the United States' 3rd Army and I was flown home to England via Brussels on 11 May, arriving at my home two days later. The following day, 14 May 1945, my parents received a telegram stating that I must now be presumed killed. . . .

Thirty-nine years later, 'Bluey' McQuilkin revisited the area where he and his crew had been shot down.

I was able to identify the hospital in Wesel where I had been treated. Later, while touring through the Reichswald Forest, I came, quite by chance, upon the British Commonwealth Cemetery. There, to my great surprise, I found the graves of my fellow crew comrades:

Flight Lieutenant J. L. Beeson, Royal Australian Air Force, pilot
Pilot Officer W. G. Bennett, Royal Air Force, navigator
Pilot Officer R. E. Jones, Royal Air Force, bomb-aimer
Pilot Officer L. J. Nichols, Royal Australian Air Force, WOP/AG

It was a moving experience, for although it may seem like a coincidence, I believe I was *meant* to find that cemetery, for I had no plans at all to visit it. . . . I have always believed, in any case, that I was spared that February night in 1945 by God's providence, and now I feel equally sure it was His guidance which led me to my former comrades' graves. . . .

Alexander McQuilkin, Kincardine, Ontario, Canada, 1984

'They Also Serve'

Alone she waited, clad
In WAAF's uniform. Her sad
Blue eyes stared in disbelief.
Eyes that could not hide her grief

Gazed as though to draw apart
The unrelenting cloud. 'Depart
Cumulus. Let him find his base,
Let me look once more upon his face.'

But the Signals WAAF already knew
There was no hope for him or for his crew.
Had heard his last despairing call:
'Mayday, Mayday, Mayday.' That was all.

Jim Brookbank*

Bill

Judge Stanley Gill (Flight Lieutenant S. S. Gill) was a 21-year-old bomb-aimer in the Pathfinder Force (514 and 7 Squadrons) around the time when the operations which stimulated this reflection were mounted.

. . . Two incidents recur to me – both, perhaps, because we must have been pretty near to joining the 10 per cent that failed, for one reason or another, to return; but we were lucky. . . .

Our rear gunner was someone I suppose Daisy Ashford would have described as an *elderly* man of about thirty! He was Bill [Parker] from Barnsley. . . . We used to call him 'the old man' and other highly respectful names, and he used to call us 'you young buggers' – it was all very friendly.

Stowed away at the back and in a turret open to the stars, for better visibility, he looked like Michelin man in his massive electrical suit. He rotated and gyrated in his turret tirelessly and vigorously until we were all sure one day he would screw himself off. He was always tranquil and alert. 'Are you alright, Bill?' Roy Worthing would call up, and back came the instant reply 'OK back here, Skip!'

One night we had to go to Nuremberg, and what with Occy, the navigator, losing consciousness as usual, and an electrical storm which somehow affected the compass, things went a shade wrong for the return trip. I was busy as usual, working the H2S† and getting some rather imaginary fixes.

After a considerable time I announced, courier-like, over the intercom: 'If you look over to starboard you may see Paris – we're passing just south of Paris.' I think we must have been flying on 'George', because Roy didn't say anything. . . . Bill from the back was the only one to show any interest. 'I say, Skip,' he said, 'what are these mountains around Paris?' I said loftily, 'There *are* no mountains anywhere near Paris – it's as flat as a pancake!' 'Well,' said Bill, 'if I put my hands out I can just about touch these. Anyway, why's Paris all lit up? Shouldn't there be a blackout?'

A few minutes later we got a good visual fix on Lausanne or Lucerne or somewhere in Switzerland, and Roy woke up and we altered course about 40 degrees north and made for home. . . .

Some months later we had to go to Kiel. We were supposed to drop hooded flares first to light up the target and, later, four x 1000-lb bombs. *Unfortunately, on our way across the North Sea, flying at 5000 feet we lost not one but two of our engines.* which Lady Bracknell would have called not so much a 'misfortune' as 'carelessness'. *The result was that we*

---

*See 'The Night I Died', page 199.
†Radar aid for navigation. (Ed.)

were unable to get up to our usual bombing height and had to go over the target at 5000 feet.' [Editors italics.]

It was an experience not to have missed: though, at the time, one gladly would. . . .

The one person who could hardly be expected to enjoy it was the rear gunner! He had . . . a fine view upwards, brilliantly illuminated from below, of a cascade of cookies, flares, bombs and incendiaries, all apparently pouring down on top of him. He had a good deal to say, but, sadly, it wasn't Bill that night for some reason. I'm sure Bill would just have said: 'I say, Skip, if I put my hands out I could just about catch the bloody lot.'

His Honour Judge S. S. Gill, Baldersby, Thirsk,
North Yorkshire, 1984

Chance is a dicer

Proverb

Prescient Power

Did some aircrew possess supernatural powers of prediction? The possibility will not be decried by those with extensive experience of operational command. Presentiments, although rare, were by no means unknown. If they presaged unfavourable events, and the 'clairvoyant' spoke openly about them, they could be disturbing to a unit; no vigilant squadron commander could allow them to go unchecked.

Miles Tripp, author of twenty-six novels and now a retired solicitor, has an authentic instance to relate.* It occurred early in 1945 while he was a flight sergeant bomb-aimer in 218 Squadron of 3 Group, Bomber Command, based, first, at Methwold in Norfolk, and, later, Chedburgh in Suffolk. Here, in a specially written narrative, he describes the circumstances.

Harry [Sergeant Harry McCalla], our West Indian rear gunner from Kingston, Jamaica, was, like most normal members of aircrew, deeply superstitious. Less normal was his ability to predict with uncanny accuracy, hours before a battle order was posted, whether we should be flying. Sometimes he would make an inspired guess at the target and sometimes he was right. His hunches came to be respected by all the crew. And then, what could have been dismissed as a series of lucky coincidences became suspect.

The CO summoned all crews to the briefing room, and told us that secret information on targets had been circulating among ground staff, and even civilians, before crews themselves knew which target they were to bomb. It was thought that someone on the squadron was responsible for these dangerous revelations, and the CO asked us to keep our ears open and report immediately any careless talk about targets.

*Miles Tripp recounted the story in detail in The Eighth Passenger, published in hardback by Heinemann (1969) and Macmillan (1978) and in paperback by Corgi Books (1971) and Robin Clark (1979). (Ed.)

Our skipper, Flight Lieutenant George Klenner, a tough Australian from Adelaide, called us together at a time when Harry wasn't around. Haltingly, and emphasising that Harry was a bloody good type, he confessed he was worried about Harry's knack of knowing when we would fly and often the likelihood of the target. It might be intuition or it might be that Harry was getting information from an unknown source.

After anxious discussion it was agreed that when the opportunity arose at least one of us would be with Harry from landing after an op until briefing for the next op. Then, at navigators' briefing, I would find out the target, join the others in a different room, and one of us would casually ask Harry where he thought we were going. Only I would know if his answer was correct and, if it was right, it was proof that his strangely accurate forecasts weren't the result of some security leakage.

I was Harry's best friend in the crew and much disliked the part I had to play, but it seemed the only sure way of proving once and for all that his 'hunches' were some sort of extra-sensory faculty.

We didn't have to wait long to put the test into effect. Dog-tired after a 9½-hour flight to Dresden and back on the night of 13/14 February, we all went straight to our hut and to bed. We were on again the following night. Harry had been with us all the time. I duly went into the briefing room to learn the name of the target. It was Chemnitz a town some miles to the west of Dresden, and a place we'd never visited before. The round trip would take 8 hours 20 minutes. I rejoined the others who were waiting in another room. It was George Klenner, the pilot, who turned to Harry and said, 'Have a shot at guessing the target, mate.'

At that point Harry knew he was on some sort of trial, but quite impassively he went across to where a map of Europe was pinned to the wall. Putting out a hand he let it stray across the map until his forefinger reached Leipzig. He paused a moment, as if uncertain, and then his hand moved on slowly across the province of Brandenburg. It continued moving until his finger reached Chemnitz; then it stopped. 'I think it'll be Chemnitz,' he said.

The rest of the crew looked at me. 'He's right,' I said.

A stunned silence was broken by the pilot exclaiming, 'Christ!' and he strode off to the briefing room to check for himself that the target was indeed Chemnitz.

Harry was upset. 'What is all this?' he asked. No one could give an adequate reply. It took time and apologies before he understood and accepted that our motives were for the best, but he never made another forecast.

I have kept in touch with him since that incident almost forty years ago. He has never been able to explain how or why his intuition worked but he told me he lost the gift after our tour finished.* As for his prediction that Chemnitz would be the target, I sometimes wonder if a form of telepathy was operating between us. I desperately wanted him to succeed in the test and he may have picked up the word which was burning in my mind. But whether it was this, or he chanced to make a lucky guess, nobody will ever know.

Miles Tripp, Brookmans Park, Hatfield, Hertfordshire, 1984

*The crew completed forty operations together. (Ed.)

Norfolk Courage

Tuesday, 2 January 1945. . . . A bleak, winter's evening at Swanton Morley, 141 Squadron's base in Norfolk, some fifteen miles northwest of Norwich. Snow was lying thinly on frozen ground. For the 'old firm' of White and Allen (Squadron Leader H. E. White and Flight Lieutenant M. S. Allen) it would be their ninety-first operation together, a night-intruder to the hostile Ruhr in support of Bomber Command's offensive.* Between them, pilot and navigator, these two made as successful and as experienced a crew as could be found in this sophisticated, night-intruding business.

But on this day there had been differences in the pair's well-tried routine. Michael Allen recalls them.

Our aircraft [Mosquito XXX No. 797] was late coming onto the serviceability state that afternoon. There was no time for an NFT† before briefing. Harry and I decided to take it on the 'op' without one. . . . We had never done this before in 3½ years of night-fighter operations. . . .

And there was another thing we hadn't done before. Around lunchtime, we tossed a coin with another crew, Dennis Welfare and 'Sticky' Clay, to see which of us should do the trip! We had had an inconclusive exchange with a Ju 88 the previous night and were dissatisfied with our performance. We wanted to go again. We won – and took off soon after briefing in the gathering dusk. . . .'

There was a third point. This aircraft had given trouble before, and had come to be regarded as something of a 'rogue'. This time the circumstances were potentially fatal. On take-off, the port engine failed at 600 feet and 140 m.p.h. The airscrew wouldn't feather.‡ A glycol (coolant) leak developed. Further, with 716 gallons of petrol on board, and darkness at hand, the chances of avoiding disaster were minimal.

With manifest skill – and some luck – Harry White manoeuvred the Mosquito into a field. Allen has the picture. 'It bumped and bounced its way across the frozen, farmland furrows and through a ditch. When it stopped, the tail unit had broken off and the wooden fuselage was severed and crumpled in several places. . . . The aircraft was by now on fire. . . .'

White was pinned in the pilot's seat which had come off its mountings with the impact. Allen was stuck fast on top of him with one foot – and flying boot – gripped inextricably by a slit in the cracked fuselage. Neither pilot nor navigator could move, and the flames were rising. Two to three minutes and the tanks must explode. Michael Allen's recollection remains sharp.

I shouted 'Help! Help!' several times at the pitch of my lungs, but the chances of anyone hearing must have been remote. We were four miles

---

*See 'Strangers in the Night', page 201.
†Night-flying test.
‡Ability to set the angle of the propellor blades to reduce the wind resistance to the minimum. (Ed.)

southwest of Swanton Morley and three miles from the nearest village. It was bitterly cold and in blacked-out England no one stayed out at night if it could be avoided. . . .

. . . I now started to contemplate what death would be like. I found myself looking forward to it and thought it would be good. . . . I would probably find out what had happened to my parents who had been killed two months earlier by a German V-2 rocket. . . . I lay there making no further efforts to get out; I was looking forward to dying within the next few seconds. . . .

Harry White, however, had other ideas. . . . He had only recently got married and felt strongly about our predicament! . . . Moreover, he was concerned about the warm glow under us and had most certainly not given up! I was shaken back to reality when I heard him shouting for the axe – a kind of fireman's axe which all aircraft carried. (I thought to myself afterwards that if it had been found he would have had my jammed left leg off in a trice!). . . .

It was at that moment of terminal despair that the miracle happened. Three men, the local farmer, Herbert Farrow, and two hands, James Andrews and 'old' Walter Ward, fortified with Norfolk's own brand of courage, had reached the scene as flames licked the port wing and bomb bay, and the ammunition was exploding.

Having wrestled with the navigator's flying boot and leg, freed him from the wreck and laid him in the ditch, they went back for the pilot. In the face of mortal danger, they released him. 'Now run for it,' White shouted, 'before it goes up.'

All four 'landed in a heap in the ditch' beside the navigator. 'Seconds later, the aircraft blew up. . . .'

The three rescuers each received the British Empire Medal. Michael Allen has recorded the rest.

'Harry and I were operational again by 14 January [editor's italics]. When my left leg had thawed out I went up to Goldsmiths and Silversmiths in Regent Street and ordered three silver tankards to be suitably inscribed . . . . With a crate of beer, and some of the squadron and the villagers of Scarning, we presented them to our rescuers. It was quite a party. . . .'

Not long ago, Michael took his wife, Pam, back to Broadway Farm. Herbert Farrow, alone of the three, was still alive.

I asked Herbert if he could remember where our Mosquito had come down. He pointed immediately to a circular patch of beet which was *light green* and some forty yards in diameter. 'There it were, my Booty!'

We squelched through the Norfolk mud . . . and there among the light green leaves of the ripening beet, we looked down and saw fragments of Mosquito 797 lying at our feet. . . .

M. S. Allen, Greycoat Place, London SW1, 1984

'Sonnet'*

I loved adventure, in my youthful pride
I challenged Fate. He let me strut and play
Awhile, till he was bored then took away
My liberty and tore me from your side.
But will you wait for me, and will you bide
Until I can with prison anguish pay
My ransom and return to you? Yet stay!
Why should you for my sake be denied
The pleasures of your youth when you can be
With many a better heart than mine which rhymes
More closely with your own; or wait for me
And innocent do penance for my crimes?
And so from all your vows I make you free
And ask but this – 'Remember me sometimes'.

P. S. Engelbach

The Cult of the Reciprocal (And Then Some) 6†

To get the taste of Charles Pretzlik's (Flight Lieutenant C. Pretzlik) horrific 'reciprocal' flown on the night of 8/9 April 1945, it is necessary to know, first, the background to his entry into the wartime Royal Air Force. Forty-five years on, the facts still seem barely credible.

In August 1939, a month before war was declared, he volunteered with half a dozen other friends to join the 115th Light Anti-Aircraft Battery, commanded by his brother-in-law, Viscount Scarsdale, at Kedleston in Derbyshire. His friends' commissions were, in due course, all gazetted, but his wasn't. There was a problem. His father, as loyal a citizen as could be found in Britain, was born an Austrian, and, in wartime, that raised questions. Charles, as British as the next man, returned to the family's business despairing of such bureaucracy.

Early in 1940 another chance came to join the army when volunteers were sought for a special skiing battalion of the Scots Guards. Training for the specially picked 600, with Pretzlik among them, took place at Chamonix, in the French Alps, 'down some excellent slopes and with plenty of champagne'. It was all highly secret, but was thought to have 'something to do with helping the Finns in their war with the Russians – and also setting about the Germans on the other side!'.

When the Finnish/Russian peace was announced, the intended expedition of the 5th Special Battalion of the Scots Guards was called off. Scarsdale thought this a propitious moment to get the worthy volunteer, Pretzlik, reinstated in his regiment as an officer. The War Office said 'no' and Charles, dismayed, returned again to civilian life.

But now the Royal Air Force wanted aircrew; Pretzlik offered his services as a pilot. Acceptance was immediate. After three months at an initial

*See 'Sonnet', page 34. (Ed.)
†See pages 47, 97, 99, 160, and 218.

training wing at Torquay in Devon, he was ready for a posting to a flying school. The CO sent for him. 'I'm sorry, Pretzlik,' he said, 'the Air Ministry's instructions are that you must be discharged at once. . . .'

999 people out of 1000 would then have told King, Government and Country to stuff it – and be fully justified in so doing, but Charles desisted and gained his reward. Three or four months later, in one of those chance meetings which occur in a lifetime, he encountered the Countess of Warwick, sister of Anthony Eden, who had recently moved from the War Office to become Foreign Secretary in Churchill's Coalition. The opportunity to unburden the story was irresistible.

In no time, I received a letter from the authorities. I was offered not one but *four* options. I could remain a civilian, join the army or the Royal Navy or return to the Royal Air Force, whichever I wanted. . . . I went back to Torquay and started all over again with the air force. . . .

On 8 April 1945, nearly five years and a great many flying hours later, Charles Pretzlik and his formidable-sounding navigator, Ian McGowan-Docherty, were at 30,000 feet over Heligoland in a Mosquito, outward bound on a deep-penetration, night-intruder operation into Germany. . . .

Ian Docherty reported a suspected enemy aircraft on the radar screen approaching from fifteen miles behind at the same height. In a moment or two the distance had been reduced to two miles. At that sort of overtaking speed, it could only have been a jet – a Me 262.
Diving from 30,000 feet down to near ground level, with the usual evasive tactics, the crew eventually threw off the persistent attacker. Climbing up again to some 15,000 feet, Pretzlik then continued on eastwards, as he thought, into Germany. In the turmoil of the encounter with the Me 262, he had, however, overlooked a cardinal point of procedure. . . .

My navigator now reported an aircraft flying at the same height, about five miles ahead, on much the same course. I concluded this must be an enemy as we were flying east and, from the briefing, I knew there should be no friendly aircraft in our area. . . .

. . . Ian Docherty gave me an excellent homing onto the aircraft and there, dead ahead in the darkness I could just pick out the silhouette some 3000 feet away. . . . With our overtaking speed, I soon had it in my sights. Pressing the gun button, nothing happened. I had forgotten to release the safety catch! I was on the point of having another go when Docherty shouted out: 'For Christ's sake don't shoot. It's a Halifax.' And there, very close now, was the British bomber, limping along on three engines, heading westwards for home, somewhere near the enemy's North Sea coast. . . .

The explanation was simple. After all the evasive action with the Me 262, I had forgotten to reset my gyro compass. The manoeuvring had thrown it all out. Instead of flying east, as I thought, I was, in fact, heading westwards on a reciprocal. . . .

It was the luckiest chance in the world that the Halifax crew escaped with their lives and I was able to live without a terrible conscience for the rest of my days. . . .

Charles Pretzlik, Isington, Alton, Hampshire, 1984

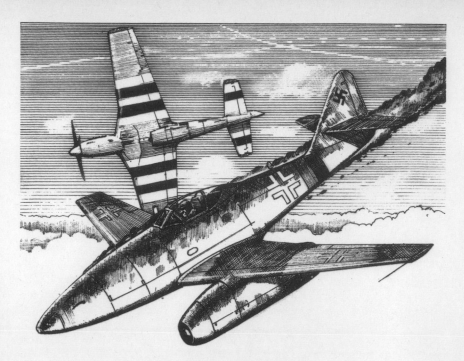

P-51 Mustang and Me 262

The Last Chance

Generalleutnant Adolf Galland, now leading JV 44, the elite Me 262 jet unit of all the talents, in the last exchanges of the war, flew his final combat on 26 April 1945. Two B-26 Marauders had fallen to his guns.

Then I was hit by Lieutenant Jim Finnegan of the United States Army Air Force (now my friend) in a P-51 Mustang, which I hadn't seen. My starboard engine was stopped, my instrument panel in the cockpit shattered and shrapnel had injured my right knee. . . .

I had to decide – bale out or go for a single-engine landing on Munich airport which was now under heavy, low-level attack. I had always had a fear of being shot while floating down in a parachute, so I took the gamble and went for the landing. . . .

It was my last chance . . . I was lucky, it was the right one!

Generalleutnant Adolf Galland, Bonn, Germany, 1984

Slanting Music

Heinz Wolfgang Schnaufer (Major H. W. Schnaufer), Commander of Nachtjagdgeschwader 4, was the Luftwaffe's most successful night-fighter pilot to survive the nocturnal holocaust of World War II. Between 2 June 1942 and the end of the war, he amassed, in the hours of darkness, a total of 121 enemy aircraft destroyed (most of them four-engined bombers). One hundred were achieved while his trusted radar operator, the exceptional Fritz Rumpelhardt (Leutnant F. Rumpelhardt), was in his Me 110 crew, and 98 of them while the faithful Wilhelm Gänsler (Oberfeldwebel W. Gänsler) was serving him as observer. They made quite a trinity, collecting between them the Knight's Cross with oak leaf, stones and diamonds for the pilot and a Knight's Cross apiece for the other two crew members.

If Schnaufer's luck had held in the long rough and tumble of war, it ran out, sadly, five years later when, in 1950, he was killed in a fatal car accident in France. It was the hell of a way for an accomplished officer to go.

To set things in perspective, two balancing points should here be made. First, the targets which Schnaufer and his crew were nightly finding were infinitely more numerous than anything the Allies had experienced in war. Second, this illustrious trio were fortunate to possess two technical attributes to sustain their record in the later stages of the struggle. They had the use of the advanced SN$_2$ radar-detection equipment, product of German inventive genius, and they could employ, in addition to the conventional aircraft armament, the lethal upward-firing cannons, codenamed 'schräge Musik' (literally, 'slanting music').

These angled guns enabled the German pilots to lay off behind and below British four-engined bombers with their most vulnerable areas exposed to attack. But that said, nothing can disguise the brilliant, professional efficiency of this outstanding crew.

It was during the two periods of darkness of 21 February 1945 – early and late – that the team's climacteric was reached. Fortune had something to do with it. Two Lancasters had been picked off in one sortie in the small hours (take-off was at 01.15), and then, in a second operation, between 20.44 and 21.03 the following evening – in nineteen crowded minutes of devastating assault – a further seven four-engined bombers were accounted for to bring the total for the two missions to a phenomenal nine. It is worth setting down the times and the positions of the conquests during that extraordinary second, nineteen-minute stretch.

Time of each four-engine bomber 'kill'	Luftwaffe fighter grid reference of position of each confirmed bomber crash
20.44	HQ – HP
20.48	HP – HO
20.51	HP – HO
20.55	HP – HO
20.58	IO – JN
21.00	JN – KM
21.03	KM – KL

Fritz Rumpelhardt, looking back across forty years, still has the clearest impression of that star-studded evening's hunting.

It was during the second sortie that chance took over from fate. I was sitting alone in the aircrew mess at Gütersloh, our airfield, gathering my strength for the anticipated night's action with a large supper. I did not realize that we had been brought to 'advance readiness', so when this was stepped up to 'cockpit readiness', followed almost immediately by take-off, I was surprised and unprepared. The squadron commander, who was, of course, all ready for action, was not very complimentary. . . .

It was fortuitous that our aircraft, the well-tried Me 110 EF, was late being got ready. The rest of the squadron had been airborne a long time so when we took off at 20.08 we were well behind. . . . We were surprised, as we followed the given course, not to see activity in the Düsseldorf area. Schnaufer was undecided about continuing on this heading when, away to the north, in the Münster vicinity, there were all the signs of strong defensive fire. . . . He at once decided to head northwest, climbing all the time, in an attempt to cut off the returning bombers. . . .

It was now that fortune favoured the crew. Rumpelhardt began getting 'blips' on his SN$_2$ screen and, as he did so, they found well above them a quite thin layer of cloud through which, here and there, the moon was penetrating. It acted like a white backcloth against which the dark silhouettes of the bombers were visible. It was the classical, set-piece situation for a 'schräge Musik' attack.

. . . Schnaufer picked out a Lancaster, flying along, no doubt quite unconcerned, slightly to our right. . . . As usual, he aimed at a point between the two starboard engines. With the location of the petrol tanks, this was where the quickest and most decisive result was always obtained. . . . It also, incidentally, gave the bomber crew the best chance of escape by parachute. . . .

. . . The first successful attack was at 20.44 hours precisely. . . . The starboard wing of the aircraft was heavily damaged by a large explosion. . . . An enormous streak of flame lit the night sky, but we thought there would be an opportunity for the crew to bale out. . . .

After that, Schnaufer had the choice of several targets. . . . Where his remarkable flying skill showed was in his ability, first, to time his attack exactly and, then, to stay with a bomber as it went through its corkscrewing, evasion tactics. . . . This way he could maintain his position without being exposed to the defending gunners. . . . He fired short bursts from close range, always withdrawing smartly. . . . He moved quickly and decisively. . . .

In those nineteen minutes of attacks, with all seven of the aircraft falling in flames, our Me 110 did not receive a single bullet from return fire, such were Schnaufer's positional skills. . . .

During an eighth attack the 'schräge Musik' failed at the decisive moment. All that was then left were the forward-firing guns in the nose of the aircraft. These also failed as Schnaufer went into the ninth attack. . . .

The strain – mental and physical – upon the captain during the time we were airborne was great. I therefore asked ground control at Dortmund for emergency landing priority back at our base, Gütersloh. . . . As we landed, taxied in and switched off the engines, there was complete silence among the crew. We were utterly drained and spent. . . . It was some minutes before we could collect our thoughts. . . .

One of the crew's victims that night was a Lancaster Jo-Z, of 463 Squadron. It had crashed on the Van Lipzig farm near Venray in Holland. The flight engineer, Stan Bridgman (Sergeant S. B. Bridgman) of Welwyn Garden City in Hertfordshire, had baled out with the rest of the crew. Through a series of chance circumstances, he made contact with Rumpelhardt a few years ago, and a meeting took place in London in 1980. Fritz Rumpelhardt's reaction was typical of the sentiments which animate old adversaries in the air forces.

. . . In our moment of success that night in February 1945, we had genuinely hoped that the crews of the Lancasters we had shot down would mostly survive by parachute. . . . When, years afterwards, I received a letter from Stan, met him later in London and exchanged gifts, a friendship developed between former enemies. It is a friendship that Schnaufer, had he lived, would have wanted to share. For us, it represents a hope fulfilled. . . .

Fritz Rumpelhardt, Kehl, Germany, 1984

POSTSCRIPT

Stan Bridgman, who suffered severe leg wounds during the attack, has added this postscript to Fritz Rumpelhardt's account:

There is no doubt Major Schnaufer's crew shot us down. Our target that night had been the Mittelland Ems Canal. It was our thirteenth sortie, we had dropped thirteen bombs (one had hung up), my Service number (1393508) began with thirteen and the numerals of 463 Squadron added up to thirteen – I might have known that we had small chance of completing our Canal mission successfully! I have since visited the Van Lipzig farm. . . . The cavity made in the woods by the crash of Lancaster, JO-Z, has been lined with concrete and is now a watering place for wildlife. . . .

It should never be doubted that the courage and tenacity of the German night-fighter crews was on a parity with that of our own bomber crews. . . .

S. B. Bridgman, Welwyn Garden City, Hertfordshire, 1984

Why Edwards Ticked

Keith Miller, the Australian journalist and cricketer, was an uninhibited and irrepressible sergeant pilot in the Royal Australian Air Force in the last years of war. He was also a close friend of the incomparable Hughie Edwards (Air Commodore Sir Hughie Edwards, VC) who, on the back of all his wartime honours, became, in time, Governor of Western Australia.

Soon after the war, Miller asked Edwards, by chance, about his wristwatch.

'Hughie,' I said, 'I'll bet that watch of yours has 'AM' [Air Ministry]* engraved on the back.' 'Keith,' he replied, 'you are the only person to notice that. I'll will this watch to you.'

Funny story about that watch. When Hughie was discharged, the only thing he wanted to retain was this watch, so he took it off his wrist and put it in his pocket. He then handed over all the rest of his gear.

'Don't worry about that lot, sir,' said the equipment officer, 'All I want is your Service watch.' 'Matter of fact,' retorted Edwards, 'I've misplaced or lost it.'

The equipment man looked at Hughie's wrist. There was a broad white band on his suntanned arm! 'All right,' said Hughie, 'how much is the watch?' 'Twenty-three pounds,' said the officer. 'Sold!'

I've got that watch still. Hughie flew with it throughout the war. It still keeps perfect time.

Keith Miller, Newport Beach,
New South Wales, Australia, 1985

Editor's note: *Just before Douglas Bader died in 1982, Keith Miller was playing golf with him and Gubby Allen, the England cricketer, at the Berkshire, near Ascot. 'I lost a ball or two that day,' Keith recalls, 'so Douglas gave me one. Appropriately, it was a Penfold Ace! I treasure it with Hughie's watch.'*

Crunch Judgement

Take off in a 'dodgy' aeroplane? Go ahead with a mission despite profound doubts about the weather on return? Continue with an operation instead of turning back when there is real apprehension about the wisdom of going on? Take a chance and trust to luck – or let discretion prevail ... ? Every pilot, every captain, every leader faced these questions at some time during the war.

Alex Thorne, for ten years editor of the Royal Air Forces' Association's journal, Air Mail, *was confronted with such a dilemma on 24 March 1945, during some critical moments before the daylight attack on the factory area of Osnabrück, in northwest Germany. Then a flight lieutenant with 635 (Pathfinder) Squadron, based at Downham Market in Norfolk, his role that day was to lead the attack and act as master bomber – a significant responsibility. ...*

To the best of his knowledge everything about Lancaster, 'D'-Dog, had been checked and made ready. The crew had climbed aboard. Understandable, in the circumstances, that the leader should want to be up and away and in the van of the squadron.

Thorne went through the flight check with Harry Parker, his flight

---

*The Air Ministry issued (very reliable) watches to aircrew. Pilots and navigators tried to 'win' them on demobilization. (Ed.)

engineer. All seemed to be on the top line – except for one small item. The fuel gauges were registering zero!

It couldn't be real. They must have stuck. He had seen the bowser leaving the aircraft the previous evening. All the obvious thoughts went through his mind. Risk it, he concluded. It was consonant with his 'press-on' spirit.

As they taxied out towards the runway, the flight engineer's voice came over the intercom. 'I don't like this, Skip. We ought to have the tanks checked. . . .'

A dipping rod was quickly found. It showed there was enough fuel for take-off, no more. Someone had boobed, but that wasn't the point now. The usual stand-by aircraft was a couple of hundred yards away. When checked, it was found to have no VHF.* No use for the master bomber who must be able to broadcast instructions to the main force. . . .

Then, suddenly, there was the faintest streak of luck. A bowser was passing 'D'-Dog. Unbelievably, it was full. In some twenty minutes 2154 gallons of fuel were injected into the Lancaster. But was it now too late to make the target – even if a direct route was flown to it? Thorne put it straight to his navigator. 'Let's start, anyway. You can be working out the answer. If it's impossible we'll have to turn back.'

Before they crossed the English coast, Boris Bressloff came back with the answer. 'We might just do it – if we get there.' He had no illusions (and neither had Thorne) about the risk of a lone Lancaster flying into the heart of Germany in daylight without escort. Some would have called it madness. If ever there was a case of 'putting it to the touch', this was it. Let the captain conclude the tale.

In the event, we had no fighter opposition, but plenty of hostility from the ground batteries, especially in the region of the Dortmund-Ems Canal. As we approached the target, the main bomber force came in behind us from the starboard side. "It might have been planned," said Jim Raymont, our rear gunner, as we circled the target area after dropping our target indicators for what was, in fact, a successful operation.

The end result was, indeed, as planned. But it followed a rare, and probably unique, omission in the servicing of an operational aircraft. It led to a chance nearly being taken which would have spelt certain disaster – and another being accepted which had a happier outcome. . . .

G. Alex Thorne, Thames Ditton Surrey, 1984

Editor's note: Some six weeks later, on VE Day, Thorne was on leave at home (and in bed with chicken pox) when a telegram arrived telling him of the award of a DSO. When, eventually, he returned to his squadron and read the citation, he found it was for a daylight attack on Nuremberg a couple of weeks after the Osnabrück affair.

A senior officer congratulated him. 'Thorne,' he said, 'we couldn't cite Osnabrück. Mistakes are not for promulgation.' What a war!

---

*Very high-frequency radio.(Ed).

Of Whittle and Aircraftman Shaw

616, the Royal Air Force's first jet squadron, was now operating its Gloster Meteor IIIs from a base near Brussels. A combination of the practical limitations of the aeroplane and the present character of the operations, gave it little chance to shine. It was an undramatic entry into a rarefied field. But if the Luftwaffe still held a massive operational advantage with its Messerschmitt 262 (and to a lesser extent with the Arado 234 and the rocket-driven Messerschmitt 163), the day of the British jet was yet to come.

It is right, therefore, to record a little-known story of how the inventive brilliance of Frank Whittle, creator of the British jet engine on which the Meteor's power unit was based, came to be unlocked. It was the result of a curious piece of misfortune which befell a man of uncommon prescience.

Sir Rolf Dudley-Williams, 1st baronet and product of the Royal Air Force College at Cranwell, sat for Exeter in the House of Commons for fifteen years. After being invalided from the Service pre-war, and before entering Parliament, he, with others, founded Power Jets Ltd, the company which then became responsible for developing Sir Frank Whittle's system of jet propulsion. Dudley-Williams's introduction to Whittle was, to say the least, bizarre.

I had intended to enter Cranwell as a cadet in January 1926. Unfortunately, I was having such an enjoyable holiday in the summer of 1925 at my uncle and aunt's cottage at Noss Mayo on the River Yealm, near Plymouth, that I forgot to send in my application for the college entrance exam. It was a devastating blow. And yet, as so often happens, this awful reverse turned out to be a well-disguised and far-reaching blessing.

By coincidence, the delay in forwarding my application meant that Frank Whittle and I became contemporaries and then close friends. Through our friendship, forged as cadets at Cranwell, I was able to play, a decade later, a considerable part in bringing Whittle's brilliant conception of the jet engine to fruition.

When Dudley-Williams's Service luck ran out and he was invalided from the Royal Air Force, he formed a base in the vending-machine business, then in its infancy. It was from here that he re-established contact with his friend, Whittle, and then set about forming and funding Power Jets and, as a managing director, injecting the drive which was to propel the company quickly forward.

And it all sprang from a chance failure to record an examination entry.

Sir Rolf Dudley-Williams, 'The Dudley-Williams Papers',
South Petherton, Somerset, 1984

Editor's note: *Unusual things — even small things — always seemed to happen to Dudley-Williams. One curious, chance episode occurred while he was still a serving officer (and, incidentally, a highly regarded flying-boat pilot and instructor) in the Royal Air Force. He was then stationed at Mountbatten, near Plymouth:*

'I was doing my rounds as duty orderly officer when I noticed a light showing in the engineering department where the maintenance of the flying-boats was undertaken. I told the sergeant of the guard that we would investigate.

Inside, I found an airman, writing. As he got up I noticed particularly that he was short of stature. When I asked him what he was doing, he replied that he had his flight commander's permission to use the office. Remarkably, I saw he was translating Homer's *Iliad*. "Why on earth are you doing that?" I asked. "Are you studying for a higher education test?"

"No," he said, he was doing it for Colonel Vanderbilt, in Boston, USA, who was paying him £600 – a lot of money then – for the translation. He added he needed the cash.

'When we got outside, the sergeant told me the airman was Aircraftman Shaw, better known as Lawrence of Arabia.'

'The Dudley-Williams Papers'

Luck Alone Couldn't Save Him

Some claim that the Deity, in His supreme judgement, never asks a victim of fate to shoulder a greater burden than he or she can accommodate. The point is debatable. What isn't arguable is that in World War II some aircrew endured punishment which would have stopped lesser men in their tracks. Jim Verran (Squadron Leader J. V. Verran), the New Zealander from Waipawa and Auckland, is as good an example as any of the rugged survivor.

He set out from his native land for the United Kingdom before the war and, on 8 August 1939, joined the Royal Air Force with a short service commission. Thereafter, he served Bomber Command and 102, 9 and 83 Squadrons through three taxing, but eminently successful operational tours during which his endeavours were rightly recognized. Yet, in the course of these duties, he withstood two experiences the like of which would have ended the ordinary mortal's flying days for good. One thing is certain – Verran enjoyed more than his rational share of luck to survive.

His long operational stretch began with Whitleys on 1 July 1940. It ended on the fateful night of 26/27 August 1944, when, on the last operation of his third and final tour, his Lancaster was shot down by a Messerschmitt 110 near Vejle in Denmark, as the crew were returning from a Pathfinder sortie to Königsberg, in East Prussia, one of the longest bombing missions of the war.

What is surprising is that, having lived through these times, Verran was still prepared, at the end of them, to devote a working lifetime to a career in civil aviation, both in the UK and overseas. Few know 'the air' like Jim Verran.

His two cataclysmic reverses bear brief reference. The first occurred between 02.00 and 03.00 on the night of 1/2 March 1943, when he and his crew were preparing to land their Lancaster in poor visibility at Waddington in Lincolnshire, at the end of a demanding attack on the German capital. Exhausted, but now looking forward to their bacon and eggs, Verran and his mates were at 800 feet on the downwind leg of the circuit when another Lancaster, captained by a Canadian, Flying Officer J. F. Greenan of 57 Squadron, hit them head on. The nightmare remains.

No explanation was ever given why this aircraft flew across the Waddington circuit. . . . Three of my crew were killed on impact. . . . The engines were scattered over a large area and the remains of the fuselage and wings caught fire. I was knocked out in the air when the fuselage section aft of the mid-upper gun turret was torn away causing the control column to snap back, striking me on the face and breaking my lower jaw. I came to in a ploughed field surrounded by bits of burning aircraft and exploding ammunition. I had been thrown clear when the remaining part of the aircraft struck the ground, propelling me through the cockpit canopy. I had, additionally, suffered a broken left femur, my right arm was paralysed and I had lacerations of the head and face around both eyes. . . .

John Moutray, my Canadian WOP/AG [see 'Making Hay', page 42 and 'Lucky Spread', page 96], walked out of the torn fuselage with minor injuries, Sergeant Chalk, the mid-upper gunner, was also relatively fortunate, but Frank Johnson, my Australian navigator, had brain damage and burns. . . . The other aircraft hit high-tension cables near Scampton, and the whole crew perished. . . .

One year and four days later, with eight months in hospital intervening, Verran was back on operations with 83 (Pathfinder) Squadron, soon to be transferred to 5 Group and Coningsby, in Lincolnshire, for both marking and bombing duties. It was with 83, on the night of 26/27 August 1944 – the concluding operation of three relentless tours – that he and his crew were raked by 20-mm cannon shells from the German night-fighter as their Lancaster crossed from the Baltic to Jutland, on the Danish coast, heading for home after the Königsberg raid. The Me 110 was itself shot down by the rear gunner before he died.

Five of the crew were eventually killed during the Me 110's attacks. Only the bomb-aimer, Warrant Officer Page, who was in the nose section, and Verran escaped injury from cannon fire. Page baled out through the front hatch. Meantime, the cockpit was on fire as the hydraulic header tank was hit, and hydraulic oil was spreading everywhere. The loss of this oil caused the undercarriage to come down and the bomb doors to open.

When Verran was finally able to bale out through the front hatch, he was immediately carried into the open bomb bay and pinned there by the tremendous air pressure. The flaming hydraulic oil was torching onto him in the bomb bay. He was only able to free himself, and drop out, when the aircraft was on the point of stall and the wind pressure dropped. . . . His release must owe something to providence, for luck alone – and his parachute – couldn't have saved him.

After landing, and despite his terrible burns and injuries, Jim Verran managed to make his way to a nearby farmhouse. . . .

. . . The occupants called an ambulance and I was taken to the local cottage hospital at Vejle, and thence to the German army hospital at Frederica where the German doctors and staff gave me the same treatment as they accorded their own nationals. On the other hand, the Me 110 pilot, whom my rear gunner had gallantly shot down before he was killed, and who was in the same hospital, refused to see or speak with me.* I gathered he thought his victory was the greater because he only had two engines whereas we had four!

A German general practitioner from Kiel carried out my skin grafts without an anaesthetic due to the shortage of drugs. They only had paper bandages. I owe my life to the GP from Kiel. . . .

In 1948 I went back to Vejle and stayed in the same farmhouse. I found that, after the Germans had buried my five crew members in a mass grave, the local people had later exhumed the bodies, given each a Christian burial and erected a headstone on each resting place. . . . I visited the cemetery. I saw also where our aircraft had crashed, and where I had landed by parachute. It was by a fjord, only 100 yards from the edge of a cliff. . . . I met again the Danish ex-merchant seaman who had driven me to the local hospital. He told me the Wehrmacht had fired on the ambulance despite its markings. . . .

Squadron Leader J. V. Verran, Bexhill-on-Sea,
East Sussex, 1985

Smoke Got in His Eyes

James Goodson (Lieut-Colonel James A. Goodson, USAAF Retd) is a versatile American. In the post-war years, his business sensitivity took him to the presidency, in Europe, of two of Goodyear's companies and of Hoover. Then ITT acquired his services as a vice-president and worldwide group executive. With that behind him, he has now turned his hand to writing books, and his Tumult in the Clouds *(William Kimber, 1983) makes one of the really arresting, first-hand accounts of the air war in Europe.*

Of course, Jim Goodson has had the material and the experience to work with. . . . Hurricanes and Spitfires in the Royal Air Force before the United States had entered the war. . . . No. 133, one of the three highly regarded American Eagle Squadrons in Fighter Command. . . . Then the transfer to the 8th United States Air Force and P-47s and P-51s with the 356th Squadron in the wonderfully aggressive 4th Fighter Group. . . . A full war ended when Goodson was hit by groundfire attacking a Messerschmitt 163 parked in a dispersal pen on an airfield near Neubrandenburg, and had to force-land.

Although wounded, he went on the run — until his luck expired and the Gestapo and the SS picked up the noted Terror-Flieger, *clapped him in prison and relegated him to a darkened cell in solitary confinement. Credited with thirty-two aircraft confirmed destroyed, and other offensive work, he expected to be shot, and in all probability would have been, but for an ingeniously contrived and certainly unconventional confrontation with the camp's Kommandant. Then a fourth talent — a propensity for blowing king-sized smoke rings from an outsize cigar — plus a nod or two from fortune, delivered him from the firing squad.*

*This was the exception, not the rule. Normally there was a chivalry between opposing aircrew which transcended wartime enmities. (Ed).

Here, in a specially adapted version of the story he tells in Tumult in the Clouds, *Goodson records his final exchanges with 'Herr Kommandant'. They took place, incredibly, over a bottle of Remy-Martin and cigars. Goodson's single aim? To get released from the cruelty of the Gestapo and be handed over to the Luftwaffe.*

. . . It was good cognac and I enjoyed it. . . .

'I see, Herr Kommandant, you have a box of Cuban cigars. I always think they go well with cognac, don't you?'

He laughed, handed me the box and took one for himself.

'You're right. I, too, enjoy a good cigar.'

He struck a match, lit his cigar and threw me the matchbox. I drew deeply on the cigar, savouring it, and then blew a thick, round smoke ring. Probably because I only smoked cigars and never inhaled them, I had formed the habit of blowing rings. The air was still in the room. The ring rolled across the table and settled and spread on the surface.

The Kommandant was fascinated.

'Do that again.'

I laughed and blew another ring.

'How do you do that?'

It was one way to gain time, so I tried to teach him. He was an apt student. The session forged a bond between us. As he wrestled with the problem, he poured me another brandy.

'Thank you,' I said. 'At least I'm going out in style.'

'Yes,' he said, 'you do have style. *Prosit!*' and he raised his glass to me.

'Is there anything else I can do for you?' he asked.

'Of course, Herr Kommandant, you could telephone the Luftwaffe!'

'No! I have no desire to make a fool of myself in front of them. I don't take orders from that lot.'

'On the contrary.' I was playing my last card. 'You would be making fools of them!'

'How?' He was interested.

'You would simply say, "We are, of course, aware of the fact that a high-ranking American flying officer was recently shot down. It has taken you so long to capture him, I thought you wouldn't mind if I mobilized my command to save further waste of time. If you wish to interrogate him, he is at your disposal. If not, I shall deal with him as I see fit." '

He continued his attempts to blow smoke rings.

'Hold the smoke in your mouth longer before blowing it out,' I said. It worked. He was delighted.

Then he looked at his watch, got up, went to the telephone on his desk and barked out an order. He hung up, came back, and poured us both another brandy.

The phone rang. He swaggered over and answered it. He repeated my suggested script almost word for word. Then all I heard was a series of '*Ja*,' '*Jawohl*', '*Ja*'.

He hung up and came back, and sat down with his brandy. . . . Neither of us spoke. He proudly blew a smoke ring. Finally, he finished his drink and stood up.

'Well, it's been a long day – and night; so if you will excuse me.' He went to the door and called for my guard, then came to attention stiffly in front of me. He shook hands with me, stepped back and saluted.

'Major, Leb'wohl!' In the doorway he turned. 'The Luftwaffe will pick you up in half an hour. . . .'

James A. Goodson, Sandwich, Kent, 1984

Partisan Preference

The relationship in World War II between Tito's Partisans in Yugoslavia and the Allied airmen who were shot down in their country was close and trusted. It was also based on immense courage. Like the underground in the occupied countries in Western Europe, these magnificent patriots ran great risks working for the Allies and against the enemy.

'Lyn' Bridge (Flight Lieutenant E. Bridge) can bear witness to this spirited cooperation. He was the 35-year-old navigator of a B-24 Liberator of 37 Squadron, captained by Flight Lieutenant Verne Cave from New Zealand, and based at Foggia, in southern Italy, which was shot down on the night of Easter Sunday, 1 April 1945, by a Ju 88 near Vinica, as the aircraft returned from a bombing raid on Graz in Austria.

Five of the crew, who hadn't been able to bale out, were killed when the bomber crashed. The Partisans got to the aircraft before the Germans and recovered the bodies. Of the remaining four who did bale out, two, Flight Lieutenant Cliff Wing and Sergeant 'Ginger' Cummings, both beam gunners, were badly wounded. They were later found and succoured by the Partisans. The other two, Bridge himself, and the bomb-aimer, Pilot Officer 'Snowy' Innes, landed, relatively intact, in a dense and dark forest. Each was caught up in high branches and neither knew of the other's proximity. 'Lyn' recalls making contact.

. . . I heard someone whistling. It was the first few bars of 'Little Sir Echo – How Do You Do' which was often played on the mess gramophone, so I knew it must be one of the crew. Then it came again, and this time I answered by whistling the next couple of bars. . . . 'Hello – hello. . . .' This spurred me to do something about getting down from the high tree. . . . Luckily, I fell on soft ground. . . .

. . . Snowy and I discussed our plight. We knew our only hope was to get to Tito's Partisans. To be picked up by Mihailovitch or the Ustashi would be as bad, if not worse, than being taken by the Germans. . . .

Getting clear of the forest, we watched the tiny village of Sinji Vrh with its fifteen to twenty cottages. . . . As the chapel bell tolled women and children appeared and went to mass. When they came out, the women chatted and the children played, there wasn't a man among them. . . . We decided to take a chance and see what reception we got. . . .

The 'Inglezi RAF' were well received. Clandestine contact was made with the local Partisans, 'all armed to the teeth', and the leader greeted them 'with a huge grin and a hearty handshake'. They had not by then found the aircraft or any of its occupants, dead or alive. After sending word to their HQ, the leader 'pointed out on a map the position of the German garrisons', but it was obvious they had little knowledge of the war beyond their own country. . . .

Later in the day, a jeep roared into the village, driven by 'Mac' (Flight Lieutenant MacPherson), a young RAF officer, the liaison between the Partisans and our HQ in Italy. He told us that Cliff and Ginger had been picked up by another band of Partisans, badly injured, and that the dead members of the crew had been taken safely away from the wrecked aircraft.

He then rushed us down the mountainside and took us to another building where there were more Partisans – and, to my surprise, a British army captain, who said we couldn't stay there and that Mac would take us to a safer place. As we left, two women on the pavement each pushed a hard-boiled egg apiece into our hands. 'Don't you realize it's Easter Sunday,' said Mac, seeing our surprise.

The two were then whisked away to another cottage up in the hills where they found 'two RAF chaps operating a secret radio'. Later, the army captain telephoned to say the Partisans were giving the dead crew members a military funeral the next day, but, for security reasons, 'Lyn' and 'Snowy' mustn't attend. He added that they would be flown out of Yugoslavia the following day and that their wounded mates, 'Cliff' and 'Ginger', would be well enough to go with them. Bridge remembers the scene on the airstrip.

. . . Cliff and Ginger were there swathed in bandages. They had with them three American aircrew. These three had been shot down over Austria almost a year before; they had walked across the Alps and then been picked up by Tito's Partisans. . . . Suddenly, as the DC-3 Dakota, with its Spitfire escort circling overhead, touched down, another jeep dashed up. Out stepped two Yugoslavs in uniform, one of them very evidently a VIP.* . . . We realized then the aircraft hadn't been sent specially for us!

After landing at Bari in southern Italy, Cliff, Ginger and the three Americans were taken away in the waiting ambulance while we were borne off to intelligence, where we were instructed to forget where we'd been and what we had seen. We were promptly posted back to the UK thankful for our good luck – and for Tito's Partisans. . . .

E. Bridge, Alnmouth, Northumberland, 1984

Editor's note: *'Lyn' Bridge, who was to spend the rest of his working life with the Rank-Hovis organization, recalls that 'Mac', the RAF liaison officer always had an Alsation dog with him. 'He told me that, when he was doing his parachute drops, he often took the dog with him. He had his own harness and parachute. Mac pushed him out of the aircraft first and jumped after him. The dog was quite unconcerned, and went on wagging his tail all the way down. . . .'*

*Believed to be Tito. Great secrecy surrounded his movements and, in those days, he had no publicity. (Ed.)

Alsatian dog in harness

The Light on the Road to Kalgoorlie*

Our job was to fly up into Albania and to Skopolje, then alter course west into the mountains of Yugoslavia to locate a pre-arranged set of fires burning in the shape of a square, circle or triangle.... Then, in the darkness, with wheels and flaps down, go as low as possible among the mountains and drop [from the B-24] our agents and supplies of arms and gold sovereigns to the Partisans....

... Women were dropped as well as men. Going back one time into the fuselage of the Liberator to say goodbye to one young woman who was to jump ... I noticed she took out a gleaming combat knife.... She brought the knife up to her face and then, turning towards the window, she used the shining blade as a mirror and applied her lipstick by the light of the full moon....

On another occasion, a Yugoslav came onto the flight deck to say goodbye before jumping! He was covered in bandoliers of ammunition, with knives and guns hanging all over him.... 'Are you going to fight the whole German army when you land?' I asked. 'No,' he said, 'the wolves.' Every full moon these trips took place....

*The editor is indebted to Air Chief Marshal Sir Wallace Kyle – 'Digger' Kyle – one of Bomber Command's wartime stalwarts and a subsequent Air Officer Commanding-in-Chief of the Command, for stimulating this story. From the war, and from his time a Governor of Western Australia, the Air Chief Marshal had come to know the special qualities of the Bishop of Kalgoorlie.

Thus wrote the Right Reverend Denis Bryant (Wing Commander D. W. Bryant, RAF), formerly Bishop of Kalgoorlie and now the Rector of St Lawrence, in Dalkeith, Western Australia. It would probably be impossible to find any Allied bomber pilot or navigator (Denis Bryant was both by trade) who equalled, let alone surpassed, the length and spread of his operational span in World War II. Listen to the record: 88 Squadron and Fairey Battles with the Advanced Air Striking Force in France in 1939 and 1940 until the collapse. . . . Then Blenheims in 2 Group of Bomber Command in 1940 and 1941 (still with 88). . . . B-24s on special duties in the Middle East, 1942 and 1943. . . . And finally, in 1944 and 1945, B-24s again, now with 99 Squadron, in India, Burma and the Far Eastern theatre. . . . There was virtually no let up until the ninetieth operation had been secured in the log book. And what operations! It makes a humbling picture of survival against the odds. . . .

Two experiences, among many, suggest that in this officer's wartime life there was a light illuminating the way. The first, paradoxically, was in the last months of war. The place: the Bay of Bengal.

Lord Louis Mountbatten, as supremo, had addressed 99 Squadron and informed us that 'this year there will be no monsoon' – meaning that for the first time ever in the Burma campaign the Royal Air Force would fly through the monsoon and the army would advance! . . . This meant often flying for hours to reach Rangoon or Bangkok or the Burma Railway under a cloud base no higher than 1000 feet above the sea. . . .

. . . Flying in 'the tunnel', I can vividly recall the 'urge' within me – almost a voice saying urgently – 'move!' – and move I did, altering course some 25–30 degrees to starboard. . . . Straightening up, and looking along the port wing, I saw a very vicious typhoon sucking the sea up into the clouds. If we had kept on course we would have flown straight into it. . . .

A similar sort of experience happened another time when moving out of formation over Rangoon, to find our two wingmen shot out of the sky by ack-ack. . . .

The second incident occurred soon after the war. Denis Bryant now had everything going for him in the Service – a permanent commission, promotion coming up, an exceptional war behind.

One Sunday, a beautiful English summer's day, when we were living in Cheltenham, I was compelled for no apparent reason other than curiosity to attend a little fourteenth-century church whose bells were ringing loud and clear at the back of our home. At this point, I had had nothing to do with the church, and hadn't even been confirmed. . . .

Then it happened! During the singing of the first hymn, the altar became a blaze of light which filled the whole church. . . . I was blinded by it. . . . Then a voice spoke . . . from the altar. 'Leave everything here at the altar. Come and follow me. . . .'

It took me two months, often walking long hours over the Cotswold Hills, to try to work out what I should do. . . . It would mean resigning my commission, losing my pension in the RAF, taking my daughter out of boarding school, sending my wife out to work, going to a theological college for three years to study a book – the Bible – which I knew very little about!

The feeling grew so strong, I had really no choice but to do it (my wife, Lin, had also had a similar experience).

Doors opened for us immediately.... I was given a place at Queen's College, Birmingham, and succeeded in passing all my exams.... Curacies in parishes in England followed.... Then one morning at breakfast, reading through the *Church Times*, an advert leapt out of the page at me: 'Pioneer priest wanted in Esperance, Western Australia....'

My wife and I looked at each other. We both said: 'That's for us!' And so it was.

The Right Reverend Denis W. Bryant, Dalkeith,
Western Australia, 1984

They Went in Threes

An impression prevailed in wartime that aircraft accidents tended to go in threes. 'That's two "gone for a Burton",' a squadron would say, 'who's gonna be third?' What substance is there for the contention? Was it fact, coincidence, superstition or fate? Or just plain baloney?

Robin Higham, of the Department of History of Kansas State University, editor of Aerospace Historian *and a member of 48 Squadron, Royal Air Force, in the final scenes of the Far Eastern war, contributes his experience.*

From my casual researches (and it could, of course, be fateful optimism at work), it does seem that accidents go in threes....

There is the case of 48 Squadron.... We had been sent out from England to take part in the invasion of Malaya. With VJ-Day, the operation was cancelled. We then replaced 486, the Canadian transport Squadron at Patenga, Chittagong. Our job was to fly in supplies to the West African Division along the Arakan Coast and to small groups in the hills and to the airfields in the Irrawaddy plain from Mingyang to Rangoon....

In the course of these operations ... 48 lost three DC-3s. In each case the wireless operator in the aircraft was not the regular crew member.

The first accident occurred shortly after most of the squadron had arrived at Chittagong. One of the crews flew up a valley on the east side of the Irrawaddy and apparently got sucked up into a cumulo-nimbus cloud until the aircraft disintegrated. The remains were found some days later.

The second aeroplane simply disappeared in the autumn monsoon (see 'The Light on the Road to Kalgoorlie', page 293), and although we and the B-24 Air Sea Rescue Flight searched for some time, no trace of the aircraft or its crew was ever found.

The third loss happened when a DC-3 was taking off, fully laden, from the 2000-yard concrete runway at Patenga. An engine failed just as it became airborne, and the aircraft came rapidly back to earth.

In the shuddering slither to a halt, the cockpit door burst open and part of the load slid through. This wedged the door against the back of the radio operator's chair, pinning him against his table and preventing him from swivelling to slide out. Almost instantaneously, the rest of the crew

– the two pilots up front, followed by the navigator from the other side of the doorway, exited through the cockpit roof hatch. . . . Moments later, the aircraft burst into flames. . . .

After these three accidents, it was rare to find a wireless operator who was not too worried or superstitious to fly with any crew but his own. . . .

Robin Higham, Kansas State University, Manhattan.
Kansas, USA, 1985

A Royal Ditching

The Fleet Air Arm's carrier-borne attacks in January 1945 on the Japanese-held oil refineries at Pangkazan Brandan, near Medan, up in the northeast of Sumatra, and at Palembang in the south – vital assets in Japan's wartime balance sheet – were among the Service's strongest, and most hazardous, operations of the war.

The assaults from the Royal Navy Task Force with its complement of four Fleet carriers – HM ships Indomitable, Victorious, Formidable *and* Illustrious *– escorted by the battleship,* King George V, *three cruisers and ten destroyers, all under the command of Admiral Vian (Admiral Sir Philip Vian), were launched as the Fleet was making its way from the Indian Ocean to the Pacific to join the United States' Fleet for the final assault on Japan.*

The escorted missions demanded a climb for the naval dive-bomber crews to some 14,000 feet over the 9000-foot Wilhelmina mountain range, followed by a run-in over 100 to 120 miles of territory, mainly dense jungle, to targets stoutly defended by enemy fighters, anti-aircraft batteries and barrage balloons.

Gus Halliday (Vice-Admiral Sir Roy Halliday), who, in due time would rise to be Director-General of Intelligence at the Ministry of Defence in London, piloting an Avenger from Victorious, *lying ninety miles offshore, was one of a force of forty-three bombers and eighty fighters which attacked Palembang in the early morning of 29 January. The target had been visited five days before, so the Japanese were on the alert.*

. . . We cleared the mountains and continued uneventfully for some thirty minutes. . . . As I saw our target, my sense of growing, but false, security was shattered by the warning of the air group coordinator's voice over the radio: 'Bogeys nine o'clock high' as a large formation of Japanese Zeros dived out of the sun.

I put my flight into echelon starboard, and as we ran up towards our diving point all hell broke loose. My air gunner in his ball turret was hammering away when he shouted over the intercom that a Zero was on our tail and, to prove it, a long, neat line of holes appeared across the top of my port wing smartly followed by a Japanese fighter breaking away. . . .

. . . Having identified the cracking plant which was my flight's target, I rolled into a dive from 14,000 feet vaguely aware of a mass of aircraft milling in all directions as our fighters were engaging the Zeros. . . . I then noticed that a flame was torching through one of the bulletholes in my wing. As I dived towards the target I saw two Avengers below me suddenly lose their wings and plummet like stones towards the ground. . . .

The reason was too apparent. The Japanese had kept their balloons floating at low level, and as we were committed to our dives they rapidly raised them to a 1000 feet or so above our bomb-release height of 3000 feet. Whether one hit an invisible balloon cable or not was pure chance. I was lucky, but glancing at my wing after I had released my bomb-load and was climbing away through clouds of black smoke, I saw with alarm, not unmixed with fear, that the flame I had noticed a few seconds before was now larger and stronger. It was about then I realized my engine had also been hit, and whenever I attempted to throttle back it misfired alarmingly. I therefore headed back towards the mountains alone since joining up and flying in formation was impossible. . . .

For Halliday, and his two crew members, the next fifty minutes were a nightmare. With a wing on fire and an engine that could be expected to quit at any moment, the chances of crossing jungle and mountains looked remote. . . . It was at the highest point over the mountains – just as the crew got their first glimpse of the sea – that the Avenger's motor finally packed up. With a steady glide, and Mayday calls and red Verey lights being fired off, pilot, observer and air gunner prepared for a ditching. Loss of hydraulics and, therefore, the use of flaps, meant that the speed of touchdown would be uncomfortably high. . . .

Nevertheless, aiming in the direction of what he took to be the silhouette of a distant destroyer, Halliday landed the aeroplane successfully twenty miles off the enemy coast, and the crew clambered into their dinghy.

Within thirty minutes, the destroyer, HMS *Whelp*, was alongside, and all our fears and apprehensions were dispelled as we were hoisted on board to be welcomed by HRH Prince Philip, who was then the first lieutenant. The attack by Japanese Kamikaze suicide planes as we rejoined the Fleet some thirty minutes later seemed of only passing importance, thus proving that everything in life is relative.

As a sequel, I should mention that production at the Palembang refinery was totally stopped for two months and, even after that, it was worked at only one third of normal capacity.

Regrettably, we lost some forty aircraft* and the Japanese a similar number. Of nine of our naval aircrew captured, all were beheaded by the Japanese – a treatment of which we were not unaware if captured.

On the lighter side, Prince Philip lent me a uniform and, together with other officers from the *Whelp*, we had a memorable 'run ashore' in Perth, Western Australia, where I disgraced myself by being sick on the ship's gangway on return.

On rejoining *Victorious* I chatted about it all with my CO, Lieut-Commander David Foster† who, among other things, subsequently asked me if I would like to go 'into soap' after the war. I politely declined. It is

*A hideous loss-rate of around 30 per cent. (Ed.)
†See 'Never Fear! But *Don't* Volunteer!', page 104.

interesting to note that Foster eventually became president of Colgate Palmolive, worldwide – another chance missed!

Vice-Admiral Sir Roy Halliday, Bank, Lyndhurst,
Hampshire, 1984

Solar Reflections

Chaos umpire sits,
And by decision more embroils the fray
By which he reigns: next him high arbiter
Chance governs all

John Milton, *Paradise Lost* (1608–74)

Meanwhile, on 1 January 1945 in an earlier Fleet Air Arm attack on Pangkazan Brandan, on the Malacca Straits, with ninety-two Avengers, Fireflies, Hellcats and Corsairs, Donald Judd's fortunes were as mixed as Gus Halliday's a month later. Bad luck, good luck gave the pair a common denominator.

Judd, leading the second flight of Avengers from Victorious, *had just crossed the Sumatran coast to a point some ten miles inland when, at 5000 feet, in the steep formation climb over the mountains, his engine started to pack up. At that moment, he had no more than 130 to 140 knots 'on the clock'. There was nothing for it but to extricate himself from the formation (an extremely tricky process in the circumstances), turn back, jettison the bombs and, by stretching the glide, try to put as much distance as possible between his aircraft and the enemy coast before ditching.*

Having made five miles or so out to sea before putting down, the crew of three got safely into their dinghy and started paddling vigorously away from the coast. The Japanese, who must have been alerted to their distress, fortuitously (in this case) didn't send a boat out for them.

Within the next hour, Hellcat fighters made their searches without coming close enough to spot the dinghy. After this false dawn, the picture, as Judd well recalls, began quickly to darken.

. . . Another thirty minutes elapsed . . . and hope had begun to ebb. We were becoming aware of the size and loneliness of the Indian Ocean. We knew well that Admiral Vian, sympathetic though he was, would not hang around with the Fleet for long for the sake of three aircrew. . . .*

[But now] Corsair fighters appeared and began to follow the Hellcats' search area. . . . [Again] they did not come close enough to see us. In desperation, I got out my Heliograph – a mirror-type, light reflector designed to attract searching aircraft. A Corsair did come close enough to notice the reflected light, but turned away. . . . We began to reach our lowest ebb. . . . Then, after a few more precious minutes had elapsed, two destroyers appeared to the south, with their attendant Corsairs. . . . Neither

*Unbeknown to Judd and his crew, Vian had already made a signal: 'If Corsairs do not locate dinghy within ten minutes, rejoin me.' There were thus very few minutes left in which to find the crew. (Ed.)

seemed likely to spot the dinghy, but with our wonderful Heliograph they were led to us, and HMS *Undine* (Commander T. C. Robinson) picked us up amid much relief and jubilation. . . .

I still treasure that Heliograph; it undoubtedly saved us from an unthinkable fate.

Donald M. Judd, Winchester, Hampshire, 1984

The Kaiten Weapon

A new, secret Japanese weapon now came into play as the United States forces were closing the ring in the Pacific. The Kaiten Weapon (literally, rotating weapon – it possessed a built-in, course-changing device) – to westerners, the Human Torpedo – was manned by volunteers who were prepared to make the ultimate sacrifice in 'a fanatical bid to smash the US Fleet in the closing months of the war'. It added another feature to the fighting in a theatre which had already witnessed suicidal endeavour.

Yutaka Yokota, a pilot and master sergeant in the air force of the Imperial Navy, was himself a Kaiten-force volunteer. He survived to tell the story* of this extraordinary development by the whim of fate or chance, certainly not by design.

Based at Otsujima and Hikari, Yokota was a member of the elite Tatara Group of volunteers who had trained in the inland Sea of Japan. As the time of the first operation approached, Yutaka wrote a 'last' letter for his family which left no doubt about his activities and expectations. It was addressed to his father, elder brother and sisters.

Please forgive me, I could not say it in Tokyo before, but now I speak my last goodbye to you. The truth is that I have not been piloting aircraft for many months. I have been training instead in a new weapon, a guided torpedo which I shall ride alone. We are going out for an attack very soon. That is why I had special leave, so I could come and see you. I am proud to be going out. What would become of God's favoured country, Japan, and her history of three thousand years, if we refused to make sacrifices for the Emperor?

I will die the moment my torpedo hits an enemy ship. My death will be full of purpose. We have been educated here to forget all small things, and to think only of the one big thing. . . . When you hear that I have died after sinking an enemy ship, I hope you will have kind words to say about my gallant death.

I have no regrets, nor anything more to say. All of you have always been very kind to me, and I have done nothing in return for this kindness. But please remember always that I thank you from the bottom of my heart.

Masakuzu and Shinji, my nephews, and Setusko, my niece, I hope that the three of you will grow into great figures, and always honour your parents. I shall be looking down on you after my death. If you want to meet your uncle, come and visit Kudan, I will be waiting there to greet you, with many smiles. . . .

**Return of the Human Torpedo*, Yutaka Yokota (Masu Printing Company, 1956).

The Kaiten Weapon (Japanese Human Torpedo)

Although it was in contradiction of his country's philosophy and code, Yutaka Yokota was 'delivered' by fortune from a premature end.

In the event, I was obliged to return on three separate occasions from planned operations due to mechanical trouble with my torpedo. The serviceability of these weapons, particularly as we neared the time of the surrender, fell far below expectations due mainly to the poor quality of the materials from which the component parts were made. Two-thirds of the weapons produced were sub-standard in this respect. . . .

Yutaka's last mission took place on 6 July 1945. For the third time, he was obliged to bring the damaged torpedo, I–36, back into port. He was in despair at his 'misfortune'.

. . . I stayed, suspended somewhere between life and death. I had been so fully consecrated to the concept of extinguishing my life, that now I did not know what to do with myself. Many of my friends had achieved their goal of glorious death, but I had not. They were at the gate of Yasukuni now, waiting for me so we could all enter together. But soon the war was over, and I had no right to enter that sacred place. Nor could I again face the world, from which I had so completely withdrawn. I was miserable, and thought of committing suicide, but I was too proud to do it. My life had been measured as worth one large American aircraft carrier, I reminded myself. How could I surrender it now to a small pistol bullet . . . ?

Yutaka Yokota, Chofu-shi, Tokyo, Japan, 1984

It Paid to Forget

Jack Rutherford – The Reverend Canon J. B. Rutherford, Vicar of Alnmouth and Lesbury in Northumberland – was a flight sergeant navigator with 110 Squadron in South Burma in mid-1945. He flew a tour of low-level operations against the Japanese in Mosquito VIs, a role which had its manifest hazards. Did this experience influence the Vicar in his post-war decision to take holy orders?

... There was no one single event which influenced me to seek ordination. Rather, it was a whole series of events all seeming to point me in that direction. ... It was the impact of all past experience, including that of operational flying which made me think things out. ... When the call to ordination came, all the past made sense in the strangest way. ...

All the same, it could be argued that there was one experience on 'a beautiful, early July morning, on the jungle airstrip at Kinmagan, forty miles north of Meiktila', which must have done something to urge the resolve to enter the Church. Jack Rutherford retains the detail.

... The time was about 06.30. A blue haze tinged the horizon above the dense jungle. ... It was the best time of the day to catch the Japs. ...

We were the last to take off. In our haste we made every mistake in the book. We forgot to remove the pitot head cover, and that meant we could not tell what speed we were doing. We also forgot to remove the ground-locks on our undercarriage, and that meant that our wheels were firmly locked in the 'down' position and would not retract.

Once we were airborne, we realized our mistakes, and called up a colleague to pace us in. That meant flying just in front of us at the required speed for landing.

We touched down, and with engines still revving signalled our groundcrew to do the necessary about the pitot head cover and the ground-locks. This done, we tore off once more down the strip. Suddenly, the port engine cut dead and we swung violently off the runway. We cut the engines and wandered disconsolately back to the flight office. Then we heard the post-mortem. We weren't the only ones to forget things that day. The groundcrew had forgotten to remove the dust pans from the air-intake and so the engines had overheated.

I often shudder to think what would have happened on that beautiful morning if we had remembered to do *our* job. We would have gone about thirty miles over the jungle and then crashed.

I also ponder on whether the good lord takes a hand in the blunders, and makes some people remember and some forget for their own good; for it was certainly for our own good that we *did* forget and had to land again. Otherwise the epitaph on our tombstone could well have read 'Gone to ground'. ...

The Reverend Canon J. B. Rutherford, Lesbury,
Alnwick, 1984

The Wounds Remain

It was right at the end of the fighting – and just after it – that the losses, when they arose, struck so hard. It was almost as if luck, having completed three, or even four, operational tours, had decided to pack it in and opt for an early release.

I. DEREK WALKER

Derek Walker (Wing Commander D. R. Walker) was commissioned in the Royal Air Force in July 1937. In World War II, he flew *four* operational tours – in Palestine, Greece and Crete, in the Western Desert and in the United Kingdom and Europe – commanding squadrons and a wing on the way. He took over the first Meteor jet squadron after the armistice. The record was undoubted, the spirit unquenchable.

Derek was killed at 14.30 on 14 November 1945, when the P-51D Mustang he was flying crashed in the circuit at Hendon, in north London, just as he was preparing to land. He had married Diana Barnato (see 'On Instruments in the 400', page 194) at Englefield Green in Surrey, in the sunshine of 6 May 1944, just eighteen months before he died.

'Derek, November 1945'

I saw you glistening in the sky
Like gleaming vapour flashing by,
I saw you next upon a marble shelf
A scorched grotesqueness of yourself.
The house you hit was still a smouldering shell
That storm we had has turned my life to hell.

I went along to see
What could be done –
The smell of singeing flesh
And jagged, ugly hunks of metal
Still remained.
The wheels were there, and bricks
And burnt-up privet hedges,
A single yellow rose
Was blooming on a blackened stem.
I stood and looked and wept
My heart cried out to Him.

And as I stood, a little man
Came up and watched as well
'Your house, Ma'am? And your garden, Ma'am?
It will all grow again . . .'
But when I turned and looked at him
Just then he understood.
He picked the rose and gave it me
'I'm sorry, very sorry, Ma'am,
I didn't know,' he said.
'Someone I love,' I cried,
'My heart sighs out for him.'

The years have passed,
My searing pains remained,
I went along again to look
And there, as in a dream,
A house of Phoenix stood,
Agleam and clean, with bright blue paint.
(The yellow rose was there)
And underneath the hedge
  of privet lay a puppy
And a battered teddybear, and close by
Stood the pram.
'Life for a life,' I cried,
And wept for freedom from my Calvary.

Diana Barnato Walker

2. 'JOUBIE', THE SOUTH AFRICAN

Ralph Fellows, from Winnipeg, Manitoba, navigator of 217, the DC-3, supply-carrying, glider-towing Squadron, based at Down Ampney, in Gloucestershire, 'veteran' of Normandy, the push up through Europe, Arnhem, the Rhine crossing, and the rest, picks up the story of 'Joubie' Joubert (Major P. S. Joubert), his pilot through all these operations and beyond.

Joubie, the South African, came to Down Ampney on 29 February 1944 and remained there until 16 August 1945, two remarkable dates – the first was the extra day of a Leap Year, the second, the day after VJ Day. Joubie was quite unique. He was old – forty-eight years old; he had amassed a great many flying hours; he had flown in the 1914–1918 encounter and wore World War I ribbons. And here he was again, this time flying Dakotas as a flight commander of 217.

There was something else quite remarkable about Joubie – he was extremely lucky. He must have been to have survived all those hours for he was, to say the least, an indifferent pilot. In a purely technical sense he was fine, but he did unusual things and at the most inappropriate moments. If that wasn't enough, he was always eager to 'have a go' and did so frequently. . . .

Two of our trips together were vintage Joubie – Joubie at his luckiest. During his time over Normandy on D-Day evening, after releasing the glider we had tugged from Down Ampney, he became so engrossed in the activity on the sea and land below us that he fairly disappeared out of his side window watching it. Eventually – and none too soon – we persuaded him to turn for home. As we swung away slowly to starboard, a piece of flak went up through our port wing leaving a jagged, gaping hole in the metal. A few seconds later in turning, and it would have blasted our cabin area.

At Arnhem, on 21 September 1944, he was even luckier. We had been detailed to drop supplies to our troops on the ground. But, due to faulty communications, and unknown to us, the designated drop zone was held by the Germans, and our fighter cover, so essential to protect us on the way in and out, was back on the ground in the Brussels area, rearming and refuelling.

The line of Daks received a terrible battering during the slow low-level drop, but Joubie held on grimly straight and level and eventually we were through. We climbed away and turned for home. Joubie put in the auto-pilot and wandered back to the cargo cabin to speak to our wonderful army despatchers.

I was busy at my navigation table when a shout from our wireless operator caused me to glance outside. FW 190s had got among our unarmed Dakotas and the sky seemed full of burning aircraft and parachutes. We, meanwhile, flew on unconcerned – on auto-pilot.

Joubie scampered back to his position and, with a fair measure of skill, coupled with his usual luck, got us home safely. It could only have happened to Joubie.

Joubie should have returned to his beloved South Africa after the Victory in Europe but he remained on with us, becoming our squadron commander. VJ Day arrived. It was all over and we, the lucky ones, had come through safely. Down Ampney celebrated and had every right to do so. Late on in the celebrations a stove pipe was produced and filled with Verey cartridges and other combustible items. Someone was needed to ignite it. No one would take the chance.

It was then that the luck that had kept Joubie safe in two world wars, and countless incidents finally deserted him. Immaculate as ever and proudly wearing his pilot wings and ribbons, he 'had a go'. It was to be his last. The contraption blew up in his face. He died the next day, 16 August 1945. . . .

Forty years have passed. I have returned to Down Ampney on several occasions. I always go into the little thirteenth-century church in the village. I always wander out to what remains of the aerodrome and read the plaque at the end of what was once a runway. And always, with sadness, do I remember Joubie. . . . And wonder why.

Ralph Fellows, Winnipeg, Manitoba, Canada, 1984

The Parabola of War: 1917–1966
1966

The parabola of war, which, in this context, began its ascent from the biplanes and the open cockpits of World War I, and then climbed up to cover the aerial developments of the second world conflict, has completed its span by settling in the age of guided weaponry and sophisticated aeroplanes which make the speed of sound seem a commonplace.

It has been quite a travel. The marvel is that its course has been contained within the period of little more than five decades.

It is right, then, that the end of the parabola should be marked by the first-hand story of an exceptional United States Air Force officer who received a direct hit from a Soviet ground-to-air missile in the Vietnam War – and survived.

The Flaming Telegraph Pole

Ken Cordier (Colonel Kenneth W. Cordier, USAF, (Retd) has been living, heavily borrowed against time, ever since 2 December 1966. That was the day in the Vietnam War when he lived through a direct hit from a Soviet SA-11 ground-to-air missile on the tail section of his F-4C Phantom jet. He was flying with the 559th Squadron of the 12th Tactical Fighter Wing, based at Cam Ranh Bay, and the mission was to provide fighter escort for a Douglas RB-66 Destroyer over North Vietnam. It involved rendezvousing with a refuelling tanker en route.

When Cordier was felled he was at 24,000 feet cruising at .8 mach or around 500 m.p.h. It was his 175th mission of the war, and he was due to return to the United States in twelve days' time. Being in the forefront of the USAF's combat pilots, his confidence at that stage was at its peak. As a 'seasoned veteran' of the fighting, he felt he was invincible.

But this day there had been portents of unease. Things hadn't gone right from the beginning. Worst of all, perhaps, was the fact that, unbeknown to Cordier, the RB-66 they were escorting was not carrying jamming equipment designed to black out the SAM radars. 'Had I known this I would have devoted a little more time to watching what was going on below. I would then very likely have seen the SA-11 (looking just like a flaming telegraph pole) coming up at me. . . .'

The events that followed in the next seconds and minutes are forever imprinted upon Ken Cordier's mind.

Ejecting F-4C (Phantom) pilot

I felt an explosion behind and under the aircraft, and faster than I can tell the sequence both engine firelights started flashing and the entire warning light panel lit up like a Christmas tree. The aircraft went into a wild fishtail manoeuvre, during which I was first pressed up against the straps and then pushed down into the seat. During this negative 'g' – positive 'g' sequence, I yelled out to my back-seater: 'We're hit. Eject!' I then grabbed the ejection handle between my legs. Later, I heard that my Gib (guy in the back) had made it out safely, too. . . .

EJECTING FROM A JET

In this ejection operation, once the handle is pulled, the seat is designed so that the remainder of the sequence is all automatic until the pilot hits the ground. After ejecting at high altitude, a small drogue 'chute deploys, which stabilizes the seat and pulls out the main 'chute after the seat falls to an altitude of about 14,000 feet. Then a barostatic device initiates the man-seat separator after which the personal parachute deploys automatically.

The fact that my own ejection occurred at some 24,000 feet meant that I would 'free fall' for approximately two miles before the automatic parachute-opening procedure came into play. After seeing my aircraft blow up, my natural reaction was to look down and see what there was below. What I saw, and what happened in the subsequent few seconds, was even more exciting than the previous moments and is *the single event in my life in which chance, or fate, played such a significant part*. . . . [Editor's italics.]

HORROR MISSILE

I looked down between my boots and saw, to my horror, a second missile (Soviet tactics at this time were to fire SAMs in salvoes of two) exploding just below and in the path of my seat! It was a red/orange and black fireball which looked like the gates of hell. It was obvious that I was going to fall into or through it. I just had time to close my eyes and hold my breath when I felt a hot flash . . . and just as quickly I was in clear air again.

I now experienced raw panic for the first time in my life. The thought flashed through my mind that the fireball must have burned off the drogue 'chute which would negate the automatic parachute-opening process and I would ride the seat into the ground if I didn't separate manually. [editor's italics.]

Our training had stressed never to open the parachute at high altitude because of the strong opening shock in still air – and yet I just couldn't wait to see, and feel, the silk canopy over the top of me. . . . So my panic-driven decision to pull the manual seat release as soon as I pushed away from the seat, and to grab the 'D'-ring to deploy the parachute, proved the correctness of what I had been taught.

FALLING FAST

The 'chute opened with such force that it sounded like an explosion, and ripped out two of the nylon panels. This allowed the air to spill out of the canopy and resulted in a faster fall which meant that I hit the ground a good deal harder than normal (editor's italics). . . . It stunned me for a few moments, but the amazing thing was that throughout this traumatic experience I suffered relatively minor injuries. My back sustained a fracture as a result of the ejection, but other than this, and the burning off of my eyelashes and eyebrows where flame had penetrated under my visor, plus powder burns on my arms, I was virtually unscathed.

The extent of my luck can be seen when the kill mechanism of a Soviet SA-II missile is explained. When the warhead detonates, the cylindrical metal casing breaks up into metal fragments which fly out in an expanding doughnut-shaped ring of shrapnel. If one is within its lethal radius, hits are virtually assured.

THROUGH THE 'DOUGHNUT'

However, the ring expands outwards and if one could pass through it along the longitudinal axis of the missile, given a bit of fortune, one should get through without a scratch, other than burns from the fireball. Plainly, this is what happened to me. Chance put me on exactly the correct flight path, at the correct speed and altitude, to fall through the hole of that 'doughnut' – and live to tell the tale. . . .

. . . All this was only the curtain-raiser for the ensuing six years and three months. What happened after I hit the ground is another story. . . . But the miraculous escape from the two SAMs convinced me that there was something else in store for me – something in the grand scheme of

307

things which I had yet to do; otherwise my story should have ended on 2 December 1966.

Colonel Kenneth W. Cordier, USAF (Retd),
Alexandria, Virginia, USA, 1985

Editor's note: *Cordier was a prisoner of the North Vietnamese for just over six ghastly, inhuman years. His courage and resilience saw him through. He eventually returned to operational flying duty with the USAF in Germany. Thereafter, he served with outstanding success as the US Air Attaché in London before retiring from the Service in 1985, at the age of forty-six, to pursue a commercial and industrial career.*

The Spirit Which Endures . . .

I am become a name;
For always roaming with a hungry heart
Much have I seen and known; cities of men
And manners, climates, councils, governments,
Myself not least, but honour'd of them all;
And drunk delight of battle with my peers . . .

My mariners,
Souls that have toil'd, and wrought, and thought with me –
That ever with a frolic welcome took
The thunder and the sunshine, and opposed
Free hearts, free foreheads – you and I are old;
Old age hath yet his honour and his toil;
Death closes all: but something ere the end,
Some work of noble note, may yet be done,
Not unbecoming men that strove with gods . . .
Tho' much is taken, much abides; and tho'
We are not now that strength which in old days
Moved earth and heaven; that which we are, we are;
One equal temper of heroic hearts,
Made weak by time and fate, but strong in will
To strive, to seek, to find, and not to yield.

Alfred, Lord Tennyson (1809–92), 'Ulysses'

Index

311

314